THE EUROPEAN MOSAIC

CONTEMPORARY POLITICS, ECONOMICS AND CULTURE

Edited by
David Gowland
Basil O'Neill
Alex Reid

LONGMAN
LONDON AND NEW YORK

Longman Group Limited,
Longman House, Burnt Mill,
Harlow, Essex CM20 2JE, England
and Associated Companies throughout the world

*Published in the United States of America
by Longman Publishing, New York*

First published 1995

ISBN 0 582 213258 PPR

British Library Cataloguing-in-Publication Data

A catalogue record for this book is
available from the British Library

Library of Congress Cataloging-in-Publication Data

A catalogue record for this book is available from the Library of Congress

Set by 7 in 10.5/12.5 Baskerville
Produced by Longman Singapore Publishers (Pty) Ltd.
Printed in Singapore

THE EUROPEAN MOSAIC:
CONTEMPORARY POLITICS, ECONOMICS AND CULTURE

Contents

Preface

In 1979 the University of Dundee set up an inter-disciplinary M.A. degree programme in Contemporary European Studies, using the contributions of enthusiastic staff from several departments. The programme has grown and flourished, always guided by the idea of promoting a pan-European view. In 1994 staff from nine departments are teaching in it, 20 Honours courses are available, and postgraduate work also flourishes. Working together has given this group an inter-connected understanding of Europe which generates its own synergy. It is that understanding which has inspired this book. The writers have collaborated extensively, so that the assignment of particular authors to particular chapters frequently leaves unmentioned the contributions of several other members of the team. The editors have tried to bring a degree of unity to the book (while leaving intact very different viewpoints) by exercising a rather strong hand in adapting the chapters as they came from other contributors. Responsibility for the content therefore rests primarily with the editors, though on the basis of the expertise of the other members of the team.

The contributors to the individual chapters are as follows:

Chapter 1   *Basil O'Neill*
Chapter 2   *David Mallion*
Chapter 3   *Christopher Bartlett, Mark Cornwall, David Gowland*
Chapter 4   *John Berridge*
Chapter 5   *Richard Dunphy*
Chapter 6   *Alan Small*
Chapter 7   *Richard Dunphy*
Chapter 8   *Alex Reid*
Chapter 9   *Charlotte Lythe, Alex Reid*
Chapter 10   *Charlotte Lythe, Alex Reid*
Chapter 11   *Basil O'Neill, Robin Adamson*
Chapter 12   *Basil O'Neill, Alison Borthwick*
Chapter 13   *Basil O'Neill, Richard Dunphy*

Chronological Table	*Christopher Bartlett, David Gowland*
Introduction and Epilogue	*the Editors*

We are particularly indebted to Jim Ford of the Department of Geography for producing excellent maps with such despatch and cheerfulness, and to Alan Small for his ready advice and help in organising the map work. We have also to thank Laura Reid and Jimmy Caird for their expert guidance in the preparation of Chapter 1. We must also express our gratitude to Dr Chris Harrison of Longman for his unfailing assistance.

Finally, the work would have been wholly impossible, from start to finish, without the unending cheerful patience and boundless efficiency of our secretary, Mrs Pam Hutton. Without her, our tempers would have been several miles shorter and our product infinitesimal.

David Gowland, Basil O'Neill, Alex Reid
School of Contemporary European Studies, University of Dundee, August 1994

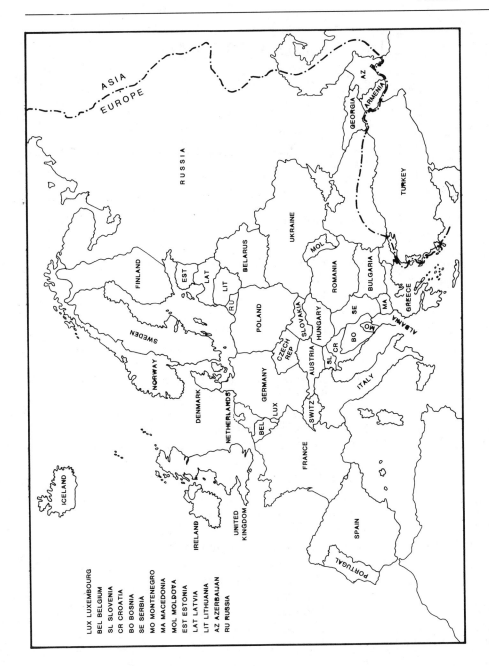

LUX LUXEMBOURG
BEL BELGIUM
SL SLOVENIA
CR CROATIA
BO BOSNIA
SE SERBIA
MO MONTENEGRO
MA MACEDONIA
MOL MOLDOVA
EST ESTONIA
LAT LATVIA
LIT LITHUANIA
AZ AZERBAIJAN
RU RUSSIA

The States of Europe 1994

List of abbreviations

APL	Albanian Party of Labour
CAP	Common Agricultural Policy
CDU	Christian Democratic Union (FRG/Germany; Hungary)
CIS	Commonwealth of Independent States
CMEA/Comecon	Council of Mutual Economic Assistance
COREPER	Committee of Permanent Representatives
CPSU	Communist Party of the Soviet Union
CSCE	Conference on Security and Cooperation in Europe
CSU	Christian Social Union (FRG)
DC	Christian Democracy (Italy)
DCR	Democratic Convention of Romania
(D)NSF	(Democratic) National Salvation Front (Romania)
DP	Democratic Party (Albania)
EAEC	European Atomic Energy Community
EC	European Community(ies)
ECB	European Central Bank
ECOFIN	European Council of Finance Ministers
ECSC	European Coal and Steel Community
ECU	European Currency Unit
EDC	European Defence Community
EEA	European Economic Area
EEC	European Economic Community
EFTA	European Free Trade Association
EMS	European Monetary System
EMU	Economic and Monetary Union
EPC	European Political Cooperation
ERM	Exchange Rate Mechanism
ESCB	European System of Central Banks
EU	European Union
FDP	Free Democratic Party (Germany)
FIDESZ	Alliance of Young Democrats (Hungary)

FN	National Front (France)
FRG	Federal Republic of Germany
FYROM	Former Yugoslav Republic of Macedonia
GATT	General Agreement on Tariffs and Trade
GDP	Gross Domestic Product
GDR	German Democratic Republic
HDF	Hungarian Democratic Forum
HDZ	Croatian Democratic Alliance
HSWP	Hungarian Socialist Workers' Party
IMF	International Monetary Fund
IU	United Left (Spain)
KKE	Greek Communist Party
KOR	Workers' Defence Committee (Poland)
KPD/DKP	Communist Party of Germany (FRG)
MDS	Movement for a Democratic Slovakia
MEP	Member of the European Parliament
MFA	Armed Forces Movement (Portugal)
MFN	Most Favoured Nation
MRF	Movement for Rights and Freedoms (Bulgaria)
MSI	Italian Social Movement
NATO	North Atlantic Treaty Organisation
ND	New Democracy (Greece)
OECD	Organisation for Economic Cooperation and Development
OEEC	Organisation for European Economic Cooperation
OPEC	Organisation of Petroleum Exporting Countries
PASOK	Pan-Hellenic Socialist Movement (Greece)
PCE	Communist Party of Spain
PCF	French Communist Party
PCI	Italian Communist Party
PCP	Portuguese Communist Party
PDS	Democratic Party of the Left (Italy)
PRNU	Party of Romanian National Unity
PS	Socialist Party (formerly SFIO, France)
PSD	Social Democratic Party (centre-right) (Portugal)
PSDR	Party of Social Democracy of Romania
PSI	Italian Socialist Party
PSL	Polish Peasant Party
PSOE	Spanish Socialist Workers Party
PSP	Portuguese Socialist Party
PUWP	Polish United Workers Party
SARK	Serbian Autonomous Region of Krajina
SEA	Single European Act
SED	Socialist Unity Party (GDR; now PDS – Party of Democratic Socialism in united Germany)
SLD	Alliance of the Democratic Left (Poland)

SPD	Social Democratic Party (FRG)
UCD	Democratic Centre Union (Spain)
USSR	Union of Soviet Socialist Republics
VAT	Value Added Tax
WEU	Western European Union
WTO	Warsaw Treaty Organisation

Introduction

The concept of a 'continent' was originally that of a stretch of continuous land, clearly bounded by sea, or at least by a narrow isthmuth. Africa, Australasia, North America, and South America satisfy this definition well enough. But 'Europe'? If you look at a large map of Asia with Europe it is obvious that there is just one landmass, which people do indeed call 'Eurasia', and 'Europe' is no more than a large peninsula projecting from it at its western side. It has no natural boundaries dividing it from Asia in the plains of Russia (the Ural Mountains have quite gentle slopes; they constitute no obstacle to the traveller). And the largest and most important state in its eastern plains, Russia, extends right across the Urals and far to the east across Siberia, out to Vladivostok on the coast of the Pacific Ocean. This situation raises two questions. First, why did anyone ever think that Europe was a separate continent? And second, why do people still think of 'Europe' as a distinct entity, and write books about it like this one? What is specially European about the territory we arbitrarily include within its boundaries, conventionally taken as running along the Ural Mountains, down the Ural River to the Caspian Sea, along the ridge of the Caucasus to the Black Sea, and then through the Bosphorus and the Mediterranean Sea to the Straits of Gibraltar and the Atlantic?

The answer to the first question is that the terms 'Europe' and 'Asia' were used by the Greek sailors of the second millennium BC, and continuing to about 500 BC, as they sailed up the Aegean Sea to the Bosphorus to trade on the coasts of the Black Sea. 'Europe' was the land on their left, where most of them lived, with the great Mycenaean cities such as Mycenae, Pylos, Sparta, Athens, Orchomenus and Thebes. 'Asia' was the land on their right, to the east, where Troy and Miletus stood and the kingdoms of the Lydians, the Phrygians, the Hittites and later the Persians flourished in what is now Turkey. They knew nothing of whether, far to the east, the land they called Europe was joined on to the land they called Asia; so they supposed that it was not, and that Europe was really separate from Asia.

Figure 0.1. The ancient Greek view of Europe

When the Greek geographer Hecataeus made a map of the world, in about 500 BC, he knew about the Caucasus and the Caspian Sea beyond it, but supposed that the salt-water Caspian stretched out into a great ocean dividing Europe from Asia. But when people give names to things they tend to think the world is arranged so that what is designated by one name is quite different from what is designated by another. And when, around 500 BC and for 20 years afterwards, the Greeks fought a great war against the Asiatic Persian Empire, successfully resisting invasions by enormous Asiatic armies, they fastened on to the idea that the forces of the Persian Empire were the forces of barbarism, of oriental tyranny and confusion, huge but culturally backward,

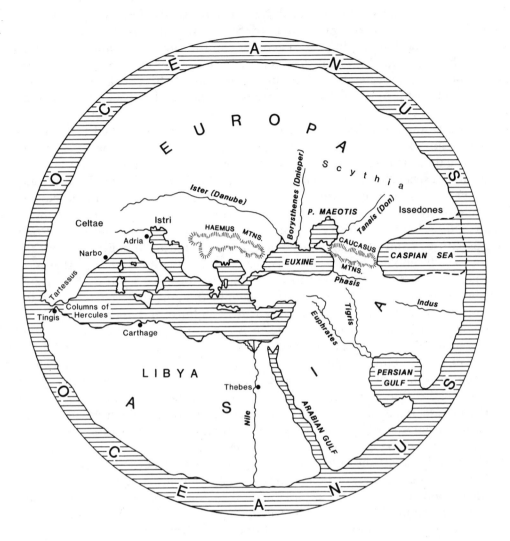

Figure 0.2. The world according to Hecataeus

lacking the capacity for self-government or the sense of freedom. This (distorted) picture of the peoples of the Persian side was labelled 'Asia'. On the other side, the Greek historian Herodotus glorified the heroic forces of the Athenians and the Spartans and their Greek allies as the forces of 'Europe', the bearers of independent-minded rationality, law and freedom. By this piece of propaganda Herodotus reclassified the Ionian Greeks who had for centuries lived on the Asiatic side of the Aegean Sea and on the islands of the Aegean, the originators of philosophy and rational science, and brave fighters in a long and heroic rebellion against Persia, as 'really' people of 'Europe', and sidelined the ancient prestige of the cultures of Phoenicia,

Babylonia and Egypt. He advanced the status of Athens, the city of culture and (relative) freedom as against that of Sparta whose citizens were good at discipline and fighting but not much else, and in this way insinuated the idea of Athens as the city which deserved to lead Greece; and he gave a further justification to the imperialist colonising activity of the Greeks all round the Mediterranean in establishing colonies on the lands of more 'barbarian' peoples.

In this way the sailors' idea of Europe as just the-land-on-the-left-hand-side-as-you-sail-North was filled with meaning; indeed, we might say, with propaganda. It became not only a label for a piece of land but also an *ideal*, centred especially in one place (Athens), where the cultural characteristics which are thought of as the ideal European ones are most fully developed; while other parts of 'Europe' only participate in this ideal by their sharing in the cultural glory of this centre or heart of Europe. In other words, not only was Europe from its inception defined in opposition to 'non-Europe', but the idea was promoted that Europe's true character is that of its 'heart', that is, of whatever centre is taken best to exemplify the idealised culture of 'Europe'. After Herodotus, for some centuries people thought more in terms of the Roman Empire, also based on a centre of culture and power (Rome), an empire which included much of North Africa and Western Asia but excluded much of what we now call Europe beyond the Rhine and Danube. Then for the next few centuries they thought more in terms of Christendom (whose range also was not synonymous with Europe except for a brief period at the end of the fifteenth century). It was in the sixteenth century, when the Portuguese, the Spaniards, the French, the Dutch and the English had become used to discovering, conquering and dominating lands across the oceans inhabited by peoples with inferior technology and no knowledge of Christianity, that the idea of Europe became important again, as the Europeans' label for the home area on maps, the Christian continent from which people sailed out to dominate the non-European lands and their 'inferior' cultures. So 'Europe' was always a word used by Europeans to bolster and celebrate their own standing and power, not just to give a label to a piece of land.

That is the answer to the first question; and already you can see how this sketch of history goes most of the way to give us the answer to the second question. Even after it had been discovered that geographically 'Europe' is only a peninsula of Eurasia, and doesn't deserve to be labelled a 'continent', still people stuck to it because to them Europe was not just a piece of land but an ideal – a place where a certain kind of civilisation was to be found (even if they disagreed greatly about what kind of civilisation this was). And for centuries now this ideal of civilisation has been located especially in the West of Europe. This is Europe's 'heart' – just as Athens was for Herodotus – and all other countries of Europe want to think of themselves as 'in Europe', as part of this European civilisation – democratic, free, individualistic, liberal, peaceful, economically efficient. But for our purposes it is most important to see that *Europe has no eastern boundaries* (except, of course arbitrary ones). We might vaguely say it gets less European as you go east, but there are no clear divisions on that journey.

This book will deal with eastern Europe as important in its own right, as it will also deal with the northern and southern parts of Europe. But it will not try to deal fully with the Baltic states or the countries of the CIS which formed part of the Soviet Union until 1991 (Russia, Belarus, Ukraine, Moldov and the war-torn and fragmented states of Transcaucasia) as this would take too much space. We shall try to give a rounded picture at an introductory level of contemporary Europe, a picture which, like Europe itself, fades out rather indeterminately to the east. We shall describe the land and the life of the people who live on it, the distribution of the population and the location of industrial complexes on the land. We try to explain the historical background to today's Europe, starting roughly from the end of the First World War but providing a more detailed treatment as we approach the present day. We pay particular attention to the historical and contemporary development of cooperative institutions set up since 1950 by western European states. These today form the European Union, a political and economic entity gathering together a wide variety of diverse states. We describe the political structures, problems and tensions of contemporary European countries grouped in four main regions. Our picture includes the character of European society, business, industry and commerce. We describe the importance of language and language differences in European life, and the rapidly changing patterns of communications which are transforming the life of Europeans. We examine Europe's post-1945 culture – the ways in which Europeans have understood their own lives and problems and found expression for these self- images in literature, music and art. We then consider the central issue of the divisions of Europe, the ideas of national identity and ethnicity which have had, and still have, so much significance for good and ill in the lives of European peoples. And we return, finally, to the nature of what it is to be European; not to sum up the book – that would be impossible – but to consider again what Europe means to Europeans, and what place it may have in the world.

We see the book primarily as a textbook for Contemporary European Studies, which is enjoying burgeoning growth in many European and non-European universities. All of us teach in this field, and all of us have felt the lack of a basic textbook which does not simply focus on European history or geography or politics or economics, but takes the widest possible inter-disciplinary approach towards making sense of contemporary Europe.

Contemporary European Studies is not a discipline in the traditional sense; it has no distinctive methods, no theories of its own, no exclusive subject-matter. What it does is to assemble, to gather together the perspectives of a range of disciplines on a complex and hugely important phenomenon: contemporary Europe and the life, struggles, hopes, efforts and achievements of its many peoples. The perspective of the political analyst is rounded out by that of the geographer, the philosopher, the sociologist, and others. In this way our understanding of Europe acquires a depth and realism which no single discipline could provide. Our hope in writing this book is that the student who reads it and uses it as part of a European Studies programme will become flexible in his or her thinking, will learn the rigour of the different disciplines and become able to shift to whatever approach seems likely to be most fruitful at the time.

This book was written by specialists who differ not only in their areas of expertise but also in their attitudes and approaches, so the student may find that different chapters have opposing perspectives on certain topics. We hope that this will be more of a stimulus than an irritation.

We also hope that the student will come to share our interest in Europe – this strange and complex phenomenon which we all think we know and which so constantly surprises us. We have no doubt that this book will be outdated even before it is printed by changes which keep happening and which are never just what we expected. The student should try to keep abreast of developments, using newspapers and journals to modify and add to the picture given here. The book is not an authority; it is a tool, a way for a student to embark seriously on the path to understanding Europe.

1 The palace and the shack: the wealth of Europe and its distribution

Introduction: Europe and the global capitalist system

For many centuries – from about 1400 to the beginning of the twentieth century – Europe (especially Western Europe) dominated the rest of the world, in power, in wealth, and in the organisation of commerce and the economy. In 1900, indeed, about 63 per cent of the world's industrial production was in Europe. Much of European thought has been based on taking it for granted that here in Europe was the leading edge of the world's civilisation. Since 1920 – and especially since 1945 – this has ceased to be so. The USA is the most powerful and richest country in the world, Japan is close to the USA in economic output, and a swathe of countries on the Pacific Rim – the eastern side of Asia round to Australia – have economies which are growing faster than any others, and rapidly catching up with Europe. This is not to say that Europe has switched from being dominant to being unimportant, but it is now just one of the major units in the world economic system.

Population

The population of Europe excluding the USSR in 1987 was 498 million, while in 1990 the 12 countries of the European Community (the EC) had 344.4 million people. By comparison the population of the USA in 1990 was 248.7 million, the USSR 287.5 million and Japan 123.5 million.

It is important to notice some important population trends. The population of the world as a whole is increasing very fast. But in Europe growth in population arising from the existing resident population has been replaced by a slow decline almost everywhere. Only in Turkey and Albania is there a strong growth rate. The decline is due mainly to a sharp drop in the birth rate. The average size of families has dropped well below the rate needed for replacement of the population (about 2.1 children per family) to about 1.75 in western Europe. In eastern Europe the effects of the dislocation of the economy and of society, combined in some cases with people postponing plans for children in order to acquire some of the material delights of the capitalist good life, have led almost everywhere to steep falls in the birth rate since 1989. In the CIS (the ex-Soviet Union) the fall was estimated at 9–10 per cent from 1992 to 1993 after a longish period of less dramatic decline. The figures for 1994 are expected to be even lower. In the five *Länder* which once constituted East Germany the birth rate slumped by a startling 65 per cent between 1989 and 1993, and demographers predict that the population may very well sink to 9 million by the middle of the twenty-first century from its previous 16 million.

If the drop in birth rate is traced to the fertility rate – the number of births per woman of child-bearing age – we can clearly identify a downward trend common to all European countries. This began in different periods in different countries but has followed a similar pattern in each one from the decade in which it began. In the 1950–70 period the trend was most marked in the UK, Scandinavia (except Finland), northern and central Italy, and Germany, but it has since spread to France, and – more recently – to Iberia, Finland, Greece, Poland and Romania. On this basis it is easy to predict that, leaving aside any effects of migration, the population will fall slowly in the next 20 years. It will fall rather faster in the UK and Germany, and probably faster still in the countries once in the eastern bloc. The scale of this fall cannot be predicted with certainty, but extrapolation from present fertility rates and death rates suggests that it might be as much as 15–20 per cent from 1990 to 2020 in the UK and Germany, rather less in other countries of western Europe, but considerably more in eastern Europe and the countries of the Commonwealth of Independent States (CIS).

It seems that conditions of family life in modern Europe, including readily available contraception, lead eventually to a fall in the birth rate to a level below that required for replacement. Whether this is inevitable in fully developed capitalist countries, or whether modernity can take other forms in its impact on society with different cultures is unclear; certainly economically advanced Islamic countries seem to show a very much higher birth rate to date. If the culture of Islam affects the fertility of a population differently from the secular/Christian culture characteristic of most of Europe, then migration of Muslims into Europe will have a definite contrary effect on its present tendency towards a declining population. But it should also be noted that the effect of AIDS on the population as a whole has so far been negligible. If gloomier predictions of its development are right, this will also increase the death rate.

But life expectancy has increased in modern European societies due to improved medical knowledge, health care and healthier living conditions. In 1990, life expectancy at birth in western European countries was between 74 and 78. The effect is not sufficient to outweigh the fall in the birth rate.

Rather, its effect is to increase the proportion of people over the age of 65 in the population. That proportion has increased in western Europe from 9 per cent in 1950 to nearly 15 per cent in 1991. For Russia the figures are not precisely comparable, but the proportion of over-60s was 13.5 per cent in 1987, expected to rise to 17.5 per cent by 2003; and those figures include the more fertile and less long-lived Asian populations, so that we should expect the figures for European Russia to show an even larger proportion of older people in the population. On the other hand, life expectancy in Russia (and the other CIS countries) has been declining for most of the past 25 years and for men is now less than 62 years. Notice that the figures we are considering are *proportions of the total population;* they are therefore affected by the lower birth rate and the resulting smaller number of children. On seeing these figures one might jump to the conclusion that the large number of old-age pensioners in the society would constitute an unprecedentedly great burden on the working population who have to produce sufficient surplus to support them. (That conclusion is often touted by politicians trying to reduce health-care provisions, etc.) But in fact the larger number of old-age pensioners is approximately off-set by the smaller number of children, so that there are at the same time fewer people under working age to support. The proportion of the population of working age remains about the same as in the mid-century. And if the older people require a larger expenditure on health care, this may be partly counter-balanced by the smaller expenditure on education for the smaller number of children and students.

The effect of continuing high birth rates in Turkey and the North African countries, however, may be considerable. This growing population already exerts a strong pressure to find outlets across the Mediterranean and the Bosphorus in the relatively rich European economies (see Chapter 13). By 1990 there were 1.5 million Turks in Germany and about the same number of North Africans (Algerians, Moroccans and Tunisians) in France. Other west European countries also have substantial Turkish and north African populations. In the UK there is also a considerable (but smaller) population of non-Europeans, mainly from the West Indies and the Indian sub-continent.

It seems very probable that this migration into Europe, especially from across the Mediterranean, will continue, regardless of government measures to stop it. Just as it has proved impossible to prevent a large influx of Mexicans and other Hispanics across the USA's southern border, so it looks likely that a great many North Africans and Turks will establish themselves in Europe, whatever governments decide. The effects of this migration may be significant, not least in reversing the trend of European birth rates and leading to a relatively stable population.

The core and the periphery

Europe's relative significance in the global economy can be illustrated by reference to gross national product (GNP). GNP reflects the total value of goods and services produced in the economy, including so-called 'invisible earnings' and profits from capital invested overseas. Gross domestic product (GDP) omits overseas earnings. The European Union (EU) countries accounted for 19.6 per cent of the world's GNP in 1993, the USA for 23.3 per cent and Japan and China each for 10 per cent. But a great deal of GNP is consumed in the home country. This is especially true of China. Europe is still a very powerful unit in the global economy. In 1992 the shares of world trade were EU 20 per cent (or 26.5 per cent counting countries which may be admitted in 1995), USA 16 per cent, and Japan 12 per cent.

It is clear that one cannot think in terms of the world as dominated by a single country or group of countries. There is a *world capitalist economic system*, in which the links of trade, finance and communications are tightly inter-dependent. It is a system characterised by very rapid change and growth, arising from the application of new technologies. Firms with branches in many different countries are now common. Europe plays a major role in this system.

There is, however, great inequality of economic power and wealth between different parts of the world. This unequal structure of the global economy is often characterised in terms of a *core* and a *periphery*. The core contains the centres of banking, finance and producer services, the headquarters of major firms, the more sophisticated high-tech industries, and has the highest standards of living and life expectation. The periphery produces food for subsistence and some for export, together with minerals, some industry based on very low wages for unskilled assembly work, and contains many of the world's poorest people, with low life expectancy and bad living conditions. The core, then, is mainly located in the northern hemisphere, the periphery in the southern hemisphere, including much of Africa, South and Central America and southern Asia. In these terms the whole of Europe is within the core. But these classifications are somewhat crude. There is also a third group of countries – the newly industrialised countries (NICs) – whose growing importance in the global economy is based on high levels of industrial development. These include South Korea, Malaysia, Mexico and Brazil.

But within Europe itself it is possible to distinguish the same core–periphery structure. We can regard the core of Europe as the broad belt of wealth, economic power and development stretching from south-east England through Belgium and the southern and western parts of the Netherlands up the Rhine valley and into Switzerland, and continuing through Lombardy and Piedmont to the Mediterranean Sea at Genoa. It includes the cities of London, Brussels, Antwerp, the 'Randstad' of the south-west Netherlands (including Rotterdam, Amsterdam, The Hague, etc), Düsseldorf, Essen, Cologne, Frankfurt, Mannheim, Strasbourg, Stuttgart, Basel, Zürich, Milan, Turin and Genoa. To this belt we should add the city of Paris and its environs, Hamburg, and

Figure 1.1. The fortress of the rich (*Guardian*, 14 February 1994)

Bavaria around Munich. This core region is thus longish but rather fat in the middle and has been called the 'Blue Banana' or 'Main-Street Europe'. By contrast some peripheral parts of Europe are economically backward and disadvantaged – average incomes in Portugal and Greece are about one-eighth of those of the cities of the core, and are even lower in Albania and Romania; while large parts of Spain, Poland, Southern Italy, and Ireland are almost as badly placed economically. (For details of *per capita* GDP in Europe see Chapter 9, Table 9.2)

This is not to say that the distribution of wealth is inevitably going to continue as it is now. Indeed, there is good reason to think that another belt of high-level development may grow along the coastal areas of the Mediterranean, in eastern Spain, southern France and parts of Italy, the so-called 'Sunbelt'.

The core areas of the world have close trading relations. One aspect of this is the transnational corporations (TNCs), the large companies whose activities and assets are spread across many different countries and possibly continents. A considerable proportion of the world's economy is now controlled by TNCs. Over a quarter of western European manufacturing production is controlled by TNCs, and the proportion is growing. With the opening up of central and

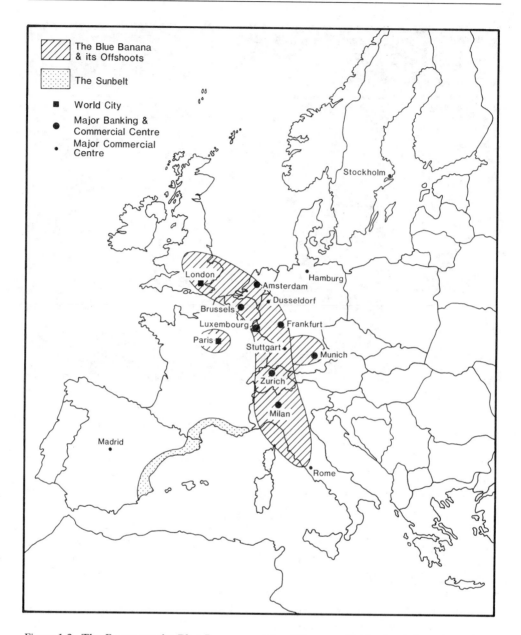

Figure 1.2. The Eurocore; the Blue Banana and its offshoots, with the Sunbelt region of possible development

eastern Europe in the early 1990s, the TNCs have capitalised on investment opportunities offered by educated cheap labour and under-developed market potential. Their headquarter offices and most of their area offices are located in the main cities of the core; in New York, Chicago, Los Angeles, Tokyo, and in the cities of Europe mentioned earlier.

These cities, then, are in constant communication with each other, and a large part of world business is controlled within them. The leading ones have been called 'world cities' – the main financial centres, New York, London, Tokyo, Hong Kong, Paris, Frankfurt, Amsterdam and Zürich. They need a host of sophisticated ancillary services – financial, legal and marketing – which add to the wealth of these cities and generate further needs – office space and office equipment, communications and transport, housing, food, and so forth, though developments in information technology are now facilitating work at home in the leafy suburbs or even the Shetlands.

High-tech developments have also been established in many regions around these cities (like those associated with the Cambridge Science Park close to London or the electronics of the area around Munich), while fashion industries are often located as close as possible to the richest markets. But a marked tendency is for the core areas to discard industry. Outside the core, land and labour are cheaper and the transport of bulk materials in and out of factories may be easier. So where production methods require substantial land, material and labour input, production is often set up outside the core, sometimes in labour-intensive 'sweatshops', but sometimes in very large-scale automated factories. Both Volkswagen and Ford operate very large car-assembly plants in Spain, taking advantage of relatively low wage rates, while assembly-based production of silicon chips and other high-tech components may be located in East Asia or Latin America.

Table 1.1. Wage rates per hour in manufacturing industry in selected countries, 1993 (or, where specified, 1992)

Japan £13.80 (may include non-manual work, but it is quite high)

Denmark £11.70

West Germany £9.10 (1992)

Netherlands £8.50

Sweden £8.30

Belgium £7.70

Canada £7.30

USA £7.20

UK £6.70

Spain £4.90 (1992)

To these statistically attested figures* can be added the following estimates:

Greece c. £3.50

South Korea c. £3.00

Portugal c. £2.50

Sri Lanka c. 35p

Bangladesh c. 25p

*calculated from data compiled by the International Labour Office, Geneva.

Industry which remains in the core areas tends to be rather technical, requiring a highly skilled and educated workforce. Manufacturing firms are often linked as parts of networks of suppliers needing to keep in close contact with each other in a complex industry. Such industries are not usually large providers of employment.

Thus the global capitalist system at the end of the twentieth century is associated with *de-industrialisation in the core areas*. The major source of employment and wealth in them is *services*. Indeed, even in the peripheral areas of Europe the proportion of employment in industry is falling, not least because modern production methods use comparatively few people in the production process, favouring rather the control and speed provided by automatic machines. But the service sector covers a very wide range of activities, from office cleaning and bar-tending to international financial negotiations and banking. In the core areas a key element is *producer services*, providing assistance to firms controlling production: advertising, banking, insurance, credit management, marketing, security services, computer services, personnel management, and so on. Such services may not provide a very large proportion of the employment in these areas, but they play a key role in the economy. In some parts of the periphery, *consumer services* play a larger role, for example, tourist-related work in hotels and restaurants, entertainment, and the like.

The economies of central and eastern Europe and the CIS have distinctive problems resulting from the overthrow of their communist regimes in 1989–1991 and the dismantling of the command economy structures of state control. These economies, currently in flux and undergoing massive restructuring (see Chapters 8–10), remain organisationally and technically backward with high levels of unemployment and poverty. But some of these countries contain significant natural resources and a high proportion of educated workers, and may follow the NICs' example of rapid progress. They may be classified as 'transition economies'.

Some major production units have been set up in these countries – often by modernising already existing plants – especially in Poland, Hungary and the Czech Republic. A notable example is the Skoda car-assembly plant in the Czech Republic, which has been taken over by Volkswagen, modernised with the help of a big injection of capital, and now has a high-volume high-quality output of small cars in a very efficient plant. Such production units may soon produce economic growth similar to that of Spain, whose economy responded well to the installation of very large production units in the 1970s.

Such regions as northern and eastern Spain are often classified as 'semi-periphery': regions of rapid economic growth, based mainly on manufacturing activity and consumer services. They do not contain the headquarters of TNCs or other large firms so they lack the economic power and infrastructural sophistication of the core areas. Such regions are essentially *branch-plant economies*, in that they depend on factories set up by large firms whose central and controlling offices are elsewhere. It has been argued that such economies are particularly vulnerable. The shift of control to comparatively remote centres means that distant managers, influenced by international factors, may determine working conditions or even shut down a production unit. But it is not easy to take such decisions, partly because they might involve the loss of substantial investment and partly because they are less independent of local conditions than has sometimes been suggested. Nevertheless, given the competitive pressures of the global economy and the mobility of capital relative to labour, the bargaining position of workers has worsened. Fast-moving shifts in strategy arising from technological change or from changes in goods manufactured or in the production process may lead firms to take drastic decisions about closures. The closure of large production units may have very serious effects on a regional economy.

Thus class inequalities in the capitalist system, which are discussed more fully in Chapter 2, may be expressed as 'spatial inequalities'. Some regions contain the wealth and also the economic power, while others are relatively powerless and much less wealthy. A critical issue for the future of Europe is whether these regional inequalities will tend to diminish as the periphery catches up with the core, or whether the unequal structure of modern world capitalism will reinforce itself. It is not at all clear that these spatial inequalities between different regions of Europe will tend to even up; they might rather become accentuated. If they do so, it seems very possible that serious political conflicts may arise from the sense of injustice and envy in disadvantaged regions, leading to racism, crime, disease, uncontrollable movements of populations seeking work, and disruption of political structures. This would have consequences even for the core, since in a modern capitalist system social and economic pressures cannot be contained within a region. It is possible, however, that intervention by national governments · or by European institutions like the EU might counter or at least limit tendencies towards unequal spatial development. Such moves may help to protect the peripheral regions and assist their development by stimulating investment and stemming the outflow of capital and population.

A feature of contemporary world capitalism is the *third agricultural revolution*: the development of agriculture – and especially food production – so systematically organised and scientifically controlled that it can be regarded as a branch of industry. Agribusiness needs very few workers and produces high-quality food on a very large scale. Crops and animals are kept in controlled conditions to optimise growth. They are looked after, harvested, packaged and prepared as foods, which are distributed for sale by largely mechanical operations and sold through large organisations, some of which are TNCs. This form of agriculture is so effective that Europe is now largely self-sufficient in foodstuffs, and the problem of agricultural policy in general is one of dealing with excess production. However, this industrialised agriculture exists alongside a very different kind of farming. Even in Europe many people in rural areas – especially in the peripheries – still work smallish farms by labour-intensive methods and live on the land. Their livelihood is threatened

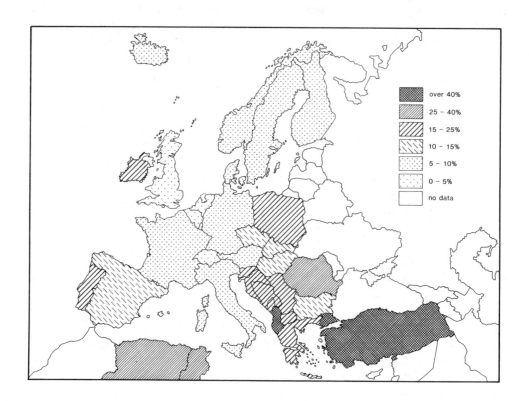

▨	over 40%
▧	25 – 40%
▨	15 – 25%
▨	10 – 15%
⠿	5 – 10%
⠄	0 – 5%
☐	no data

Figure 1.3. Percentage of workers employed in agriculture, 1989–90

by industrialised agriculture which needs so few workers. If the agricultural sector in Europe were completely uncontrolled, whole regions would be swiftly depopulated, and unemployment and dislocation would be enormous, with major political consequences.

The EU operates a system of controlled prices and partial protection for rural areas – the *Common Agricultural Policy (CAP)* – to deal with the problem of rural depopulation, but of course it does so at the expense of putting up food prices and directing subsidies to inefficient farmers. CAP is based on three main principles: (a) a single market for the free circulation of agricultural goods within the EU; (b) a Community preference in that market based on a system of import levies on non-EU agricultural products and export subsidies to EU farmers; and (c) joint financial responsibility for CAP via the European Agricultural Guidance and Guarantee Fund. CAP came to be widely regarded as an impossibly expensive policy because subsidies had grown unchecked. In the late 1980s CAP was modified to set limits to such subsidies and to reduce total expenditure on CAP within the EU budget. A policy of setting land aside to avoid over-production was instituted. However, it still absorbs two-thirds of the EU budget, and it may well be further modified in the next few years.

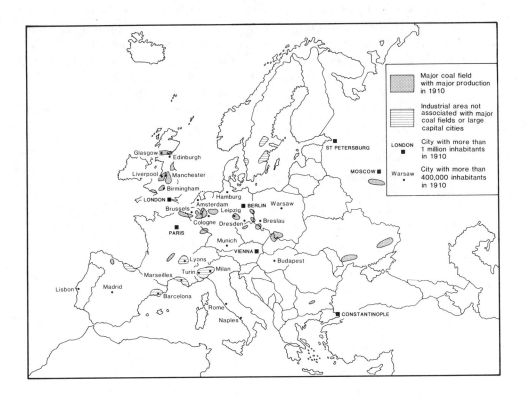

Figure 1.4. Europe: Major centres of population in 1910, showing coal fields

The third agricultural revolution has further integrated agriculture and food production into the framework of global capitalism. The impact of such industrialised agriculture on the transition economies of central and eastern Europe will probably be severe, since they contain a larger proportion of agricultural workers and peasants than any western economy except Greece. They have considerable potential for increased agricultural production, but its impact will depend on whether the EU admits them to its food markets and how far they can achieve the necessary readjustment of their methods.

If it is now asked what determines the location of wealth, economic power and industry within such an economic structure, the answers will be very different from what they were for eighteenth and nineteenth century capitalism. In the first industrial revolution the crucial factor for the location of industry was proximity to energy supplies, especially coal. Consequently many of the major centres of population in Europe were on or close to major coal fields, and a large part of their activities was in the heavy industries of coal-mining, steel production, and engineering. To these centres of population in 1914 should be added the capital cities of the larger countries, like London, Paris and Berlin.

In the late twentieth century transport and communications have become much easier and cheaper, and though coal is still quite important much of it is used for the generation of electricity which is now easily transmitted over great distances. (The efficiency of electricity transmission has vastly increased since 1950.) Energy is also obtained from oil and gas, which can be transported very cheaply through pipelines or by sea in giant tankers, and from nuclear power stations producing electricity. So the crucial factors determining the location of wealth in today's Europe are rather:

1. *Labour*: different kinds for different purposes: professional for producer services and corporate management; skilled for high-tech and R and D (research and development), production and services; semi-skilled/unskilled for assembly-line production and consumer services. Attitudes and habits of the workforce are also important; managers seek hard-working, disciplined and cooperative labour, not prone to major strikes.
2. *Major lines of communication* (especially significant where different lines of communication converge) for:
    (a) *Information*: telecommunications – including computer facilities for large-scale control of information traffic, postal services – depending partly on air services;
    (b) *People*: passenger transport by air, rail, and road (note the problem of congestion);
    (c) *Goods*: air, rail and road, but also by sea, where port facilities are vital;
    (d) *Energy*: electricity supply grids; oil and gas pipelines; oil refineries; port and rail facilities for oil and coal.
3. *Proximity to markets* – especially for rapidly changing markets and markets with specialised kinds of demand.
4. *Proximity to producer services,* for example:
    (a) *Financial services*: banking, insurance, credit, security, management consultants;
    (b) *Information services*: computers and computer analysis, access to databanks;
    (c) *Research and design*: universities and science parks, specialised technical advice companies.
5. *Attractive living conditions* – for the staff and for visitors: e.g. good infrastructure, pleasant climate, good urban conditions, good educational facilities.

All five factors may favour established centres of population, especially the richest ones. These will tend already to have the best communications and are themselves large markets. Producer services tend to gather in them, and (in some cases) they have already developed the best urban environments for living. In effect, the structure of contemporary capitalism works according to the biblical saying, 'Unto everyone that hath shall be given, and he shall have

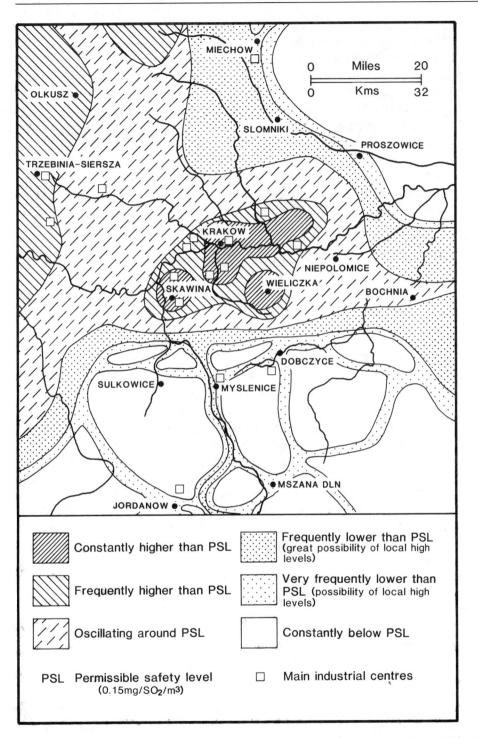

Figure 1.5. The 'Black Triangle': severely polluted area around Cracow (southwest Poland), showing sulphur dioxide pollution. (Other impurities are distributed similarly.)

abundance, but from him that hath not shall be taken away even that which he hath' (Matthew 25:29); or, to use the jargon of geographical economics, it works according to the *regional multiplier*. In this way, the distribution of wealth and population established in earlier ages is – very approximately – preserved and accentuated.

But the tendency is not quite as simple as that. For one thing, the means for very large-scale movements of goods or very rapid and efficient movement of passengers are not set up everywhere. Older communications systems may be inadequate, and their very existence may lead to indefinite postponements of decisions to build up-to-date systems. For example, airports are widespread, but only a small number of international airports are capable of taking the large number of passengers required for world cities. Moreover, the regional multiplier tends to favour capital cities or anyway international trading cities, rather than the old industrial cities.

Older centres of population and wealth tend to decline in competition with the leading cities and regions. With their ugly and polluted environments, few amenities and large numbers of unemployed workers, they are unattractive to producer-service and high-tech industries. The old industrial regions of northern England, Scotland, Wales and Northern Ireland are declining and disadvantaged regions for these reasons, and qualify by relative poverty and unemployment for EU regional economic aid. A similar situation may be developing in the coal and steel regions of northern Spain. We may expect such problems to arise also in many of the old industrial areas of central and eastern Europe, compounded in the case of the Silesian region of Poland by very severe pollution problems arising from the use of their own local impure brown coal (lignite) as their main source of power (see Fig. 1.5).

But even the core regions of Europe contain seriously disadvantaged regions which often qualify by poverty, unemployment, etc. for EU regional assistance grants (see Fig. 1.6). This is true of the Nord region of France and the adjoining Belgian coalfields, the Lorraine iron region and the Saar coalfield, and parts of the Ruhr coal and steel region. But other cities of the Ruhr (like Düsseldorf and Essen) have become successful core cities with international importance, partly because massive war-time damage made it necessary almost totally to reconstruct the urban environment after 1945.

The reasons why geographers expect a major development along the Sunbelt of eastern Spain, southern France and north-central Italy are that, apart from excellent living conditions, communications are good, the burgeoning tourist trade to the Mediterranean resorts has brought in both capital and workers, and there has been development of large branch-plant production in eastern Spain.

There may also be considerable scope for development towards world city status in the case of certain cities of eastern Europe: Prague, Warsaw, Budapest, St Petersburg, Moscow and Kiev. In western Europe it is the capital cities – like London, Paris, Copenhagen, Madrid, Stockholm, Athens – which have come to dominate the commercial and financial activity of their countries and their international links; and this tendency may be expected also in eastern Europe as it moves more and more effectively into the global economy.

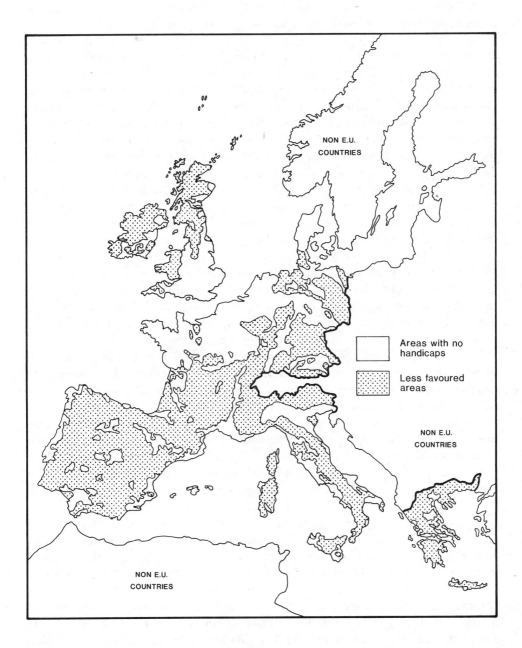

Figure 1.6. The EU's less favoured areas (1994)

Energy

A major problem for any advanced economy is energy supply. Until 1950 Europe obtained most of its energy from coal, a growing proportion of which was converted into electricity. Only in Italy and Norway was there any considerable development of hydro-electric power. But it became apparent that energy from oil was considerably cheaper and was rather easier to handle by automatic procedures. Consequently there was a great expansion of its use as a source of energy at the expense of coal. By 1972 oil provided 65 per cent of western Europe's energy needs and coal a mere 22 per cent. Nearly all this cheap oil was imported. After the 1973 Arab–Israeli War, however, the Organisation of Petroleum Exporting Countries (OPEC) increased the price of oil more than fourfold; while in 1979–80, the price more than doubled again. Since then it has fallen again in real terms to slightly below the 1973 level, but the sense of insecurity and uncertainty about possible devastating price-shifts led western Europe to try to reduce its dependence on imported oil.

Energy policy changes have included (a) a halt to the hitherto continuous expansion of demand for energy (by technical improvements in energy use, energy-saving measures, etc.); (b) a diversification of energy sources; and (c) the development of home sources of energy, notably North Sea oil and natural gas. Currently the sources of western Europe's energy are: oil 53 per cent, coal 19 per cent, natural gas 19 per cent and primary electricity 9 per cent (primary electricity is electricity generated from nuclear power and from hydro-electric power; where the electricity is generated from oil, coal or natural gas it is included in the figures for these sources). Notice that the proportion supplied by coal is even smaller than its level in 1972.

In central and eastern Europe, however, in 1982 coal made up a much larger proportion of total energy consumption (54 per cent), while oil and gas together contributed 40 per cent. Poland's dependence on coal was as high as 76 per cent. Energy was used much less economically throughout the eastern bloc.

Natural gas has been developed as a source of energy largely since 1950. Resources, often associated with oil deposits, are very large and natural gas has become a major source of energy notable for its ease of management. By 1990 it was being transported mainly through pipelines, and the technology for using it efficiently (mostly in power stations for generating electricity) was well developed.

It is still true that Western Europe imports most of its oil (about 60 per cent) and gas from various sources, but the Middle East now provides less than 40 per cent of the oil. The north African countries provide a greatly increased share, assisted by an oil and a gas pipeline from Algeria to Sicily and thence to the rest of Europe, and extensive terminal port facilities in southern France (Lavera, near Marseilles) and Italy (Genoa and Savona) for both oil and liquefied natural gas. The Middle Eastern pipelines from the Gulf oil-fields to the Mediterranean in Egypt and Turkey provide some security against sudden withdrawal of supplies from that source.

In the longer term the large oil and still larger natural gas reserves (40 per cent of world reserves) of Russia and other CIS countries may meet a sizeable proportion of the needs of Western Europe; indeed, even in the late 1980s when the Iron Curtain supposedly kept eastern Europe separate from the West, 14 per cent of western Europe's energy needs were supplied by the Soviet Union. But from the late 1980s Russian oil production has been sharply diminishing as a result of obsolescent technology and economic dislocation in the transition to a market economy. (Gas production, on the other hand, was holding steady in the early 1990s.) It seems certain, however, that in the longer term production will recover and that exports to western Europe will become very significant, thus enabling Russia to earn the hard currency it needs to provide the large-scale investment required for modernisation. The largest Russian reserves are in the far North, in the Pechora region and beyond the Urals near the mouth of the river Ob (the Tyumen region), but there are also very large reserves in the region around the South of the Urals and towards the Volga, as well as some in Arkhangel'sk Oblast' and the Caucasus. All are connected by a network of pipelines to the population centres of Russia and the Ukraine, and thence to central and eastern Europe and the West, connected through Poland to Germany and through Hungary to Austria and Italy.

But the most remarkable development in European energy supplies since 1960 has been the discovery and exploitation of large oil and gas reserves in the North Sea. These began in 1959 with the discovery of the Slochteren gas-field (now called the Groningen field) in Dutch territory, but through the 1960s and 1970s large fields were discovered, mostly in a belt running northwards through the centre of the North Sea to well north of the Shetland Islands. They fall almost entirely within the territories of the UK, Norway and the Netherlands. As a result these countries are able to provide quite a large proportion of their energy needs from their home supply, thus saving imports; the Netherlands gets over half its energy needs from its own natural gas. Most of the oil and gas is now transported by undersea pipelines to the nearby mainland. It is certain that the fields already discovered contain extensive reserves, adequate perhaps until 2010 or later, while further exploration is almost certain to reveal major new fields to exploit, not only in the North Sea but also in the Irish Sea, in the Bay of Biscay, and in several areas of the Mediterranean, Adriatic and Aegean Seas around Spain, Italy, Albania and Greece. Thus the potential for European energy supply from oil and gas is very promising.

At the height of the panic induced by the 1973–74 oil crisis and the resulting recession in the European economy, great efforts were made to find alternative sources of energy, especially in countries like France and Germany which had no working oil and gas sources, and nuclear power was extensively developed. So by the 1980s a considerable number of such plants were operating throughout Europe, providing electricity for the grid. By 1989 this source provided 34 per cent of western Europe's total electricity generation (and an eighth of its primary energy). The proportions for different countries ranged from 75 per cent of electricity generation for France and 61 per cent for Belgium, to 45 per cent for Sweden, 41 per cent for Switzerland, 39 per cent for Spain, 35 per cent for West Germany, to 22 per cent for the UK and 0 per cent for Italy. France gets more than 30 per cent of its total energy needs from nuclear power. French policy has shown little inclination to heed warnings from environmentalists about the dangers of nuclear power. Electricity thus generated is also exported, much to the UK and Italy, and some to Germany, while Switzerland exports to Italy and Germany. Since the Chernobyl accident of 1986 in which the control-system of a Ukrainian nuclear power station failed and quantities of toxic materials were emitted into the atmosphere and deposited on the region around and even thousands of miles away, public hostility to nuclear power has increased and its expansion has slowed. But the European Commission's medium-term objective for the EU is

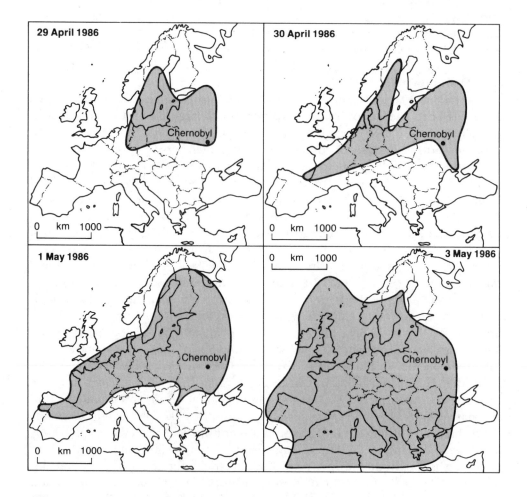

Figure 1.7. Radio-active pollution from the Chernobyl accident

to increase the proportion of energy supplied from nuclear power by about half, to 17 per cent. This is not necessarily driven by financial rather than safety measures; constructions already established or under way will tend to raise the amount produced from present levels in any case. Nuclear power has a very long planning cycle; it is many years after major construction has begun before it can come on-stream, and many years after a decision has been taken to close down a power station before it is technically or economically possible to do so.

Coal and lignite were once thought to be the main indigenous energy resource for safeguarding Europe against further price rises in imported energy like that of 1973. But even then, coal was considerably more expensive, awkward to transport and use, and dirtier than oil or gas. Reducing coal production by closing the less productive pits therefore continued all over Europe, despite considerable improvements in productivity. Coal production in western Europe dropped by 24 per cent from 1973 to 1989, and it seems likely that the cut-back would have been even larger but for the political sensitivity of putting miners out of their jobs. Europe's total coal consumption amounted in 1990 to only 19 per cent of energy supplied. Moreover, some foreign coal supplies were very much cheaper than western European coal – costing as little as half the price, so that even the coal western Europe was still using included 34 per cent of imported coal in 1989, some from Poland, some from the USA, and some from Australia. Greater reliance on coal (arising from improved technology) would probably benefit overseas rather than domestic coal producers.

Lignite or 'brown coal' is dirtier and less pure than hard coal. It is present in great deposits in the Rhineland and Saxony (Germany) and Silesia (Poland), and also in Spain and Greece. The older heavy industries of these regions made extensive use of lignite, but the resulting pollution and its inefficient energy production led to steep falls in its use in West Germany before 1989 and less dramatic reductions in Spain. But East Germany and Poland continued to use it, with serious environmental pollution in south-west Poland and adjoining parts of eastern Germany. Unification trebled Germany's lignite reserves, but burdened it with the former GDR's inefficient and polluting power stations. It seems certain, however, that lignite production will be drastically reduced and the power for local industries found in more modern ways.

Hydro-electric power is important in some limited areas of Italy, Norway and Spain, but for Europe as a whole its contribution to energy supplies is small. The attractions of obtaining energy from a renewable resource rather than burning a fossil fuel (as with oil, gas or coal) or generating long-term dangerous waste by the production process (as with nuclear power) are obvious enough, but so far the practical problems of getting enough power from available sources have proved too great except for limited developments. Possibly improved uses of wave, tidal and solar power will allow these sources to make a substantial contribution, but we are far from that as yet. A more immediately viable way of preserving the earth's resources of energy is to reduce further Europe's energy needs. The technology for doing so already exists, but it has been more extensively utilised in some countries, including those of Scandinavia, than in others like the UK.

Structure of Firms and Industrial Production

The development in the USA of the method of mass production in the 1920s was especially associated with the name of Henry Ford and with the production of cheaper motor cars. Thus such production methods are called 'Fordism'. Standardised products are produced in a large factory from materials and components kept in store, on an assembly line kept continuously moving by watchful supervisors. The assembly-line workers perform simplified, repetitive tasks; no scope exists for variation of their work or for individual initiative, since the mass production system requires each worker to perform just one stage of a pre-set process, and works well only if there is no variation from that process. The work is unsatisfying, mindless, but at least reasonably undemanding. The employer has greater control over the system of production and it requires only cheap semi-skilled labour.

Such mass production methods are still used, but less often now. They involve several disadvantages. Quality control is difficult. Production cannot be speeded up beyond the capacity of the workers on the most time-consuming stage of the process. It is difficult without wasteful waiting time to coordinate the output of different lines of production, so that a great quantity of components and materials may need to be stored until needed on the assembly-line. But the most serious disadvantage is the uniform character of the products. Such production methods are designed for high-volume output of a few lines and for long runs.

Such uniformity is unsuited to an industry in which technological, design or fashion changes require rapid product change, which applies to most industries in the 1990s. Furthermore, the market increasingly requires differentiated products to meet individual consumer tastes and as inputs to other production processes. Modern production, therefore, is characterised by flexible control systems, highly responsive to the market and to technological development. This reduces time wastage in production and delays before sale to a minimum. Such production systems are labelled 'just-in-time' systems (for production in immediate response to demand) and 'just-in-case' systems (for products adapted to the precise requirements of the consumer). What makes them possible is (a) highly controlled production processes, often by robots or other highly automatised machines and machine systems; and (b) rapid transfer of information and its linking to the production process itself, both made possible by computer systems.

Thus the production system is essentially an *information system*. It is the flow of information which determines the effectiveness of the production process and its link to its market; and this information system, in turn, is closely tied to the financial control of the firm. Such information systems may operate globally thanks to the speed and scale of modern telecommunications (using satellite communications for many of the greater-distance links). Some TNCs use such systems to control from their headquarters production planning, cost accounting, marketing, customer services and the management of the workforce. Levi Strauss's jeans production is aimed at ensuring that every time a customer buys a pair of jeans of given design and size in a shop anywhere on earth, the production of a replacement (unless plans for change of design supervene) will be triggered in one of its factories and the order will automatically be added to the batches for delivery at the earliest possible date. The Tokyo headquarters of the Mitsubishi Corporation receives from and sends to its many branches all over the world more than 4.5 million words every day. Benneton of Italy produce clothes in precise response to a rapid, computerised flow of information from all their retail outlets in Europe.

It is easy to see why such a system will reduce employment in manufacturing: very little labour is required for it to work. It may not be quite so obvious why information-governed production tends to reduce demands for energy. Computer-aided design tends to reduce the size and weight of moving parts of machines, and to minimise energy use in the production process itself. The production system has been called 'lean production', a system which uses information flow through computers and automatic, flexible production processes to achieve maximum economies in the use of labour, materials, energy, and indeed capital (since virtually no capital is locked up in storage or waste). But a particularly significant effect is to encourage the separation of different elements of the production process. Thus sub-contracting has become a major feature of industrial organisation. Flexibility is often obtained by the specification of standard components which can be assembled in different ways to produce different products. Once the design has been determined, the firm may find it cheaper and more efficient to sub-contract the work of producing particular components to other firms. Thus inter-locking contractual arrangements result in many relatively small firms producing components which other firms assemble. The effect on the spatial distribution of industry is that different parts of a complex product may be produced in locations around the world and transported to an assembly site.

But although such possibilities seem to favour the dispersion of productive industry, especially to those parts of the world where wages are lowest, in practice technical demands and the need to keep in touch with designers, suppliers, services of all kinds and the market tend to encourage locations fairly close to one another. Thus, in Europe at least, many of the more technical industries are growing fastest in or near the core areas. Production may indeed be dispersed in smaller production units for components and for specific stages of production, but this dispersion is for the most part to parts of the European core. The production of a single European aircraft, for example the European Airbus, involves the separation of its components into different parts produced in Manchester, Filton near Bristol, Hatfield near London, Dordrecht in the Netherlands, Charleroi in Belgium, Bremen, Hamburg, Laupheim near Stuttgart, Augsburg in South Germany, Nantes, Les Mureaux near Paris, Toulouse, Madrid, and Seville. Most of these sites are close to or in the core. In many of these cities and regions, other similar kinds of high-tech production will be under way, creating a network of highly skilled workers able to inform and influence each other.

This concentration of human resources has become government policy in the idea of science parks, units of interaction between universities and research institutes and industry which, if successful, generate an impetus for technically developed production linked to research. This has happened in Grenoble, in Munich, at Sophia Antipolis on the Mediterranean coast of France, around Utrecht and Amsterdam, in Cambridge, and in the development corridor along the M4 from London to Bristol. The wealth of technological knowledge and talent in Russia, once largely harnessed to the Soviet defence programme, is also beginning to be gathered in similarly fruitful concentrations in locations there.

But it is not clear that the present degree of spatial concentration will continue. The further extension of fast communications in Europe may spread the core and make its interactions effective over greater distances. The presence, among the centres for aircraft production for the Airbus, of Nantes, Augsburg and Seville might suggest that such a development is possible.

Communications

Here some notable features will be selected for comment rather than attempting a rounded picture of the whole structure of communications in Europe.

Ports

The free and cheap movement of goods which is such an essential pre-condition for the global economy we have been describing is to a considerable extent achieved by transporting goods pre-packed in very large units, in containers or in giant tankers for oil. To accommodate these on their arrival or departure, ports were needed with special facilities for loading and unloading and for further despatch of cargoes. Older port facilities were quite inadequate for this, and in many cases the existing harbour locations were too built-up for the extensions needed. In this way some older ports, like Liverpool, have failed to adapt to the conditions of modern capitalism, while others, like Hamburg, Marseilles and Gothenburg, have done so by abandoning their old port areas and constructing new port facilities close by.

Europe's leading port, Rotterdam, has successfully used its position at the mouth of the Rhine in a sheltered estuary where deep channels could be dredged, building extensive port facilities and large factories and oil refineries to process some of its bulk imports. Such facilities provide a growth-point for certain types of industry involving bulky goods. Like Rotterdam, most of the top 20 European ports, including the seven largest container ports, are located around the southern end of the North Sea. Such a location provides direct access to the European core at a centre for land communications and close to major cities. For the Mediterranean trade, apart from Barcelona and Valencia, most of the big ports are gathered at the head of the Ligurian Sea – Marseilles-Fos, Genoa, La Spezia, and Livorno itself.

Air

Here a comparison with the situation in the USA is instructive. The American air transport system is considerably cheaper than the European one, more widespread, and subject to fewer problems of congestion. The European airlines are each protected by their governments, so each can to some extent escape the pressures of competition. Fares are fixed by international agreements. Air traffic control is not fully coordinated between the systems of the different European countries. Air transport is in this way a prime example of the disadvantage which Europe suffers in the global economy from the political division of its economic system. The European Union's competition policy is intended to overcome these obstacles. As with many such policies, it is a long way from intention to achievement. Within Europe the major airports clearly reinforce the dominance of the core, and especially of the world cities. Foreigners arrive in a country at its major airports, which will normally be close to the capital city. (Only the federal systems of Germany and Switzerland have significant dispersion of major airports.) Of western European airport cities, much the largest is London, followed by Paris, then by Frankfurt, Amsterdam, Rome, Copenhagen and Zürich.

Rail

A notable development is the French network of high-speed trains – '*Trains de Grand Vitesse*' (TGVs) – which strongly competes with air transport for comfort and city-to-city speed since it takes passengers direct to city centres; journey times are only about 50–60 per cent of those taken by express trains. The system is planned to extend throughout continental Europe, but like other developments across national boundaries it is taking some time to organise. It has had a beneficial effect on the amenities and economic prospects of the cities and regions it serves, and could be a considerable factor in any 'spreading of the core'.

Road

The motor car is wonderful – except for all the other people who own them. The mobility it has conferred on private and commercial users has filled Europe's space with a dense network of roads, well suited to the rapidly interacting environment a modern economy requires. Unfortunately, however, the dense mass of other road-users, especially 44-ton lorries, makes it difficult to get where you want to go. In particular this congestion damages the environment and renders cities far less effective as sites for the concentration of human activity. Building more and wider roads only leads to greater traffic; building by-pass roads around major cities (as in the Boulevard Périphérique round Paris or the M25 round London) only leads to increasing blockages.

One response is to build more and more facilities – hypermarkets, leisure centres, industrial workplaces, offices, and of course homes – outside the city centres. Another is to force cars out of cities (by forbidding them to enter, or taxing them highly for coming in), providing much-improved public transport within the cities, and thus seeking to re-establish a form of urban living independent of the car. Of course these policies may be combined. But it is hard to see how the mobility essential for a modern economy can be preserved without extensive use of the car.

Apart from these problems, the road system of western Europe is adequate. In eastern Europe and even more so in Russia and the CIS, roads and support services are more seriously deficient. Improvements are getting under way and are an essential step in establishing the modern infrastructure which eastern Europe needs.

Telecommunications

The network of telecommunications is developing extremely fast, both in the installation of fibre-optic cable through urban areas and in establishing new forms of electronic communication, like cellular mobile telephones and facilities for video conferences. Computer connection makes possible the forms of inter-communication between and within firms which this chapter has described. For a more detailed description of developments, see Chapter 11, but it should be stressed here that much the largest volume of information transmitted is commercial and financial, and the operation of international finance and business is essentially dependent on international (and indeed inter-continental) telecommunications, which are set up mainly for their benefit.

The speed and flexibility of telecommunications networks means that they can perform their role from any region which is adequately provided with links to satellites and fibre-optic cables, but such provision is not uniform over Europe, nor even over western Europe; and the world cities of London, Paris, Frankfurt, Amsterdam and Zürich operate the fullest capacity of international connections. Moreover, this traffic is expected to increase greatly in the coming decade, and competition for it is intense. It is interesting, as an example of the forms of global corporative interaction, that the three main competitors in this field in mid-1994 were three TNC consortia, each gathering into a single group major companies from the USA, Europe and Japan.

Further reading

Clout, H., Blacksell, M., King, R. and Pinder, D. (1994) *Western Europe: Geographical Perspectives*, Longman, Harlow, Essex.

Dicken, P. (1992) *Global Shift: the Internationalization of Economic Activity*, Paul Chapman, London.

Hoffman, G. W. and De Souza, A. R. (1989) *Europe in the 1990s: A Geographic Analysis*, Wiley, New York.

Hull, A., Jones, T. and Kenny, S. (1988) *Geographical Issues in Western Europe*, Longman, Harlow, Essex.

Knox, P. and Agnew, J. (1994) *Geography of the World Economy*, Edward Arnold, New York and London.

Masser, I., Sviden, O. and Wegener, M. (1992) *The Geography of Europe's Futures*, Belhaven Press, London.

Minshull, G. N. (1990) *The New Europe: Into the 1990s*, Hodder and Stoughton, Sevenoaks, Kent.

Pinder, P. (1990) *Western Europe: Challenge and Change*, Belhaven Press, London.

2 The pecking order: social inequality and politics in Europe

This chapter begins with a brief review of theories of inequality in modern societies and then examines how well they fit the facts of twentieth century Europe. The impact of industrialisation on the occupational structure for men and women is emphasised. The resultant pattern of inequality is shown to be partly influenced by the development of democratic states and the moderation of the impact of market forces by the spread of social welfare provisions.

Theories of class and inequality in modern society

There are two main approaches to explaining social inequality in modern industrial societies. The *liberal view* was promoted by the rising middle classes who first challenged the agrarian elites ruling Europe before the industrial revolution. Liberals fought against inherited wealth and power, championing the idea of equality of opportunity. They saw the prospect of opportunity for all to compete on equal terms as the capitalist economy swept across Europe from the north and west towards the east and south. A free labour market would allow workers to sell their talents to the highest bidder rather than be tied to a particular landlord. Although trade and manufacturing would create fortunes for some and penury for others the rewards would be fairly distributed on merit.

The *socialist view* was most potently expressed by Karl Marx (1818–83). Recognising the material progress facilitated by modern industrial capitalist development, he believed that eventually the new methods of production would be harnessed for the benefit of all, but not under capitalism. Although capitalism was a necessary stage in human progress, it would have to be replaced by a socialist system before the full democratic potential of modern industrialism could be realised.

Marx thought that liberal capitalism was not much less oppressive than the preceding feudal regimes it had replaced. In the past a minority ruling class had exploited the mainly agricultural workforce by various forms of compulsion. When workers moved from the domination of their local landlord to make an apparently free contract to work for the factory owner, they entered a new form of 'wage slavery' from which they had little possibility of escape. Forced to accept whatever wages were on offer, they did not really share the new freedom enjoyed by their middle-class employers.

Marx predicted that the gap between the wealthy owners of capital and their workers would increase under capitalism, although overall living standards might rise. Wealth would become concentrated in an elite, for small business-people or independent artisans would be unable to compete with large monopoly companies. Skilled workers would be replaced by machinery, and the working class would become a mass of unskilled and alienated drudges struggling to survive on minimum wages.

The horrors of the capitalist labour market would force workers to organise into trade unions and then into their own political parties to fight for reform. But reform would be blocked by the capitalist class who would dominate the state. Social inequality would be intensified by periodic booms and slumps. Social protests would rise until the labour movement was strong enough to lead a revolution to sweep away capitalism and replace it by a socialist system based on common ownership.

Liberals and Marxists both recognised the international dimension of modern society. Marx lived long enough to see large-scale capitalist organisations encircling the globe, employing new means of communication to link together producers and consumers in many countries. Given such a powerful enemy, he argued that workers could not defeat it at local or national level. The socialist revolution might start in one country, probably in one of the most advanced capitalist societies, like Britain or the USA, but it would have to spread throughout the world. Workers of the world would have to unite as effectively as the capitalists had done on an international scale. As one later sympathiser put it, capitalism was a tiger and it was impossible to tame it claw by claw!

Among modern critics of Marx, *functionalists* argue that a complex industrial society is bound to develop inequalities because there will always be a need for leadership. Qualified experts in positions of authority have to be rewarded for exercising their talents and are bound to become the new elite. Functionalists point to what happened under the Soviet brand of state socialism, where getting rid of capitalism did not prevent senior party members awarding themselves all sorts of special privileges.

Pluralists accuse Marx of over-simplifying the link between economic wealth, social status and political power. They prefer to follow Max Weber (1864–1920), who accepted that social class was a major cleavage in modern society but not the only one. Pluralists point to conflicts within classes, between one trade and another, or between rival regional, national, ethnic or religious groups, as in Northern Ireland, Italy, Spain, and various parts of central and eastern Europe today. Although they do not accept the classical liberal model of a society of competing individuals, they reject the two-class model and stress the plurality of social conflicts. Politics is not a simple football match between two sides, capital and labour. Political parties are seen as shifting coalitions of interests seeking a share of power. The parties have even been likened to firms competing for customers.

These rival theories of modern capitalist society offer different interpretations of the same facts. The next section looks at how well the theories fit the available facts about social inequality in modern Europe.

Democracy adapts to modern industrialism

It is difficult to generalise about social inequality and conflict in modern Europe. The battle between, and sometimes within, the classes has taken place against a kaleidoscopic background of social upheaval induced by economic and political change. The First World War dealt a severe blow to hopes for the international solidarity of workers, as they rallied to their countries' flags. Their national loyalties may have been strengthened by social reforms conceded or promised by pragmatic governments. In the closing decades of the old century and the opening decades of the new, the extension of the franchise to all men and eventually, in most countries, to all women, was completed (see Table 2.1).

Table 2.1. Introduction of universal franchise in Europe

	Universal male suffrage	Universal adult suffrage
Belgium	1894	1948
Netherlands	1918	1922
France	1848	1945
Italy	1913	1946
Germany	1871	1919
Ireland	1918	1923
UK	1918	1928
Denmark	1849*	1918
Norway	1900	1915
Sweden	1909	1921
Finland	1907	1907
Austria	1907	1919
Switzerland	1848	1971

* = With significant restrictions
Source: extracted from C. Pierson (1991) *Beyond the welfare state?*, p 110, Table 4.3

Table 2.2. Introduction of social insurance in Europe

	Industrial Accident	Health	Pension	Unemployment	Family Allowance
Belgium	1903	1894	1900	1920	1930
Netherlands	1901	1929	1913	1916	1940
France	1898	1898	1895	1905	1932
Italy	1898	1886	1898	1919	1936
Germany	1871	1883	1889	1927	1954
Ireland	1897	1911	1908	1911	1944
UK	1897	1911	1908	1911	1945
Denmark	1898	1892	1891	1907	1952
Norway	1894	1909	1936	1906	1946
Sweden	1901	1891	1913	1934	1947
Finland	1895	1963	1937	1917	1948
Austria	1887	1888	1927	1920	1921
Switzerland	1881	1911	1946	1924	1952

Note. These dates include schemes which were initially voluntary but state-aided as well as those that were compulsory.
Source. extracted from C. Pierson (1991) *Beyond the welfare state?*, p 108, Table 4.1

This period also saw the first phase in the establishment of state welfare systems. Many countries passed legislation introducing basic measures of social security to insure workers against such hazards as industrial accidents, ill health, unemployment, retirement in old age and the cost of rearing children. State expenditure on the provision of education, housing, health and other social services for the working classes steadily rose, although not yet to the more generous levels which were reached after the Second World War.

Some of these reforms were deliberately introduced by right-wing leaders like Bismarck to undermine the appeal of working-class radicals and were accompanied by attempts to crush growing labour movements. The gradual consolidation of trade unions and labour parties brought pressure on governments for further reforms, especially after the franchise was widened. Employers and military leaders could also see the sense of maintaining a healthy and better educated citizenry to compete more effectively with rival nations in work or in war. Social legislation was also, in many cases, motivated by genuine concern, especially as the extent of the deprivations of the poor were more fully revealed. In 1949 T. H. Marshall, a leading writer on social policy in Britain, saw the provision of social rights to welfare as an extension of the rights of citizenship; they should not be understood as merely civil rights to equality before the law and rights to vote and to participate in politics.

While motivations for such measures varied, there was a functional necessity for such innovations in any advanced industrial state. The demands of urban living and exposure of families to the inherent risks of the labour market created new social problems for which new remedies had to be found. During the inter-war period, however, economic and social problems accumulated faster than many governments could learn to cope with them. The nineteenth century faith in the efficiency of market forces began to be undermined. Pressure built up for governments to intervene on a wider scale, not just to deal with the casualties of economic collapse but to prevent them occurring by more effective planning or steering of economic development. Governments of all persuasions began to intervene in the running or closer regulation of major industries and public services, directing resources to regional black spots and seeking to create employment by public works such as road building and electrification. Unfortunately, as each country erected tariff barriers to protect its own industries from foreign competition, the general effect was to reduce world trade and deepen the recession.

Class and capitalism since the Second World War

The two world wars and the unsettled economic and political circumstances of the period between them did not stop the process of modernisation. The whole of Europe continued along the path of industrialisation although some regions followed generations behind the leaders. One way in which we can gauge the extent of development is by examining the shift in the occupational structure. As a country industrialises, workers are drawn from the land to work in industry and in the various private and public service occupations necessary to support a modern society: clerical work, administration, work in consumer services like restaurants, transport work, education, and so forth.

At the more mature stages of industrialisation, technological progress raises productivity and the proportion of service jobs increases because fewer people are needed in manufacturing, and fewer still in agriculture. Chapter 1 describes the deindustrialisation of post-industrial society which arises as these processes continue, and which is now extending widely in the core countries.

In Fig. 2.1 the shifting pattern of occupations is shown for each of the geographical regions of Europe up to 1980. Western Europe (here defined as Austria, Belgium, West Germany, France, the Netherlands, Switzerland, Ireland and the UK) had clearly advanced furthest and was well into the late industrial stage. The third of its working population engaged in agriculture in 1910 had shrunk to nearer 5 per cent by 1980. There was some variation between countries in this region; the UK had the smallest agricultural population, 3 per cent; France and Austria had more significant farming minorities of 8 per cent and 9 per cent respectively, and Ireland had no less than 18 per cent in 1980. However, western Europe's industrial workforce had remained at about 40 per cent throughout this period, the excess labour being absorbed by services, which had grown from under 30 per cent to over 50 per cent. The 1980s has seen further decline in industrial employment, since more is produced by fewer workers because of technological progress.

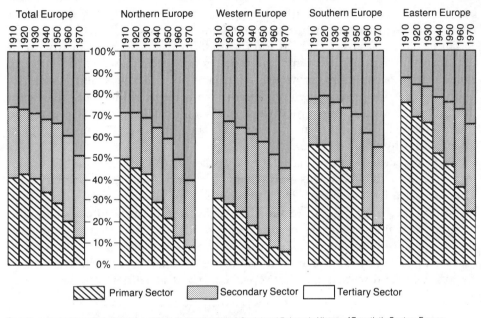

Source: extracted from G. Ambrosius and W. H. Hubbard (1989) *A Social and Economic History of Twentieth-Century Europe*
      p. 57, Figure 2.4

Figure 2.1. Sectoral distribution of the working population by region, 1910–80 (per cent)

Northern Europe had a far larger agricultural sector in 1910, employing nearly half of the labour force, but this had shrunk to about 8 per cent by 1980. Its manufacturing sector has grown only modestly, from a little over 20 per cent to 30 per cent, while its tertiary sector has doubled from nearly 30 per cent to 60 per cent.

Southern Europe (Greece, Italy, Portugal and Spain) developed along similar lines, but a generation later than the north and west. The eastern bloc lagged even further behind. Both these regions began the post-war period with agriculture as their leading source of employment but have since made rapid strides towards a modern employment pattern. Southern Europe's distribution of employment in the 1980s resembled western Europe's in the mid-1960s but had a slightly larger agricultural population. The eastern bloc in the 1980s largely resembled western Europe as it was in 1930s.

It is not easy to translate these sectoral shifts in employment into changes in class structure. Broadly speaking the increase in the service sector means more non-manual office jobs. But as manufacturing has become more technologically sophisticated it too employs many administrative workers and technicians who are classified as non-manual. The services sector also includes many physically demanding jobs such as nursing, furniture-moving and refuse collection, not to mention ballet dancing and all-in wrestling. However, on balance, the shift from manufacturing to services increases the number of people who work with their heads rather than their hands.

These changes have tended to erode traditional class distinctions between the horny-handed labourers and the more genteel occupations. The entry of women into occupations previously restricted to males has also upset the pecking order. Because women have traditionally received lower pay than men the influx of women into office work has somewhat lowered its status. The traditional male 'white-collar' worker has been increasingly replaced by a lower-paid 'white-blouse' worker.

Marxists focused on the male factory worker as the typical member of the working class exploited by his class enemy, the ruthless capitalist (see Fig. 2.2). They expected class inequality and conflict to escalate to the point of revolution. However, instead of the class structure polarising into a small elite dominating a mass of unskilled labourers, the middle ranks of the occupation structure have expanded. The mature industrial workforce is usually represented by a pyramid-shaped hierarchy of occupations graded by skill and responsibility and rewarded by appropriate pay and social status (see Fig. 2.3).

Figure 2.2. The nineteenth-century image of the ruthless capitalist
Source: J. Vaizey (1971) *Revolutions of our Time: capitalism,* Weidenfeld and Nicolson, London, p.38

Figure 2.3. The modern hierarchy of occupations

This pyramid model is misleading in several ways:

1. The base is too broad. Unskilled jobs began to be eliminated by labour-saving machinery. The pyramid ought to be redrawn as a diamond or a pear.
2. There has always been some overlap in pay, with skilled manual workers earning more than the lowest level of white-collar workers.
3. Such a diagram might suggest that everyone is employed. It leaves out not only the self-employed (small business-people, shop owners and artisans) but also a more significant minority, the 'idle' rich who could live off 'unearned' dividends from large fortunes, generally inherited. However, many of these hold well-paid directorships or even managerial posts in their own or other companies, so they reappear in the diagram within the managerial class, but in a way which does not show their special position.

However, the pyramid model does highlight the large part played in modern society by white-collar workers at all levels, from humble clerks to senior managers and professionals. The expansion of officialdom, which was a feature of large organisations in the private and public sectors of all European countries, is shown in Fig. 2.4.

At the start of the post-war period, the UK was slightly ahead of Sweden, with nearly 30 per cent non-manual employment, compared with about 20 per cent in West Germany, France and Italy. Czechoslovakia and Hungary trailed well behind with about 15 per cent and 10 per cent respectively. By 1980 Sweden had overtaken the UK with nearly 60 per cent non-manual workers, but the UK had moved to 50 per cent, closely followed by West Germany, France, and probably Italy too (there are no comparable data for Italy in 1980). Even Hungary had nearly 40 per cent, four times more than in 1950.

These figures have to be read with some caution as there are regional variations within countries and different proportions of women workers in each country. In the UK, for example, recent figures reveal that a slight majority of men are still in manual jobs (55 per cent) although over two-thirds

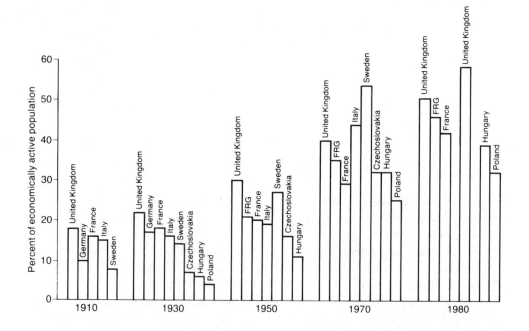

Figure 2.4. Expansion of non-manual employment in various European countries, 1910–80 (as percentage of working population)
Source: G. Ambrosius and W. H Hubbard (1989) *A Social and Economic History of Twentieth-century Europe*, p. 64, Figure 2.5

of the female workforce is non-manual. This raises difficulties in categorising the social class of families in which the husband is a manual worker and his wife or daughter is an office worker. However it is clear that the polarisation of society into two distinct classes has not occurred.

A managerial revolution?

Writers such as James Burnham and J. K. Galbraith have claimed that modern societies, whether capitalist or communist, have been taken over by bureaucrats, who dominate economic and political decision-making. Critics of capitalism are sceptical of this supposed divorce between ownership and control and point out that few business managers could survive for long if they failed to show a profit on their shareholders' investments. Studies of elite groups have also revealed the ability of leading families to dominate decision-making at the top of giant corporations; even if they own a minority of the total shares they can influence decisions far more than the scattered thousands of smaller investors. The idea of a managerial takeover might have been more relevant to the Soviet system but even there the reins of power were held by those in the higher echelons of the Communist Party; we might say that their 'capital' was political.

However, if managers have not exactly staged a revolution they have established themselves in a way that makes it hard to draw a sharp line between capitalists and workers. Many managers and professionals have savings and investments to supplement their considerable salaries and fringe benefits, and they clearly have a stake in the continuation of a system that rewards them so well. This blurring of class-interest has extended also to a wider group, including most white-collar workers above the lowest levels and some of the highest paid manual workers. With savings and investments, company pensions, their own houses, cars and other consumer durables, not to mention holidays abroad, these new beneficiaries of the post-war boom are not likely supporters of a revolutionary movement. However, research on the so-called 'affluent manual workers' has revealed a continuing awareness of class differences and a willingness to support trade unions to defend class interests. Their voting behaviour tends to favour socialist parties but responds to government performance: they will support any party which offers them a better deal, provided they think it can deliver. Although broadly supportive of state welfare they are resistant to paying for it by heavier tax deductions from their own pay packets and they tend to oppose 'welfare scroungers'. Their behaviour fits the pluralist model of competing interest groups better than the Marxist theory of class conflict.

Social mobility and equality of opportunity

One result of the expansion in the numbers of white-collar jobs was to make it more likely that the children of manual workers would end up in occupations considered superior in social status. With a shrinking demand for manual work in general, and unskilled work in particular, many children would need a more extended education to qualify for technical, supervisory and managerial posts. Modernisation has triggered off an explosion of educational provision at all levels. Surveys conducted in the 1960s and 1970s show between a quarter and a third of the sons of manual workers obtaining white-collar jobs. In addition, especially in the newly industrialising countries, there was a considerable movement from agricultural families into both manual and non-manual jobs in industry, commerce and public services.

Do we then have equality of opportunity? Children from middle-class families continue to have much better prospects than those from the lower classes and boys in every class have a slight edge over girls. There has been some variation. The most open society has been Sweden, with its long history of labour governments, and the more closed are Germany, Italy, Spain and France, possibly as a result of their histories of more right-wing governments. Study of entry into the very top elites of societies, as opposed to movement between lower and middle-class occupations, has revealed a much greater degree of social closure. Although there is more 'room at the top' in all societies, and some sons (and, more rarely, daughters) of peasants or factory hands can find their way into comfortable managerial or professional occupations, there is not such easy access to the boardroom or to very senior government posts. Wealth, private education, and family influence still count at the peak of capitalist societies.

The end of the post-war boom

The post-war boom from about 1950 to 1970 encouraged optimism among the aspiring lower classes that they or their children could 'get ahead'. Even most of those who remained manual workers could look forward to full employment, improved living standards and the security of living in a welfare state.

In the 1990s prospects are less rosy. With slower growth since the mid-1970s but continuing advances in productivity, mass unemployment at levels around 10 per cent have become the norm, even in the prosperous countries of the North and West. The prospects of young people have been dented and there is mounting resentment as more and more education and training is demanded for relatively humble career openings. Among those who fail to secure education or training, a pool of long-term unemployed is being created, some of whom have never had secure jobs. It has been suggested that this situation is a factor in rising rates of violence, crime, and drug abuse.

Those lucky enough to find permanent jobs may continue to rise on merit thereafter, but the struggle to find work is fiercer. Added competition from migrants from other parts of Europe and beyond intensifies ethnic and racial conflicts. Demographic factors may ease the problem a little, as birth rates dip in the more advanced countries, but employment prospects may continue to decline in the peripheral countries of Europe. Unless they can modernise their educational systems and work attitudes, and so attract more inward investment, this will be particularly true for the CIS countries. Within the EU countries, Spain, the southern parts of Italy, Portugal, Ireland and the former East Germany have much higher rates of youth unemployment than the rest. Youth unemployment in Spain can reach as high as 60 per cent, especially in large cities. Immigrants, often concentrated in urban ghettos, are twice as likely to be unemployed as others.

In northern Europe, education or training continues for many beyond the age of 20. In the south, most have finished schooling by the age of 17. Although state educational provision has expanded in most countries over the last couple of generations, the rate of take-up of further education is still strongly influenced by home background, so that in most countries the working-class taxpayer effectively subsidises the further education of the middle classes. Even if access to education can be improved so that all pupils fulfil their potential, in a tight labour market family influence may continue to tip the scales of justice in the allocation of jobs. Children of disadvantaged groups may have more chance of success in small businesses and in careers where formal qualifications are less important.

Social democracy and welfare capitalism

Before the end of the nineteenth century Marx's prediction of a socialist revolution seemed unrealistic. However, many believed that socialism might be achieved gradually by democratic means. Extension of the franchise allowed working-class parties to establish a considerable parliamentary presence. By 1920 they were securing 20–40 per cent of the vote and had shared in government in many countries. As the process of industrialisation gathered pace the working class was expected to keep on growing and give socialist parties an overall majority of votes. It is easy to understand why this expectation was dashed in countries where the democratic system collapsed in the period to 1940, since in them genuinely democratic trade unions and labour parties were brutally suppressed. But where democracy was preserved or restored after the Second World War, why did left-wing parties not do better than shown in Table 2.3?

Table 2.3. Socialist/Social Democrat and Communist/other left parties: percentages of vote at national elections by decade

		1940s	1950s	1960s	1970s	1980s
Austria	Soc	41.7	43.3	43.3	50.0	45.4
	Com	5.3	4.3	1.7	1.2	0.5
Belgium	Soc	31.2	37.4	31.0	27.0	28.0
	Com	10.1	3.4	3.7	2.9	1.4
Denmark	Soc	36.4	40.2	39.1	33.6	30.9
	Com	9.7	4.2	10.2*	11.3*	15.4*
Finland	Soc	25.7	25.3	23.4	24.5	25.4
	Com	21.8	22.1	21.6	17.6	16.0*
France	Soc	20.9	15.0	16.0	22.1	35.6
	Com	27.0	23.9	24.2*	25.3*	13.5*
Germany	Soc	29.2	30.3	39.4	44.2	39.4
(FRG)	Com	5.7	2.2	–	0.3	0.2
Greece	Soc	–	–	–	19.5	43.5
	Com*	–	12.9	13.6	10.8	12.0
Ireland	Soc	8.7	10.9	14.8	12.7	8.6
	Com	–	–	–	–	–
Italy	Soc*	21.9	18.1	17.2	13.8	16.5
	Com	20.6	22.7	26.1	30.7	28.3
Netherlands	Soc	27.0	30.7	25.8	28.6	31.0
	Com*	9.2	6.2	6.2	4.7	3.1
Norway	Soc	43.4	47.5	45.5	38.8	37.4
	Com	9.7	4.2	10.2*	11.3*	15.4*
Portugal	Soc	–	–	–	35.2	27.5
	Com	–	–	–	16.1	16.1
Spain	Soc	–	–	–	30.4	43.4
	Com	–	–	–	10.1	5.9
Sweden	Soc	46.1	45.6	48.4	43.7	44.5
	Com	6.3	4.2	4.2	5.1	5.6
Switzerland	Soc	26.8	26.5	25.1	24.1	20.7
	Com	5.1	2.7	2.6	3.8*	2.6*
UK	Soc	48.0	46.3	46.1	39.1	39.9*
	Com	0.4	0.2	0.2	0.1	0.0

* = split between two or more parties

Source: Extracted from Jan-Erik Lane and S. Ersson (1991) *Politics and society in Western Europe*, 2nd edn., Sage: London, pp.140–3, Table 3.13

Some of the reasons have been examined already in the changing shape of the class structure:

1. Manufacturing now accounted for less than half the workforce (see Fig. 2.1 above). The working-class proportion stopped growing and even shrank.
2. Even within the manufacturing sector, more workers became administrative, technical or managerial personnel – seldom eager supporters of socialism. Manual workers within the growing services sector (except for public service workers) were harder to recruit into trade unions, and rural labourers often had a deferential attitude or a religious aversion to socialism.
3. Socialist parties failed to secure the allegiance of all industrial workers, although they received some compensating support from radicals in the middle and upper classes.
4. Labour movements were sometimes split into rival Communist, Social Democratic, and other factions (especially in France and Italy) or into rival linguistic or religious groupings (as in Belgium and the Netherlands).
5. Right and centre parties could count on considerable support from industrial workers who shared their economic, religious or nationalist beliefs.

The precise fate of working-class parties depended upon many variables: the array of left, centre and right parties in each country and the shifting alliances between them, the system of voting and constitutional rules about the formation of governments, the success or failure of incumbent governments and the occurrence of crises or scandals, to say nothing of the personality of party leaders. President Mitterrand, for example, was able to unify the normally divided French left to win power in the 1980s against a divided and discredited right.

Working-class parties were most successful when they broadened their appeal beyond the industrial worker, as the West German SPD did after 1959, when they abandoned their Marxist ideology. The Labour Party formed the government in the UK from 1945 to 1951 and again intermittently in the 1960s and 1970s. The Swedish Social Democrats held power from 1932 to 1976 and 1982 to 1991 and led the way towards the development of welfare capitalism. They expanded state welfare services whilst nurturing a successful capitalist economy, combining full employment with an active labour market policy to phase out old industries and retrain workers for new ones. The growth of welfare services provided jobs for many women and helped others to get the education and child care they needed to work elsewhere.

The political basis of such welfare capitalism was a social contract between the state, employers' associations and trade unions, often labelled 'corporatism'. It allowed wages and prices to be held in check, employment and investment to be planned, and taxation and welfare expenditure to be agreed. Other western states attempted variations on this formula, even under conservative or liberal governments, but apart from Austria, few succeeded in maintaining the necessary degree of cooperation. Nevertheless, welfare states blossomed. From 1960 to 1975 the average country in western Europe increased its spending on welfare from 15 per cent to 27 per cent of GDP. Social welfare provisions were transformed from minimal concessions to the poor into universal public services (including education, public housing, social security, health and social services) on which everyone might have to rely at some stage in their life.

Criticisms of the welfare state: from left and right

Marxists condemned social democracy as a sell-out. Although the workers benefited from improved social security and social services, so did the middle classes. Employers were assured of a healthy, educated and well-housed labour force. Professionals gained well-paid state posts. There was no major redistribution of wealth. The state taxed the young and healthy in all classes to support the old and sick and other dependents.

'New Right' thinkers inspired Margaret Thatcher, followed by other European leaders, to attack state welfare in the name of market forces. State spending was condemned for pushing up taxes, creating bureaucratic inefficiency, and encouraging dependency. People were encouraged to fend for themselves, by house-purchase, and by private education, health insurance and pensions. It was argued that the state should provide only a minimal safety net for those who could not afford private services.

Although few governments dared to slash welfare spending as harshly as the New Right advocated, there was a worldwide cut-back, especially in the 1980s. Even socialist governments in France and Spain adopted Thatcherite policies. Social expenditure growth in the OECD countries, which had averaged around 8 per cent *per annum* from 1960 to 1975, slowed to about 4 per cent thereafter. Even Sweden, the citadel of social democracy, succumbed to periods of conservative government.

Beyond the welfare state: disorganised capitalism?

Since the mid-1970s the post-war boom appears to have ended and the prospects for social democratic reforms have worsened for a number of reasons:

1. The return of mass unemployment reduced the tax base, putting pressure on government spending. Paying for millions on the dole without increasing taxes meant less for other social policies.
2. Demographic trends threaten a gradual increase in the elderly population, the main recipients of welfare spending. More has to be put aside to

support them; but further tax demands invariably meet resistance from taxpayers. Defenders of state welfare point out that, if the state does not raid our pockets, the private insurance companies will. Shifting the burden to the private sector does not diminish it, especially when allowance is made for the extra administrative costs and profit margins of private alternatives.

3. Unemployment and tighter labour laws have weakened the trade unions throughout Europe after a generation of post-war growth. The unemployed cannot afford subscriptions, while those who remain employed grow less militant, afraid of victimisation. Some former strongholds of the union movement have been especially hard-hit by recession and government cut-backs or privatisation. The process has gone furthest in the UK with the privatisation of former nationalised industries such as gas, electricity and steel, a shift away from public provision in bus transport and even some social services, and restrictive trade union legislation. Unions have lost bargaining power with employers and government. Apprenticeships have given way to state education and training schemes in which employers have gained more influence. Young people who are unemployed or in casual jobs have little opportunity to join a union and may become a 'missing generation' for the labour movement.

4. The globalisation of capitalism has accelerated recently. TNCs now switch investment around the world in search of cheap labour and sympathetic governments. Even with socialist parties in government, states often find it harder to tie employers down to corporatist agreements of the kind that Sweden once exemplified. The proliferation of trading blocks such as the EU may be interpreted as the political adaptation of capitalist nation-states to new economic realities. There is little sign so far of the labour movement gearing up for effective international resistance. Most trade unions are fiercely protectionist and suspicious of cooperation with fellow workers abroad, fearing (often rightly) that they may be after their jobs. The struggles over the Social Chapter in Europe could be the first signs of a new continental labour politics which might attempt to establish corporatism on a continental scale. But the differences in living standards of workers throughout Europe will make it difficult for labour to achieve international solidarity in negotiations with employers or governments.

5. New social movements are competing with class politics. Feminism, gay and lesbian rights, anti-racism, the peace movement, and ecological protest could be aligned with the left (sometimes with difficulty). Nationalism, regionalism and religious revivals might undermine this 'rainbow coalition'. There are ominous signs that the far right is becoming more attractive to the dispossessed and insecure, partly by appeal to racism.

6. Traditional class loyalties are weakened by the collapse of old industrial communities. Support for established class-based parties is weaker than it was at the height of the post-war boom. Although class is still one of the

best indicators of how a person will vote, there are increasingly marked divisions within the working class, as already explained. However, divisions in the working class have occurred throughout its history without destroying all sense of unity. Polls show continuing strong support for state health and welfare provisions (though they also show support for tax cuts).

7. It has been suggested that the more affluent workers may be tempted to support centre or right-wing parties and to shun the so called 'underclass' of permanently unemployed or casual workers and those kept out of the labour market by lack of skill, single parenthood, sickness or disability. The presence of immigrant minorities may strengthen this tendency unless strong government action is taken to combat discrimination and conflict. However the notion of an underclass is a rhetorical device that lumps together many disparate tendencies in modern society. There is little in common between so many disadvantaged groups. The Marxist response is to argue that apart from a small elite we are all one pay-cheque away from the dole queue and there is no difference between the underclass and the rest of us. Perhaps the social division between men and women is more important.

Gender and inequality

Although formal inequality between women and men was eroded by the move to universal adult suffrage (see Table 2.1 above) it took some time before women's new electoral strength was translated into greater social equality. In the peasant economies of pre-industrial Europe many women worked on the land, and when industry developed they quickly took up factory work, especially in textiles. But the tradition of their role as mothers and housewives was strong both among the peasants and in the middle class. Traditional gender roles tended to persist, especially in late-industrialising countries or those with strong religious and legal support for male supremacy.

The cause of women's emancipation was taken up by a radical minority, often led by middle-class women who had struggled to enter the professions, but it was wartime experience which helped loosen stereotypes, as women took on formerly male occupations. Longer term demographic trends towards smaller families, reinforced by the legalisation of abortion and advances in contraception, probably had a greater effect, freeing women at an earlier age from the burdens of child rearing and opening up prospects for a return to full-time employment. The spread of household equipment such as washing machines and vacuum cleaners may have helped but standards of house-keeping often kept pace, off-setting possible reductions in hours of housework. Changes in family law have improved women's property rights and made separation and divorce easier. The growth of state welfare benefits and services also made it more feasible, though still not easy, for a woman to exit from an intolerable marriage, although there was still strong economic pressure to marry or remarry.

Since 1945 there has been a general rise in women's participation in paid work, especially by married women. By the late 1980s about one-third of women in the EC were employed, but with considerable variation between countries: activity rates were nearly 70 per cent for Danish, about 50 per cent for British, and less than 30 per cent for Spanish women. The sectoral distribution differed between men and women. Less than 10 per cent of either sex worked in agriculture but only two out of ten women worked in industry and seven in services. By contrast, 40 per cent of men worked in industry and 50 per cent in services.

There is much variation in women's employment between and within countries according to the stage of industrial development and the state of the labour market. However, a common feature is for women to be concentrated in industries and occupations which reflect their traditional caring roles: for example, nursing, primary school teaching and social work, catering and cleaning, textiles and clothing manufacture, hairdressing. Even when employed in general office work they are often confined to junior posts serving the needs of male bosses. These jobs are identified as 'women's jobs' and consequently carry poorer pay and promotion prospects. Even where women compete on equal terms with men their domestic ties and male prejudice may prevent them getting top jobs. Women are also more likely than men to work part-time, particularly in the UK, and this often entails poorer pay and conditions and less chance of continuous employment and an occupational pension. However, the European Court of Justice has built upon the Treaty of Rome principle of equal pay for equal work, to exert pressure against gender discrimination in employment and other spheres (see Marshall case, Chapter 4).

The impact of marriage on women's working life can be seen in Fig. 2.5, which also shows the contrasting pace of change in Poland, West Germany, Sweden and Italy between 1950 and 1982. Whereas in Sweden in 1950 most women left the labour force on marriage, by 1982 they continued in work with activity rates almost as high as those of men. The generous provisions of the Swedish welfare state no doubt supported this trend: better education and child care, and a tax and benefit regime which encouraged both parents to work full-time, and provided parental leave entitlement for fathers as well as mothers.

Women in the eastern bloc were encouraged to perform paid work but the 'emancipation' of Soviet woman was not accompanied by the domestication of Soviet man. He expected his wife to combine a full-time job with all the duties of the traditional wife, and her situation was further burdened by the shortage of consumer goods in the shops and the need to spend hours in queues. Creches, nursery schools and other forms of support for mothers and children were provided – to an especially high level in East Germany and Hungary. Since the collapse of state socialism these welfare measures have been drastically slashed.

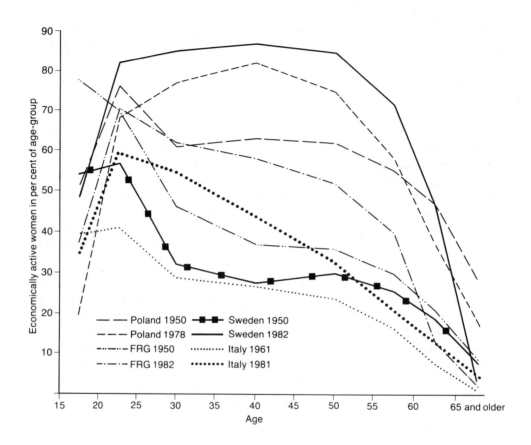

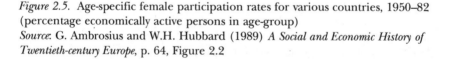

Figure 2.5. Age-specific female participation rates for various countries, 1950–82 (percentage economically active persons in age-group)
Source: G. Ambrosius and W.H. Hubbard (1989) *A Social and Economic History of Twentieth-century Europe,* p. 64, Figure 2.2

The revival of religion in some countries has also tended to reverse some of these gains, such as liberal provision of abortion facilities and easy divorce. Galloping unemployment has affected women more than men. Some women have been driven into prostitution as their only means of support.

In the long term, Europe will have to come to a new social consensus on the gender roles and relations. If Europe recovers fully from the prolonged recessions of recent years, a real alternative to the male breadwinner/female housewife tradition could open up, one in which both husband and wife do paid work – full-time or part-time according to the needs of the family. The burden of care for young children and elderly relatives or other dependents might be shared equally between the sexes. However, we seem to be stuck half-way to this new regime; women are more involved in paid work outside the home, but many men are not yet willing to reciprocate by taking more responsibility for housework and caring tasks, which are still regarded as 'women's work'. It is not yet commonplace for a 'working husband' to feel comfortable phoning his boss to say that he must take the day off because his children are ill.

The dual-career household is, in any case, unlikely to be a standard pattern. As at present, there will also be couples both of whom are unemployed, single-parent households, and some in which one of a couple works. Moreover, the children of couples in work are more likely to find employment themselves. Employment and unemployment seems to run in families, leading to a greater polarisation of the workforce into the 'haves' and 'have-nots'.

An egalitarian family structure would require considerable changes in social policy. The state would have to introduce new patterns of taxes, welfare benefits, and social services at affordable cost to support two-earner families as well as single parents who wish to work. It would also have to monitor occupational training, recruitment, promotion, pay and pensions to ensure equality of opportunity between the sexes. As most of our existing welfare states were built at a time when the male breadwinner was the norm, there is much rethinking to be done. So far the UK seems to differ from most of its continental neighbours, relying on women taking part-time jobs, and failing to deliver sufficient child-care facilities to allow them to compete with men on fair terms for full-time careers. However, an EC survey of social attitudes in 1987 indicated a more egalitarian outlook on women's roles in the UK, France, Denmark and the Netherlands than elsewhere in western Europe, especially in the FRG and Luxembourg. It also showed a nostalgia for traditional family role models in Ireland, Belgium, Spain, Portugal, Italy and Greece. But there seemed to be no consistency between ideals and social realities, with many unexpected variations in practice. The only consistent feature was that women were generally under-represented in positions of power, in politics and in the workplace.

There is a protracted debate among feminists about where private enterprise stands on the gender equality issue. Some maintain that capitalist employers are 'gender blind' and will hire whatever labour is cheapest, most flexible and adequately skilled. Others argue that capitalism takes advantage of older patriarchal traditions, continuing to pay women less than men, and using them as a 'reserve army of labour' that can be drawn on in a boom and discarded in a recession. The role of trade unions is somewhat ambiguous. They have a long history of male domination which has sometimes caused them to see women as unwelcome competition for skilled jobs. More recently many have taken a more progressive attitude, especially as unions have fought against declining membership. However, because women are more likely to work part-time they are harder to recruit into trade unions. Their domestic commitments make it harder for them to attend union meetings or hold office, even if they are bold enough to brave male prejudice.

More women will be needed in government, industry and trade unions before their needs are fully embodied in social policy. The EU has accepted the principle of equal opportunities for men and women but it remains to be seen how effectively such a principle can be implemented, given the competing pressures of legislation, public opinion and market forces. The British government's dismantling of minimum wage legislation, which protected workers in low-pay industries, has weakened the position of women, who are concentrated in them. The other EU members have retained minimum wage laws, and have committed themselves to reinforcing protection of the workers in the Social Chapter of the Maastricht Treaty.

Conclusion

Social inequality in Europe has taken directions which nineteenth century liberals and Marxists were unable to predict. The 'middle way' of social democracy seemed to offer a compromise between capitalism and socialism until the 1970s, since when it has been on the defensive. In the early 1980s there were still predictions of a convergence between East and West, as a reformed eastern Europe appeared to be heading in the social democratic direction. Now Russia and the other CIS states have taken the plunge into the icy waters of market capitalism, at the cost of greater social inequality. If this proves too bracing there may be a turn to the left, or perhaps to the far right. Meanwhile the future of social democracy in the West is still being debated, with as much attention to gender and race as to class.

Further reading

Ambrosius, G. and Hubbard, W. H. (1989) *A Social and Economic History of Twentieth-century Europe*, Harvard University Press, Cambridge, Massachusetts.

Bailey, J. (ed.) (1992) *Social Europe*, Longman, Harlow, Essex, especially chapters on social inequality, gender, race and trade unions.

Cochrane, A. and Clarke, J. (eds) (1993) *Comparing Welfare States*, Sage, London.

Hamilton, M. and Hirszowicz, M. (1993) *Class and Inequality: Comparative Perspectives*, Harvester Wheatsheaf, Hemel Hempstead, especially chapters on inequality in communist and post-communist societies.

Meehan, E. (1993) *Citizenship and the European Community*, Sage, London, pays particular attention to the rights of women.

Padgett, S. and Paterson, W. E. (1991) *A History of Social Democracy in Postwar Europe*, Longman, Harlow, Essex.

Pierson, C. (1991) *Beyond the Welfare State?*, Polity Press, Cambridge.

Wise, M. and Gibb, M. (1993) *Single Market to Social Europe*, Longman, Harlow, Essex, especially Chapter 5, 'Towards a social Europe', and Chapter 6, 'A social charter for a European social market?'.

3 Continuity and change: Europe since 1918

Introduction

The aim of this chapter is not to narrate the history of Europe since 1918, but to highlight those events, issues and developments which throw most light on the Europe of today. In many ways this task is much more straightforward in the case of western than of eastern Europe. While some reference to the history of the inter-war years in the former is appropriate (including the rise and defeat of Fascism), most attention is given to the movement towards, and the debates surrounding, the creation of the European Communities (EC) – subsequently the European Union (EU). The history of the west European states is examined with particular reference to the emergence of new forms of cooperation since 1945. More detailed treatment of political development in these states is provided in Chapters 5–7.

In the case of central and eastern Europe due attention has been given to the confused and troubled inter-war period. Many of the political, social and economic tensions of that era have a distinctly contemporary ring to them – especially in the case of the former Yugoslavia. This chapter also explores the post-1945 division of Europe into two camps, and examines the communist takeovers in so much of eastern Europe. Chapter 8 will consider the years of communist power and decline.

Between two world wars

The choice of a starting date for the history of contemporary Europe must necessarily be an arbitrary one. But the similarities between the political map of Europe created by the peace settlement at the end of the First World War and that of 1990 are sufficiently striking for this to be a convenient point of departure. The First World War also brought to a head the internal tensions within tsarist Russia, which, after much bitter conflict, led to the establishment of a communist regime and the Union of the Soviet Socialist Republics (USSR). Finland and the Baltic States secured their independence. The multi-racial empire of Austria–Hungary collapsed to be replaced by the states of Austria, Hungary and Czechoslovakia; other slices of its former territory were added to Romania, the new state of Yugoslavia, and the revived state of Poland. The latter also secured land from Germany and much more from the former Russian empire. Alsace and Lorraine reverted to France, while Italy secured some additional territory. Europe, however, had not been divided neatly into nation-states. Many were profoundly dissatisfied with the settlement.

Of particular significance was Germany. Although somewhat reduced in size, and burdened with war reparation payments to the victorious powers, this was still potentially a most formidable state. Democracy in the new Weimar Republic was a fragile growth, and it was not to be expected that one of Europe's most dynamic peoples would accept for long the many constraints imposed upon them by the Treaty of Versailles. Even in the 1920s successive ministries strove to revise its terms and to greater or lesser degrees thought in terms of territorial revision and the restoration of Germany as a great power.

This is not to say that the Nazi takeover or the Second World War were inevitable, but the Germans – the most numerous European people after the Russians, and with major resources and skills at their disposal – were bound to prove increasingly restless neighbours. The dangers, however, were dramatically accentuated by the Great Depression from 1929. Hitler and the Nazis had become the leading force in the German government by 1933, and this meant that changes to the map of Europe which might have been attempted with care and patience under the politicians of Weimar were pushed through in the later 1930s with extraordinary speed and ruthlessness. The more ambitious schemes of Hitler and his colleagues to make Germany the leading power in Europe and to extend German influence and territory deep into eastern Europe and Russia were not unknown among many of the right-wing traditionalists, but again – as one can see from the thinking of the military within this group – they were rarely prepared to pursue their dreams with the same single-minded determination and impatience as Hitler.

His task was made easier not only by Germany's rapid economic recovery after 1933, but also by the conditions which prevailed elsewhere in Europe. Eastern Europe was fragmented, with the mysterious and menacing (but as yet mostly internally preoccupied) USSR beyond. To the south, Italy's internal problems had already brought a Fascist regime under Mussolini to power as early as 1922, although it was not until 1935–36 that this regime began to move decisively into line with Nazi Germany. Even then Italy was a relatively weak and unreliable ally, but nonetheless it added to the problems of Britain and France.

France, which had been the strongest power in continental Europe in the 1920s, suffered increasingly from political instability, a low birth rate, a loss of national confidence, and a horror of another major war. Even before Germany

Figure 3.1. The peace settlement in central and eastern Europe 1919–1923

rearmed in the 1930s, the French had begun to commit themselves to a defensive strategy with the building of the Maginot Line. Moreover they were not disposed to take any major initiative without British backing.

The British, however, were no more willing to fight than the French. Their leaders were eager to believe that not even Hitler could be so irrational as to make a bid for German hegemony in Europe, and perhaps even further afield. That Hitler might be willing to risk a major war seemed almost inconceivable. War could be accepted by the British government only if continued acceptance of Hitler's aggressive acts threatened to prove even more catastrophic to British interests than the continuance of peace. Therefore, much was surrendered to Hitler until the decision in March 1939 to uphold Poland's integrity – probably in the mistaken hope that this would persuade Hitler to limit his ambitions and negotiate in good faith. In fact Hitler was so determined to have his way that he offered the USSR the eastern regions of Poland and other advantages in eastern Europe. He was, however, disappointed in his hope that the Nazi–Soviet Pact of August 1939 would persuade the western powers to give way yet again. The latter chose to fight even though (having failed in their own tentative efforts to win the USSR) they could not save Poland.

In the 1920s the eastern Europeans had enjoyed a brief period when they were relatively free from Russian and German power. Some had also been looking westward with hopes of French support in an emergency. But French readiness to resist Germany had fallen away sharply and reached its nadir with the transfer of the Sudetenland from Czechoslovakia to Germany in 1938. Even before this, German economic influence had been rapidly spreading in eastern Europe.

Eastern Europe between the wars

Some general histories touch only lightly on the subject of eastern Europe between the wars. The collapse of communism since 1989 means that the inter-war history of these states has acquired a new relevance – in some ways even more important than that of western Europe.

Despite or because of the emphasis after 1918 on self-determination, national and ethnic conflicts endured within and between many of the states of eastern Europe. Yugoslavia, for instance, began life after 1918 as the Kingdom of the Serbs, Croats and Slovenes. It included Montenegro plus the Bosnian parts of Austria–Hungary. The key to future tensions lay in the fact that Serbia did not see the new kingdom as a 'voluntary union' but rather as a 'conquest', or the 'prize' for its contribution to the allied victory. It thought in terms of Greater Serbia. A similar attitude was taken by the Romanian leaders who now expanded their state to embrace the former Hungarian province of Transylvania, and gave short shrift to the Hungarian minority therein.

In the 1990s, especially when considering the wars in Yugoslavia, commentators have often suggested that the states of eastern Europe were created by the victorious western allies after the First World War. This was what many western politicians proposed at the time, and it was a view often endorsed by east European politicians; for it suggested on the one hand that the new states were in a fundamentally subordinate position to the western powers in the new Europe, and on the other that states in the East could expect special assistance and patronage from the West. In fact, east European states like Czechoslovakia, Poland and Romania were primarily responsible for creating themselves in 1918–19, seizing power and occupying territory with little regard to Allied feelings. They knew of course that they had western sympathy for many of their actions, but there was little that the West could do, if it had wished, to prevent the so-called 'Balkanisation' of Eastern Europe which had occurred by 1919. Where the West was influential, however, was in providing the model of a democratic political system which would be adopted by almost all the countries of eastern Europe in the 1920s. It was, moreover, the western allies who through the peace treaties put their stamp of approval on the east European settlement, confirming or redrawing borders in the region, and singling out certain states (Germany, Austria, Hungary and Bulgaria) as guilty parties who needed to be punished.

Eastern Europe in the 1920s experienced a decade, not repeated until the 1990s, when both Russia and Germany were somewhat distracted from the region by their own domestic difficulties. But just as post-war Germany and Italy found the sudden imposition of democracy destabilising, so the experiment in democracy in eastern Europe in the 1920s was to prove a disaster. In some cases the main reason was that the old privileged elite was still in power in the new states. In Hungary, for example, democracy was never really an option after the chaos at the end of the war: under the influence of Count Bethlen (who wished, like the elite in Germany, to put the clock back) the old pre-war political system had effectively been reintroduced by 1922. In Bulgaria events took a similar turn, since there too the old elite retained crucial positions in society. In the face of a democratic electoral system which brought the peasantry *en masse* into politics, and with rumbling discontent at the terms of the peace treaty, the Bulgarian elite moved swiftly in 1923 to remove the peasant leader, Stamboliyski and impose a semi-authoritarian regime. In Romania the fate of democracy was slightly different, but here again the old elite acted to protect their interests when democracy threatened: they carefully 'controlled' the elections, ensuring both that the peasantry had no real voice and that King Carol could quite easily assume greater powers from 1930. Indeed, it might be said that democracy on the western model was never fully implemented in Romania: in the 1920s, as after 1989, the authorities presented to the west a facade of democracy to conceal corruption and the perpetually unsolved issues (such as land reform) which continued to fester under the new regime.

In other parts of eastern Europe, it proved to be even more difficult to impose a western-style system on new countries created from different nationalities and provinces. Although the states of eastern Europe were in theory national states, born from the multi-national Austro-Hungarian empire, most of them (except Hungary) contained substantial national minorities. The peacemakers in Paris had realised this and had set up a 'Minorities Section' in the new League of Nations in Geneva; all the new states of eastern Europe were obliged to sign a Minorities Treaty guaranteeing the rights of national minorities within their borders. The inter-war period was to be the only time in the twentieth century that national minorities were given special protection in international law, for the system was abandoned in the late 1930s. Even if such laws are finally adopted again in the 1990s (notably with Bosnia in mind), a general system of 'minority protection' would be a highly unlikely development, for the inter-war system was generally felt to have failed.

Nevertheless, it had some influence. The Hungarians in Romania and the Sudeten Germans in Czechoslovakia were probably treated slightly better because of the international pressure from Geneva upon the Romanian and Czech governments. However, a major fault in the system was that it did not apply to older states like Germany, which in the 1930s was free to treat its large Jewish population as it wished without international censure. Furthermore the presumption that minorities should be protected had its own dangers; it provided ample opportunity for disaffected states like Germany or Hungary to interfere in other European countries where they had national minorities. Memories of this interference have not died; they are, for example, clearly evident in the furore which erupted when the German Chancellor, Helmut Kohl, alluded to the present-day German minority in Poland, or when Prime Minister Jozsef Antall of Hungary drew attention to the Hungarian minority in Romania. For the complex national mosaic in Eastern Europe has of course resurfaced in the 1990s, having been suppressed under communist rule. It is this and the long historical memories surviving in Eastern Europe which make the inter-war period highly relevant to any discussion of present-day Europe.

One country where the inter-war system of minority protection most failed to make a mark was Yugoslavia. The three main nationalities – the Serbs, Croats and Slovenes – were supposed to be equal partners in the new state and none of them in international law could claim to be national minorities; only the Muslims in the new state were singled out for special protection in Yugoslavia's Minority Treaty. The new states of Yugoslavia and Poland offer prime examples of the immense difficulties which arose in the 1920s when a western-style system was imposed on new multi-national states, containing regions thrown together from different empires and different historical traditions. In Yugoslavia, at its creation in 1918, one can already discern many of the nationalist frictions which would cause the state's destruction in the 1990s. While the Serbian authorities tended to view the new state as a Greater Serbia, the Croats under their popular peasant leader Stjepan Radič wanted substantial Croatian autonomy within it.

In other words, by 1919, the wartime idealism which had envisaged the new Yugoslavia as a nation of equal partners was already seriously under threat. In the Serb–Croat struggle, it was the Serbs who were victorious: they managed to impose a Serbian constitution on the country in 1921, which effectively meant a centralised state run from Belgrade for the next two decades. Ironically (in view of present-day events) the constitution was only voted through with the help of the Muslims of Bosnia; for the next 20 years they, like the Slovenes in the north-west of the country, would tend to support the Serbs in return for special privileges. But it was the Serb–Croat conflict which undermined Yugoslavia from the very beginning. The Croat Peasant party was never reconciled to the 1921 constitution and its mass membership enabled it seriously to disrupt Yugoslav politics in the 1920s. Indeed, the clash of Serbian centralisation against Croatian semi-independence caused the breakdown of democracy by 1929; King Alexander imposed a dictatorship, trying – like Tito after the Second World War – to dampen down nationalism and create in its place a 'Yugoslav nationalism'. As we know, these efforts failed; it would have needed a very long time for Serb, Croat and Slovene nationalism to weaken and blend into a common Yugoslav identity.

By the late 1920s western-style systems of government had broken down in most of central and eastern Europe. The problem of creating a democratic structure when much of the old regime was still in place was evident in Germany, Hungary and Bulgaria. In some European countries dictatorships, even if somewhat benevolent in nature, were already in place: in Spain, under Primo de Rivera (a precedent for General Franco's later dictatorship); in Albania under King Zog; in Italy under Mussolini; in Yugoslavia under King Alexander; and in Poland under Marshal Pilsudski. Poland, as we have mentioned, had similar problems to Yugoslavia: it was created from former empires, each with its own historic tradition; it contained sizeable minorities – in this case the Ukrainians, Germans and Jews – and its 1922 constitution set the stage for political instability. With a system of proportional representation and massive powers given to parliament, it proved impossible to preserve political stability. The final result was the coup by Marshal Pilsudski in 1926. Like King Alexander in Yugoslavia, Pilsudski was primarily concerned to remove the political chaos at a stroke and give the country some stability. As in so many other countries of Europe, it had been rapidly revealed that Poland's problems of post-war reconstruction, economic crises, national minorities and different historic traditions, left it unprepared for the imposition of a western-style system of government.

Indeed, apart from France and Scandinavia, one of the few continental countries where a democratic system seemed to be flourishing by the 1930s was Czechoslovakia. Here in the 1920s a multi-party democracy developed, aided by a stable system of coalition governments drawn largely from the middle strata of society. However, Czechoslovakia too had its share of domestic instability, which at a time of international crisis might be exploited by hostile neighbours: the so-called Sudeten Germans of Czechoslovakia were never fully reconciled to their sudden position of subservience in a Czechoslovak national state and they appealed in vain to the League of Nations for a solution to their grievances. Similarly, some Slovak Catholic leaders were dissatisfied with the idea of a 'Czechoslovak' nationality, so favoured by Czech leaders, for it always seemed to place them as the junior partner. As in Yugoslavia, the seeds of the eventual break-up into two separate states (January 1993) were present already in the 1920s. But these seeds were only able to grow boldly during times of international strain: notably, during the Second World War when the Nazis dominated eastern Europe, and in the 1990s when the Soviet iron glove was finally withdrawn. In both cases Slovak nationalists were able to reassert themselves and break away from Czech influence to create a separate Slovakia. In their first such appearance, as a Slovak puppet state under Monsignor Tiso (1939–45), they proved to be useful allies to Hitler's Germany.

War and the division of Europe

The military might of Germany proved irresistible in the first stages of the Second World War. Spectacular victories in Scandinavia, the Low Countries, and above all against France in the spring and early summer of 1940 encouraged Fascist Italy to join the conflict on the side of Hitler. Even Britain's survival was for a time in doubt. Russo-German differences, however, were increasing over the future of eastern Europe, and these were among the reasons why Hitler attacked the USSR in June 1941. At first all went well, but in December 1941 the Russians were able to halt the advance on Moscow. In the same month Germany also became involved in war with the United States. From 1943 the tide turned decisively against Germany. The war ended in May 1945 with the allies provisionally splitting their vanquished enemy into four occupation zones. By then the war had wrecked or seriously damaged the economies of all the main belligerents except that of the United States. On the other hand the war had left the USSR as the main land power in Europe, with its armies having advanced west of Berlin and Prague.

The USSR was thus well placed to influence the political map in the east. Its own territory was again advanced westward (as in 1939–40) at the expense of Poland, Romania and the Baltic States. Poland was partly compensated with German territory east of the Oder–Neisse line. In the course of 1949 two Germanies were created – the German Democratic Republic (GDR) in the east tied to the Soviet bloc and the Federal Republic of Germany (FRG) aligned with the West. Meanwhile an 'Iron Curtain' had descended across Europe, with the communists securing supreme power in the years 1945–48 in Poland, Romania, Bulgaria, Hungary and Czechoslovakia – with varying degrees of assistance from the USSR.

Communism had also been established by 1945 in Yugoslavia and Albania, largely by the efforts of local communists. In Yugoslavia, Marshal Tito had been victorious partly through British military backing from 1943. But his

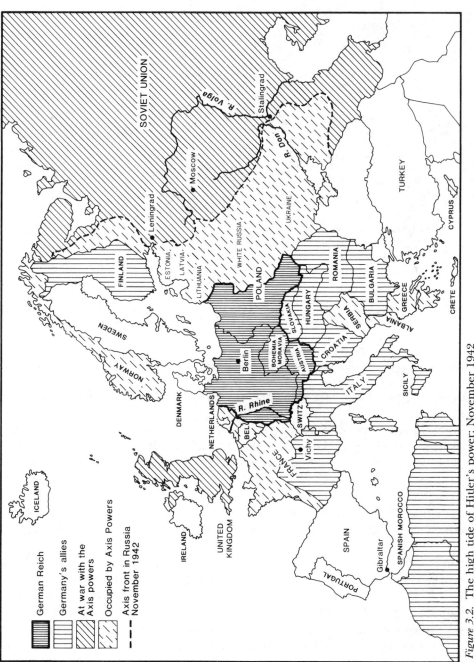

Figure 3.2. The high tide of Hitler's power: November 1942

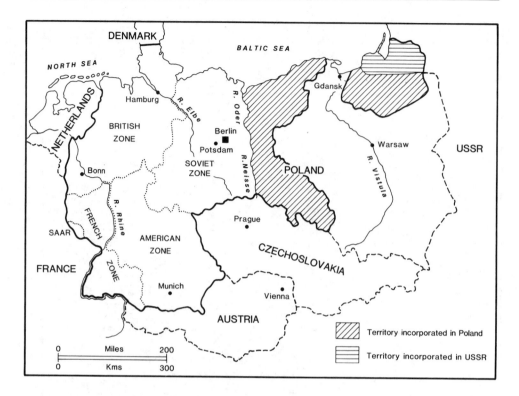

Figure 3.3. Germany: allied occupation zones 1945–49 and losses of German territory

movement also gained support from those who felt revulsion at the ethnic atrocities committed in Yugoslavia during the war; in particular the Ustasha regime in wartime Croatia had carried out a policy of genocide against Serbs. This was a horror which would remain in Serb minds for decades, an experience far more traumatic than Croat memories of inter-war Serb domination of Yugoslavia. Tito after 1945 aimed to remove these ethnic tensions and tried to forge a new 'Yugoslav nationality'. But his independence and ambition led to a crisis with the USSR. Stalin wanted loyal and obedient 'Stalinists' in power, and although he failed to bring down Tito (Yugoslavia survived with Western help despite its expulsion from the Soviet bloc and various efforts to subvert its regime), he was able to ensure that docile 'Stalinists' ruled elsewhere in eastern Europe. Stalin's prime aims in Europe from the end of the war were to prevent the formation of a new threat to the USSR on its western borders and to secure resources wherever he could to assist in the rebuilding of the war-shattered economy of the USSR. There was probably no master plan shaping the communist takeovers in eastern Europe, and the USSR proceeded with a certain amount of discretion and flexibility. It did not, for instance, enforce a communist regime in neighbouring Finland. Influence over Finnish foreign policy and its economy was enough. In contrast there was a speedy communist takeover in Poland, the German highway into

Russia in the two recent wars. The pace varied elsewhere in eastern Europe, and was much influenced by local circumstances as well as by Soviet assessments of American intentions.

Of the states which became communist, it must be emphasised that except for Czechoslovakia all had had short or troubled histories as parliamentary democracies. This had made them very susceptible to Nazi influences during the war, and from 1945 the communists found it relatively easy to remove those people who had been or who were accused of collaboration with the enemy. In addition (apart from Czechoslovakia) the eastern states had tended to suffer from massive rural under-employment between the wars, and in many regions peasants were clamouring for land reform. The communists were able to take full advantage of this. The old order, its institutions and personnel were often ill-equipped to resist the dynamic and ruthless challenge of the communists, who were highly organised and adept at securing control of the police and other key departments when entering into coalitions with other parties. Always, too, there was the shadow – and sometimes the physical presence and activities – of the USSR to take into consideration.

Stalinist conformity was imperative in Eastern Europe until his death in early 1953. The new Soviet leaders then hesitantly and erratically began to experiment with less totalitarian methods at home, and to allow the eastern European regimes rather more discretion in their domestic affairs. The limits of this more liberal approach were demonstrated in eastern Europe by the Soviet reactions to a number of crises and incidents in 1953, 1956, 1968, 1970 and 1981–2 (see Chronological Table). Above all they drew the line at any threat to the communist monopoly of power or the departure of any state from the Soviet bloc. Nevertheless some diversification was occurring in the communist states of eastern Europe, and this was to accelerate from the 1960s. (See Chapter 8.)

In 1949 close defence ties were established between most western states (West Germany was not added until 1955) under the North Atlantic Treaty Organisation (NATO). But serious military preparations against the USSR did not begin until the Cold War took a turn for the worse in the early 1950s, due to the Korean War and increased western suspicion of Soviet aims in general. Between 1958 and 1961 there was serious East–West tension over the future of Berlin and related German issues. This reached a climax in August 1961 with the building of the Berlin Wall to stop the exodus of East Germans to the West. Paradoxically this led in due course to sufficient stability and confidence in East Germany for a dialogue of sorts with its western neighbour to become possible. Intensive diplomatic activity in the early 1970s between the eastern and western blocs led to some formal acceptance of a divided Europe and to various efforts to regulate tensions. On the whole, detente in Europe survived the renewal of the Cold War by the superpowers from 1979 with a fair measure of success. The climate changed rapidly from 1985 with the emergence of Mikhail Gorbachev as the new Soviet leader. It was not, however, until late 1989 that the vulnerability of communism in eastern Europe was recognised.

By the end of the year the Berlin Wall had been demolished, and the two Germanies were moving towards unification.

Projects of West European Reconstruction 1945–50

In 1945 the major European states emerged from the war with greatly reduced power and influence. Britain confronted the immediate price of victory in the form of the largest external debts (£4.7 billion) in its modern history. France had lost great power status as a result of military defeat by Germany in 1940. Defeated and occupied Germany was a mere object in the international system, and lost territory in the East (see Fig. 3.3). Italy was adjusting to the collapse of Mussolini's Fascist state.

The spectacle of a politically and economically exhausted Europe gave rise to a widespread view that Europe's recent history of war, nationalism and economic rivalries offered no model for constructing a prosperous, peaceful and free continent. Radical programmes of political reconstruction reflected a general desire to break with the disastrous past, as if 1945 represented 'Year Zero'. Most prominent among such programmes was the idea of European unity, which was pursued with a new seriousness of purpose and a mixture of idealistic and realistic motives. It was hoped that a new European community would permanently contain the dangerous force of nationalism and would integrate the European nations so effectively that war would be 'not merely unthinkable, but materially impossible' (Robert Schuman, 1950). Moreover, it would offer a framework to accommodate the defeated states rather than leaving them with a permanent sense of aggrieved isolation. Support for European unity was most marked at the unofficial Congress of Europe in May 1948 at which the dreamers of a federalist Europe found a platform for their views. By this time, however, expansive schemes for pan-European unity were crumbling away, because the mutual hostility (Cold War) of the two superpowers, the USA and the USSR, was dividing Europe and Germany.

The earliest post-war forms of cooperation between the western European states arose out of their extreme economic and military weakness in comparison with the superpowers. They cooperated in being supported and strengthened by the USA, and in resisting the threat of the USSR. All European states to a greater or lesser extent faced considerable difficulties in financing their recovery programmes; in particular they lacked dollars (the so-called 'dollar gap') to pay for imports. Secretary of State George Marshall offered substantial American aid to assist the rebuilding of Europe (June 1947) and in the resulting four-year European Recovery Programme ("Marshall Aid"), $12,534 million was distributed. American insistence that the sixteen west European recipients of this aid use it for recovery in a co-ordinated way impelled these states into forming the Organisation for European Economic Co-operation (OEEC), the first major effort at post-war

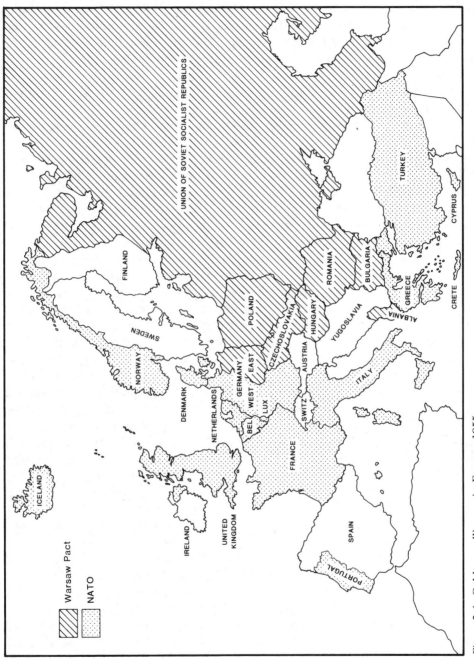

Figure 3.4. Cold war alliances in Europe 1955

economic cooperation between the west European states. This pump-priming exercise helped to lay the foundations of sustained economic recovery and growth in western Europe over the next two decades. It also marked the beginning of long-standing American support for political and economic integration in western Europe in order to create a more free, multilateral international economy in place of the highly fragmented European economy of the interwar period.

Another important influence in promoting cooperation between the west European states was widespread fear of the Soviet threat to western Europe, particularly pronounced at the time of the Berlin blockade (see Chronological Table). In 1948, Britian, France and the Benelux states (Belgium, the Netherlands and Luxembourg) formed the Brussels Treaty Organisation. This mutual security pact served as a catalyst for the creation of NATO a year later, comprising the USA, Canada and ten west European states. The idea of west European unity thus appeared partly as a by-product of the Cold War.

Early post-war west European organisations operated on the principle of intergovernmental cooperation and involved no loss of national sovereignty. This arrangement suited some states more than others and gradually produced a basic, enduring division over the organisation of western Europe. One set of states, led by Britain and including the Scandinavian countries, supported a limited, practical and intergovernmental approach that opposed both federal political structures and proposals for a European customs union. Britain was reluctant to enter into any new, binding European commitments beyond those needed to organise west European defence co-operation, to qualify for European Recovery Programme aid and to ensure American support against the USSR; the Empire and Commonwealth – together with efforts to restore the 'special' Anglo-American war-time relationship – took precedence over Europe in the order of British external priorities. The Scandinavian countries were also disinclined to involve themselves too tightly; they rejected proposals to create a nordic customs union in the 1950s and restricted their Nordic Council (established in 1953) to very modest functions.

A second set of states, led by France, advocated a more closely integrated European grouping. France was particularly concerned to avert any future military threat from Germany; there had been three German invasions of France, in 1870, 1914 and 1940. After Germany's defeat in 1945, France initially aimed to maintain a weak, divided Germany, with plans for dismemberment that echoed Clemenceau's comment 'I like Germany so much that I want as many Germanies as possible'. But it was the Cold War that determined the more limited partition of Germany into two states, which included a potentially powerful, partially-sovereign West Germany (FRG, 1949). France then faced the unattractive prospect of FRG participation in the western international system without any specifically European controls.

The Origins of the European Communities

Against this background Robert Schuman, the French Foreign Minister, presented a proposal to place all Franco-German coal and steel production under a common High Authority in an organisation open to other European countries (May 1950). France and five other states – FRG, Italy, and the Benelux states – supported this Schuman Plan, signed the Treaty of Paris (April 1951) establishing the European Coal and Steel Community, and thus as the 'Six' laid the first building block of the European Communities. Schuman and Jean Monnet, the author of the Plan, launched the enterprise as the first step towards a European federation and the elimination of Franco-German antagonism. The distinctive feature of the Plan was its emphasis on the supranational principle in the form of a High Authority with powers independent of the governments of the member states. The idea of integrating first just one sector of the western European economy – coal and steel – promised a 'spill-over' effect leading to the integration of other sectors and ultimately to political integration. The choice of coal and steel reflected the high degree of interdependence of the member states in this sector.

The motives of the states which adopted the Schuman Plan were reminiscent of Bismarck's remark: 'I have always heard politicians use the word "Europe" when they were making requests to other powers which they did not dare formulate in the name of their own country.' France sought to anchor the FRG in a French-led European system, thereby allaying fears of a revanchist Germany, enhancing France's status as a European power and challenging the prevailing notion of a British-organised west European bloc. Besides protecting French access to German coal, the Plan also marked the beginning of a longer-term trend linking the modernisation of the French economy to the idea of an economically integrated western Europe. West Germany's support was guaranteed by its first Chancellor (1949–63), Konrad Adenauer, who envisaged a western European federation based on a close Franco-German relationship and membership of the western alliance, thereby advancing FRG claims for full sovereignty and equality without arousing the bogey of German nationalism. Meanwhile, the Italian government aimed to restore the country's European credentials and to reinforce its authority in the face of a large, hostile communist party. The positive response of the Benelux states reflected both their heavy dependence on the German economy and their support for close inter-state economic ties which had already led them to form the Benelux customs union in 1948.

The Course of European Integration 1954–1961

The progress of western Europe towards integration has been constantly marked by setbacks. For example, shortly after the launching of the Schuman

Plan an American proposal for a major west European rearmament programme (September 1950), including the FRG, exposed the European states' mutual suspicions. France was particularly determined to prevent the formation of a German national army and aimed to do so by proposing the creation of a European Army including German troops (Pleven Plan, October 1950). This plan formed the basis of a supranational European Defence Community treaty signed by the Six (1952). But eventually France was not prepared to surrender its national sovereignty in order to contain the FRG, and refused to ratify the treaty (1954). This major setback to the Community method of integration confirmed British doubts about the Six's unity of purpose and provided an opportunity to reassert British leadership in western Europe. In 1955 a sovereign, rearmed FRG joined NATO. It was also incorporated into an enlarged version of the Brussels Treaty Organisation, the Western European Union (WEU), which followed the British preference for non-supranational European cooperation. (Thereafter the WEU had very little significance until the 1980s when it became the focal point of a revived interest in developing defence links exclusively among western European states. It has since emerged as the possible defence arm of the EU, with its current commitment to a common foreign and security policy.)

It was in these seemingly unfavourable circumstances that the Six embarked on the 'relaunching of Europe' in 1955. The Messina conference of foreign ministers (June 1955) opened negotiations that resulted in the formation of the European Economic Community (EEC) and the European Atomic Energy Community through the Treaties of Rome (March 1957). The failure of the EDC proposal was partly responsible for this successful initiative. The Community idea was no longer plagued by the issue of German rearmament, so attention was focused instead on the economic track to integration. During the period 1953–58, intra-Six trade was already rapidly expanding, at more than 10% per annum. A developing improvement in Franco-German relations greatly assisted the outcome. The formation of WEU and British military guarantees helped to reconcile France to a rearmed Germany. The Saar settlement (1956) also removed a contentious issue from Franco-German relations as this territory, under French supervision since 1945, was now reunited with the FRG. Thereafter, the rapport between de Gaulle (first President of the Fifth Republic, 1958–69) and Adenauer resulted in the Franco-German Treaty of Friendship (1963) that symbolised the post-war rapprochement between the two states. Meanwhile, a common market offered France an assured outlet for its mounting agricultural surpluses, and assisted the burgeoning export-oriented industrial production of the FRG.

The EEC was designed to form a common market with free movement of goods, capital, labour and services. Phased progression towards a customs union was identified as a major goal, and the introduction of a common agricultural policy also emerged as an immediate priority. The underlying political purpose – 'to establish the foundations of an ever closer union among the European peoples' – accommodated different views about integration and avoided any specific reference to the supranational principle expressed in the ECSC treaty. The four main institutions collectively expressed an assortment of emphases. The Commission represented a supranational dimension as the guardian of the Community ideal with particular responsibility for recommending policies and administering the treaties. The Council of Ministers, as the organ of national governments, was empowered to act as the decision-taking body. The Court of Justice served to establish a new legal order independent of the member states. The Common Assembly (later European Parliament) was primarily a consultative body.

The successful negotiation of the Treaties of Rome sharpened and eventually formalised the division of western Europe into two trading blocs. Fears of a widening gulf between the Six and the rest of western Europe prompted a British attempt to devise a European Free Trade Area including the Six. France rejected this idea, and effectively strengthened its leadership of the Six while undermining British influence in Europe by terminating negotiations (December 1958). The UK and six other states – Austria, Denmark, Norway, Portugal, Sweden and Switzerland – then established the European Free Trade Association (EFTA) in 1960 with no provisions for closer economic or political unification beyond a free trade area in manufactured goods. Western Europe thus entered the 1960s at 'sixes and sevens'.

The Crises of the 1960s

There have been many debates in the years since 1960 over the pace and direction of the development of the EC. These have focused on the relative importance of apparently conflicting goals: inter-governmental cooperation and supranationalism; limited and expansive visions of the EC's global identity; political and economic integration; enlargement of EC membership and deepening of its functional integration. Some would see the last two of these pairs of goals as complementary rather than conflicting.

During the 1960s major clashes over these issues left a mixed record of achievements and failures. In its 'honeymoon period' the EEC accelerated the tariff-cutting programme (1960), launched political union negotiations (1961), attracted applications for membership from three EFTA states – UK, Denmark and Norway – and Ireland (1961), and concluded the first agreements on the Common Agricultural Policy (1962). During the rest of the decade the most notable developments were the completion of the customs union, the full implementation of the Common Agricultural Policy and the emergence of the EEC as a single actor in international trade negotiations. In the meantime, however, a series of crises dashed hopes of political union (1962), blocked enlargement (1963) and even threatened the EC's survival (1965–66).

These crises arose out of a clash between French policy under de Gaulle and the policies of the other member states. Gaullist emphasis on national independence involved intransigent opposition to supranationalism, and also presented a vision of Europe – 'from the Atlantic to the Urals' – freed from superpower rivalries. This 'European Europe' opposed the prevailing view of an integrated western Europe in the western alliance, and eventually led to France's withdrawal from NATO in 1966. The political union project collapsed as a result of irreconcilable differences between France and the other member states over NATO ties and the status of the EC relative to its member-states. Enlargement plans were also blocked when de Gaulle unilaterally vetoed two British applications for membership in 1963 and 1967. Gaullist opposition to the Commission's supranational pretensions, especially its plan for automatic funding of the EC, resulted in a French boycott of all EC institutions in July 1965. The eventual settlement, the Luxembourg Agreement of January 1966, effectively amounted to an agreement to disagree between France and the other member states on the right to exercise a national veto in the Council of Ministers.

Renewal and Recession 1969–1984

Changing international conditions by the late 1960s – including de Gaulle's retirement in 1969 – gave renewed momentum to the EC. First, President Pompidou, de Gaulle's successor, broke the log-jam on enlargement, allowing for the accession of three new members in 1973 – UK, Ireland and Denmark – while the fourth applicant – Norway – rejected membership in a referendum. This reversal of French policy was due to mounting anxieties about West German economic power and strategic objectives, and to a consequent recognition of the value of British membership as a counter-weight to West Germany. It was true that the FRG, 'and economic giant but a political pygmy' (Willy Brandt), could not take the diplomatic initiative in European affairs. But there was no denying the FRG's standing as Europe's leading power in the industrial and financial markets, since it now accounted for some 20 per cent of total world trade, possessed the strongest currency in Europe, and emerged as the EC's 'paymaster'. Changes in FRG policy towards eastern Europe also alarmed Paris. The Ostpolitik (policy towards the east) of the Brandt Administration (1969–74) abandoned the previous policy of non-recognition of the eastern European states, and aimed for the normalisation of relations. This aroused French fears of a neutralist FRG drifting away from its western ties.

Secondly, the European states feared that the superpowers intended to reach agreements about European issues with little or no reference to the European governments. Accordingly they were more inclined to strengthen their own unity so as to form an effective power structure with which to bargain about their own affairs. De Gaulle's hope that the grip of the super-powers on Europe might loosen had been shattered by the Soviet invasion of Czechoslovakia (1968), while the quickening pace of detente at the super-power level by the late 1960s exacerbated the Europeans' fear of being left out.

In this new atmosphere the Hague Summit of EC leaders was held in December 1969. Its programme of 'completion, deepening and enlargement' included undertakings to open negotiations with the applicant states, to develop new common policies, to forge a monetary union by 1980 and to

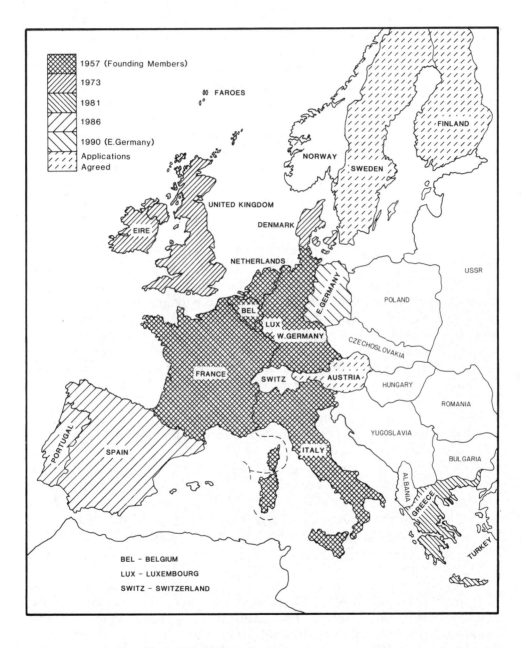

Figure 3.5. The enlargement of the European Community

explore the possibility of political cooperation. Shortly afterwards in 1970 a process of continuing consultation, European Political Cooperation, sought to coordinate the foreign policies of the EC states. This was further assisted by the emergence of the European Council (1975), which formalised the hitherto *ad hoc* 'summit' meetings of EC heads of government.

In some respects the crises of the 1960s merely postponed agreements until the 1970s, as in the case of enlargement. The question of the EC's funding, for example, was finally settled in 1970; all revenue from tariffs on manufactured goods and from levies on agricultural imports – together with up to 1 per cent of value added tax (VAT) collected by member states – became the EC's automatic revenue. In other respects, however, the EC emerged from this period in a different form from that visualised by some of its federalist-minded founding fathers. The Commission, for example, was now overshadowed by the Council of Ministers whose intergovernmental conduct of business resulted in extremely slow decision-making ('Eurosclerosis').

More difficult economic conditions during the 1970s strained the European economies, blocked the more ambitious plans for integration which had evolved from the Hague summit, and put the EC's decision-making system under great strain. High economic growth rates in the 1950s and 1960s ended in 1973–74 with the quadrupling of the price of oil by the Organisation of Petroleum Exporting Countries (OPEC); the average annual growth rate (in GDP) of the leading four west European EC states slumped from 4.6 per cent (1960–1973) to 2.2 per cent (1973–80). The consequent rise in inflation and unemployment undermined the economic aspects of the Hague programme and exposed problems of cohesion as the EC economies were very differently affected by recession. As a result the notion (so important in the 1990s) of a fast and slow lane to integration emerged. The Hague Summit's project of economic and monetary union (Werner Plan) was an early casualty of these new conditions, as the collapse of the dollar-based fixed exchange rate system (1971) resulted in floating currencies.

While economic and monetary union failed to materialise by 1980, the European Monetary System (EMS) of 1979 provided for closer co-operation in monetary policy. This Franco-German initiative developed out of a renewed emphasis on the Bonn/Paris axis at the centre of the EC; the French and West German leaders, Giscard d'Estaing and Helmut Schmidt, forged a close working relationship during the period 1974–81, in contrast to the preceding ten years of troubled relations. The EMS aimed to create a 'zone of monetary stability' in western Europe and survived to provide the base for economic and monetary union plans in the 1990s.

The economic recession and the more protectionist climate of opinion in this period, however, limited EC progress on other fronts. Member states responded to the oil crisis of 1973–4 by concentrating on national efforts to safeguard their oil supplies. The planned progression from 'negative' integration (the removal of existing restrictions) towards 'positive' integration (new common policies) ran into increasing difficulties. The absorption of 90 per cent of the EC's budget by the Common Agricultural Policy seriously impeded any new spending initiatives, while widespread government efforts to curb public expenditure created a further obstacle. The customs union survived, but non-tariff or invisible barriers continued to block the emergence of a common market.

Enlargement also presented the prospect of a weaker EC. Britain's protracted adjustment to membership occupied much time, as the Labour Government conducted a 're-negotiation' of the terms of entry (1974–75) and the Thatcher Administrations of 1979–84 sought to reduce the UK's net contribution to the EC budget. However, enlargement continued with the accession of Greece in 1981 and of Spain and Portugal in 1986, following the collapse of their dictatorships. The EC thus became more representative of western Europe, comprising some 90 per cent of western Europe's population and accounting for 88 per cent of the area's GDP. These developments underlined the problem of decision-making and increased the pressure for institutional reform.

Mixed results emerged from attempts to develop an EC political identity on the international stage in the 1970s and early 1980s. The American idea of a 'Year of Europe' (1973), intended to revive the western alliance, met with limited European interest and exposed divisions between the EC states over transatlantic relations. Their reaction caused the American Secretary of State, Henry Kissinger, to observe that Europe had no single telephone number. The fluctuating state of East-West relations from detente in the first half of the 1970s to the 'second cold war' (1979–85) did produce a common EC response. This was first evident in the Helsinki Conference on Security and Co-operation in Europe (1973–75), which resulted in East-West recognition of the territorial and political status quo in Europe, and held out the possibility of peaceful change and growing links between the two halves of Europe. A common west European interest in maintaining improved relation with the eastern bloc was also evident as superpower relations deteriorated in the early 1980s; the EC states gave only qualified support to American toughness against the USSR. At this time support for a more distinctive 'European voice' in the security and foreign policy fields found expression in the European Council's 'Solemn Declaration on European Union' (1983).

The Drive to Closer Union 1985–1992

Increasingly it was felt that the immobilism of the EC was damaging western Europe's economic performance. Its share of world trade in manufactured goods fell from 45 per cent to 36 per cent in the period 1973–85. The USA and Japan were ahead of Europe in the technological revolution, while the new industrialising countries of the Far East were posing a growing threat to European industry.

Against this background, new efforts were made to rejuvenate the EC. The Milan European Council (June 1985) convened an intergovernmental conference to consider the future of the EC and a possible revision of the founding treaties. The immediate consequence of this 'second relaunching' of Europe was the Single European Act (1986) and the commitment to create a Single European Market by the end of 1992. This market would be the largest frontier-free market in the advanced industrial world, accounting for some 22.5 per cent of the world's GDP and 19.5 per cent of world exports (1991).

The institutional provisions of the Act established a key new principle in the decision-taking procedure of the EC. The Council of Ministers was now empowered to take decisions by qualified majority voting, thus overcoming the use of the national veto. The European Parliament, a directly elected body since 1979, acquired greater influence. The European Council and European Political Cooperation were formally incorporated into the EC. However, the EC retained its hybrid character, reserving substantial powers for member governments. For example: the Parliament still lacked the legislative competence required to reduce the 'democratic deficit' in the conduct of EC affairs, while defence and security issues remained matters for inter-governmental co-operation.

The significance of the Single European Act for the future development of the EC gave rise to a fierce debate. Some saw the Act as a means of promoting further political, economic and monetary integration. This view was strongly championed by Jacques Delors. His Presidency of the Commission (1985–94) restored its role as a dynamic force in promoting new schemes, most notably a three-stage plan for full economic and monetary union and a Social Charter of workers' and citizens' rights. The strongest counter-blast to the Delors vision came from the British Prime Minister Margaret Thatcher, whose Bruges Speech (September 1988) rejected the notion of a European superstate and insisted that the achievement of a single market and foreign policy co-operation between the member states sufficiently defined the EC's objectives.

This debate over the EC's future beyond 1992 assumed even greater importance following the dramatic transformation of the central and eastern European political landscape in 1989 with the rapid collapse of communist governments and the opening of the Berlin Wall. The subsequent unification of the two Germanies in 1990 and the break-up of the Warsaw Treaty Organisation and the Yugoslav and Soviet states in 1991 presented altogether unfamiliar conditions for determining the EC's future. The EC states reflected divisions of opinion over issues like enlargement and integration in their responses to these events. Britain and France, for example, had different priorities: the former emphasised enlargement and thus hoped to slow the pace of integration, while the latter supported further economic and monetary integration, partly to reinforce the EC ties of a united Germany.

The prevailing view on the order of priorities at this time was to postpone enlargement until after the completion of the single market. One long-standing division disappeared with an EC-EFTA agreement of 1992, creating the European Economic Area. This was only an interim arrangement since Sweden, Norway, Finland and Austria were expected to join the European Union in 1995. Meanwhile, some of the central and eastern European States – Czechoslovakia, Hungary and Poland – concluded association agreements with the EC (1991) that provided for free trade within ten years and the possibility of eventual membership. In April 1994 Hungary and Poland formally applied for full membership.

The events of 1989–90 immediately strengthened pressures for synchronising the processes already under way and working towards further political and economic integration. The European Council agreed in April 1989 to convene an Intergovernmental Conference to draw up a treaty on economic and monetary union. A comparable advance towards political union was particularly assisted by a joint appeal for European Union (April 1990) issued by President Mitterand and Chancellor Kohl. This demonstration of the continuing importance of the Franco-German axis in the EC was followed by a European Council decision (June 1990) to establish a second Inter-governmental Conference on political union. Consequently two Intergovernmental Conferences, one on political union and the other on economic and monetary union, were convened in December 1990 and culminated in the Treaty on European Union signed by the EC heads of state and government in Maastricht in February 1992. The substance and significance of this Treaty are discussed in the next chapter. Some of its main provisions – the agreement to create an economic and monetary union by 1999 and the commitment to a common foreign and security policy – have been sorely tested by subsequent events.

At a comparable, uncertain stage in the EC's development during the early 1970s, one commentator likened the member states to a bag of sticky yet individually identifiable marbles involved in a journey to an unknown destination. Since 1986 the journey has been faster and more stressful for the marbles. Will they break apart from the mass under the strain? At any rate, the Maastricht Treaty on European Union represents one guide – if only a vague one – to the next destination.

Further reading

Crampton, R. J. (1994) *Eastern Europe in the Twentieth Century*, Routledge, London.

Heller, A. and Feher, F. (1990) *From Yalta to Glasnost*, Blackwell, Oxford.

Story, J. (ed.) (1993) *The new Europe: Politics, Government and Economy since 1945*, Blackwell, Oxford.

Swain, G. and Swain, N. (1993) *Eastern Europe since 1945*, Macmillan, London.

Urwin, D. W. (1995) *The Community of Europe: A History of European Integration since 1945*, 2nd edn, Longman, London.

Young, J. W. (1991) *Cold War Europe 1945–1989: A Political History*, Edward Arnold, London.

4 Composition of an unfinished symphony: the European Union

Europe has rarely experienced such sustained and heated debate on an international treaty as that which raged on the Treaty of Maastricht in 1992–93. Unfortunately, after the tumult and shouting had died away, most people were still woefully ignorant about the Treaty – not surprisingly, since the debate had in many countries been more concerned with internal partisan politics than with the real issues. The general impression given in the UK, for example, was that despite valiant British opposition more sovereignty had been lost to 'Brussels'. This impression has little to do with reality, and obscures a situation which appears to be very complex but is basically quite simple. Since the purpose of this chapter is to enable readers to understand what the European Union is and how it works, it will have to begin and end with Maastricht. On the way, it will be necessary briefly to consider what sovereignty really means.

Some simple points should be clarified first. 'Brussels' is far too complex a term to be used as a catch-all expression covering anything from a bunch of unelected international bureaucrats trying to impose unnecessary rules to a group of enlightened visionaries trying to bring some order into chaos. Those who praise or blame 'Brussels' for a decision may in fact be referring to the Commission which made the proposal, the European Parliament committee which examined it, the Council of Ministers which took the decision, or the officers in a Directorate-General who actually put it into operation; all too often it is a vague derogatory term of general application, aimed at the Community as an entity. It is very important to remember that the decision is finally taken by ministers of all the member states in the Council of Ministers. So, if governments represent people, in that sense 'Brussels' is us. A second term that is bandied about too easily is 'sovereignty', which has almost opposite meanings when used in an internal or international context. *Internally* – that is, applied to a nation state – it means the seat of final authority, on behalf of the people in whom that authority may be theoretically vested. That means a hierarchy of authority, in which order is maintained and sanctions may be applied by governmental authorities on behalf of a sovereign people.

In *international* terms, though, when politicians speak of defending Britain's sovereignty they mean defending Britain's right to act according to its own interests and without regard to others. That means in theory that every state, large or small, rich or poor, is the equal of every other state, and has the right to behave accordingly. So whilst in international society sovereignty means a community of equals, with individual states behaving according to self-interest, in a nation state it means a pyramid of authority to which the individual is subject. If the international definition of sovereignty were applied inside the nation state it would be called anarchy.

In practice, of course, states cannot behave just as they like. It would be quite impossible for Liechtenstein to threaten to invade Germany to force withdrawal of a tariff; but changes in Liechtenstein's internal laws could have a dramatic effect on the commerce of other states, whose business people have taken advantage of low business taxes and incorporation laws to establish 25,000 holding companies there. In reality there is an inevitable inter-dependence between states which forces them to develop various forms of cooperation; one of the most advanced and complex of these is exemplified by the European Community and the European Union.

The present degree of European cooperation stems from the conditions in which Europe found itself after the Second World War, and has its roots in defence, economics, and idealistic views of how nations ought to behave. The way these pressures led to the formation and early development of the EC is explained in Chapter 3.

A common market implies a great deal more than the removal of internal tariffs and quotas and the erection of a common external tariff. Its declared aim of removing *all* barriers to trade and ensuring the free movement of people and capital as well as goods and services takes it into non-economic areas. People cannot move around freely in the common market if they need work permits or visas for another member state, or if a mining engineer's British degree is not recognised in Belgium. That means getting rid of internal passport controls and reaching agreement on the content of degree courses, so there is a strong and inevitable integrationist tendency which attracts the idealists as well as the economists. Eventually the degree of cooperation inherent in a common market leads to consideration of a common foreign policy, and consequently to a common security policy. This is the stage we have reached with Maastricht, which has brought together the economic, idealistic and defence considerations in one treaty, including the building of links with other organisations such as NATO.

In this chapter the EU and the EC are described and analysed as they are in 1994 – that is, after the Treaty on European Union (commonly called the Maastricht Treaty) came into force.

The Organisational Structure of the European Community

The organisational structure of the Coal and Steel Community formed a model which was followed closely, seven years later, by the European Economic Community and the European Atomic Energy Community. Each Community had a Council of Ministers and an Executive (the High Authority for the ECSC, Commissions for the other two) but they shared a Court of Justice and the parliamentary body known as the Common Assembly. In 1967 the three Communities were merged, so though the three treaties and the three Communities still existed inside the EC, the Merger Treaty created one Commission and one Council of Ministers alongside the Common Assembly and the Court of Justice, so the same four institutions now served all three Communities.

This organisational pattern reflected the demands, on the one hand, of the basic philosophies of the six parliamentary democracies which made up the original membership, and on the other of the requirements of political and organisational reality. Though democratic theory predicated some representation of the peoples of the member states – through the Common Assembly, which eventually became the European Parliament – political reality meant that nothing would really happen unless the governments were able to discuss issues and come to an agreement; hence the Council of Ministers. But the international nature of such a complex organisation demanded an international executive – hence the Commission – and an independent and international Court of Justice was obviously necessary so that there could be some means of settling disagreements arising from the Treaty. As will become clear, the Treaty was essentially a constitutional document for a political system, which had misleading similarities to the political systems of the member states but was in fact significantly different.

The basic organisational relationship of the four major institutions can be stated quite simply. *The Commission* puts forward the ideas, *the European Parliament* gives its opinion on the proposal, *the Council of Ministers* takes the final decision and the *Commission* is then responsible for putting the agreed policy into operation. *The Court of Justice* is not directly involved in this decision-making circuit but is vital to its operation; without it, there would be no final and authoritative interpretation of the Treaty and the powers of the institutions. This explanation is over-simplified, but the reader who keeps this basic relationship firmly in mind will have little difficulty understanding more detailed explanations of the Community's operations. It is important to recognise that this is a power-sharing structure in which each institution has exclusive powers and cannot proceed without the others: the Commission to make proposals, the Parliament to comment, the Council to decide and the Commission to put into action (Fig. 4.1).

In essence, this organisational structure has survived to the present day, creating a political system in which power is shared between governments, elected representatives and an independent executive, with a Court of Justice

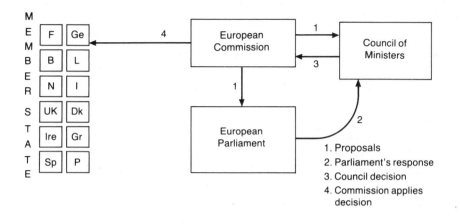

Figure 4.1. The European Community: the decision-making process

able to settle any question which might arise concerning the extent of the powers and duties of any institution. With regard to the Treaty of European Union of 1992–94, that statement has to be qualified in some important respects, because the new sections of the Treaty on Foreign Policy, Security and Defence, and on Justice and Home Affairs, have largely avoided the power-sharing system. But for the rest it holds good, and even with these qualifications, the EU is best understood if that framework is kept in mind.

Since the Treaty of Paris in 1951 (the ECSC), the Treaties of Rome of 1957 (the EEC and the EAEC) and the Merger Treaty of 1967, there have been a number of other treaties which were in effect additions and amendments, the most recent and most extensive of which is the EU treaty. There was a major amendment of the treaties in 1986 through the Single European Act (SEA), by which the governments of the member states set a date for the completion of the Internal Market (1 January 1993) and agreed on a number of other steps to help bring this about. The biggest and most recent amendments were contained in the Maastricht Treaty, which will require separate analysis later on. Suffice it to say for the moment that Maastricht created a new institution, the Committee of the Regions, provided for a European Central Bank (ECB) and a common European currency, and further substantially increased the powers of the European Parliament. It also added two completely new areas of activity – to develop a common foreign and security policy, and provide for cooperation in the fields of justice and home affairs – but in the main these are not covered by the Community mechanisms and procedures that are about to be examined here, and will have to be analysed separately. It is very important, however, to clear up one common misunderstanding about Maastricht: the European Union does not replace the European Community, but extends it and adds to it. Article A of the EU Treaty states: : 'The Union shall be *founded* on the European Communities, supplemented by the policies and forms of cooperation established by this Treaty' (my italics).

Strictly speaking, therefore, the EU is comprised of the European Communities (all three of the original Communities) plus extra bodies and procedures concerned with foreign policy, security, defence and justice and home affairs, whilst the term 'European Community' is to be applied to what used to be the European Economic Community. We therefore have a confusing plethora of treaties, so for clarity, throughout this chapter, 'EC Treaty' means the consolidated series of treaties (ECSC, EEC, EAEC, plus all amendments up to but not including Maastricht); 'Maastricht Treaty' means the amendments to the original treaties plus the new material negotiated at Maastricht, and 'EU Treaty' means the consolidated treaty – the EC treaty plus the Maastricht amendments and new material.

There are aspects of the SEA and the Maastricht Treaty, over and above the amendments made to the original treaties, which must be looked at more carefully. But in order to understand their significance it is necessary first to examine and analyse the way in which the Community, rather than the Union, works, and for the purpose of this analysis it is the structure and procedures of the Community after the amendments of the SEA and Maastricht that will be examined.

Anatomy of the European Community

The common classification of international organisations into inter-governmental, supranational and non-governmental is not very useful for analysis, and certainly needs further refinement if the European Community is to be analysed properly. It is really more accurate to speak of inter-governmental and supranational *elements* in organisations than to label the organisation as a whole; any organisation formed by means of a treaty signed between states (governments, *de facto*) is in that sense an inter-governmental organisation. But it may well have institutions or offices whose officials do not belong to or represent governments, and whose powers, within defined limits, override those of the national member governments and therefore have to be regarded as supranational elements within the organisation. There may be others which are simply inter-governmental, with no supranational or internationalist elements at all, and yet others where the treaty was signed by governmental representatives but which carry out most or all of their work at the technical and professional level. In any case, one extra label is necessary – to define those bodies which do not, in the main, see themselves as representing national interests, and certainly not the interests of their governments; in this chapter, the term 'internationalist' will be used to describe such bodies.

In the European Community, the inter-governmental organ is the Council of Ministers, whilst the Commission, the European Parliament and the Court of Justice each dispose of some supranational powers. In addition, the Commission has to be regarded as an international and independent body, serving the Community as a whole, whilst the European Parliament certainly sees itself as having a collective role which is internationalist. This perception by each institution of its own, and others', roles stems from, interprets and develops the clear constitutional statements about institutional powers and duties laid down in the treaties. The ink is hardly dry on the documents before the institutions are trying to interpret them in the light of their own role-perception, sometimes culminating in a Court of Justice ruling and not infrequently in a revision of an agreed interpretation. It is through this constant synthesis of ideas and interpretations that Community procedure is refined and developed, and in order to understand it a study of the major institutions and their powers and duties is needed. It would be very neat and tidy if one could study the institutions and then study the procedures of the Community but, as will be seen, the two are so inter-mingled that it really is not possible to separate them. What should stay with the reader, at the end of the day, is an impression of institutional inter-dependence, and that is a very accurate reflection of what the Community is and how it works.

The inter-relationship of the four major institutions

The Council of Ministers is the meeting-place for the governments of the member states. Each government is represented by one minister, served and supported by a delegation of national civil servants and an international secretariat. Unlike national governments, however, the Council is not the author of the proposals it considers. That role is reserved for the European Commission, an executive body originally appointed by the governments acting together but thereafter independent of them. The European Parliament, directly elected by the people of the member states since 1979, does not see itself as representing states or governments; individually, Members of the European Parliament (MEPs) see themselves as representatives of their electors, and collectively as the guardians of democratic oversight of the European Community as a whole. These three institutions, as we shall see, effectively share the decision-making power of the Community between them. The fourth major institution, the European Court of Justice, takes no direct part in this power-sharing structure, but is nevertheless vital to its operation. Although appointed by joint action of the governments in the first place, the Court is a totally independent body composed of jurists of the highest international reputation, and its ruling on any dispute – which might include an argument as to the limits of an institution's powers – is final. A slightly more detailed diagram of the Community (Fig. 4.2) may help in understanding this and the following sections.

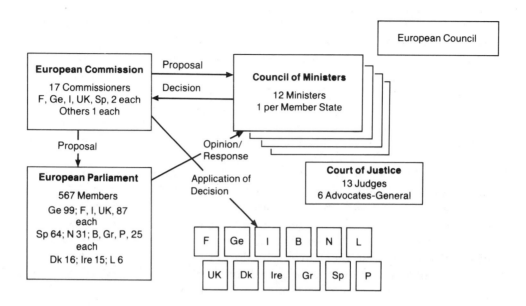

Figure 4.2. Internal relations in the EC

The Council of Ministers

The diagram Fig 4.2 shows the Council of Ministers spread out like a pack of cards on a table; this is because the Council is actually several Councils, depending on what subject is being discussed. The Agricultural Council, the Energy Council, Education Council, Social Affairs Council, and so on, are all composed of one minister from each state relevant to the subject under discussion, but they are all called 'the Council'. Some titles are less obvious – the Trevi Council, for instance, comprises the immigration ministers – and there are 'special' councils from time to time. The 'senior' council comprises the foreign ministers, whilst the Finance Council (ECOFIN, composed of finance ministers) and the Agricultural Council are also considered to rank higher than the others. Whatever form it takes, the Council is the decision-taking body of the Community, considering proposals which have been made by the Commission and deciding on them after obtaining the opinion of the European Parliament.

There is one other body in the diagram which has not yet been explained – the European Council. This is the Council of Ministers meeting at Heads of Government level – popularly termed the European Summit – at least twice a year. The role of the European Council has grown, particularly in providing general guidelines as to the direction in which the member states wish to see the Community (and now the Union) develop.

The Presidency of the Council is held by each member state for six months at a time, rotating between the member states in alphabetical order. The first six months of the year always provides much more opportunity of getting things done, since August is not a working month and the holidays tend to spill over to some extent into July and September, so from 1993 the cycle has reversed pairings of countries to ensure that states get a summer Presidency and a winter Presidency alternately.

The Presidency country takes the chair of the Council and of its committees and working groups, and is generally responsible for leading and facilitating the Council's work during the period of its Presidency. Considerable political and diplomatic skill is involved, since the Presidency has to try to reconcile the positions of 12 member states, which may have widely differing positions on an issue. Time will always be a problem; Presidency countries naturally want to be able to point to some definite achievements after their term in office, and six months is really a very short time to conclude matters of importance.

Table 4.1. The political complexion of member states' governments in July 1994

Member State	Government
Belgium	Centre-left coalition
Netherlands	Centre-left coalition
Luxembourg	Centre-left coalition
France	Right-wing coalition
Germany	Christian Democrat/Free Democrat coalition
Italy	Forza Italia/Northern Leagues/National Alliance (Right-wing coalition)
Denmark	Social Democrat-led coalition
United Kingdom	Conservative
Ireland	Fianna Fail/Labour coalition
Greece	All-party coalition
Spain	Socialist (minority)
Portugal	Social Democrat

Note that the Council is *not* a European Government or Cabinet; it could hardly be, since the ministers round the table come from different political systems and political parties. Six of the 12 member states are monarchies and six republics. Their governments are of varying political persuasions, as shown in Table 4.1.

It is important to notice that though the Council has decision-making powers, it *does not have the power of proposal.* Almost all of the time it has to work on proposals from the Commission, which it can only change by unanimity – that is, a vote in which all states vote in favour. To an increasing extent, too, it has to work in conjunction with the European Parliament, whose powers have been significantly increased through the Single European Act and the Maastricht Treaty. Thus, although media commentators frequently say that the *real* power (of decision) lies with the Council, the exercise of that power depends absolutely on the complementary roles played by the Commission and the Parliament, with the Court in the background to make sure that nobody pretends to a power not given by the Treaty. Though we shall qualify this later so far as the EU is concerned, the Community therefore has to be seen as a power-sharing system, which is arguably more democratic than the political systems of some of the member states.

It may now help to list the sort of legislation that emanates from the Council after the procedure which has been described. These instruments may be regulations, directives or decisions:

- *Regulations* are directly applicable in all member states. They are binding in their entirety – that is to say, both as to the end to be achieved and the means by which it is to be achieved.
- *Directives* are binding as to the end to be achieved on all member states to whom they are addressed, but the means is left to each member state.
- *Decisions* are binding in their entirety on those to whom they are addressed – that is, both ends and means.
- The Council can also make *recommendations* and express *opinions*; these have no binding force, though depending on the circumstances they may have considerable influence.

A great deal of anguish, especially in the UK, has been expended on the system of voting in the Council. Originally most decisions required unanimity, which effectively meant that each country had a veto; if all states did not vote in favour, the motion was lost. Difficult enough with six states, this became more and more difficult as the Community expanded until it virtually brought things to a standstill. To try to speed things up without reluctant states being steamrollered by the majority, a system known as Qualified Majority Voting (QMV) was introduced, weighting the votes in the Council roughly in proportion to the size of the member state, as set out in Table 4.2. Which system of voting is used in the Council on a particular matter depends on the legal base – that is, whatever procedure is laid down in the treaty. For some things (accession of new members, for example) unanimity is required, but for others, including most matters concerning the Internal Market, QMV is specified.

Qualified majority voting provides the Council with a means of coming to a conclusion without being hampered by the need for unanimity but with safeguards to prevent the contentious and divisive atmosphere which could result from a simple majority in which five states were against and seven in favour. As can be seen, the number of votes is in proportion to the size of the state; in addition, however, 54 votes in favour are required for a successful vote, whilst any coalition of ministers assembling 23 votes can stop the decision being taken. A simple calculation reveals the sophistication of the QMV. It can be seen that the five biggest countries voting together cannot carry the day; that only amounts to 48 votes, so another six votes are needed – which means two more states. Conversely, two big states plus one of the smaller states, or a variety of other combinations, can put together 23 votes and block the decision. Concern about being 'outvoted in Brussels' should be evaluated against this background.

Table 4.2. Qualified majority voting in the Council of Ministers

Member State	Number of Votes
Belgium	5
The Netherlands	5
Luxembourg	2
France	10
Italy	10
Germany	10
Denmark	3
United Kingdom	10
Ireland	3
Greece	5
Spain	8
Portugal	5
Total number of votes	76

It would be misleading to leave this account of the Council under the impression that only ministers were involved. Ministers, after all, have important and time-consuming jobs to do in their own countries, and meetings of the Council which actually involve ministers last only for a day or two at a time. In any case, as a permanent institution the Council needs staff of its own to arrange the meetings, provide agendas, take the minutes and generally see to it that the affairs of the Council are provided for while the ministers are not in Brussels. This is done by the permanent staff of the Council in the Council's Secretariat-General. Ministers need deputies, too; the Council could not do its work if everything had to be left until the ministers themselves met, so each member state maintains a Representative Delegation, under an Ambassador to the Community and a Deputy Ambassador. Collectively the delegations are known as COREPER (from the initials in French) or the Committee of Permanent Representatives. Officials from all 12 delegations meet in working parties to try to hammer out as much as possible in between ministerial meetings. These are *national* civil servants following the policy of their governments, so to a considerable extent they are able to act on behalf of the ministers. By the time the ministers actually meet, the agenda has been reduced to those matters which could not be agreed by the civil servants, if necessary by consultation with their head office. This machinery obviously throws civil servants of different nationalities together, and there are some useful side effects, the most obvious of which is that people discover that 'foreigners' are not aliens from another planet. In addition, since many countries have similar problems, civil servants from one state learn that others are solving the problems in quite different ways, so there is a mutual exchange of ideas. The overall structure of the Council is summed up in Fig. 4.3.

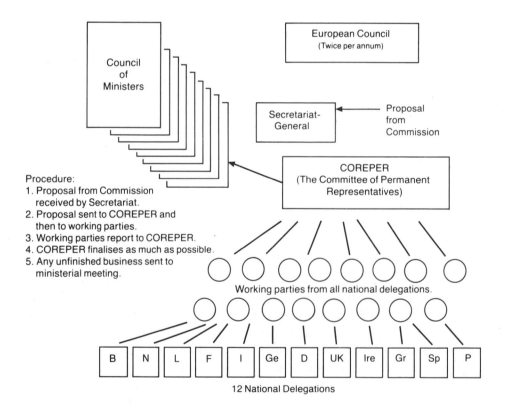

Figure 4.3. How the Council of Ministers works

The Commission

The Commission is the executive of the Community, with powers to make the proposals and to execute them when decided upon. 'The Commission' is the title of the collegiate body of 17 commissioners, but is also used to describe the whole of the bureaucracy, organised in 23 Directorates-General, over which the commissioners preside. There must be at least one national from each member state amongst the commissioners; in practice there are two from each of the larger states (Germany, Spain, France, Italy and the United Kingdom) and one from each of the others. A tempting analogy would be to say they are international civil servants, but that is misleading in the British context because each commissioner is finally responsible for his or her own portfolio and does not work to a minister, whilst collectively the commissioners have a joint responsibility for the collegiate decisions of the Commission as a whole. Commissioners therefore are a cross between a British permanent secretary and a minister; like a permanent secretary, they head and administer one or more departments (the Directorates-General) but, like a minister, they have the final responsibility for their policies and they are overtly political in the interests of their own Directorate-General and of the Commission collectively. The Commission meets weekly, taking its decisions by simple majority. It has to publish annually a General Report on the activities of the Community, not later than a month before the opening of the European Parliament session, so that Parliament can in effect debate and comment upon the overall activities of the Community in addition to the specific controls set out below.

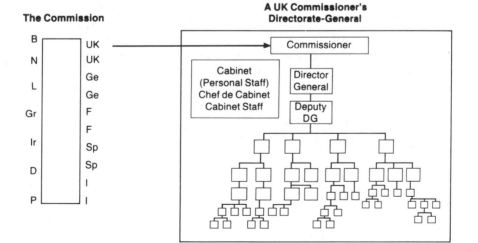

Each Commissioner is responsible for one or more Directorates-General. The diagram shows a typical Directorate-General, in this case under one of the UK Commissioners.

Figure 4.4. The European Commission

There is a President of the Commission, who is responsible for the general direction and oversight of the work of the Commission as a whole. Though this is a position of considerable power and influence, it does not enable the president, even together with the Commission, to 'rule Europe from Brussels'. The Commission is one institutional facet of the Community's procedure; it cannot do anything without the input of the Parliament and the Council, and would be subject to the judgement of the Court should it grow 'too big for its boots'. Certainly the president cannot 'go it alone', though inevitably the impact of a particular president is what the incumbent is able to make of it; the immediate past-President, Jacques Delors, maintained a high profile and had a considerable impact upon the European scene. One effect of this was to provide the Eurosceptics with a bogey-man and scapegoat around whom to weave the often fanciful stories about the evils of 'Brussels rule', but there is little doubt that the Commission now needs a firm hand at the helm if it is to maintain its position in a structure which member states' governments are always keen to dominate through the Council.

The term of office of the Commission has been extended by the Maastricht Treaty from four years to five, so that it is now coincident with that of Parliament, whose powers and duties relative to the Commission have been emphasised in other ways. The member states' governments will still nominate the President of the Commission, but they now have to consult the European Parliament first, and the whole Commission needs a vote of approval by Parliament before they are actually appointed (Article 158,1). (The President appointed in 1994, Jacques Santer, was almost rejected by the vote of the Parliament; the closeness of the vote will certainly strengthen the Parliament's position with regard to future appointments.) This new power indicates the way in which the Community develops. Parliament has always wanted the power to *appoint* the Commission, and lobbied vigorously to that end, so this amendment in Maastricht represents a compromise. Parliament retains its power to require the resignation of the whole Commission via a motion of censure carried on a two-thirds majority of the votes cast (Article 144). Though it remains doubtful how effective this would be if the governments were simply to reappoint the same Commission, the Commission would then once again require a vote of approval, so it is arguable that in this respect power has shifted slightly towards the Parliament.

The European Parliament

The European Parliament has been directly elected since 1979. The Members of the European Parliament (567 MEPs from 1994) are elected by the citizens of Europe. Before 1979 the Assembly was appointed, theoretically by and from member states' parliaments and generally in proportion to party strengths within those parliaments. But even the appointed Assembly exuded a robust internationalism which put pressure on member states and the Council to strengthen the Community, and in particular pressed for more powers for the European Parliament. It was the appointed Assembly which eventually forced the Council to institute direct elections for a Parliament with a fixed term of office of four (now five) years, though that Parliament has not yet succeeded in forcing through a standard system of election for all the member states. The most glaring anomaly is the UK, which is the only state not using a proportional system; the result is that until the 1994 election all but one of the British MEPs were Labour or Conservative, despite the fact that other parties polled percentages that would have won them seats in any other member state.

The membership of the Parliament is roughly in proportion to population size, though a glance at the table will show that the big states were determined to prove that they were all equal! This of course does not apply to Germany after the 1994 election, where the numbers have been adjusted to allow for the re-unification.

Table 4.3. Composition by nationality of the European Parliament

Member State	Year of entry	Pre 1994 election	Post 1994 election
Belgium	Founder	24	25
Netherlands	Founder	25	31
Luxembourg	Founder	6	6
France	Founder	81	87
Italy	Founder	81	87
Germany	Founder	81	99
Denmark	1973	16	16
United Kingdom	1973	81	87
Ireland	1973	15	15
Greece	1981	24	25
Spain	1986	60	64
Portugal	1986	24	25
Total		518	567

The seating plan is a hemicycle, with the focal point the President's chair and the Party Groups occupying segments of the hemicycle. To the right of the President the front seats of the hemicycle are for the Commission; on the left, for the Council, since both of these groups can have representatives in the Chamber to explain their points of view on the matter under consideration.

The Council representative answers questions for an hour at every session, the President of the Council gives an account of a 'summit' after the meeting, and the President of the Foreign Affairs Council outlines the Council presidency's programme at the start of a presidency and reports on it at the end. Commissioners have the right to speak to explain and defend the proposal under discussion, and to answer questions, but neither the Commission nor the Council has the right to vote in the Parliament.

The European Parliament differs from any National Assembly, in one very important respect. *It does not support a government* – there is no European Government, drawn from the majority party in the European Parliament, so there is not the same compulsion to maintain party discipline. A vote against the motion before the House does not bring down a Government or induce an election – it could not do this, in any case, because the term of office for the European Parliament is fixed at five years. There are other factors which weaken the tendency to toe the party line which is the norm in the UK; the semi-circular design of the chamber itself does not encourage confrontational or nationalistic politics, nor does the seating plan. MEPs sit in Party Groups – not necessarily with the same names as national party groups – and in alphabetical order within those groups, so Labour's Mr Black will probably be next to a German Socialist, Herr Becker. Stemming from the lack of compulsion to maintain party discipline and the fact that they do not sit together by nationality, block voting as a national group is quite rare – and difficult to detect if it does happen, as a member state's MEPs will be distributed over a number of Party Groups. Within those Groups, voting discipline is also weaker than in the UK parliament – there is a whip, but it is difficult to enforce and there is really little attempt to do so, because there is no 'government' or 'opposition' party to support. Obviously it is also more difficult to agree upon and enforce a 'party line' in the Socialist Group (for instance) which is composed of MEPs from every member state, and where the brand of socialism varies sufficiently to make it more difficult to find binding agreement on a party line. The fact that the Group is not supporting or opposing a government also makes the point of having a 'line' less obvious. So the following aspects of the European Parliament should be noted:

● Weaker group discipline
● Commonality of interest – Parliament sees itself as having a purpose and corporate role much more clearly than, say, the UK Parliament. It tends to be an institution which tries to push the development of the Community forward, and therefore has more in common with the Commission than with the Council.
● Weaker national identification
● Voting tends to be on the merits of the question

The European Parliament works roughly on a four-week cycle, as shown in Table 4.4. Group and committee meetings are in Brussels, and plenary sessions are in Strasbourg, whilst the administrative headquarters of the Parliament is in Luxembourg. Although the Parliament's strong preference is to centre everything in Brussels, this has so far foundered on the self-interest of France and Luxembourg, who do not wish to lose the status and economic spin-off that result from being the site of a major institution.

Table 4.4. Meeting-cycle of the European Parliament

Week 1	Week 2	Week 3	Week 4
Group Meetings	Plenary Session	Committees	Constituency

The European Parliament's work is focused on its committees (18 of them, though this is not a number fixed by statute). Unlike the UK Parliament, proposals go to the committees before they come to be considered in plenary session, which has the considerable advantage that all proposals have been dissected and examined in detail before Parliament as a whole considers them. The committee appoints a *rapporteur,* whose job it is to draft the Report of the Committee on the proposal it is considering – in a way that reflects the view of the committee, not his or her own. The committee votes on the report (by simple majority) and it is that report, with the committee's recommendations, which then goes before Parliament in plenary session, where the committee spokesperson presents it and outlines the committee's views. The report is then debated and voted upon. Voting is by show of hands or if requested, electronically – there are buttons to record votes on each MEP's desk in the chamber. The Parliament is then able to notify the Council of its position and carry the process of legislation a step forward.

This method of procedure, together with the system of voting and the fact that because of the lack of need for partisan support there is little party point-scoring, means that the flow of business is quite fast – incredibly fast, to anyone used to the Westminster pace of life; and the European Parliament gets through a lot of work in a session. The other profound difference between the European and British Parliaments is that whereas in the UK MPs virtually always vote with their party, MEPs feel no such compulsion.

The extent of Parliament's control over legislation stems from the treaties, and could be said to cover four areas. The phrase 'The Council, acting on a proposal from the Commission and after consulting the European Parliament, shall decide ...', which is frequently the legal base of an action, sums up the essential relationship between the institutions admirably. The treaties specify the circumstances in which Council is required to act unanimously or by qualified majority vote. As a result of amendments in the Single European Act and the Maastricht Treaty, parliamentary influence has been strengthened. In certain circumstances Parliament can even reject proposed legislation outright. Finally, in various Articles (e.g. the accession of new member states) the actual *agreement* of Parliament is required. Coupled with the comparative absence of partisan voting, these procedures mean that it can be argued strongly that the European Parliament effectively exerts more control over Community legislation than the House of Commons does over the British government. One example which may be cited is the Budget; both Parliaments have to pass the respective Budgets before they are legal, but whereas the Westminster Parliament makes a lot of fuss and noise but then will almost always vote loyally on the party line, the European Parliament has thrown the Budget out completely on two occasions.

Parliament tends to have a natural alliance with the Commission and has a tendency to view the Council with, at best, a stance of armed neutrality. Governments and governmental bodies do not like to see obstacles placed in their way, and since the Parliament as the watchdog of Community interests does not shrink from such obstructive activity, the increase in parliamentary powers has usually been achieved in conflict with the Council. Gradually conciliation procedures to deal with disagreements between the Parliament and the Council have been established, but for the Parliament this is not enough. It wants some machinery to negotiate points of probable disagreement *before* the disagreement occurs. There has been an increase in dialogue between the two bodies (not negotiation, but discussion), for example before the Budget; and since 1981 this has become the Trialogue – the Presidents of the Council, the Parliament and the Commission. This meeting has actually negotiated an Inter-Institutional Budget Agreement which all three institutions then approved, but the practice has not so far been extended outside the budgetary field.

The Court of Justice

It has already been stated that while the Court of Justice does not take part in the decision-making cycle of the Community, its existence is essential to the system. Some authoritative and final ruling on interpretations of the treaty, and a means of settling disputes between institutions, member states, commercial organisations and other interested parties (and/or any permutation of these bodies), has to be not only available but accepted by all parties if the system is to work at all. In its absence, the whole structure could grind to a halt or malfunction as a consequence, let us say, of an argument over the right of the Council to come to a decision before it had received the opinion of the Parliament. Such a dispute did actually arise, and the Court's judgement substantially affected the balance of power in the Community in favour of Parliament.

The Court is composed of 13 judges and six Advocates-General, each of whom must be qualified to hold the highest judicial office in his or her own country or be a jurisconsult of recognised competence, whose independence and impartiality is beyond doubt (Article 167). They are appointed by 'common accord' of member states, but once appointed they are totally independent of governments or other institutions of the Community. The statute of the Court provides for the immunity of judges in the performance of their duties, requires them to take an oath of impartiality, forbids the tenure of any political or administrative office, and provides when appropriate for their retiral and, *in extremis*, removal. As can be seen, therefore, great care has been taken to make this institution a completely independent and impartial body – a necessary precaution, when one considers its very considerable powers.

The main points of Article 177, which lays down its jurisdiction, show how important the Court is to the operations of the Community:

- It may interpret the Treaty, in cases of doubt as to its meaning.
- It may rule that the action of an institution is, or is not, valid and within its powers; if the institution has exceeded its powers, the Court can declare the action void.
- It may (and under some circumstances *must*) hand down a ruling on request from a court or tribunal of a member state, if that court or tribunal considers it needs such a ruling to enable it to give judgement.

The Court's judgements are enforceable under Article 187, and a state found wanting will inevitably comply, albeit after a certain amount of huffing and puffing to satisfy whatever internal political pressures caused it to offend in the first place. The Court is in fact available to 'any natural or legal person' – European institutions, governments, companies, EU staff, and even ordinary citizens of a member state – provided that a breach of the Treaty is alleged. There have in fact been a number of successful actions by citizens against their own governments under these provisions.

Three examples will show why the Court is so important to an understanding of the way the Community works. They illustrate how a state or an institution can be called to account if a breach of the Treaty is alleged; one concerns an institution purporting to have a power which it did not have, one a state in breach of treaty regulations, and one a state whose internal regulations breached treaty provisions.

In what came to be called the 'Lamb War', the French Government halted consignments of English lamb at the Channel ports. This would of course be illegal under common market regulations had it been done to protect French agricultural interests, and in truth that was the real reason for the French action in response to heavy political pressure from the French lamb farmers. The French Government, however, maintained that it was acting in the interests of public health and hygiene, and had a responsibility to inspect the lamb to make sure it was fit for Gallic stomachs, which was *not* illegal. By the time some sample lorry-loads of lamb had been unloaded from their refrigerated trucks, taken to laboratories some distance away, tested and returned, the whole consignment had of course gone off and could not be sold. There was outrage in Britain, fanned by the tabloid press, whose three-inch headlines screamed indignation and abuse ('Hop Off You Frogs' was one tabloid's contribution), whilst the French press expressed mild surprise at the British lack of concern for public hygiene. The Commission and the British Government therefore took the French Government to Court, alleging a breach of the Treaty, and were successful. The French Government was ordered to desist, and did so after a certain amount of blustering.

Some months later the British Government found it necessary, of course in the interests of public health, to stop and inspect imports of French apples; this time the seven-centimetre headlines were in French papers, but the outcome was the same and this time the British Government had to back down. Both incidents illustrate the degree of national chauvinism lurking below the surface, if somebody – usually a government responding to internal political pressure – chooses to stir it up. The Community can be a useful and convenient scapegoat to take electors' minds off the internal political situation if a government is suffering adverse criticism.

The other two cases are perhaps even more important. In the Marshall case a British woman maintained that the Treaty had been breached by the British Government because British women were required to retire at the age of 60 whilst men could go on to 65, which effectively breached the equal pay provisions. The Court held in her favour and the British Government was obliged to re-examine its legislation on the retirement age; it has taken a long time, but finally the retirement age has been settled at 65 for both men and women. The case illustrates the circumstances in which Community law can cause a change in national law where the two are in conflict, and also provides an example of an individual citizen taking her own government to Court. The Iso-glucose case, on the other hand, is an important example of an inter-institutional dispute between the Council and the European Parliament. The Council purported to enact a regulation imposing a levy on glucose; it did so after asking for the opinion of the European Parliament, as it was required to do by the Treaty, but without waiting to receive it. The Council maintained that whilst the Treaty required that the European Parliament should be consulted it said nothing about having to wait for the opinion. The Court, however, held that the meaning of the Treaty was that the opinion had to be asked for *and received* before the Council could proceed, and annulled the regulation. The power of Parliament was thus effectively enhanced. Since the Council could not proceed without its opinion, it could drag its feet when faced with a regulation or directive it disliked, thus putting pressure on the Commission and Council to compromise if they wanted to get the instrument passed.

The Effects of the Treaty of Maastricht

The overall effect of Maastricht, in stark contrast to what some governments have suggested, is to reinforce inter-governmental cooperation outside the framework of EC/EU institutions. In two important sectors of the Treaty, Foreign Policy and Justice and Home Affairs, control is firmly in the hands of the governments via the Council and the European Council, with Parliament and the Commission relegated to the sidelines and the Court totally excluded. In other respects, however, the structures of the Community have been strengthened. The major points of the Treaty can be summarised as follows:

1. Two new areas of cooperation of member states are added:
   (a) Foreign Policy, Security and Defence
   (b) Justice and Home Affairs.
2. The intention to establish a single currency, the ECU, common monetary and exchange-rate policies, and the establishment of a European System of Central Banks (ESCB) under a European Central Bank (ECB).
3. The introduction of the concept of subsidiarity, in an attempt to define the areas of competence and responsibility which fall to the Community and the member states respectively.
4. The establishment of a Citizenship of the Union, whereby every national of a member state becomes also a citizen of the European Union.
5. The establishment of a common Social Policy between 11 of the member states, the UK having opted out.
6. An increase in the powers of the Parliament, enabling it to appoint an Ombudsman, appoint Committees of Enquiry, receive petitions and request the Commission to make a proposal (which goes a little way toward the Parliament's long-standing desire to be able to initiate legislation).
7. The creation of a new institution, the Committee of the Regions. This gives the regions of Europe a direct representation and bypasses their governments.

Some of these provisions could be of great significance. Take, for example, the complementary impact of subsidiarity and the Committee of the Regions. Subsidiarity is defined in Article 3b in terms intended to suggest that power will be shared between the EU and member states, with the balance in favour of the states, but elsewhere in the Treaty it means that 'decisions are taken as closely as possible to the citizens' – which clearly could mean at a sub-governmental level. Put that together with direct regional representation to the Committee of the Regions and the result could be that centralist national governments might find it difficult to resist pressures for devolution or the establishment of a federal state.

But perhaps the thing that most encapsulates the hopes and fears of the Europhiles and Europhobes is the establishment of a single currency. Everyone who has been abroad on holiday will have experienced the fumbling with a pocket calculator when shopping, the irritating refusal of the banks to change the pocketful of pesetas or francs left over at the end of the holiday, the hassle of changing from one currency to another and the payment of commission to the banks at every change. The costs of commission were vividly illustrated recently by a journalist who visited each of the 12 member states in turn, changing £100 into francs, then guilders and so on. He ended with just over £40, having done nothing with his £100 except change it into other currencies. Multiply that by the enormous number of business transactions that take place every day, and the reason for the desire to establish a single currency becomes obvious – as do the problems of making the change. Billions of pounds, francs, deutschmarks and so on are added to the costs of business transactions every single day. A single currency would produce enormous savings which could be used to reduce the costs of production and therefore the price to consumers. Opposition to the proposals is concentrated in two areas – banking, which stands to lose large profits, and the ordinary citizen, frightened by tales of a strange new currency and the alleged loss of sovereignty. So considerable lobbying is going on to try to slow up progress towards a single currency or drop the idea altogether, to oppose other aspects of European monetary policy, and generally to resist integration. Nevertheless the EU Treaty lays down a firm timetable for the achievement of a European Monetary System (EMS) and the establishment of the European System of Central Banks (ESCB) and the European Central Bank (ECB).

The European Monetary Institute (EMI), the forerunner of the central bank, has already been established in Frankfurt in January 1994 as the start of the second stage towards monetary union. The importance of this progress in financial cooperation is that the ECB stands alone amongst the changes made by Maastricht in one crucial respect: it is supranational, not under the control of any institution or agency. Its model is the Bundesbank, which operates independently of the German government and which in the opinion of many people is the reason for the stability and strength of the deutschmark. No other institution in the EU has this status, which explains why such bitter battles are raging around the issues of monetary policy.

A great deal depends on developments in the second half of the 1990s. The next inter-governmental conference, to review and if necessary to revise the Treaty, is scheduled for 1996, so there will be a great deal of manoeuvring for position before then. High noon is set for 31 December 1997 at the latest; if by that time the date for the beginning of the third stage (the setting up of the ECB, the ESCB and the irrevocable setting of the conversion rates of the ECU into the other currencies) has not been set, the third stage will start anyway on 1 January 1998, and member states will have to decide where they stand.

Further reading

Clesse, A. and Vernon, R. (eds) (1991) *The European Community after 1992: A New Role in World Politics?*, Institute for European and International Studies, Association Luxembourg-Harvard, Luxembourg.

Commission of the European Communities (1994) *Treaty on European Union*, Office for Official Publications of the European Communities, Luxembourg.

European Parliament (1992) *Maastricht: The Treaty on European Union. The Position of the European Parliament*, Office for Official Publications of the European Communities, Luxembourg.

Freestone, D. A. C. and Davidson, J. S. (1988) *The Institutional Framework of the European Communities*, Croom Helm, London.

George, S. (1991) *Politics and Policy in the European Community*, 2nd edn. Oxford University Press, Oxford.

Nicoll, W. and Salmon, T. (1994) *Understanding the New European Community*, Harvester Wheatsheaf, Hemel Hempstead.

Williams, A. M. (1991) *The European Community*, Blackwell, Oxford.

5 The core democracies of Western Europe: France, Italy, Germany and the United Kingdom

Introduction

Despite their differing historical paths and cultures, the four major democracies of western Europe have confronted many similar problems and challenges since 1945: democratic consolidation and economic reconstruction; the building of political and social consensus; urbanisation, modernisation, and changes to the social structure; the impact of recession and economic crisis since the 1970s, and in particular the growing burdens on the welfare state; the increasing internationalisation of both politics and economics, and the challenges associated with moves towards European integration in particular. All of these developments have been associated with major transformations in cultural and social life – for example, the almost universal decline in the social and political influence of the main churches through widespread secularisation; the move from large-scale and labour-intensive manufacturing industry to light industry, computerisation, and the service sector, with a concomitant decline in traditional working-class sub-cultures and in the relationship between social class membership and political behaviour; the greater political attention paid to women with moves towards increased gender equality in at least some aspects of life; the changing ethnic and racial composition of societies; and the momentous challenge posed by the growth in the power of the mass media and the impact of new forms of marketing and communications upon politics.

More recently, the collapse of communist rule in eastern and central Europe, and the reopening of old and seemingly intractable conflicts which had lain dormant for decades there, as well as the eastern countries' need for economic aid, have added to the debate about the future of western European democracy. Traditional parties and ideologies have been forced, with varying degrees of enthusiasm and success, to respond to new political agendas, centred on ecological concerns, race and ethnicity, regionalism, and gender politics, for example; and to organise around new socio-political cleavages, many of which are as yet only semi-formed. Whereas some parties have sought to transform their ideologies and structures totally, others have been content to adapt to change rather more slowly. New political forces have sought to enter the mainstream – the Greens, for example, but also, most dramatically in the early 1990s, a resurgent extreme right in several countries. Everywhere, politicians and commentators alike agree that the major European democracies face mounting evidence of voter volatility, unrest, and disenchantment. Demands for institutional and political renewal can be heard, and concern is voiced that, in the absence of successful renewal, the future stability and health of European democracy may be threatened.

This chapter seeks to present a very brief synopsis and analysis of the main contours of political developments in each of the four major western European democracies since 1945. It begins by examining each country in turn, before turning to a comparative analysis of the challenges confronting the major democracies in the 1990s.

France

The experience of war, occupation, and eventual liberation left deep scars upon the French body politic: in 1945 the country was divided between those who had resisted the Nazis and those who had collaborated either actively or passively. This political dichotomy was compounded by divisions within the victorious resistance movement between a nationalist right-wing, loyal to General Charles de Gaulle, and a communist-led left-wing. The French Communist Party (PCF) emerged in elections held in October 1945 as the biggest single party with 26 per cent of the popular vote. However, the political life of the Fourth Republic – inaugurated in October 1946 – was to be dominated by a series of shaky coalition governments, often led by the moderate and pro-western socialist party (SFIO); and both the Gaullist and communist movements were to experience marginalisation, following de Gaulle's withdrawal from active politics in 1946 in disagreement with the new constitution and the PCF's removal from the post-war government in 1947. Importantly, the war-time experience had discredited those substantial sections of the French right which had collaborated with the Nazi occupation, and which adhered to an almost pre-revolutionary creed which conflated racial purity with 'true Frenchness', and national glory with respect for hierarchy. Although such sentiments would resurface in the 1950s in the form of the far right Poujadiste movement, and even in some parts of the Gaullist movement, and again in the 1980s in Jean-Marie Le Pen's *Front National*, for the most part the post-1945 French right would embrace a conservative or bourgeois variant of the democratic republicanism of 1789.

A key priority of the governments of the Fourth Republic was economic reconstruction. From 1945 to 1947, the National Resistance Council nationalised many key industries as well as banking and insurance concerns. Although the pace and direction of nationalisations changed after the PCF's removal from government in 1947 – partly in response to receipt of US support in the form of Marshall Aid – state intervention and direction remained a cornerstone of the French drive to rebuild and modernise the economy. A modernisation plan was launched by Jean Monnet in 1945, based on the premise that the only way to catch up with countries such as the UK and USA was through development of large corporations which could introduce technological innovations and benefit from economies of scale. From 1946, governments sought to raise investment and production in the private sector by assistance and encouragement of mergers. A series of five-year plans from 1947 prioritised industrial growth, to be achieved initially through the development of French industry behind the barriers of protection. Politicians such as Pierre Mendès-France and Guy Mollet sought to speed up modernisation throughout the 1950s. Industry grew rapidly, living standards rose, and from 1952 increased urbanisation began dramatically to change the social structure. On the negative side, rural depopulation saw many small farmers forced off the land, small businesses suffered from the policy of industrial and commercial concentration, and the new city-dwellers frequently suffered from urban congestion. Moreover, the planning process was entrusted to civil servants and technocrats who were to be increasingly accused of top-down and authoritarian management. The *dirigiste* foundations of French-style corporatism were laid in this period, preempting later Gaullist tendencies to bypass traditional interests and elites by dealing with sympathetic professional associations.

The Fourth Republic was politically unstable. A strong parliament, inclusive of all shades of opinion through proportional representation, had been envisaged. However, parties within parliament remained deeply polarised. Weak governments, unable to straddle the great political cleavages, further reproduced chronic party instability. The weakness of cabinet government and the high degree of party control over the day-to-day workings of the state led to no fewer than 25 governments and 15 prime ministers between 1945 and 1958. Even more worrying, from the point of view of the political establishment, was that by 1951 nearly half the electorate was voting for parties – either the PCF or the extreme right – which rejected the post-war political system altogether; indeed, the 1950s saw a rise in support for the right-wing Poujadiste movement which appealed to those lower-middle classes adversely affected by economic restructuring. The crisis in politics contrasted with the professionalism of technocratic and civil service groups which represented elements of stability and continuity.

It is possible that the Fourth Republic might have endured longer, but for the crisis which erupted in Algeria in 1954. The outbreak of a violent and bloody colonial war there had a profound effect upon French society, polarising the country again between supporters and opponents of French imperial rule. By 1957–58, it was clear that elements of the French military were dangerously out of control, and willing to resort to open rebellion and threats of assassination against cabinet ministers; France's moral standing in the world was collapsing as reports of torture of Algerians reached the outside; and right-wing terrorist groups at home were targeting opponents of the colonial war. Fears rose that the civilian authorities were in danger of losing power to the army in a coup.

When a coup came, in May 1958, it did not inaugurate a military-style dictatorship. Rather, Charles de Gaulle, helped by his war-time prestige and by the fact that he had stood above the chaos of the Fourth Republic, took power, promising a new constitution for a Fifth Republic. That Constitution, promulgated in September, introduced a strongly centralised presidential democracy with a directly elected president as executive head of state (de Gaulle became president in December). The powers of parliament vis-à-vis the executive were reduced. De Gaulle consolidated his position by removing the military threat to democracy, and ended the war in Algeria, granting that country independence.

The Gaullist decade saw substantial elements of continuity in economic policy. State direction of private sector operations through technocratic planning continued to act as a motor force of economic development. With the foundation of the EEC in 1957, the French economy was opened up, step by step, to greater competition; however, caution and compromises with those business interests which felt threatened by international competition were necessitated by political as well as economic criteria. In 1963 a new regional planning agency was created – DATAR – with the intention of further bypassing local elites and developing the more backward areas of the country. Its operations also tended to undermine political parties and reinforce the irrelevance of parliament as a forum where regional problems could be aired and resolved. Throughout the 1960s, the regime sought to strengthen industry by encouraging mergers and shut-downs which led to mounting unemployment and a lengthening of the working week – the longest in Western Europe by 1968.

Economic modernisation was not accompanied by a modernisation of social structures. Indeed, Gaullism exuded paternalism and populist appeal to traditional morality, patterns of social behaviour and respect for authority. The combination of rapid economic growth with social stagnation created several sources of powerful discontent. Workers, especially the newly urbanised, were angered by rising unemployment, low wage increases, public spending cuts on health and housing, the perceived failure of wage increases to match economic growth, and the effects of cuts in public spending on health and housing after 1963. Students railed against a university sector in which numbers had expanded rapidly without a corresponding increase in spending on education. Small farmers also grumbled. These grievances came to a head in May 1968 when France was rocked by virtual revolution. Tens of thousands of students and workers occupied universities and factories, and for a period it seemed as if the Fifth Republic would fall. Eventually, de Gaulle called a general election which was won by the right-wing parties, capitalising upon the fear of revolution and chaos. However, the regime had been badly shaken, and in April 1969 de Gaulle resigned the presidency, being succeeded after elections by Georges Pompidou.

May 1968 represented a revolt against the stifling paternalism of post-war French society. In the early 1970s, French governments moved to introduce a number of changes, including greater trade union rights, educational reforms, and progressive social legislation including the legalisation of abortion and freer access to birth control. However, under both Georges Pompidou's presidency (1969–74) and that of his successor, Valéry Giscard d'Estaing (1974–81), France remained a highly centralised state.

During the 1970s a number of important developments changed the nature of political competition. First, the end of the hegemony of Gaullism on the right of the political spectrum meant that the remains of the Gaullist movement had to compete with a non-Gaullist right which saw itself as more modern, liberal, pro-European and less nationalist. Such forces were organised by Giscard d'Estaing into the Union for French Democracy (UDF), a centre-right coalition which supported his presidential bid. Gaullist forces, reorganised by Jacques Chirac into the Rally for the Republic (RPR) in 1976, would have to both compete against and cooperate with this new centre-right in order to hold on to power.

Second, 1972 saw the Communist and Socialist parties sign a Common Programme of the Left which was to facilitate greater left-wing cooperation from which the Socialist Party (PS) of François Mitterrand would emerge as the main victor. Despite a flirtation with the more open-minded and independent (from Moscow) positions of 'Eurocommunism' during the 1970s, the French Communists, under Georges Marchais, had reasserted their hard-line and sectarian reflexes by the end of the decade and were unable to compete with Mitterrand's PS. It was the PS, preaching social modernisation, regional reform, workers' self-management, and redistribution of wealth, which benefited most from the post-1968 change in atmosphere.

Positive election returns for the left in 1978 were followed by Mitterrand's election in May 1981 as the first Socialist president of the Fifth Republic. The PS then achieved a majority in parliament and a government which included four Communist ministers took office.

The early Mitterrand government had many radical innovations to its credit. Among the measures introduced were: a strengthening of workers' rights and a raising of the wages of many workers; attempted reflation of the economy through increased public spending; increases in social welfare provision; the introduction of legislation to increase women's rights in the economic and social spheres; and long-overdue regional reforms – named after the minister responsible, Gaston Defferre – which, though criticised in their implementation, provided for democratically elected regional authorities for the first time and represented a step away from the Jacobin tradition of centralising all power in Paris.

By early 1983 the reform programme was in trouble. The international climate worked against radical economic policies which depended upon increased borrowing and higher taxes, and in 1983–84 Mitterrand effectively backed away from Keynesian economics in favour of austerity. Realisation that the government could not deliver socialism whilst ignoring external pressures also led to a greater enthusiasm for European cooperation and integration from 1984. In July 1984, the Communists resigned from government, Mitterrand replaced his prime minister, Pierre Mauroy, with the young technocrat, Laurent Fabius, and the administration moved towards the centre. Elections in 1986 returned a right-wing parliamentary majority and a period of cohabitation between a right-wing government (with the Gaullist, Chirac, as prime minister) and a Socialist president began. Although the new government carried out some privatisations, the ground had already been prepared by the Fabius administration, and the U-turn was less dramatic than might have been expected.

Mitterrand's reelection in 1988 brought the PS back to office. But this time, there was little of the earlier idealism; the Communists – reduced to less than 10 per cent of the vote – remained firmly in opposition; and Mitterrand included several centre-right figures from the UDF in his new, pragmatic administration. His appointment of a succession of moderate prime ministers – Michel Rocard, Edith Cresson, Pierre Bérégovoy – seemed to confirm to some commentators that French politics was undergoing a process of de-ideologisation, with a pragmatic centre-left and a pragmatic centre-right cooperating, whilst agreeing on the fundamentals of policy. To others, the impression was created of a Socialist Party unsure of how to react to the country's economic problems or (after 1990) the challenge of a united Germany.

A wild card in French politics was a resurgent extreme right in the form of the racist *Front National* (FN), led by Jean-Marie Le Pen. Benefiting from the inability of the established parties to produce solutions to mass unemployment, and the decline of the PCF as an effective vehicle for the protest vote, this force, preaching hostility towards immigrants and calling for social authoritarianism, was to achieve 10–15 per cent of the vote in elections from the mid-1980s. Its rise succeeded to some extent in setting the political agenda in the early 1990s, tempting politicians such as Chirac and Cresson to utter anti-immigrant remarks and to promise tough action on illegal immigration. The FN also sought to exploit growing fears of a loss of national sovereignty which it claimed was inherent in the Maastricht Treaty on European Union; the Treaty was only very narrowly approved by the French in a referendum in September 1992 following a campaign against ratification by the FN, the PCF, and some Gaullists.

Although a mass anti-racism movement was formed in response to the FN, there was a clear turn to the right in the early 1990s, and this was confirmed by the election of a right-wing government in March 1993, under the Gaullist Edouard Balladur. Another period of cohabitation began. Nevertheless, the volatility of the political situation meant that by the end of 1993, the new government had already been forced to stage two humiliating retreats in the face of popular opposition to its education reforms and its plans to reduce the wages of young workers. Local elections in early 1994, which saw a left-wing revival, seemed to confirm the impression of volatility.

Politics and society in France in the mid-1990s appeared diversified and fragmented with the contours of future political competition difficult to predict. On the left, a battered Socialist Party faced competition from left-radicals, Greens, Communists, and a populist Citizens Movement formed by a former Socialist cabinet minister, Jean-Pierre Chevènement. On the right, both the Gaullist and non-Gaullist movements were divided over the direction of economic policy and the future of European integration; and the Front National remained a challenge. Although the logic of presidential elections makes for alliances of convenience, French society is scarcely less fragmented politically than in the days of the Fourth Republic.

Italy

From Mussolini's downfall in July 1943 – after which he fled behind German lines, presiding in name over a Nazi puppet regime – until final liberation from Fascism on 25 April 1945, Italy was involved in civil conflict, although the increasing domination of the Germans over the remnants of Italian Fascism allowed the conflict to be articulated by the anti-Fascist side as a war of national liberation. Indeed, both the Communist and Christian Democrat wings of the Italian resistance movement were to emphasise the patriotic nature of the anti-Fascist struggle. Democratic patriotism was seen as a useful way of constructing a new Italian national identity which was not merely post-Fascist but decidedly anti-Fascist, thus denying the hard right any nationalist or patriotic legitimacy in post-1945 Italy.

Whilst such political myths played a positive role in binding some of the wounds of the previous 20 years, the reality was a lot more complex. An extreme right, nostalgic for Mussolini's rule, was to remain an enduring force in Italian politics, albeit a minority one; reorganised in December 1946 as the Italian Social Movement (MSI) in order to circumvent the constitutional ban on the old Fascist party, it would wait for nearly 50 years until the collapse of the Christian Democratic system of power in the early 1990s gave it an opportunity to expand its social base, entering the Italian Government in May 1994 with five cabinet ministers.

The Italian people voted in June 1946 to abolish the monarchy. A new constitution established Italy as a democratic republic. The Christian Democrats (DC), under Alcide de Gasperi who became prime minister in December 1945, engineered (with Washington's approval) the expulsion of the Italian Communist Party (PCI) from the post-war government in 1947, and in 1948 the long period of Christian Democratic dominance began in earnest when the party won general elections with nearly 50 per cent of the vote. The

DC would remain in power, at the head of a series of mostly coalition governments, until its collapse amid massive corruption scandals in 1993–94.

Italian economic policy after 1945 sought regeneration through integration with the world capitalist economy. An 'open-doors' policy was pursued which emphasised competition in external markets. Northern Italian industry was encouraged to take advantage of low wages paid to southern migrant labour, and to act as the motor force of a growth drive led by exports. This policy necessitated internal migration from south to north, heavy external emigration of 'surplus' workers, weakened trade unions, and relative neglect of agriculture, especially the notoriously inefficient southern agricultural sector.

After 1953, the DC felt that political circumstances necessitated greater state intervention in the economy. General elections in 1953 saw the DC slide to 40 per cent of the vote, and the PCI increase its vote to nearly 23 per cent, eclipsing the Socialists on the left. The DC failed to change the electoral law so as to award two-thirds of the seats in parliament to the winning party or coalition. Having failed in this attempt at manipulation the DC moved to entrench itself in power against the danger of an eventual left-wing victory at the polls by exploiting the full potential of giant state corporations created during Fascism – such as the Institute for Industrial Reconstruction (IRI) – or instituted by the DC – such as the State Hydrocarbons Corporation (ENI), which emerged in 1953. Public works programmes contributed to the economic boom in the 1950s and 1960s. Significantly, the DC under Amintore Fanfani brought the state and semi-state sectors under party political control, patronage becoming a mainstay of the party's system of power. Public sector jobs were increasingly awarded on the basis of political loyalty rather than merit.

In the period from 1957 to the mid-1960s high growth rates transformed Italy into a modern industrial economy. But serious negative features of the society and the economy were exacerbated during the 1960s. In the cities appalling conditions and low wage rates prevailed for many of the hundreds of thousands of newly urbanised poor. The long-standing imbalance between the rich north and the under-developed south became, if anything, even more critical as Italy emerged as a major economic power. Unemployment in the 1950s reached four times the European average. Social problems were neglected – provision of public housing was negligible and no national health service existed until the late 1970s.

From the mid-1960s, when wages began to pick up, the trade union movement became more vocal. The DC responded to a perceptible rise in support for the PCI by seeking to isolate the Communists through incorporation of the Socialist Party (PSI) in coalition government from 1963. This move was facilitated by the election of a more liberal-minded Pope, John XXIII, in 1958; his predecessor, Pius XII, had vigorously opposed any opening by the DC to the centre- left. However, this merely encouraged expectations of social reforms which, ultimately, the PSI was unable to deliver whilst the DC controlled the purse-strings. In the longer term, the PSI was to be drawn into the web of patronage and corruption which came to characterise the Italian political class, a process which was facilitated by the election of Bettino Craxi as PSI leader in 1976.

By 1969, the economic miracle was in trouble. Attempts to buy social peace and political stability by expanding the numbers in higher education and in the state bureaucracy, and by paying hidden subsidies to dependent social groups (in the form of 'invalidity' payments to semi-employed small farmers, for example) could not prevent a social explosion in 1969. The so-called 'Hot Autumn' of that year saw massive industrial unrest, with more hours lost in strikes than in any other country in the developed world.

The early 1970s saw some social reforms which strengthened workers' rights, establishing a new institutionalised role for the trade unions. The perceived shift in the balance of power towards the labour movement, together with continuing good election results for the PCI, provoked an extreme right-wing backlash: neo-fascist terrorists bombed civilian targets from 1969, hoping to provoke political chaos and calls for an authoritarian government, and both far right and far left terrorism plagued Italian politics during the 1970s and 1980s.

The 1970s was a decade of social change. Despite opposition from both the DC and the Vatican, a clear majority of Italian voters approved the legalisation of divorce (1974) and abortion (1981) in referenda. Together with evidence of falling attendances at church services, and growing political diversification within the ranks of the Catholic clergy, these developments highlighted the widespread secularisation of Italian society. The election of a conservative Pope, John Paul II, in 1978 failed to reverse the trends; indeed, the Pope's Polish background perhaps underlined his sometimes clumsy interventions in Italian politics. During the 1970s a large and vocal feminist movement campaigned successfully for changes in family law and in the laws on rape, which had effectively condemned women to second-class citizenship. However, it was to prove more difficult to change societal attitudes, especially in the conservative south.

In the wake of the social and economic change which characterised the early 1970s, electoral support for the Italian left grew impressively. The PCI scored more than 34 per cent in elections in 1976, drawing close to the DC on 38 per cent. The PCI, pioneers of independent-minded reform-communism long before Gorbachev, called for a 'historic compromise' with the DC. A powerful array of forces – the economic and financial establishment, the Church, the DC and its allies, the security services, the American Embassy, the Mafia, and the shadowy far-right Masonic lodge known as P2 (to which nearly 1,000 of the most influential figures in Italian public life were known to belong) – opposed the election of any left-wing government. According to PCI leader Enrico Berlinguer, a successful democratic reform of the Italian state, to tackle corruption and the Mafia (a powerful criminal organisation) and to strengthen democratic institutions, could not be undertaken by the

Communists alone in the face of such opposition. It required the two big parties to work together. If the DC would commit itself to political reform, the PCI would agree to put socialism on the back burner. A period of 'national solidarity' opened during which the DC, under the wily Giulio Andreotti, continued to exclude the Communists from government; but obtained their support in parliament in return for consultation. Such a formula caused considerable tension within both parties: the right-wing of the DC resented and opposed any 'legitimation' of the Communists; and the left-wing of the PCI feared that their party would simply be used by the establishment to undermine the gains of the labour movement, and then be cast aside. The murder in 1978 of leading DC reformer Aldo Moro, an advocate of dialogue with the PCI, was followed by a turn to the right. Moro was kidnapped and murdered by the left-wing terrorist group, the Red Brigades. However, subsequent revelations suggested that elements of the state security services and some of his own DC colleagues were implicated in the events leading to his death.

The 1980s opened with the PCI back in opposition and very much in isolation. The Communists' loss of any sense of strategic direction was bitterly exposed after the tragic death of their leader, Berlinguer, in 1984; thereafter, open factionalism gradually robbed the party of its once proud unity of purpose. The party's defeat in a referendum on wage cuts in 1985, and its inability to halt job losses or privatisations, was followed by an electoral set-back in 1987, when the PCI share of the vote fell back to 26.6 per cent.

In 1983, the DC agreed to the appointment of Socialist leader Bettino Craxi as prime minister, although Christian Democrats continued to dominate the cabinet. Craxi had led the PSI steadily to the right, acquiring a reputation for fierce anti-communism and ruthless pragmatism. He sought to project the PSI as a decisive force for change, attractive to the young upwardly-mobile professionals and middle classes and contemptuous of 'old-fashioned' Marxist ideology and political moralism – which he associated with the PCI. During his four years as prime minister and subsequently, the Socialists played a double role in government. They claimed to be a more modern alternative to both the Communists and Christian Democrats, yet cooperated closely with the latter who were convinced that Craxi was a necessary coalition partner if the Communists were to be kept isolated. They demanded economic rationalisation, yet became ever more embroiled in the system of corruption and patronage with which they came to be as closely associated as the Christian Democrats. Craxi's party succeeded in winning wealthy backers, such as the media mogul Silvio Berlusconi. Nevertheless, for all its new influence and powers of patronage, the PSI was unable to exceed around 15 per cent of the popular vote.

By the early 1990s, the Italian political system was showing signs of considerable strain. No real change of government had been achieved since 1947. The Mafia remained a powerful threat, not only to democracy and the rule of law, but to the very survival of the Italian state. The system of political patronage, based upon high levels of public spending, was difficult to sustain in times of economic recession and Italy entered the 1990s with the highest level of public debt – around 100 per cent of GDP – in western Europe. The decision of PCI leader Achille Occhetto to rename and relaunch the party as the post-communist Democratic Party of the Left (PDS) in February 1991 was intended to break the log-jam and create a new centre-left majority. In the event, the party split, with radicals leaving to form the Communist Refoundation Party, and a divided left suffered further losses in elections in 1992.

Meanwhile, a revolt against the high levels of public spending necessary to keep the government parties alive got under way in the north. The populist Northern Leagues, centred in wealthy Milan and led by the outspoken Umberto Bossi, exploited the well-documented connections between government parties and the Mafia to accuse the Roman establishment of draining the north of resources and pumping them into the Mafia-infested south, where the Christian Democrats (and increasingly the Socialists too) had their power base. The Leagues veered between calls for a new federal Italy, and threats of outright northern secession. Appealing to the self-interest of the northern middle classes, but capturing working-class support also with a heady mixture of regionalist fervour and hostility towards 'immigrants' from the south, the Leagues won nearly 9 per cent of the total national vote in 1992.

In 1991–94, a series of investigations into political corruption by a number of outstandingly brave Italian magistrates – their resolve strengthened, if anything, by Mafia assassination of several of their colleagues – revealed massive networks of bribery and theft of public funds and ensnared hundreds of leading politicians. Virtually the entire ruling political elite was exposed as corrupt. The left opposition parties hoped that popular anger might sustain support for a thorough democratic revolution, perhaps involving a move to the left (and in particular towards new left-wing movements such as the anti-Mafia Network, founded by the anti-Mafia campaigner, Leoluca Orlando). However, as some former Communist politicians were also cited in corruption investigations, evidence mounted of a growing exasperation with all politicians and with politics in general – expressed in a longing for a 'saviour' from without who would smash the old system. A popular referendum on electoral reform in June 1993 produced a massive majority in favour of a move away from proportional representation – seen as leading to weak and corrupt cabinets – towards a more British-style electoral system. Alarmingly, serious discussion of the implications of various reforms tended to get brushed aside by a tidal wave of negative feeling towards the entire political class.

Local elections in November 1993 produced victory for a left-wing alliance, led by the PDS. However, a huge increase in the neo-fascist vote was also recorded; the neo-fascist MSI was visibly replacing the crumbling Christian Democrats as the main right-wing force in the south of the country. The DC was now disintegrating, with a rump renaming and relaunching itself early in 1994 as the Italian Popular Party.

In February 1994, Silvio Berlusconi launched a new political movement, Forza Italia, with the intention of blocking an anticipated left-wing victory in general elections scheduled for March. The movement was aggressively right-wing, preaching free market economics, business success, anti-communism, and promising instant cures to the country's economic and political crises. It benefited from the backing of Berlusconi's vast media and business empire. Although Berlusconi was associated with the old regime – a member of the P2 Masonic lodge, and a friend to many of the disgraced political elite – he managed to project an image of success and dynamism. In alliance with the Northern Leagues and the neo-fascists, his movement harnessed a popular mood of weariness with political squabbling, desire for strong government, and longing for economic prosperity, to inflict a heavy defeat on the left-wing alliance in March; Berlusconi subsequently became prime minister.

His cabinet was the first in any European country since 1945 to include fascist ministers, causing concern in many European capitals. Moreover, it represented an unprecedented concentration of political, economic, and media power in the hands of one man. Given the volatility of Italian politics, the degree of political polarisation, and the enormous problems confronting the country, further party upheaval seems likely.

Federal Republic of Germany

After the defeat of the Nazi regime in 1945, Germany found itself under the military and political sway of the four liberating allied powers – France, the UK, the USA, and the USSR. Although the preservation of German unity remained on the agenda in the immediate post-war period, western reluctance to accept Soviet demands that any united Germany should be neutral and demilitarised, together with the dynamics of the Cold War which soon developed, effectively sealed the division of the country.

The new Federal Republic of Germany (FRG) adopted a Basic Law in May 1949. This provided for a parliamentary democracy, with a cabinet government accountable to parliament. The country was divided into states, or *Länder*, governed by their own parliaments and enjoying considerable powers. At the federal level, a two-chamber parliament consisted of a lower house (*Bundestag*), directly elected every four years by the people, and a much smaller upper house (*Bundesrat*), comprising representatives of the various state governments. A federal president is elected every five years by the lower house of parliament, augmented by an equal number of *Länder* representatives. The head of government, the Chancellor, enjoys considerable authority. A dual electoral system provides for half the seats in the *Bundestag* to be filled on the basis of a constituency-based vote, and half on the basis of a party list system. However, parties polling less than 5 per cent of the total national vote are excluded. This measure, it was claimed, would ensure stability and governability; it also, of course, penalises smaller parties and narrows the range of views which are represented in parliament.

One of the first tasks to be faced by the new Germany was de-Nazification – the removal from positions of authority and bringing to justice of those guilty of crimes under the Nazi dictatorship. However, de-Nazification soon fell victim to the logic of the Cold War. Although some 13 million people had been screened by 1949, less than 2,000 were considered major offenders. As the USSR came to be regarded as the new enemy, and the FRG as being on the front line of the new East–West potential conflict, fierce anti-Communism, rather than thorough-going catharsis *vis-à-vis* the Nazi past, came to characterise the political life of the FRG. The Communist Party of Germany (KPD) was banned in 1956 – although it soon resurfaced under a new name, the DKP.

Until 1969, the political life of the FRG was dominated by the Christian Democratic Union (CDU) and its conservative ally in Bavaria, the Christian Social Union (CSU). The CDU/CSU was a centre-right force, firmly committed to the Western alliance under American leadership and strongly anti-communist. Although it embraced capitalist economic rationale and was committed to private sector-led economic growth, it also sought a measure of social partnership between employers and trade unions, and articulated the concept of a social market economy. This was in essence a kind of paternalistic capitalism, in which the state assumed some responsibility for regulating prices in the housing and farm sectors, for social insurance, and for offering protection to the lower income groups.

The CDU leader Konrad Adenauer was Chancellor from September 1949 until October 1963. The period witnessed the consolidation of CDU supremacy as the party led the FRG through a sustained economic boom. The model of economic management adopted allocated huge powers to an independent central bank, the *Bundesbank*, which was charged with keeping inflation under control at all costs. A strongly centralised trade union movement, the DGB, was enlisted by the state to assist in guaranteeing labour discipline in return for a recognised place at the negotiating table; collective bargaining over wages was regulated by law.

The period of economic success and capitalist stabilisation and the growing consolidation of CDU power forced a historic rethink within the ranks of the main opposition party, the Social Democratic Party (SPD). A growing moderation on the part of the SPD had seen the party drop its support for widespread nationalisation of the economy, accept the capitalist market economy, and abandon its militant secularism, accepting religious instruction in schools. This process of change within the SPD came to a head at the party congress in Bad Godesberg in 1959, when the SPD turned its back on Marxism and embraced reform-socialism. The following year saw the SPD effectively accept the main outlines of Adenauer's foreign policy.

In 1960–66, the CDU governed in coalition with the centrist Free Democrats (FDP). As elsewhere in western Europe, the decade saw considerable social and cultural change which presented a challenge to the CDU. In 1963 Adenauer was succeeded as Chancellor by Ludwig Erhard. Policy divisions within the government, the growing confidence of the SPD (which elected Willy Brandt as its leader in 1963), and the easing of the Cold War in the 1960s all contributed to a CDU loss of confidence in 1966 which was followed by a period of 'grand coalition' between the CDU-CSU and the SPD. In 1969, the popularity of Brandt's policy of improved relations with the East (*Ostpolitik*) saw the SPD clinch victory. An SPD–FDP coalition followed with Brandt as Chancellor. The SPD remained in power until 1982, Brandt being succeeded as Chancellor by Helmut Schmidt in 1974. The 1970s saw substantially improved relations with the USSR and eastern Europe, including the GDR.

While consensus among the main parties, political stability, and mounting acceptance of the FRG internationally, combined with substantial economic recovery, represented a success story, there was of course another side to West German life. Revolt against the stifling conformism and orthodoxy of politics and society was commonplace in the late 1960s and early 1970s among young people, and especially students. In its most extreme manifestation, this led to urban terrorism by far left groups, such as the Baader–Meinhof gang. The heavy-handed response of the authorities included much-criticised police measures, and the introduction of notorious laws banning left-wing radicals from holding public sector jobs. Such measures caused concern amongst intellectuals and civil liberties groups about the extent to which authoritarian impulses still characterised the official response to political dissent.

In the 1970s, the FRG, in common with its partners throughout western Europe, suffered the effects of the oil crisis and recession. A nuclear energy programme was one response to this situation. Opposition to nuclear energy, to growing involvement in NATO, and to the environmental pollution caused by industrial growth, produced a vocal Green movement in the early 1980s. The West German Greens soon established a reputation as among the most politically effective and formidable of European environmental movements, heralding a new brand of politics which soon found echoes in other European countries. Mobilisation against NATO plans to modernise nuclear weapons on FRG soil gave the Greens a popular cause, and in 1983 they entered the national parliament.

In 1982, the FDP moved to the right, responding to a combination of circumstances – the ascendancy of 'new right' ideas elsewhere, the renewed Cold War following the Soviet invasion of Afghanistan and martial law in Poland, and clashes with the SPD over the funding of welfare programmes. As a result, the FDP brought down the SPD-led government and returned the CDU, under Helmut Kohl, to power. The new government reduced social welfare spending and increased incentives to the private sector. Throughout the 1980s, the Kohl administration's primary objective was to maintain the country's economic standing in the face of international recession and mounting unemployment at home. The FRG had established itself as a highly successful exporter, dominating the markets of its neighbours. Not surprisingly, the Kohl governments would display support for the completion of a unified European market, and by the end of the 1980s European political union had become a key and strategic policy goal.

The collapse of the GDR in 1989 presented the FRG with unanticipated challenges and opportunities at the beginning of the 1990s. Economic union of the two Germanies in July 1990 was followed by political union in October. Kohl's promises of instant economic improvements to the people of the East, the prestige he enjoyed as the man who presided over unification, and the hesitancy and uncertainty of the SPD in the face of unification, all contributed to a CDU victory in all-German elections held in December 1990. However, by the mid-1990s it was clear that united Germany faced a number of difficulties which may yet blight the consolidation of the new all-German democracy and hold serious implications for Europe as a whole.

First, unification has plainly not involved a fusion between two equal partners; rather, it has resembled a takeover of the GDR by the FRG – symbolised by the simple extension of the FRG's Basic Law to cover the GDR, rather than the promulgation of a new Constitution for the united Germany. The impression of Western arrogance and insensitivity led to resentment among those strata in the East likely to suffer economically, at least in the short to medium term. A backlash in the East against perceived neglect by West Germany has seen some rise in support for the former GDR Communists, now renamed the Party of Democratic Socialism (PDS). In early 1994, the PDS scored impressive local government gains. Reactions amongst the FRG establishment, involving threats to proscribe the PDS, cast doubt upon the willingness or ability of some in the corridors of power to tolerate dissent or diversity which might challenge the hitherto prevailing consensus.

Second, unification imposes heavy economic costs on the German economy at a time of recession. Many Westerners are unwilling to pay higher taxes or suffer reductions in living standards in order to help subsidise the recovery in the East. Reports of resentment towards Easterners, stereotyped as lazy or parasitical, underlined the scale of the effort required to build a truly unified nation.

Third, unification has seen an alarming rise in neo-Nazi violence and racist propaganda, with an escalation of murderous attacks upon immigrants, Jews, homosexuals and other vulnerable groups, calling into question the willingness or ability of the authorities to respond decisively to right-wing violence. Whilst electoral support for the far right remains as yet slight, the potential for such groups to exploit economic hardship in order to undermine democracy clearly exists.

Finally, the costs of unity have cast a shadow over German enthusiasm for European unity. Opinion polls on the eve of the 1994 European Parliament elections showed a clear drop in public support for the Maastricht Treaty on

European Union and a growing unwillingness to sacrifice the deutschmark for any single European currency. Although the government remains committed to European economic, monetary, and political union by the end of the twentieth century, the growing sense of uncertainty engulfing Europe and the growing economic burden at home mean that it will have to calculate carefully whether Germany can afford the risks involved in pushing ahead with a European union for which it may well have to foot more of the bill. Germany made a net contribution of around DM25 billion (£10 billion) to the European Union budget in 1994 – a figure which could treble if poorer states in the East become full EU members. Whilst the prospect of Germany becoming semi-detached from the European project and rediscovering the pursuit of national self-interest may alarm its neighbours and partners and lead to much debate and soul-searching within Germany itself, it seems likely that such a scenario will increasingly compete with the European vision of successive German chancellors for dominance of the political agenda.

United Kingdom

Alone among the major west European democracies, the United Kingdom entered the post-war era without having to embark on the search for new political institutions. The UK had experienced neither Fascist dictatorship nor enemy occupation (apart from the Channel Islands). Nor, for that matter, had it experienced a far-reaching democratic political revolution in modern times; a hallmark of the UK political system has been its gradualist evolution, embracing democratic reforms without ever fully shedding its aristocratic and elitist origins. The UK, for example, does not have a written constitution; the upper house of its two-chamber parliament is an unelected House of Lords; and although its constitutional monarchy is politically powerless and largely symbolic, the prime minister, or head of the executive, can exercise considerable powers of patronage and decision-making in the name of the Crown prerogative (i.e., outside parliamentary accountability). The political system has been praised for stability and durability, but criticised for secrecy, elitism, and centralisation of power.

In 1945 the UK entered an era of long-term decline as a world power, although the extent of this was only to become apparent later. Although Conservative Prime Minister Winston Churchill presided over victory in the Second World War, the radicalising and levelling effect of the war upon British society, and the enormous hopes raised for social progress in the post-war era, delivered election victory in 1945 to the Labour Party led by Clement Attlee. Committed in theory to wholesale nationalisation of the economy, Labour has in practice always followed a much more moderate course, embracing the mixed economy but dedicating itself to social amelioration through welfare provision and wealth redistribution. The new Labour Government carried out a number of major social reforms, including most famously the foundation of a National Health Service to provide free and comprehensive health coverage to all. In many respects, Labour was building on earlier reports produced by the national coalition government of the war years (and enjoying Conservative and Liberal support) which had recommended the formation of a welfare state to provide health care and education, and insurance coverage 'from the cradle to the grave'. The Attlee government also strove to deliver full employment.

Inevitably the cost of such measures forced a devaluation of the currency in 1949 and a reduction in the UK's overseas and defence commitments. The period from 1945 through to the 1960s saw the UK withdraw from, and preside over the dismantling of, its empire. Decolonisation and close and growing dependence on the USA tended to dominate British foreign policy. The UK mostly stood aside from efforts at European cooperation in the 1950s.

Internal divisions within the Labour Party over cuts in social welfare spending and foreign policy led to the return of the Conservative Party to power in 1951. Four subsequent Conservative prime ministers – Churchill (until April 1955), Anthony Eden (April 1955–January 1957), Harold Macmillan (January 1957–October 1963) and Alec Douglas-Home (October 1963–October 1964) – presided over administrations which followed consensus politics – accepting the welfare state, pursuing stability and partnership between government, employers, and the trade unions, and seeking to build upon economic growth. Realisation that industrial growth necessitated entry to European markets led to an application to join the EEC in 1961, which was vetoed by France until 1969.

Following the collapse of the Conservative government in 1964, amid economic woes and moral scandal, Labour returned to power. The new prime minister, Harold Wilson, captured the imagination of the country with a call for a scientific-technological revolution. The 1960s saw far-reaching social change. The rise of a youth culture and the challenge of the women's liberation movement both confronted old, traditional values. The so-called sexual revolution saw greater access to birth control while a consumer boom partially transformed the nature of domestic labour for many women by bringing labour-saving machinery within their budgets. Educational reforms included the foundation of the Open University, extending the possibility of participation in third level education.

Despite a generally favourable economic situation, Labour lost in 1970 and a Conservative government led by Edward Heath took office. The 1970s were to prove a disastrous decade for the UK economically. Recession and the impact of the oil crisis forced power cuts and the introduction of a three-day working week in late 1973; wages and prices were temporarily frozen. Conflict with the trade unions over Heath's 1971 Industrial Relations Act culminated in a miners' strike which eventually brought his government down in 1974.

Back in power between 1974 and 1979, Labour faced mounting economic problems. High inflation, faltering productivity, rising unemployment, and the widespread perception that trade unions enjoyed too much power bedevilled efforts at recovery. Labour was forced increasingly to borrow heavily from the International Monetary Fund and to plead with the unions for social peace. By 1979 the Labour government had ceded effective control over its economic policy to the IMF, and had to introduce monetarist policies which bitterly divided the Labour Party. The Conservatives then fought an aggressive campaign which returned Margaret Thatcher to power as the country's first woman prime minister.

Until her removal from office in November 1990, Thatcher, a free market right-winger, presided over a series of governments which set out to change the face of the UK, abandoning consensus politics. In her economic policy she sought to reduce public ownership, embarking on a sustained programme of privatisation of hitherto nationalised industries; she cut income tax, raised indirect taxes, and removed controls on prices and wages, leaving the free market to determine their levels. A monetarist policy saw public spending attacked and efforts to control the money supply prioritised. The trade unions were targeted by measures which sought, for example, to reduce their right to secondary picketing and to regulate their internal affairs.

Politically, Thatcher earned a reputation as a British nationalist and a centraliser of power. Hostile to demands from Scotland and Wales for regional devolution, she considerably reduced the powers of local government. Engaging in fiercely nationalistic rhetoric, she attacked the threat to UK sovereignty allegedly posed by the European Community. Returned to power in 1983, following victory over Argentina in the Falklands War, she cultivated strong personalistic leadership. Calls for a return to 'traditional family values' and attacks on the rights of homosexuals and other groups brought forth accusations of moral authoritarianism. However, the rhetoric and the reality were not always matched. By the end of her prime ministership in 1990, the economy was again in recession. Manufacturing output had decreased considerably, and evidence suggested that both regional and social class inequalities had grown. Inflation had indeed been reduced. The trade unions had been greatly weakened (perhaps her most lasting achievement). But nothing like the promised economic miracle to restore lost national greatness had materialised. Unemployment, which had stood at one million in 1979, had by 1990 reached between three and four million.

Thatcher fell from power when her own party became convinced that the vastly unpopular poll tax, which she had introduced to finance local government, would cost it the next election. But her successor, John Major, retained power with a much reduced majority in 1992. His government continued with Thatcherite policies in most spheres, but was plagued by indecisive leadership, splits over policy (especially on European unity), various minor moral and political scandals, and a general air of incompetence and loss of direction. The Conservative vote fell to 27 per cent in local government elections in May 1994, and they suffered serious losses in European Parliament elections the following month when their 28 per cent vote was their worst national election result for more than a century.

The 1980s was a traumatic decade for Labour. In the early 1980s, under the influence of its left wing, the party embraced policies such as opposition to membership of the EEC and support for unilateral nuclear disarmament which proved unpopular with the electorate. Internal divisions culminated in a split in 1981, when several Labour right-wingers formed the breakaway Social Democratic Party (SDP). This short-lived phenomenon eventually merged with the Liberals to form the Liberal Democrats in the late 1980s. However, the split certainly damaged Labour. Under first Neil Kinnock (1983–92) and then John Smith (1992–94), Labour sought to modernise and moderate its image and programme, supporting European integration, accepting that an immediate reversal of all Conservative economic changes was not feasible, and seeking to appeal to the middle classes. Defeat in 1992 was a bitter blow to the hopes of Labour's modernisers, but by the mid-1990s under its new leader Tony Blair it appeared a more credible party of government than it had done for many years.

From the perspective of the mid-1990s, the UK faced several formidable challenges. While some of the country's severest economic problems – such as endemic mass unemployment – could be said to reflect international realities, in several other respects the UK was in danger of falling behind its partners and competitors: for example, in education and training, investment in public transport and infrastructure, and provision of social services. The Conservatives, kept in power due to their dominance in the heavily populated south of England and never polling more than 43 per cent of the vote since 1979, faced deep-rooted resentment in the north of England and in Scotland and Wales.

Demands for regional devolution, especially in Scotland, continued to go unheeded, provoking worry in some quarters that a build-up of frustration might eventually threaten the unity of the UK. Calls for modernisation of the political system, including electoral reform, came from civil liberties groups, opposition parties, and campaigning movements. However, many people feared that any electoral reform in the direction of proportional representation might fragment the Conservative and Labour parties and lead to a much more diversified party system, in which both Greens and extreme right groups could exert influence. In 1994, however, the long-standing murderous conflict in Northern Ireland (arising from disputes between 'Nationalist' – mainly Catholic – groups wanting to unite with the Republic of Ireland and 'Loyalist' – mainly Protestant – groups wanting to stay in the UK) seemed at last set on a path to settlement and peace. There may well be further implications for other components of the UK, and for the UK's post-war and post-imperial identity crisis in general. Divisions over European policy and the celebrations of the 50th anniversary of D-Day highlighted the Janus-like nature of so much of UK political culture: one face turned with nostalgia towards the past, another with a mixture of trepidation and hope towards an uncertain future.

Into the 1990s: the challenges facing the major multi-party democracies in comparative perspective

Western Europe's four biggest democracies, in common with their smaller neighbours, face a number of considerable challenges in the years ahead.

The European economy has undergone a period of prolonged recession, which may be intensified in the short to medium term by uncertainty about the pace and outcome of European monetary and economic union and the demands of lesser developed countries in eastern and central Europe. A key factor undermining economic security for many has been mass unemployment, which is estimated at 20 million in the European Union in 1994. Of course, Europe in the post-war period has known economic restructuring and upheaval before – the 1950s and 1960s were decades of rapid economic change when millions of people were uprooted. Then, however, the problem was one of the imbalances caused by societal modernisation and economic growth, the mood was generally one of optimism for the future, and politicians could point to the promise of future rewards. Now, no easy solution to mass unemployment seems at hand – indeed, for many people no solution at all seems possible. Not since the 1930s has economic insecurity and uncertainty so greatly coincided with political pessimism.

Economic crisis is accompanied in many countries by a growing sense of political crisis. The main parties of both left and right face the consequences of the perceived failure of their ideologies to make sense of reality. The growing complexity of policy-making and the globalisation of economic processes contribute to a sense of parties being unable to deliver their election promises. Although centre-right parties which are prepared to 'go with the flow' of the international markets are perhaps less immediately challenged by such developments than left-wing parties which see their dreams of radical social change through controlled economic management implode, in the longer term all democratic parties must struggle to convince the electorate that democracy can still deliver in sufficient measure for people to feel that they have a stake in its defence and preservation. Cynicism and nihilism are directed at politics in general and there is mounting evidence of voter alienation, volatility, and protest voting.

The secularisation of society, the rise of a market-based consumer culture, and the erosion of long-standing political identities and sub-cultures, are spreading a sense of loss of identity and of moral values. It is perhaps those social groups adversely affected by economic decline that are most vulnerable to moral panic.

This combination of circumstances creates a potentially lethal cocktail of resentment, despair, and sullen alienation on the part of millions of Europeans which extremist groups who do not share the values of European liberal democracy seek to exploit. The spectre of communism may no longer stalk Europe, but the spectres of racism, neo-fascism, and intolerance would appear to be back. Neo-fascist parties have scored considerable electoral success in France and Italy; in Germany and in the UK, there has been a marked increase in extremist violence against minorities. The search for scapegoats is on.

Of course, it does not pay to be too pessimistic. The political culture of the major European democracies has proved very resilient. Europeans have fought and died for the values of pluralism, democracy, and individual and collective liberties, and those values will not be surrendered easily. But the challenges facing the major democracies are obviously great.

An overriding concern must be the popular feeling, evidenced by opinion polls, that political systems are remote from the lives and concerns of ordinary people. This may be related to the declining ability of national governments to deliver desired policy outcomes whilst, at the same time, the business of building a European Union remains very incomplete, fraught with obstacles, and insufficiently engaged with the peoples of Europe. One possible response, as argued in Chapter 13, could be greater regional decentralisation, though this might of course spark off a nationalist reaction. Another response would be political reforms aimed at increasing citizen participation and involvement in politics, strengthening civil society, improving accountability of decision-makers to society, and harnessing new forms of political communication.

Western Europe's four major democracies have considerable achievements to their credit in the post-war era, not least the attainment of greater security for the mass of their citizens, the preservation of basic civil liberties, and the acceptance of norms of at least minimum social justice and social responsibility. The struggle to defend and build upon those achievements may well be the overriding priority in the coming years.

Further reading

Black, C. *et al* (1992) *Rebirth: A History of Europe Since World War II*, Westview Press, Boulder, Colorado.

Childs, D. (1992) *Britain Since 1945: A Political History*, Routledge, London.

Ginsborg, P. (1990) *A History of Contemporary Italy: Society and Politics 1943–1988*, Penguin, London.

Hancock, M.D. *et al* (eds) (1993) *Politics in Western Europe*, Chatham House, London.

Mény, Y. (1993) *Government and Politics in Western Europe: Britain, France, Italy, Germany*. Oxford University Press, Oxford.

Smith, G. *et al* (1992) *Developments in German Politics*, Macmillan, Basingstoke.

Stevens, A. (1992) *The Government and Politics of France*, Macmillan, Basingstoke.

6 Reluctant Europeans: Norden

Introduction

The word 'Norden' is used to describe the north European group of countries comprising Denmark, Finland, Åland, Norway, Sweden, and the Atlantic islands of Iceland, Faroes and Greenland. The Atlantic islands, which form part of this group through their historical connections rather than their geographical characteristics, will not be considered in any detail in this chapter.

The histories of the Nordic countries have been inter-linked since 1397, when Denmark, Sweden and Norway were united under the Danish crown. In 1523 Sweden (incorporating the south-west part of modern Finland) separated from Denmark, and in the early nineteenth century lost Finland to Russia, but gained control over Norway. Norway obtained independence in 1905, Finland in 1917.

Table 6.1. Area and population 1991

Country	Area	Population	
	1,000 km^2	000	per km^2
Denmark	43	5,154	120
Sweden	450	8,617	19
Finland	338	5,029	15
Norway	324	4,241	13
Iceland	103	258	2.5
Faroes	1.4	47	34
Greenland	2,176	56	0.03

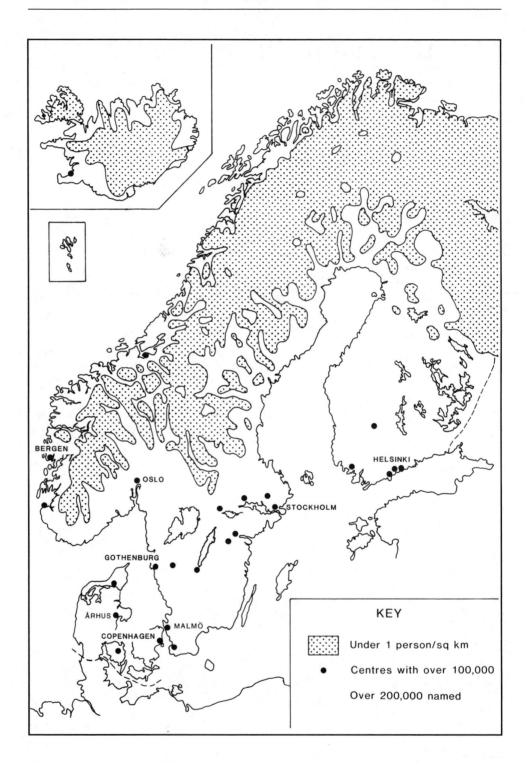

Figure 6.1. Norden: population density

Only occasionally have the Nordic countries played a major role on the European stage. This marginality is partly the product of their peripheral location. Copenhagen, at the southern end of Norden, lies some 880 km from Strasbourg, and from there Norden stretches north to the North Cape some 2,000 km away. This distance factor strongly affects people's attitudes to European institutions. Norden's resources are limited, and its populations are small compared with those of the major powers of Europe.

Neutralism

Thus it is not surprising that the wars and power-struggles of European history have not on the whole been fought for control of Norden, and the invasion-routes of the great armies have generally remained on the south side of the Baltic Sea. Attempts by kings of Denmark and Sweden to make great conquests and establish empires outside Norden have always eventually ended in failure, and the failures have in the last 250 years led to the overthrow of Danish and Swedish absolute monarchies and the establishment of a strong populist – and subsequently democratic – tradition in Nordic politics. In Norway and Finland the recent memories of the popular struggles for independence have encouraged a similar tendency towards constitutional rule and democracy, combined with a tradition of suspicion of great powers and militarism.

This tradition has become associated with a policy of neutrality in relation to the great powers of Europe (a policy formally announced in 1914 and reaffirmed in 1939). For small peripheral powers such a strategy seemed to work best, and its occasional partial failures – such as the British retaliations against Sweden during and after the First World War for supplying Germany too enthusiastically with armaments – only convinced most Nordic people that the balancing-act of neutrality must be very careful and cautious. The policy has always been combined with sizeable armed forces, to convince any ambitious great power that invasion of a Nordic country would be a costly business. One notable success story of such a policy is that of Finland, which has to contend with a great power to the east – Russia, or until recently the Soviet Union – with a strong strategic interest in controlling Finland for the sake of its access to the Baltic. Indeed, Finland was part of the Russian Empire from 1809 to 1917, and has since then fought a war (the Winter War of 1939–40) and later joined Germany's war against its huge neighbour, in order to resist Soviet claims on its territory. But when the Soviets backed off from trying to convert it into a puppet-state, the Finns negotiated a Treaty of Friendship, Cooperation and Mutual Assistance in 1948 which nevertheless gave the USSR substantial advantages. Finland had to concede a Soviet naval base on its territory in the Baltic, and a considerable loss of land to the East and North (Karelia and Petsamo, including access to the Arctic). It accepted also a policy of avoiding any major anti-Soviet positions (such as membership of any organisation which might be thought to be directed against the USSR), and an obligation to resist any incursion of armed forces passing through its territory to attack the Soviet Union. (This obligation was invoked by the USSR during the 1980s when it barred the use of Finland's airspace to the passage of NATO's cruise missiles.) But Finland remained independent, and retained trading links with the West. In this way the Finns avoided being sucked into the Eastern Bloc, essentially by maintaining a neutral balance tilted somewhat in the Soviet direction.

Denmark and Norway, on the other hand, have maintained since 1945 a kind of near-neutrality tilted towards the West. Both became members of NATO, and both applied for membership of the EC (following Britain's lead) in 1970 (though Norway withdrew its application after a referendum). The reason for allowing themselves to be so closely linked to the West was the changing strategic situation: the threat to Denmark from Soviet troops in East Germany, and the fact that Norway's coastline was a major strategic asset and prize for any possible submarine warfare between NATO and the USSR. But both states continued to keep their distance from the Cold War power-struggle; they refused to allow the installation of NATO bases or the entry of nuclear weapons or Nato ships into their territory, and imposed strict limits on NATO exercises in their seas. (However, bases in Greenland and Iceland enabled the NATO navies to control the approaches to the Atlantic from the North.) Sweden maintained a complete neutrality, seeking to defuse any fears by either great power about this northern area. The strategic differences among the four states have meant that they have found little reason to cooperate on mutual security.

Political and social character of Norden

The Nordic peoples are predominantly Protestant (Lutheran), and in the twentieth century they have come to share a social-democratic direction in their politics. Norway, Sweden and Denmark are constitutional monarchies, Finland a republic. The parliaments of all four countries are unicameral. Multi-party systems with proportional representation ensure that most administrations are coalitions. (Norway, however, has a modified system, in which parliamentary bodies work in two separate chambers when dealing with certain issues. This tends to give special weight to established special interest groups.)

Social Democratic parties are the largest in all four Nordic countries and have had the preponderant influence on government until the 1980s. In Sweden, for example, the Social Democratic Party has held power for 55 of the 63 years from 1932 to 1994. All four states have developed strong social welfare provisions and an egalitarian and liberal tendency in their policies. All four have multi-party democracies in which social democrats usually held most power within coalitions at least until the early 1980s. More recently financial strains have led to a retreat from some social welfare provisions in order to prevent taxes from rising too far, and participation in a global (or anyway European) free market has led to more competition which could lead to greater inequality. As a result, more right-wing coalitions have held office. Conservative administrations ruled in Denmark in 1982–93, in Sweden in 1976–82 and 1991–94, and in Norway in 1981–86. The Finnish government is invariably a coalition of the four major political parties, but its complexion has been more right-wing and financially cautious in the 1980s, and the 1987 elections produced a majority for the non-socialist parties. But Denmark's and Sweden's 1994 elections restored the Social Democrats to power, though without overall majorities. The pressures which the mobility of capital exerts on political and social policies in the 1980s and 1990s were well shown during the 1994 Swedish election campaign; the Wallenberg organisation threatened to take its business out of Sweden if any new Swedish government raised taxes to pay for social welfare. That pressure failed to persuade enough Swedes to vote against the Social Democrats to deprive them of power, but may yet influence the policies they adopt. In Norway the Labour Party has retained power since 1986 under Mrs Gro Harlem Brundtland (except for a short period in 1989–90), though partly by modifying its position and always with the support of other parties. Green or Ecology parties made a strong showing in Norden in the late 1980s; they obtained 20 seats in the 1988 Swedish election. However, despite the continuing strong environmental ethic in all four countries their strength has waned in the 1990s.

Agriculture and Forestry

The fertile undulating plains of Denmark provide a remarkable agricultural contrast to those of the other Nordic countries where poor soils and a shorter growing season in the colder climates restrict arable farming to a few favoured areas. Although Denmark has increased its forest area since the Second World War it is in Sweden and Finland that forests cover more than half the country (see Table 6.2). With a more rugged mountainous landscape Norway is the least well endowed, with two-thirds of the country unsuitable for either agriculture or forestry.

Denmark is an extension of the North European Plain and 64 per cent of its land is arable. Lacking mineral resources and with a temperate climate compared to other Nordic countries, it developed during the nineteenth century by far the most export-orientated agricultural economy in Norden. A cooperative farm system made intensive dairy farming and pig rearing economic for the traditional small family-owned Danish farm. Since 1945, however, small farms have proved unable to adapt sufficiently to modern methods of farming within cooperative systems, and farm consolidation has been intense. Today the average arable area of a farm is 38 hectares – the second largest in the EU after the United Kingdom. The social consequences of this shift are considerable; Denmark has changed from a society of independent farmers to a modern industrial and service economy, in which over three-quarters of the workforce is employed in the service sector.

Agricultural products were exported mainly to the rapidly industrialising nations of western Europe, and particularly to the United Kingdom. This led to the development in the twentieth century of a major west coast port – Esbjerg. The dependence of Danish agriculture on exports and the importance of the British market led Danish farmers, unlike their Norwegian counterparts, to support entry to the EC in 1973 along with the United Kingdom. Membership secured access to important markets for Denmark's very efficient agriculture, which now employs only 5.6 per cent of the workforce (Table 6.3) but still produces 24 per cent of exports, though only 3.4 per cent of its GDP.

Table 6.2. Percentage land utilisation in Denmark, Finland, Norway and Sweden

	Arable	Permanent pasture	Forest	Remainder
Denmark	59.4	4.9	11.4	24.3
Finland	7.6	0.4	59.3	32.7
Norway	2.8	0.4	30.4	66.4
Sweden	6.4	1.3	50.7	41.6

Norwegian agriculture is still dominated by the small family-owned dairy farm with a small area of arable or pasture land and a much larger area of forest. In open competition with Europe's efficient farmers most of these farms could not survive, which is why rural areas voted strongly in 1972 against Norwegian entry to the EC. The contribution of agriculture, forestry and fishing to Norway's GDP was estimated at 4.4 per cent in 1990. These sectors employed 5.8 per cent of the labour force in 1991. Less than 3 per cent of the land surface is cultivated, and the most important branch of agricultural production is livestock. From 1986 to 1989 agricultural GDP increased by an average of 5.8 per cent each year.

A major part of Norwegian subsidies go to support the farmers. But this is not entirely political string-pulling. To hold Norway together as a country the life of its remoter regions must be maintained. Its great length and the difficulty of communications from the south-east to the rest of the country mean that to avoid depopulation many of its regions need substantial support. In Norway the periphery is not only distant from the core; it suffers greater physical and climatic disadvantages and is heavily dependent on primary activities which provide increasingly fewer employment opportunities. Although the larger peripheral towns continue to expand, the population of rural areas in the west and north is declining and ageing, which is strategically awkward as the threatened regions adjoin the sea route which leads to the Russian Arctic and to the gas reserves and fisheries of the Barents Sea. But establishing local industries is very difficult.

In Sweden, too, agriculture has been concentrated in larger farms, but not as part of an exporting industry. During the 1980s agricultural production rose by 0.5 per cent a year, but has since declined somewhat. The most important feature of Swedish and Finnish land-use is forestry. Almost 70 per cent of the land surface in both countries is forested, and products deriving from forestry – notably paper – accounted for 17.3 per cent of Swedish exports and 36.6 per cent of Finland's in 1992; 22 per cent of Finland's manufacturing output is derived from forestry products. But in both countries the proportion of the workforce engaged in agriculture, forestry and fishing together was quite small: 3.3 per cent and 8.6 per cent respectively.

Fishing

Danish fish landings tripled during the 1960s. Access through EC membership to formerly restricted waters then facilitated a further 50 per cent increase. With a landing of 1.96m tonnes in 1988 Denmark exceeded Norway's catch for the first time. The fishing industry accounted for about 5 per cent of Denmark's export earnings in 1992.

Fishing accounts for only about 1 per cent of Norway's GNP, but provided 6.5 per cent of total export revenue in 1991. It is important in terms of regional policy as the key fishing areas are in the Lofoten Islands and off the northern coasts. Many settlements have no other employment opportunities, and it is partly for this reason that Norway in 1993 resumed catching small numbers of minke whales despite protests by the international Green movement. Fish-farming has also been intensively developed since the early 1970s.

Declining fish stocks in European waters suggest long-term problems. The seriousness of the situation has made all countries aware that international cooperation is necessary. Whether fishing can be controlled sufficiently to restore the stocks is at present an open question.

Industrial development and services

In common with many western European countries employment patterns in the Nordic countries are characterised by a rapid decline in the primary sector, particularly that of agriculture, and a spectacular increase in the service sector which now accounts for more than 60% of all job opportunities in

Table 6.3. Economically active population (percentages)

		Agriculture Forestry Fishing	Mining Manufacturing	Construction	Services
Denmark	1960	17.6	29.8	7.5	45.1
	1970	10.7	26.9	9.2	53.2
	1980	7.7	20.3	7.6	64.4
	1990	5.6	21.1	6.3	67.0
Finland	1960	35.2	21.8	8.7	34.3
	1970	20.2	26.0	8.3	45.5
	1980	12.5	27.3	7.1	53.1
	1990	8.3	21.2	7.5	62.8
Norway	1960	19.4	27.0	9.5	44.1
	1970	11.6	28.5	8.7	51.2
	1980	7.6	25.5	8.8	58.1
	1990	5.8	16.8	6.5	70.9
Sweden	1960	13.8	36.0	9.1	41.1
	1970	8.1	30.5	9.7	51.7
	1980	5.5	26.2	7.2	61.1
	1990	3.2	21.2	7.1	68.5

Norden. There has also been a significant decline in industrial employment figures reflecting the changing nature of industry and the adoption of less labour intensive processes. Finland tended to lag behind the general Nordic trend in the post-war years but in the last decade has rapidly caught up and now shows the same predominance of the service sector and a relative decline in the primary sector (see Table 6.3).

Denmark has developed its sector of North Sea oil and gas so successfully that it can supply 50 per cent of its energy needs. But the economy is now more technologically developed and requires more energy, so Denmark remains vulnerable to sudden rises in oil prices as in 1973 and 1979. Having decided against nuclear energy, the country is also pursuing a vigorous alternative energy programme.

Danish industry is dominated by the processing sector. Once key sectors, ship-building and textiles have now been virtually eliminated by competition from the Pacific Rim. Denmark today has a wide variety of relatively small-scale industrial plants. In the past these were located mainly in the ports (particularly Copenhagen) but regional policy has encouraged a wider spread throughout the 1980s. In 1992 industry employed 26.6 per cent of the workforce and produced 26.7 per cent of GDP. In the 1990s the downturn in the world economy has caused difficulties for Danish industry and threatens the country's high standard of living and excellent welfare provision.

Norway's traditional economy began to change in the late nineteenth century, when cheap hydro-electric power became available and led to the establishment of high energy-using industries such as aluminium-smelting. Hydro-electric power still provides much of Norway's domestic energy needs and 99 per cent of its electricity production. But Norway remained a poor country until the discovery of off-shore oil in the late 1960s. The oil and gas are mostly exported and accounted for 49 per cent of exports in 1991; revenues have at times exceeded 18 per cent of GNP. This has enabled Norway to make major improvements in infrastructure – particularly roads and bridges – and to subsidise the ailing agricultural and industrial sectors of the economy and improve social benefits generally. Oil-related industry has also expanded, especially in the boom-town of Stavanger but also in the Oslo area. Norway's industrial and service core remains in the east, where the major pulp and paper mills and engineering and chemical sectors are located. Today the engineering sector encompasses a wide range of export-orientated electrical and high-technology businesses. As in Denmark, the ship-building industry suffered from Pacific Rim competition in the 1980s. While still important, it has had to concentrate on oil-related and specialised vessels.

Industrial production accounted for 35.8 per cent of Norway's GDP in 1990 and employed 23.2 per cent of the workforce in 1991. During the late 1980s industrial output grew in real terms at an average of 4.6 per cent per annum. But the sharp drop in the price of oil since 1986 has put the Norwegian economy increasingly under pressure. The currently exploited oil fields will eventually be exhausted. New fields may be opened further north, in the Barents Sea and the north Norwegian Sea which have shown small quantities of oil and vast reserves of gas. World gas supplies are extensive and market conditions difficult, so Norway is still trying to find more oil and to sell more gas. A further complication is the dispute between Norway and Russia (and maybe also Finland, if it should recover its Petsamo corridor to the Arctic) over rights to the sea and the sea-bed in the Barents Sea.

Sweden is Europe's fifth largest country, possesses Norden's largest population and has its most successful economy. This success is based mainly on industry, and more recently on a great expansion of the service sector, which now employs about three-quarters of the workforce. The post-1945 socio-political environment has facilitated smooth economic development and the evolution of what was seen as a model welfare state, based on full employment, high social welfare spending, large public sector employment and a preference for a consensus/compromise style in politics. However, Sweden's high wage economy has recently shown signs of strain because of international competition and the world recession; and the model has lost something of its cult status.

The development of hydro-electric power in the late nineteenth century helped Sweden become a significant industrial economy. But lack of adequate domestic energy sources has always been a problem. The oil crises of the 1970s, when Sweden was importing some three-quarters of its energy supply, forced it to seek greater energy efficiency and alternative energy sources. By 1991 the establishment of nuclear power provided about 18 per cent of the total energy supply and 52 per cent of electricity production; oil and natural gas accounted for 43 per cent, hydro-electric power 15 per cent and coke and coal 7 per cent. But parliament has been persuaded by environmental interests to close all nuclear plants by 2010. Other energy sources will have to be found – probably gas from Norway and/or Russia. Hydro-electric expansion is unlikely due to development costs and strong environmental objections.

The economy has nevertheless grown at an impressive rate, and Sweden now has one of the highest living standards in the world. This is mainly due to its record in industrial exports: the motor industry exports three-quarters of its output. But the drop in world demand for steel has seen a once-major iron and steel industry decline considerably while the chemical and plastics industry, including pharmaceuticals and biotechnology, have expanded. As in Norway and Finland there is a diverse engineering sector with particular strengths in the electrical and electronic fields from televisions to electric generators and from industrial robots to household appliances. Saab, Volvo, Aga and Electrolux are household names throughout Europe and North America. The pulp and paper industry, the fourth major manufacturing sector, faces a world over-capacity and is restructuring. Significant mineral reserves include 15 per cent of the world's uranium.

Finland's national anthem laments its poverty; and indeed by the 1950s Finland had only a semi-industrialised economy with 46 per cent of the population engaged in farming and forestry. Since then the country has been transformed. Agriculture accounted for 8.6 per cent of employment in 1992, industry for 27.7 per cent and services 63.7 per cent. Income per capita in 1985–90 was the second highest in Europe, just ahead of Sweden and Denmark, but by 1992 it had dropped to sixth place and last in Norden.

Finland had to pay reparations to the Soviet Union until 1952, mainly in the form of metal and engineering products. A highly efficient engineering and metal goods sector then sought other outlets. It found them in the Soviet Union and the EFTA countries. By 1993 these industries employed 30 per cent of the workforce and provided a similar proportion of exports. Other key products include agricultural and forest machinery, electronic equipment and ships, particularly icebreakers and cruise vessels. The chemical industry which, in addition to the basic areas of oil refining and fertilisers, now includes significant pharmaceutical and techno-chemical products, has expanded rapidly. Food processing provides 16 per cent of exports, while paper and wood products, though currently in recession, have made substantial gains.

Finland is less well endowed with domestic energy supplies than either Norway or Sweden. More than 30 per cent of its needs are met from hydro-electric, peat and forest waste sources and 15 per cent from nuclear power in which Finland invested when oil prices rose in the 1970s. As in

Sweden this policy has been criticised, especially after radioactive pollution from Chernobyl in 1986 blighted Finland. In 1985 the ruling coalition threatened resignation (and likely political chaos) to force opposition parties to withdraw a motion calling for the closure of Finland's nuclear power plants. Oil, which is currently cheap, still provides nearly 30 per cent of Finland's needs; but Finland would be vulnerable to a rise in world prices.

The economic and political situation of Norden in the 1990s, and involvements in international economic organisations

The Nordic countries have been cautious from the start about committing themselves to the EC (and later the EU), even though all of them have substantial trading links with EU countries. This attitude derives partly from the tradition of neutrality, with the fear that the long-term consequence of membership could be a political and then military entanglement from which its members would be unable to extricate themselves. In the case of Finland this consideration precluded all possibility of membership, and Sweden too felt obliged to keep its distance, though even here Olof Palme promoted the idea of membership with safeguards for neutrality during 1970 and 1971, until it became apparent that there was too much opposition to the policy. But these considerations had less force for Norway and Denmark, and when EC membership negotiations got under way in 1970 their leaders felt that they could maintain within the EC the position of limited military involvement they had established with NATO. Norway's 1972 referendum forced its government to withdraw its application, though Denmark entered the EC in 1973. Another reason for Nordic caution about the EC was the strong tradition of national independence. In all four countries industrial and financial interests tended to favour EC membership, while organised labour was wary. Farming interests were usually strongly opposed, fearing the loss of their protected positions (except in Denmark where the farmers wanted access to European markets for their exports).

All four Nordic countries, however, joined EFTA in 1959, confident that this would not lead to any political interdependence. Within the Nordic region itself the different states felt the need to establish an organisation to facilitate cooperation. In 1953, Denmark, Iceland, Norway and Sweden set up the Nordic Council, and were joined in 1955 by Finland. Since then they have set up a free labour market, an agreement on cooperation on transport, a Nordic Investment Bank, a Nordic Social Security Convention (1955) and a Nordic Passport Union (1958). The Nordic Council was supplemented by the Nordic Council of Ministers in 1971, which can make binding decisions in the sphere of Nordic cooperation, subject to unanimity and parliamentary approval. Denmark, Norway and Sweden have jointly owned and run the successful Scandinavian Airlines System since 1951. Denmark and Sweden have agreed in principle to build a huge bridge and tunnel which should drastically reduce travel times between Copenhagen and Malmö. Construction has begun on the Danish side, but environmental protests have hindered Swedish efforts. So there are many contacts, and in some fields there is substantial cooperation; but it is determined case by case where it seems likely to be beneficial to all parties, not as part of a general framework of supranational authority. Most of its benefits are small-scale, like the agreement to develop cooperation, transport links, and trade between mid-Norway and mid-Sweden.

The Council also maintains an active interest in the Arctic, where fragile eco-systems have been severely damaged by Soviet naval and air bases in the Kola Peninsula and by unrestricted development of the Russian oil and gas fields in western Siberia. International cooperation (between the Nordic countries, Canada, the USA and Russia) is obviously extremely urgent in the Arctic, but will be difficult to establish for an area so sensitive in military and development terms. In 1993, the Nordic states and Russia signed an agreement establishing a Barents Euro-Arctic Council to cooperate in environmental protection, but so far little has been achieved other than agreements to exchange information.

Relations with the EC have been close, even for the three countries which declined to apply for membership. Agreements signed in 1972 secured free trade with the EC in industrial products for Norway, Sweden and Finland, and these countries have increasingly sought to adjust their financial policies to keep their currencies in line with the main EC currencies, just as the EC countries themselves were obliged to do as part of the transition towards a single currency. (The policy broke down, as it did for the EC countries, in the general financial chaos of 1992, but it seems certain that it will be resumed.)

This structure of international links has worked rather well. Nordic economies have grown satisfactorily, trade has developed, while politicians have avoided disturbing the status quo. But in the late 1980s and early 1990s increasing pressures for change have become manifest. First, the structure of the global and European economy has become markedly more large-scale and integrated (see Chapter 1). In many industries firms based only on single countries (especially small ones) now seem too small to survive world competition. A straw in the wind is the (unsuccessful) attempt of the highly successful Swedish car producer Volvo to merge with Renault of France, in 1993. Successful though they are, Volvo clearly reckon that they are not big enough for the competition now gathering. The structure of trade, also, favours close international links within organisations like the EU, and the Nordic countries' trade with EU countries is now 150 per cent greater than that among themselves. Financial markets show a greater instability, from which some protection may be found in closely integrated international financial structures (such as an EU common currency). Second, the industries which once were content with domestic markets are now often able to produce on a larger scale and so seek wider markets.

Third, the collapse of the Warsaw Pact after 1989 and the subsequent disintegration of the Soviet Union in 1991 has weakened the long-cherished

Nordic tradition of neutrality. 'From what are we now being neutral?' they ask. The concerns which previously favoured neutrality now rather indicate involvement in international structures, to reduce the risk of instability and to keep a powerful united Germany within a peaceful and strong international framework. Finland's obligations to avoid international connections which might worry the Soviet Union were dissolved in three treaties with Russia in 1992 which merely guaranteed non-aggression and friendly relations between the parties.

Fourth, in the case of Finland, the economic collapse of the Soviet Union and consequently of some of its markets for Finnish goods has led to a dramatic drop in Finland's trade with Russia, previously more than 20 per cent of its exports, but less than 5 per cent by 1993. (The USSR had in any case been overtaken by the FRG as Finland's chief trading partner in 1988.) Finland has had to seek a great expansion of its trade with other countries, primarily the EU, to make up for the loss, and its economic motives for entry into the EU have correspondingly grown stronger. Similar considerations apply to Sweden, where government opinion in 1989–90 moved rapidly in favour of EC membership as economic indicators plummeted and the Single Market threatened.

Fifth, the concerns of social democrats and labour parties in Norden that the EC might work to the disadvantage of workers' interests were partly alleviated by the EC Council agreement in 1989 to a Social Charter of workers' rights.

As a result of these factors all three non-member Nordic countries applied for membership of the EU, applications which the EU has accepted. The applications were dependent on ratification by referenda in autumn 1994. In Finland and Sweden these showed clear majorities for the applications (by 57 per cent and 52.3 per cent respectively); but Norway rejected membership of the EU. What the consequences for Norway will be is as yet unclear. For Sweden and Finland admission is set for 1995. But even in these countries the continuing existence in the public's mind of suspicions and anxiety about membership of the EU, in spite of the fact that all the main political parties and industrial leaders gave it their support, will probably continue to shadow their political involvement in the EU.

The Nordic country which *has* been a member for a considerable time, Denmark, caused considerable disturbance in EU politics by rejecting the Maastricht Treaty, which its government led by Paul Schlüter had accepted, in a referendum held in June 1992. The majority against ratification was very small (50.7 per cent to 49.3 per cent) but its effect was to block the Maastricht Treaty altogether for the whole EC. Frantic political manoeuvrings in the autumn produced an agreement by other EC states to insert a protocol in the Treaty allowing the Danes to opt out of the single currency, the common defence policy and common European citizenship and, with this addition, the Treaty was accepted in a referendum in May 1993, by 56.7 per cent to 43.3 per cent. In fact it is not clear that concerns about national sovereignty which these exemptions might meet were what worried all of the No-voters; some were certainly concerned rather about the so-called 'democratic deficit', the limited powers of the European Parliament under the Treaty.

Figure 6.2. Norwegian cartoon: 'No to EU!' The organisation 'No to the EU' has created some unlikely bedfellows in Norway. The cartoon shows an ageing conservative farmer with his privately owned farm flying the national flag, and 'No to EU' cut in his hayfield. He is arm-in-arm with a youthful urban female punk, with spray-can, spraying graffiti 'No to the EU' and 'Down with Wealth' on the wall. They are chorusing 'Let us say no together'.
Source: Oppland Arbeiderblad

But it is not unlikely that the traditional Nordic tendency towards neutralism and separate national identity may appear again as factors in the politics of the EU. As a Swedish official is reported to have said: 'Have you asked Belgium or Portugal whether they are really ready to help defend Finland's border with Russia?' One likely new area of cooperation in the post-Cold War period is the Baltic Sea region: the first session of the Ministerial Council of the Baltic Sea States was held in March 1992. This grouping will tend to weaken any Nordic unity since it does not include Norway but does include several non-Nordic states. Norway's absence from the EU may also to some extent pull the Nordic countries apart.

Further reading

Derry, T.K. (1979) *A History of Scandinavia*, Allen and Unwin, London.
Fullerton, B. and Knowles, R. (1991) *Scandinavia*, Paul Chapman Publishing, London.
Glyn Jones, W. (1986) *Denmark, A Modern History*, Croom Helm, Beckenham.
Hodne, F. (1975) *An Economic History of Norway 1915–1970*, Tapir, Bergen.
Hodne, F. (1983) *The Norwegian Economy 1920–80*, Croom Helm, Beckenham.
Johansen, H.C. (1986) *The Danish Economy in the Twentieth Century*, Routledge, London.
John, B. (1984) *Scandinavia – A New Geography*, Longman, London.
Lane, J-E. (1991) *West European Politics* Vol 14, No 3. Special Issue on 'Understanding the Swedish model'.
Varjo, U. and Tietze, W. (eds) (1987) *Norden: Man and Environment*, Gebrüder Borntraeger, Berlin.

7 Escaping from the jackboots: Spain, Portugal, Greece

Introduction

During the mid-1970s, Spain, Portugal, and Greece emerged from the shadow of right-wing dictatorships. Spain and Portugal had been governed by authoritarian regimes since the victory of General Franco in the Spanish civil war in 1939 and the ascent to power of the Portuguese dictator Salazar in 1926; in Greece, a military dictatorship which seized power in 1967 had been preceded by almost two decades of quasi-democratic rule during which entrenched discrimination against left-wingers – the losers in the Civil War of 1946–49 – was commonplace.

Although factors particular to each country were important in their respective democratic transitions, similar processes of social and economic change contributed to the dictatorships' downfall. Moreover, the fact that all three embarked upon the transition within a three-year period (1974–77) can scarcely be coincidental: the international context exerted an influence. The concept of southern Europe as a distinct regional sub-system has facilitated comparative analysis of the emergence and consolidation of new political systems. Aspects of this regional sub-system which have been highlighted include: relative economic under-development, delayed political modernisation, cultural distinctiveness, and particular exposure to international influences.

Relative economic under-development is manifest in late and partial industrialisation, with the southern European countries remaining more rural and technologically backward than northern Europe. Some writers have argued that their economies are distorted by chronic unevenness and structural dependency.

At the political level, southern Europe was a late-comer to mass democracy: Spain's brief experience of democracy was stamped out by Franco's victory in 1939; Portugal and Greece only really achieved the status of functioning pluralist democracies after 1974. Moreover, all three countries have exhibited weak civil societies, with a relative lack of a participatory culture, the persistence of traditional elites and of pre-modern forms of political organisation, and clientelism as a defining characteristic of the political systems. (Clientelism means a system of political relations based upon the exchange of favours by politicians in return for the procurement of a political following. This does not necessarily imply corruption.) Efforts at creating strong and autonomous interest groups and social movements have been patchy; and parties tend to remain relatively weak in terms of their roots in society and their effective articulation of societal interests. Moreover, the line between party and state is frequently traversed; for example, a party membership card often facilitates a job in parts of the public sector.

Culturally, southern Europe has continued to be more influenced by forms of traditional religion, although Spain in particular has recently undergone substantial secularisation. This point refers not simply to the fact that southern Europe tends to be Roman Catholic (or in the case of Greece, Orthodox) whereas northern Europe tends to be more Protestant; rather, it refers primarily to the traditional and more mystical forms which Roman Catholicism takes in Portugal or Spain, as opposed to Catholicism in, say, Britain or the Netherlands. Attention has also been paid to another cultural aspect with clear political implications: the greater importance of the family (including the extended family) in social life. Although rapid urbanisation in recent decades has disrupted traditional patterns of family life, the economic importance of the family as a buffer against unemployment and poverty in societies with relatively under-developed social welfare systems remains significant.

Finally, southern European countries are weaker powers which have been increasingly vulnerable to economic and cultural penetration in the latter half of the twentieth century and to the political influence of stronger powers. Throughout the immediate post-war decades, the United States exercised a clearly decisive influence over Greece, especially; more recently, the EU has probably replaced the US as the primary external political influence throughout the region. External influences can crucially condition the options available to policy-makers and political and social forces.

Having embarked upon the transition to liberal democracy within a few years of each other and joined the EC during the 1980s, these three countries can be seen as sharing a common path and facing similar challenges.

The crisis and downfall of the dictatorships

Portugal

The Portuguese dictatorship, overthrown in April 1974, had been in power since 1926. António Salazar was the regime's strongman until September 1968. He was succeeded by Marcelo Caetano, whose attempts to preserve power through controlled liberalisation ended in failure. The dictatorship followed a parliamentary, but not democratic, republican regime (1910–26).

Salazar's advent to power represented a triumph for the land-owning class over more urban and modern strata. The regime attempted until the 1960s to preserve a conservative, Catholic Portugal based on the economic power of large land-owners. Ideologically, it reinforced itself by reference to myths of rural purity and the degradation of urban life, the alleged decadence of the modern ideologies of liberalism and socialism, Roman Catholic beliefs and morals, and Portuguese nationalism. It was opposed to modernity, and reflected a curious blend of rural nostalgia and fundamentalist Catholicism.

It would be wrong to think that Salazar possessed no industrial policy. Behind tariff barriers, modest but important industrial growth was encouraged in the 1930s and 1940s. State investment in public works provided employment and laid the basis of an infrastructure which was to permit the economic U-turn of the 1950s and 1960s. During the 1950s the economy was gradually permitted to take advantage of favourable world conditions. In the 1960s an economic take-off, partially financed by inflows of foreign capital, transformed Portuguese society. Urbanisation and modernisation rendered the regime ideologically bankrupt and politically isolated.

It has been argued that the attempt to create the so-called New State (*Estado Novo*) came to an end in the early 1960s. At the start of the decade, Portugal was still a largely rural society with nearly half of its labour force employed in agriculture. Compared to northern Europe, high levels of illiteracy and low standards in health care and provision of basic sanitation prevailed. Political repression weighed heavily, with containment of dissent entrusted to the secret police. Throughout the 1960s three developments contributed to worsening social tensions: increasing integration with the world economy (above all with northern Europe), the mounting burden of colonial wars in Africa, and a growing crisis of ideology and of legitimacy.

The dictatorship had negotiated EFTA membership in 1958. This marked the beginning of a retreat from protectionism and isolation. It has been estimated that almost one million people – one-eighth of the total population – emigrated (mostly to northern Europe) during the 1960s. The outflow of people was matched by a huge increase in inflows of foreign capital; by 1970, foreign capital invested in Portugal had increased nearly thirty-fold. Colonial wars added to the pressure for change. Liberation struggles against Portuguese imperialism began in Angola, Guinea-Bissau and Mozambique in the early 1960s. The dictatorship responded with a military build-up which resulted in a largely conscript force of almost 250,000 by the early 1970s. In relation to the country's population, this military machine was surpassed only by North and South Vietnam and by Israel. One in four men of military age ended up in an army which was increasingly enmeshed in futile and brutal colonial wars. The burden on the exchequer was vast. Spending on the military consumed half of total public expenditure by the late 1960s.

As the regime sought to improve living standards in order to maintain both its own legitimacy and support for the war effort, a programme of bringing in foreign capital became essential. The structural reorientation of the economy was radical. A small, protected home market gave way to emphasis on export-centred manufacturing industry, with foreign companies taking advantage of low wages and a union-free environment. Emigration and conscription soaked up potential unemployment and emigrants' remittances helped with the balance of payments. The country was increasingly dependent on foreign capital and on northern Europe. By the 1970s employment in agriculture had dropped to one-third of the labour force.

Ideologically, the project of a rural, Catholic, anti-modern and isolated Portugal was dead by the late 1960s. However, the regime had no new vision to put in its place. A new urban working class had emerged. It was poorly paid and badly housed, its working conditions were harsh, and it was denied trade union rights. In a sense society was undergoing a profound identity crisis. Uncontrolled economic growth both raised expectations and created new problems of pollution, poor sanitation and housing conditions, and growing inequality.

From September 1968 until April 1974, the regime veered shakily between controlled liberalisation and bouts of increased repression. Some exiles (including the future president, Mário Soares) were permitted to return home, and a 1972 trade agreement with the EC encouraged the regime's technocratic advisers to hope for full EC membership. Realisation that this would be facilitated by a transition to democracy increased pressure from within for further change. In 1973 Caetano resorted to repression in the face of industrial unrest. This coincided with discontent within the military where younger officers had founded a radical Armed Forces Movement (MFA). War-weariness by now united broad sectors of society, including many conservatives. In April 1974 the MFA seized power, ending nearly 50 years of dictatorship. The new government ended the wars in Africa, granting independence to the colonies. On virtually every other issue, however, both army and society were divided. For the next two years, politics swung back and forth between left and right.

Between April 1974 and the summer of 1975, the Portuguese Communist Party (PCP), the best organised opposition force in the dying days of the old dictatorship, sought to capture the leadership of the revolution. It supported the appointment of a left-wing army officer, Vasco Gonçalves, as prime minister in July 1974, and the formation of a Revolutionary Council in early 1975. This body nationalised banks and insurance companies, broke up the large landed estates and distributed land to the peasants. It was envisaged that the Revolutionary Council would guard against capitalist or Fascist restoration.

From mid-1975, events moved against the left. Whilst the majority of Portuguese had welcomed the demise of dictatorship, many – especially in the Catholic north – remained conservative. Moreover, there was a widespread fear that the pro-Soviet PCP would simply replace one form of dictatorship with another. The PCP's tactics earned it the hostility of the Portuguese Socialist Party (PSP) led by Mário Soares. Pro-western technocratic elements within the power structures, together with moderate army officers, began to regroup.

Elections to a constituent assembly were held on 25 April 1975, and disappointed the communists who won just 12.5 per cent of the vote. The PSP emerged as the only really national party with 37.9 per cent; conservatives took 34 per cent. In April 1976 the PSP won general elections and in July the period of revolutionary turmoil ended when Mário Soares became prime minister.

Spain

In many ways the path of the Spanish dictatorship has been strikingly different from that of Portugal. In power since 1939, Franco imposed a highly centralised and authoritarian regime. He shared with Salazar a hatred of socialism, communism and liberalism, and was also concerned with repressing every sign of social or ethnic pluralism. Ethnic groups such as the Basques and Catalans bore the brunt of a repression which drove their languages and cultures largely underground. The Spanish dictatorship drew upon the support of rural landowners and the Roman Catholic Church. It also appealed to the army's self-image as the protector of a unified and centralised Spain and its hatred of regional autonomy. The army was used to repress those who had supported the left in the Spanish Civil War and the divisions of that war were effectively institutionalised.

Franco's regime, although the most classically Fascist of the three dictatorships, represented a coalition of forces which was riddled by contradictions. Monarchists, Fascists (the *Falange*), rural landowners, technocrats, nationalist soldiers, and Catholic clerics, coexisted sometimes uneasily inside the National Movement, the regime's political party. Franco, proclaimed *Caudillo* (Leader), presided over this coalition, mediating between its often warring components. It was the *Falange* which provided the Fascist trappings – a uniformed mass movement complete with Roman salute, quasi-corporatist doctrines of social organisation, and authoritarian nationalism. But the *Falange* was never more than one part of the movement.

From 1939 until the mid-1950s, the regime pursued economic and social policies similar to those followed in Portugal. Trade unions were smashed and replaced by Fascist corporations; political repression was employed to keep workers in line; low wages and high food prices meant that the spending power of most people was limited and little existed by way of demand-led growth. The power of the big landowners was reinforced and agriculture remained notoriously inefficient. Marshall Aid was not offered in 1947, and Spain remained isolated internationally.

By the early 1950s problems were mounting, with shortages of food and technology necessitating imports. A major economic debate divided the ruling party between opponents and advocates of the development of free market capitalism. The latter won through; economic and military agreements with the US in 1953 were followed by membership of the International Monetary Fund in 1958. A Stabilisation Plan in 1959 aimed at attracting foreign investment and modernising the economy whilst retaining political repression.

As in Portugal, the 1960s and early 1970s witnessed growing involvement with foreign markets, penetration by foreign capital, and moves to draw closer to the EC. Spain requested associate EC membership in 1962. The regime hoped that full membership could eventually be achieved without democratisation. Growth rates rose dramatically in the 1960s, especially in the north. This rapid and uneven development generated social and economic problems – above all the uncontrolled growth of urban centres as people flocked from agriculture into industry with consequent hardship for the newly urbanised workers.

Four important contradictions surfaced during the decade. First, a growing urban working class began to find its voice. The illegal but active trade unions organised strikes from 1962. The regime's ability to keep workers passive depended on rising living standards. However, a reformist path was opposed by those who had reluctantly conceded the economic U-turn when assured of growing army representation in government and increased repression to avoid political change. Second, the balance of forces within the National Movement shifted away from the landowners and *Falange* towards an alliance of more internationally inclined forces – technocrats, bankers, and financiers. Third, attempts at limited reform in the mid-1960s with a slightly relaxed press law simply encouraged the underground opposition forces to organise against repression. Finally, as society secularised, with falling rates of church attendance in urban areas, the Catholic Church began to distance itself from the regime. Progressive priests and bishops condemned torture and repression of workers' rights. In 1971 the Church actually apologised to the Spanish people for the support hitherto given to Franco.

As the 1970s got under way, the regime's backers were hopelessly divided. Two broad groups emerged. Hard-line falangists favoured continuing repression; reformists favoured controlled liberalisation and an opening to the opposition forces. This latter group included Adolfo Suárez, who was to preside over a new centre-right political formation in the mid-1970s, the Democratic Centre Union, and was to become prime minister of post-Fascist Spain. Some of the regime's leading members veered between repression and reform. These included Fraga, who later emerged as founder of the Popular Party (PP), the main conservative party in present-day Spain.

In 1969 the ageing Franco appointed as his successor Prince Juan Carlos, son of King Juan in whose name Franco had ruled. Political instability and street protests increased in 1973, when the assassination by Basque gunmen of the regime's second-in-command, Admiral Luis Carrero Blanco, prompted reformists within the regime to move into dialogue with the (still illegal) opposition parties. Following Franco's death in November 1975, Juan Carlos was crowned king and the way was cleared for a democratic transition. Adolfo Suárez became prime minister in 1976, and despite opposition from hard-liners, political parties were legalised from February 1977. The moderate tactics of the opposition parties – including the Spanish communists – were decisive in enabling a transition to democracy, without anything like the rupture which occurred in Portugal. Democratic elections in June 1977 gave victory to the centre-right UCD with 34 per cent of the vote; the socialists led by Felipe González gained 28 per cent; the communists led by Santiago Carrillo won 10 per cent; and Fraga's conservatives won 8 per cent.

Greece

The short-lived Greek military dictatorship came to power at a time when the international climate was less tolerant towards Fascist regimes than it had been in the 1920s and 1930s, and it had little time in which to consolidate its authority. Nevertheless, the Greek dictatorship enjoyed the support of the USA, which was more concerned with securing a solid anti-communist ally in an area judged vulnerable to Soviet influence than in defending democracy inside Greece.

In 1945, the Allies had agreed that Greece should belong to the western sphere of influence. Stalin did little to help the Greek Communist Party (KKE) when it attempted to seize power in 1946. The communists had played a leading role in the anti-Nazi resistance movement and resented signs of a conservative restoration under British–American influence. British military intervention helped to secure the defeat of the communists and the imposition of a conservative regime after a bitter and bloody civil war (1946–49). The civil war left deep wounds on the body politic and helps explain the highly partisan nature of political alignments ever since. From 1949, anti-communism was adopted as an instrument of state policy and the KKE was banned.

Although Greece was formally a parliamentary regime, real power lay outside parliament. Alongside the fairly liberal constitution of 1952, a largely unwritten code operated, which accepted the army as the guarantor of the established social order. Repressive laws were directed against those suspected of communist sympathies. The civil service and the teaching professions were purged. Suspected left-wingers could be deprived of a passport, a driving licence, or a public sector job. In administering this system of discrimination, the police built up a huge network of spies.

Power was exercised by a triarchy of monarchy, army and the parliamentary right. Any attempt to open up politics to the centre-left risked jeopardising this balance and calling into question the role of the army as custodian of the *status quo*. (This is what happened in the mid-1960s, prompting the military coup in 1967). After 1952, British influence was superseded by US influence. The Greek economy was opened up to foreign (largely American) capital much earlier than the economies of Spain or Portugal. Greece joined NATO in 1952. Its vulnerability to outside influence was intensified by the situation in Cyprus, where extreme Greek nationalists were pressing for union with Greece and the situation exploded into violence in the mid-1950s.

In the 1958 election a reviving left braved discrimination to poll 25 per cent

of the vote. More significant was the formation of a Centre Union in 1961
under the leadership of George Papandreou and his son Andreas. The Centre
Union combined elements of political liberalism, economic Keynesianism,
radical popular nationalism and old-fashioned clientelism. It posed a real
challenge to the dominance of the right. Elections in October 1961 returned
the right, led by Constantine Karamanlis, to power. An association treaty with
the EC in 1962 was intended to anchor Greece in the western camp. In
November 1963 elections returned a centrist government led by George
Papandreou, and Karamanlis left for voluntary exile in Paris.

Further elections in February 1964 gave Papandreou a clear mandate for
change. Social reforms followed, including raising the school-leaving age from
12 to 15 and launching a campaign against illiteracy. Keynesian inter-
ventionism in the economy sought to raise wages and boost demand. Political
prisoners were released. It seemed as if the centrists were moving towards full
democracy by opening up the political system to the lower social classes and
overcoming the civil war divisions. However, such changes alarmed the military
and powerful business groups.

In the summer of 1965 King Constantine II forced the Government's
resignation, to appease the military. A right-wing cabinet was installed,
presiding over mounting social unrest before agreeing to hold new elections
in May 1967. To forestall these elections the military seized power on 21 April
1967. A junta led by Colonel George Papadopoulos suspended human rights,
banned political parties and strikes, proclaimed martial law, and sent
thousands into internal exile.

Although ferocious anti-communist rhetoric was a hallmark of the junta,
there is no doubt that their real target was the centrists; the military feared any
threat to their privileged position. From 1967 to 1974 traditional values were
extolled, but the corrupt lifestyle of the military leaders – soon enjoying the
'good life' on luxury yachts donated by grateful Greek shipping tycoons –
belied their pious, moralistic propaganda.

The junta's contemptuous attitude towards all politicians alienated the
traditional political establishment and even the king, who attempted an
unsuccessful counter-coup in late 1967 before fleeing to Rome. Thereafter, all
power was concentrated in military hands. The regime was isolated and
discredited; it lacked internal unity or ideological coherence; and it was
concerned with little more than its own privileges. It stumbled on with
American support until 1974. Repression kept opposition contained until
March 1973 when Athens students staged an uprising. A further uprising in
November was brutally repressed; 34 students were killed and scores wounded.
Soon afterwards, a hard-line coup inside the junta brought intensified
repression.

In April and May 1974, the junta staged a military escapade in Cyprus,
apparently hoping that conflict with Turkey would shower it with patriotic
honours. On 20 July Turkey invaded Cyprus, the island was divided into two
zones, and the Greek army retreated in a shambles. The junta lost American

sympathy; Washington certainly had no desire to see two NATO allies at war. On 23 July, the junta withdrew from politics in disarray. Karamanlis, who created a new centre-right party called New Democracy (ND), returned from Paris to preside over a transition to democracy. This time, the measures which had enshrined military power in the 1950s were ended, the communists were legalised, and full parliamentary democracy under civilian rule was achieved.

Dynamics of the democratic transitions

None of the democratic transitions in southern Europe was the outcome of a spontaneous mass revolution. In all cases, the actions and interactions of key elite groups, social and political forces (including parties, trade unions and churches), and state institutions (especially the army) significantly determined the nature of the transition. It is essential, therefore, to study the social and political context which shaped these actors' perceptions of what was desirable and possible.

In Spain, it is clear that sections of the old regime came to embrace the need to enter into dialogue with opposition forces and to abandon repression. By the early 1970s technocratic and business elites were beginning to accept the need for a democratic transition after Franco's death, though they often disagreed on how far democratisation should go. In Greece, the dictatorship isolated itself from traditional conservative elites, and apart from key business backers, such as the shipping tycoons, had a limited support base. In Portugal the loss of military confidence in the dictatorship was decisive.

So why did the dictatorships disintegrate from within? Economic change since the 1950s involved greater dependence on foreign trade and foreign capital. Potential conflicts between manufacturers geared to supplying the restricted needs of a protected home market and of multinational corporations and bankers and financiers had intensified. The suppression of trade unions and opposition parties alienated the workers, and the absence of channels of communication and negotiation dented support from business groups. The dictatorships did not permit real representation of diverse interests even within the ranks of their own supporters. Conflicts intensified and industrial relations deteriorated. A section of the dominant economic elites came to recognise the need for at least a limited pluralism. This was necessary both to achieve social and political stability, and to allow renegotiation of the alliance between the component parts of the ruling bloc. But even a limited pluralism was thwarted by the elimination of genuinely representative parties and interest groups. Attempts at half-hearted reform floundered, as the regimes realised that they risked losing everything once reform got under way. This, in turn, helped to convince some elites that only a transition to liberal democracy could secure stability and economic growth.

External pressures were also important. The incentive of EC membership seemed to offer a guarantee of greater prosperity, less dependence on US capital and influence (especially in Greece), and political stability through anchorage in the family of established western European democracies.

The relative weakness of mass opposition reduced the likelihood that the dismantling of the dictatorships might threaten the capitalist order and undermine the power of existing elites. Popular pressure from below for change certainly existed in all three countries – as was shown by strikes and demonstrations. Certain social groups in particular gave vent to this pressure – workers in Spain, students in Greece, young soldiers in Portugal. But there was never any real threat of left-wing revolution, except perhaps from sections of the Portuguese military. Pressure from below for change conditioned the actions of elites, but rarely set the agenda.

Mass opposition was probably strongest in Spain where the complex interactions of parties, trade unions, employers' organisations, political elites and the army was of critical importance. The moderate tactics adopted by the left-wing parties helped to reassure dominant groups and to facilitate a smooth transition to democracy. The Spanish Communist Party (PCE) found itself electorally and politically weakened by the dynamics of subsequent democratic consolidation, but its moderation and pragmatism were crucial in strengthening the hand of reformists such as Adolfo Suárez and in reducing military opposition to the transition. Similarly, the unions were prepared to demand sacrifices of their members and enter into agreement with the employers to guarantee the conditions for democratic stability.

The role of the military was decisive everywhere. The Spanish military had been interwoven into the fabric of the Franco dictatorship, enjoying a privileged position since the Civil War, and regarding itself as the defender of Spanish unity. In Portugal, the military's involvement in colonial wars was to prove the catalyst of the dictatorship's downfall. Only Greece approximated to a pure military dictatorship. Although the military possessed its own concerns, it exhibited also many of the tensions and contradictions present in society. Nowhere was the military a monolithic bloc. In Portugal, internal divisions rendered the post-1974 army an unstable political instrument; the PCP for example found its attempts to use the Revolutionary Council to push for more radical transformations of society frustrated by the inability of the military to act cohesively. In Greece, military divisions forced the dictatorship to withdraw from the political stage. Even in Spain, many younger and better educated officers perceived their role as a force of modernisation rather than crude repression. A Military Democratic Union was formed in 1974 to push for changes. The number of senior officers favouring legalisation of the PCE rose from 5 per cent to 30 per cent in 1975–76. The lesson from southern Europe seems to be that in times of rapid social and economic change precipitating a crisis of political legitimacy the military can become an arena for internal conflict. Much depends on the strength of civil society, the tactics and strategies of social and political forces, and external pressures.

The consolidation of new political institutions

Clearly, a distinction exists between transitions to democracy and the subsequent consolidation of new political systems. Admittedly, it is not always easy to state where transition ends and consolidation begins. Nor is it clear what time scale should be adopted. Moreover, the struggle to defend and reinvigorate democracy is a continuous one which every generation faces. Bearing this in mind, it might still be argued that a qualitative step forward has been taken on the road away from authoritarian regimes when the values and ground rules of the new democratic political system gain widespread acceptance and new political institutions begin to function smoothly.

Democracy can be consolidated only through a number of processes. The powers and role of the state must be delineated, allowing an autonomous civil society to flourish. The new constitution must be accepted by a majority of citizens and political actors. The different interests and views in the society must be effectively represented by parties which are autonomous from the state and accountable to citizens. Governments must be formed on the basis of a majority, and power must alternate peacefully between government and opposition. The party system must be stabilised, and anti-democratic parties must become marginal, preferably through lack of support. The armed forces must be subordinated to the democratic civilian authorities. Channels of communication and negotiation must be established between the state, parties, and major interest groups. A civic culture must be established in which the concept of citizenship rights and obligations is accepted and understood.

Spain, Portugal, and Greece have come a long way in achieving democratic consolidation. Civilian dominance over the military has been established. This happened relatively early in Greece, where the military discredited itself comprehensively; attempts to plot against the new government in 1974–75 foundered when a large majority of the officer corps remained loyal to the elected authorities. In Portugal the military continued to play a significant role in politics into the 1980s; nevertheless, the Revolutionary Council was disbanded in 1982 and in February 1986 a civilian – Mário Soares – finally became head of state. In Spain the civilian authorities had to make considerable concessions to secure the military's withdrawal from politics. These included increased defence spending and soft-pedalling on regional reforms. An attempted military coup in February 1981 collapsed following the personal intervention of the king. Since then, the military has stayed out of politics, although threats to Spanish unity can still provoke its unease.

Relatively stable party systems now function in all three countries. The only really 'anti-system' party is the Basque *Herri Batasuna* (political wing of the ETA terrorist organisation). Support for far-right or neo-fascist parties has been insignificant up to 1994. The communist parties all operate within the democratic system. In Portugal a short-lived Democratic Renewal Party was founded by elements close to the military in 1985 but collapsed in 1987. Political competition since then has been between four relatively stable forces:

centre-right liberals (PSD), centre-left socialists (PSP), conservatives (CDS) and communists (PCP). In Spain, considerable turmoil in the mid-1970s has given way to a three-party system – socialists (PSOE), conservatives (PP), and communists and allies (United Left – IU). The remaining 20 per cent of voters support regional parties which mostly accept the Spanish constitution. In Greece, there is a similar three-party system of conservatives (ND), socialists (PASOK), and communists. However, signs of upheaval within the Greek party system appeared with a split within ND in Spring 1993 leading to the formation of another right-of-centre party called Political Spring. Led by Antonis Samaras, it benefited from an upsurge in Greek nationalism following international recognition of the Former Yugoslav Republic of Macedonia (FYROM).

Survey evidence suggests that popular support for the new political systems is relatively high. Moreover, the recourse to referenda to abolish the monarchy and establish a republic (as in Greece in 1974), or to approve legalisation of parties (as in Spain in 1976), helped to confer legitimacy.

Nevertheless, a number of negative phenomena threatening the consolidation of democracy can be observed. The persistence of charisma as a key political asset is a double-edged sword. Whilst the enormous popularity of certain leaders has helped to stabilise democracy, it may mean that some parties find it difficult to survive intact after the death or retirement of their leaders. The personalisation of politics can also accentuate rivalries and feed demagogic and authoritarian tendencies. Parliaments remain weak and executives retain a considerable degree of autonomy from parliamentary supervision; this, however, is a problem common to all European democracies. The weakness of civil society manifests itself in a number of ways. Parties are seldom mass organisations, despite the use of state patronage. Trade unions remain weak – only 10–15 per cent of the labour force in Spain and Portugal – and plagued by political rivalries. Employers' organisations lack internal coherence. The relative weakness of channels of communication and negotiation between the state and the main interest groups has meant that industrial relations have recently been plagued by conflict. Finally, evidence of corruption has come to light. The ruling parties in Spain and Greece ended the 1980s embroiled in scandals involving allegations of embezzlement of state funds. Although the multi-faceted crisis of parties is a feature of all western democracies, the distinction between party and state in southern Europe has arguably been blurred to an even greater extent than in northern Europe. On the other hand, it might be argued that most examples of clientelism, as distinct from corruption, are fairly harmless and have helped to secure the new democratic systems.

Party competition since the transition to democracy

Party competition in southern Europe since the mid-1970s has been characterised by the dominant role of conservative and socialist parties, the deradicalisation of the socialist parties, the struggle of the conservative parties to modernise, and the decline of the communist parties, split everywhere between reformers and traditionalists.

The socialist parties were the dominant force in Spain and Greece during the 1980s, and to a lesser extent in Portugal from the mid-1970s until the mid-1980s. In Spain, the Socialist Workers' Party (PSOE) won elections in 1982, 1986 and 1989, polling 40–48 per cent of the vote. PSOE returned to power as a minority government with 38.8 per cent in June 1993, despite losing seats and votes. In Greece, the Pan-Hellenic Socialist Movement (PASOK) was founded by Andreas Papandreou in 1974 and won power in 1981 with 48 per cent of the vote. PASOK held office until June 1989 and returned to power in the elections of October 1993. In Portugal the PSP has been less successful electorally, but it held the premiership in 1976–78 and 1983–85 and has held the presidency since 1986.

The character of the socialist parties has changed enormously. Early radical aspirations have been abandoned in favour of moderate social democracy. PSOE dropped its commitment to Marxism in 1978, thereafter evolving steadily into a centrist party in terms of economic policy. During the 1980s it was even accused of favouring Thatcherite economics. At the end of the 1980s the trade unions accused PSOE of betraying the unemployed through its deflationary policies. Unemployment has remained the weak point of the party's record and probably helps to account for its recent electoral losses. The Spanish economy has grown under PSOE direction but monetarist policies have brought about this growth. Even if the retention of the state's controlling share in many industries renders the charge of Thatcherism less than accurate, few would deny that the results achieved have little to do with socialism as the party once envisaged it. In foreign policy too Felipe González abandoned former socialist policies in 1986, and secured NATO membership and entry into the EC. PSOE's most radical achievements in government have perhaps involved reducing the Church's influence in education and introducing social reforms such as divorce and abortion legislation.

In Greece PASOK in opposition called for withdrawal from NATO and opposed EC membership. It advocated an independent foreign policy sympathetic to Third World causes, social reforms aimed at achieving gender equality, comprehensive health and education programmes and widespread socialisation of industry and financial institutions. The first PASOK government attempted many reforms, but was forced to moderate its foreign policy stance, especially with regard to the American military presence and membership of the EC. Papandreou made much of renegotiating the terms of EC membership so as to obtain a better deal for Greece, but achieved little by doing so; moreover EC aid probably created a dynamic of dependency. In the mid-1980s PASOK adopted austerity measures which weakened trade unions and effectively shelved Keynesian-style spending plans.

In Portugal the PSP has sought to project itself as the party of EC-sponsored modernisation. In practice this entailed reversing many of the nationalisations of the early revolutionary period and implementing measures to attract foreign investment. The party has been open to coalition with the centre-right PSD which supported Soares' presidential re-election in 1991.

A number of factors explain the rightwards move of the socialist parties. The 1980s saw the rise of New Right ideas internationally and the vulnerable position of the southern European economies left the socialists exposed. There was a strong temptation to embrace the free market modernisation promised by the EC as the only basis upon which to build for future prosperity. Moreover, there was a need to reassure dominant economic and social groups that democracy would not result in upheaval and revolution. Once the task of democratic consolidation was perceived as vital, a move away from radicalism was inevitable in some form. The socialist parties all had fairly weak links to organised labour, which reduced internal organisational resistance to the rightwards move. The parties were centralised machines in which a cult of leadership facilitated policy U-turns. Papandreou, for example, regularly purged the PASOK leadership almost at will. It is true that resistance in PSOE to González's policy changes has sometimes been forthcoming from a populist wing associated with Alfonso Guerra, but in March 1994 González was able to orchestrate a leadership reshuffle which reduced Guerra's influence. Finally, socialists have faced weak competition on their left flank.

A balance sheet of the socialists' performance in southern Europe must record a number of substantial achievements: democratic consolidation, EC membership, extension of civil liberties and women's rights, and economic growth. But the socialists' loss of any clear radical or reforming commitment now poses identity problems, as does their growing involvement in scandals and clientelist politics.

The socialists' move towards the centre and market-led economics has also created identity problems for the right-wing or conservative forces, especially in Spain. In both Spain and Greece conservative parties played the dominant role in government during the 1970s but lost power in the early 1980s. The right has been more successful electorally in Portugal.

In Greece, ND, in power from 1974–81, embraced welfare policies and a consensus approach to industrial relations; it enjoyed business backing whilst speaking of the need for social democracy. However, the moderate image was not accepted by all its members and a backlash by right-wingers intensified after it lost power in 1981. During the 1980s, ND moved further to the right, calling for privatisation of state-owned industries and strict control of the money supply. Greece's crippling burden of debt, allegations of abuse of state funds by PASOK, and the perceived need to meet EC conditions for aid, all created a climate in which calls for fiscal rectitude gained a receptive audience. ND defeated PASOK in June 1989, but without gaining a majority in parliament. A year-long coalition with the communists – to tackle corruption – ended when ND gained a one-seat majority, ruling on its own until October 1993.

In the early 1990s, ND's economic policies provoked industrial and student unrest. The party backed down in 1991 in the face of opposition to its education reforms. It was further forced to abandon plans to pardon the imprisoned leaders of the old military junta, and was placed on the defensive over the crisis in Macedonia. A split in 1993 showed how vulnerable it was to internal party conflict. Defeat by PASOK in October 1993 was followed by the election of a new leader, Miltiades Evert, a moderate who had previously clashed with the right-wing of his own party. Having lost internal unity, it is clear that the Greek conservatives are far from achieving a position of dominance.

In Spain, two main rightist formations emerged during the mid-1970s: the centre-right UCD, led by Suárez, and the more conservative PP, led until 1990 by Manuel Fraga. Political polarisation during the early 1980s badly squeezed the UCD and permitted the rise of PP. Paradoxically this may have sealed the electoral fate of the right throughout the 1980s, for many Spaniards were clearly unwilling to trust PP, given some of its leaders' past associations with hard-line elements of the Franco regime.

The Popular Party has continued to suffer from factionalism, a failure to modernise its image and ideology, and difficulty in adapting to social change. It has been unable to attract any significant working-class support and has been thwarted by the fact that many conservative voters continue to favour regionalist parties. The election of José Maria Aznar as leader in 1990 heralded a serious attempt to address these concerns. Aznar pushed through reforms in February 1993 aimed at increasing the PP's appeal to women and young people, and introduced mandatory dismissal for corrupt office-holders. A concerted drive in June 1993 to project the PP as a modernising, young, and attractive alternative to a tired socialist Government ended in disappointing failure: it polled a mere 34.8 per cent, 4 points behind PSOE, and was again condemned to opposition. Clearly, the Spanish right continues to suffer from problems of identity, legitimacy, and credibility.

Portuguese conservatives have been more successful. The centre-right PSD has dominated politics since the mid-1980s, balancing a neo-liberal, market-led approach to economics with the pursuit of consensus with the socialists. Led by Aníbal Cavaco Silva, the PSD has held power since 1987. Nevertheless, it faces a challenge from the more orthodox right-wing CDS – a party with 10–14 per cent of the vote. Moreover the PSD in power has not always been as willing to push through the privatisation its rhetoric had suggested. Critics have sometimes alleged that the patronage potential of the public sector is one reason why this is so; another may be an unwillingness to face deteriorating industrial relations.

The record for the southern European conservatives is mixed. Nowhere has the right achieved real political dominance, although in Portugal it has come close. In Spain conservatives continue to suffer from association with the authoritarian past, although it must be expected that this will ease as time passes. In Greece the right resembles a shaky coalition of potentially divergent interests. The dilemma everywhere is clear: should the right pursue consensus with the centre-left or aim for dominance, through conflict if necessary? Consensus may be a safer option, guaranteeing social stability and democratic consolidation. The pursuit of dominance may be a high-risk strategy in countries where socio-political cleavages formed in the pre-democratic past still run deep.

The third main political force in the region has been the communists, although several such parties have now evolved into post-communist parties. The communist parties all resisted the old dictatorships and the Iberian parties especially were important actors during the democratic transition. Since then, however, they have faced marginalisation. Two types of response have been characteristic. The first has involved a reformist strategy which prioritised democratic consolidation, isolation of the extreme right, and establishment of the democratic credentials of the communists themselves. The second has involved an attempt to move the transition process along quickly, under communist leadership, in the direction of socialist revolution.

The majority of the Spanish communists chose the first response, contributing to democratic consolidation but paying an electoral price. Disappointing election results, the top-heavy leadership style of PCE boss Carrillo, and direct interference from Moscow, all contributed to a severe internal party crisis in the early 1980s. The PCE split into several warring factions, sunk to a mere 3 per cent of the vote and almost disintegrated in 1982–86. The Greek communists had split as far back as 1968 into a pro-Soviet hard-line KKE and a moderate minority faction which took a democratic line. The Portuguese party remained wedded to Soviet orthodoxy.

Until the early 1990s the PCP and the KKE maintained an electoral presence of around 10 per cent, a strong base within sections of the trade union movement, and a loyal working-class following. However, since the collapse of the USSR these parties have struggled to come to terms with the implosion of their ideology. Severe internal splits led to expulsions from both parties in the early 1990s. Not even the election of new leaders – Carlos Carvalhas (PCP) in 1992 and Aleka Papariga (KKE) in 1991 – has stemmed the haemorrhage of voters, members, and influence. In October 1993, the KKE saw its share of the Greek vote fall to around 5 per cent. Both the KKE and the PCP will struggle to maintain even their current diminished status in the future.

The PCE drew back from the brink of disaster in 1986 by joining with dissident socialists, pacifists, feminists and others to launch the United Left (IU) coalition. Conceived as a broad front of anti-NATO radicals, the IU has consolidated itself as the third force in Spanish politics. In June 1993 it polled just under 10 per cent. Provided the IU can avoid splits, it has a good chance of occupying the space on the left vacated by PSOE. It seems clear that the IU is now a post-Marxist phenomenon which articulates the concerns of the Green, feminist and peace movements.

The moderate Greek communists launched the Greek Left (EAR) in 1987. Again, this is very much a post-communist party committed to gender equality and radical reforms rather than classic Marxism. The retreat of the KKE into sectarianism in 1990–92 left the EAR, together with KKE dissidents and others, fighting under the banner of the 'Coalition of Left and Progress' (*Sinaspismos*). This formation polled 2.9 per cent in the October 1993 elections, narrowly missing the 3 per cent required for representation in the Greek parliament. Since the Spanish IU and *Sinaspismos* are rooted in significant social movements, and articulate concerns which many feel have been neglected or betrayed by the socialists, they have the potential to be dynamic (if minority) political forces in the 1990s. However, they have yet to develop a strategy which does not condemn them to merely reacting to a pace of events set by the socialists.

The impact of the European Community

Greece joined the EC in 1981, Spain and Portugal in 1986. There is no doubt that EC membership has had important economic, social, political and cultural effects. Those who supported membership enthusiastically – the centre-right parties, and the Iberian socialists – argued that the EC would assist democratic consolidation, bring prosperity, and achieve cultural reintegration into the European mainstream. EC aid would facilitate infrastructural improvements and industrial modernisation; and the discipline of membership would force the southern European economies to bring inflation and budget deficits firmly under control. In other words, a powerful external guarantee of both democratic consolidation and balanced growth would result. Those who opposed EC membership totally – chiefly the KKE and PCP – argued that the EC would accentuate uneven development and suck their countries into increased dependency upon northern European (and American) capital. Membership would erode national sovereignty and imperil the recently won democratic freedom by shifting real power away from national governments and parliaments to Brussels. A third group – comprising the moderate Spanish and Greek communists – accepted EC membership as a guarantor of democracy and as a progressive development, but opposed the free market logic inherent in the EC and argued for a struggle to transform the Community from within. This would involve left-wing forces battling within a strengthened European Parliament to achieve a much stronger social Europe. PASOK, in Greece, has moved from outright hostility to qualified acceptance of EC membership.

There can be little doubt that EC membership has helped to stabilise democracy. On the other hand, southern Europe has found itself battling for a

greater share of EC resources and for increases in social spending. Greece has
benefited from the EC's Integrated Mediterranean Programmes (IMPs) which
had their origins in PASOK's renegotiation of membership terms in 1982–83.
Under the IMPs, southern Europe has picked up payments to assist with the
readjustment of small businesses, agriculture, and tourism to the requirements
of participation in the European single market. Portugal has gained
significantly from EC structural funds, picking up some £666 million between
1988 and 1992. Greece and Spain have benefited from agricultural subsidies.

Nevertheless, there have been difficulties in adjustment, and it remains
unclear how the region will fare when the last of the special transitory
protective arrangements for fruit and vegetables expires. Familiar problems
remain: high foreign debt, high inflation (except in Portugal), very high
unemployment and the threat of growing regional imbalances. Mass tourism
has damaged the Mediterranean coastline and overloaded waste disposal and
sewage systems. The Mediterranean is the dirtiest sea in the world with few
under-developed coastal areas left. This could endanger the tourist trade.

Although southern Europe is relatively more prosperous now than it was
prior to EC membership, its overall position as a poor and dependent region
has not changed. Much now depends on the unpredictable nature of the EC's
development. If a two-track or even three-track European Union develops,
then it seems certain that southern Europe will find itself more dependent
than ever on decisions taken in the developed core. Spain, Portugal, and
especially Greece are hopelessly ill-equipped to meet the criteria for monetary
and economic convergence; the enthusiasm of governments in the region to
do so risks rising unemployment and mounting social tension. The ability to
tackle inflation and debt is hampered by political factors. People may resent
cuts in living standards and real wages, and reduced expenditure on health
and education provision, and this may lead to political instability. Measures to
raise revenue by widening the tax base and tackling fraud, evasion, and
corruption risk alienating farming and professional support for the ruling
parties. If people are to accept such measures there has to be a major change
in political culture.

Conclusion

Spain, Portugal, and Greece face a number of difficult challenges. Their
democratic political systems are all but secure. Nevertheless, as in northern
Europe, signs of political malaise are evident. Irredentist nationalism which
threatens to drift across the Balkans towards Greece, and the growing
incidence of racially motivated attacks on immigrants in Spain, present a
challenge to democratic leadership. Political elites have yet to face up fully to
the task of carrying forward the modernisation of politics and political systems.
This is not merely, or primarily, a generational question. The relative weakness

of civil society, the persistence of clientelism, and the tendency to resort to populist demagogy challenge the ability of political systems to express through democratic channels new socio-political cleavages as they arise.

Economically, southern Europe's fate is now firmly inter-twined with that of the EC. Should the EC back away from the pursuit of a socially integrated political union, the region may suffer. Southern Europe now faces competition from eastern and central Europe, both in the export market and in the scramble for financial assistance from the EC. Finally, the Mediterranean region remains a potentially explosive area in the post-Cold War era, and the maintenance of political stability on Europe's southern flank is scarcely less crucial now than before.

Further reading

Danopoulos, C. (1991) 'Democratising the military: lessons from Mediterranean Europe', *West European Politics*, 14 (4) pp. 25–41.

Ethier, D. (ed.) (1990) *Democratic Transition and Consolidation in Southern Europe, Latin America and South-East Asia*, Macmillan, Basingstoke.

Gillespie, R. (1990) 'The consolidation of new democracies' in Urwin, D. and Paterson, W. (eds), *Politics in Western Europe Today*, Longman, London.

Liebert, U. and Cotta, M. (eds) (1990) *Parliament and Democratic Consolidation in Southern Europe*, Pinter, London.

O'Donnell, G., Schmitter, P. C. and Whitehead, L. (eds) (1986) *Transitions From Authoritarian Rule: Southern Europe*, Johns Hopkins Press, Baltimore.

Payne, S. (1986) 'The concept of "Southern Europe" and political development', *Mediterranean Historical Review* 1, pp. 100–15.

Pridham, G. (ed.) (1990) *Securing Democracy: Political Parties and Democratic Consolidation in Southern Europe*, Routledge, London.

Pridham, G. (ed.) (1991) *Encouraging Democracy: The International Context of Regime Transition in Southern Europe*, Leicester University Press, Leicester.

Urwin, D. (1989) 'The Extension of Democracy in Southern Europe', in *Western Europe since 1945: A Political History*, Longman, London.

8 The cockpit: central and eastern Europe

Introduction: central and eastern Europe in the 1950s

Chapter 3 traced the early history of the people's democracies through to Stalin's death. The summer of 1953 brought workers' strikes and demonstrations in several countries, especially East Germany, but the most dramatic protests against the crumbling Stalinist system followed Khrushchev's February 1956 denunciation of Stalin at the Twentieth Congress of the Communist Party of the Soviet Union (CPSU). It was in Poland and Hungary that the issues of the time came to a head. Yet while the Polish October and the Hungarian uprising arose from similar grievances, their outcomes and the two countries' subsequent developmental patterns were very different.

The Polish Party, with workers' hero Wladyslaw Gomulka restored to its leadership, persuaded Khrushchev that it was still in control of the situation, but the gains of October including the workers' councils were then steadily eroded as Gomulka proved less a radical, nationalist reformer (as the workers had seen him) than a relatively humane, but orthodox, Marxist–Leninist. In 1958 economic reform plans were shelved, leading to successive confrontations between regime and workers into the late 1980s.

In Hungary the Soviets judged that premier Imre Nagy, pushed by popular pressures, had jeopardised Party rule by agreeing to reinstall a multi-party system. His announced withdrawal from the Warsaw Treaty Organisation (WTO) was the last straw. Soviet troops 'restored order' and Party First Secretary Janos Kadar began the process of 'normalisation'. Nagy was executed in Summer 1958. Yet five years later the initially detested Janos Kadar launched the programme of 'goulash communism' that made Hungary the most tolerable Soviet bloc country to live in.

The personalities of the two leaders were significant factors. Unlike many of their elite colleagues, both had modest life-styles, were basically honest and wanted to provide a viable socialist system for the ordinary citizen, but Gomulka often made up his mind too quickly and then stuck to his decision. While Kadar was a model *apparatchik*, once he had satisfied the Soviets as to

Figure 8.1. Central and eastern Europe 1994 (Yugoslavia = Serbia, including Kosovo, and Montenegro)

'normalisation' his aim was what would later be called 'socialism with a human face'. But he moved cautiously, reassuring the Soviets that the Party's leading role was not threatened and heeding their calls at times for caution.

Elsewhere too, a Party leader's personality could profoundly affect domestic and foreign policy developments – and long periods at the top were common. As in the USSR, no country had any formal means for transferring power to a successor, and an incumbent's death (or less commonly removal) provoked a succession struggle and a rather uncertain period while the victor was consolidating his power.

Albania

Enver Hoxha led the Albanian Party of Labour (APL) from its founding in 1941 till his death in 1985. Albania's post-war direction always reflected his struggle to maintain its territorial integrity against a perceived Yugoslav threat. Albania came under Soviet patronage until Khrushchev's rapprochement with Tito went too far. In April 1961, the Soviets and their allies reneged on promised credits and began pulling experts and advisers out of Albania. But the Chinese took Albania under their protection, as an outpost of pure Stalinism against Soviet revisionism. At the 22nd CPSU Congress in October 1961 Khrushchev labelled the Albanian leadership Stalinist (i.e. 'pro-Chinese'), and the USSR and other WTO members broke off diplomatic relations (though Romania soon restored normal relations).

Chinese protection and aid lasted till 1977, but relations deteriorated after President Nixon's 1972 visit to China. Meanwhile, nepotism and the blood feud remained endemic, culminating in the mysterious death in 1981 of Mehmet Shehu, who was subsequently accused of plotting Hoxha's assassination after 28 years working beside him as Prime Minister. All Shehu's many relatives and close associates in high posts were quickly removed.

On Hoxha's death in 1985, his successor Ramiz Alia tried cautiously to foster relations with other European countries and to ease some domestic restrictions without compromising the Party's Stalinist ideals. Greek television programmes, which could now be received in Albanian towns across from Corfu, showed how far living standards lagged, but little real opposition was apparent till Summer 1990.

In December 1990 the APL responded to the demands of a fledgling Democratic Party (DP) for genuine, multi-party elections by removing five leading hardliners and scheduling multi-party elections in two months' time. But open criticism of the APL remained banned. Shedding their fear of the security police, the masses demonstrated against the APL in all major cities. The first statues of Enver Hoxha were toppled. Tanks were sent in and an APL Conference was hastily convened. A month's postponement of the elections barely increased opposition campaign possibilities, but the 1966 ban on religious worship and observance was revoked and the first political prisoners freed.

Rural support ensured an APL electoral victory, but the DP won in the cities. A deteriorating economic situation and growing anarchy in the north next to Yugoslavia's Kosovo Province (where the predominantly Albanian population was oppressed by the Serbs) brought fresh elections in February 1992, which were won by the DP. Sali Berisha resigned as party chairman when elected president in April 1992, after constitutional changes had greatly increased presidential powers.

Table 8.1. Albania: Elections to National Assembly, March 1992 – total seats obtained

Party	Directly Elected	Proportional Representation	Total
Socialist Party of Albania (SPA) (former Albanian Party of Labour)	90	2	92
Democratic Party (DP)	6	32	38
Social Democratic Party	1	6	7
Human Rights Union	2	–	2
Republican Party	1	–	1
Total	231	19	250

Life has become little easier for the urban masses since then, and indeed worse for the unemployed (approximately 40 per cent of the adult population in 1992). The new centre-right administration ended the previous guarantee of 80 per cent of their former wages to the unemployed. Output remains low, but transnational companies are vying to develop Albania's off-shore oil and gas deposits and its substantial under-developed mineral resources. By late 1993, inflation was down to 1.5 per cent per month, the lek was steady against the US dollar, exports had increased 259 per cent over their 1992 low, agricultural output was up by 20 per cent and even industrial production had shown some signs of recovery. GNP in this way rose by 8 per cent. The number of motorised vehicles approached 150,000, a 400 per cent rise in two years. The IMF and the World Bank have acknowledged these efforts, and also recent human rights legislation, including a law rehabilitating former political prisoners, but practice has a long way to go to catch up with the new principles.

A vast gulf now separates the DP from all opposition parties. The APL was renamed the Socialist Party of Albania (SPA); its daily newspaper *Zeri i Poppulit* still has the biggest circulation, and constantly criticises the government's 'inhumane' economic policies. In April 1994, its leader Fatos Nano was sentenced to 12 years in prison and fined the equivalent of US$725,000 for alleged corruption during his brief spell as prime minister in 1991. Witnesses at what was virtually a closed trial included Ramiz Alia, brought from his cell for the occasion. The government banned the ASP from holding any form of public meeting in Tirana for seven months and settled scores with many leading members of the old regime, including Hoxha's widow, sentenced to 11 years in jail for misuse of government funds. Political democracy lags behind economic progress. Even the DP's coalition partner, the Social Democratic Party, boycotted parliament over delays in drafting a new constitution.

Relations with Greece have deteriorated. Many illegal immigrants have been repatriated to southern Albania/northern Epirus, especially after the Archimandrite Chrysostomos was deported for allegedly subverting its Greek community. Greece has also been wary of Albania's decisions to join the Organisation of the Islamic Conference and seek closer relations with Turkey. (In July 1994 Greece vetoed a proposed EU development loan to Albania of US$42 million.) Relations with FYROM Macedonia and Yugoslavia are also difficult; ethnic Albanians in Macedonia continue their campaign for greater autonomy, and the Kosovo issue remains potentially explosive, though Berisha has rejected any use of force in settling it.

Yugoslavia and its successor states

As stated in Chapter 3, Yugoslavia was ethnically the most fragile of the countries created after the First World War. The 1991 census showed a total population of 23.5 million, of whom 34.9 per cent were Serbs, 19.0 per cent Croats, 8.6 per cent Muslims (a category created for Bosnians and Hercegovinians), 7.5 per cent Slovenes, 7.4 per cent Albanians, 5.7 per cent Macedonians, 2.5 per cent Montenegrins and 1.8 per cent Hungarians (almost all in Vojvodina). Only 3 per cent identified themselves as Yugoslavs, while there was a wide range of other minority nationalities. The territory was divided into six republics and two autonomous provinces (Vojvodina and Kosovo), both constitutionally part of (Greater) Serbia.

Tito had hoped to turn this hotch-potch of peoples into Yugoslavs by institutionalising a system requiring consensus on decision-making among the republics and autonomous provinces. However, Croatia and Slovenia, the two richest republics, increasingly felt they were being exploited by Serbia and the others to develop the poorer territories of Montenegro, Bosnia-Hercegovina, Macedonia and Kosovo, whose *per capita* income averaged less than 60 per cent of the average for Yugoslavia in 1966. In fact, these southern regions were no better off by 1989. But increasing Croat demands for separation led Tito to purge the Republican Party leadership of Croat separatists and carry out precautionary purges elsewhere from 1971.

Tito was the thread that held the fragile federation together. His system, which enshrined the divided interests of constituent parts so separate in wealth, culture, religion and attitude, limped along for 10 years after his death while tensions mounted. In Kosovo a young, largely Albanian population had increasingly demanded the republican status which the Constitution denied them, but until Aleksander Rankovic's fall in 1966 they were suppressed. For 20 years thereafter Serbs lost leading posts in Kosovo, were discriminated against in everyday life, and left in droves. Then, from late 1987, Slobodan Milosevic, the new neo-Stalinist General Secretary of the Serbian Party, coercively reasserted the pre-1966 Serbian dominance. This was formalised in February 1989 by amendments to the Serbian Constitution. There were immediate strikes throughout Kosovo, and the Yugoslav presidency was forced to send in troops.

Yugoslavia was polarised as, especially in Slovenia and Croatia, Serbia pushed for a crackdown on dissenters who were accused of supporting counter-revolution in Kosovo. The Serbs were supported by a puppet Vojvodina, and by Macedonia and Montenegro, both concerned about their growing Albanian populations.

In September 1989, the Slovenian parliament voted for a multi-party system and the right to secede from the Federation. Yugoslavia, since 1950 eastern Europe's most open country, was now lagging in the reform movement sweeping the bloc. The Congress of the League of Communists of Yugoslavia (LCY; the communist party) agreed in January 1990 to give up its monopoly on power, but when their demand that the Republican Leagues of Communists be independent was rejected, the Slovene delegates stormed out, quickly followed by the Croats. Non-communist governments were elected in Slovenia and Croatia, where large majorities in year-end Republican referenda supported independence. Both declared independence in February 1991.

After invading and hastily retreating from Slovenia in June 1991, the Serbian-dominated Yugoslav army attacked Croatia with its large Serbian minority, especially concentrated in Krajina. A Serbian autonomous region of Krajina (SARK) had seceded from Croatia in February. A savage war, ended by a cease-fire in January 1992, was soon followed by the ruthless struggle (still going on in 1994) for the partition of Bosnia and Hercegovina, where Serbs, Croats and Muslims had lived in relative harmony for decades.

The Yugoslav Federation now consists only of Greater Serbia and an increasingly unhappy Montenegro, which fears loss of statehood under Serbian proposals to divide the rump Yugoslavia into regions. As December 1993 elections showed, military successes have won greater support from Serbs for Milosevic's policy, though the Republic's increasing impoverishment may eventually prove his downfall. Passions have been inflamed everywhere. Europe's worst post-war atrocities have been committed, and memories are long. With his rump Yugoslavia shunned by western countries, Milosevic has been seeking support elsewhere, including Romania and parts of the former USSR.

Table 8.2. Elections to Lower House of Yugoslav Assembly, December 1992 – seats won

Party	Seats
Socialist Party of Serbia (SPS) (ex-LCS)	47
Serbian Radical Party (SRS)	34
Depos Opposition Bloc	20
Democratic Party of Serbia	17
Democratic Party (DS)	5
Socialist Party of Montenegro	5
People's Party	4
Democratic Community of Vojvodina Hungarians (DZVM)	3
Other coalitions	3
Total	138

Table 8.3. Serbia: Elections to Serbian Assembly, December 1993

Party	Seats
Socialist Party of Serbia (SPS) (ex-LCS)	123
Depos Opposition Bloc	45
Serbian Radical Party (SRS)	39
Democratic Party (DS)	29
Democratic Party of Serbia	7
Democratic Community of Vojvodina Hungarians (DZVM)	5
Party for Democratic Action–Democratic Party of Albanians	2
Total	250

Note: In the December 1992 elections to the Montenegrin Republican Assembly, the Democratic Party of Socialists of Montenegro (former League of Communists), the ruling party, retained that position, winning 42.5 per cent of the votes.

Slovenia's lack of a significant Serbian minority made diplomatic recognition and admission to international organisations easier, and its economy has suffered less than elsewhere. President Milan Kucan was re-elected by a landslide in December 1992, and a broad-based centrist coalition rules (see Table 8.4). Relations with Croatia have deteriorated since the independence struggle. The Slovenians resent the Croats' passivity when Yugoslav tanks rolled into Slovenia in 1991, while Croats remain aggrieved by Slovenia's continued trade with Serbia at the height of the war in Croatia. Slovenia virtually sealed its borders against Croatian refugees and is delaying completion of the highway linking Croatia with Austria. There has effectively been a trade war between the two new states. Commercial inter-dependence has brought moves towards conciliation, though Slovenia's improving economic prospects have encouraged stronger outside links, including a December 1993 agreement to eliminate tariffs on 80 per cent of Czech–Slovenian trade.

Table 8.4. Slovenia: Elections to National Assembly, December 1992

Party	Elected		Total Seats	% Votes
	Directly	By PR		
Liberal Party (LDS)	17	5	22	23.7
Christian Democratic Party (SKD)	8	7	15	14.5
United List (incl. former League of Communists)	8	6	14	13.6
Slovene National Party (SNS)	3	9	12	9.9
Slovene People's Party (SLS)	2	8	10	8.8
Democratic Party (DS)	–	6	6	5.0
Greens (ZS)	–	5	5	3.7
Social Democratic Party of Slovenia (SDSS)	–	4	4	3.3
Others	–	–	–	17.9
Total	38	50	88*	100

* Total of seats was 90, with one each reserved for non-elected representatives of Hungarian and Italian minorities

Croatia's Upper and Lower House speakers, vexed by President Franjo Tudjman's autocratic style and his earlier eagerness to follow Serbia in partitioning Bosnia at the expense of the Muslims, led a break-away from the ruling Croatian Democratic Alliance (HDZ) and established an Independent Democratic Party in early Summer 1994 when continuance of the HDZ's parliamentary majority till 1996 looked uncertain. Tudjman's term as president runs till 1997.

Macedonia was admitted to the UN in 1993 as FYROM, but recognition by the EU remains blocked by Greece which seeks to force it to change its name, not mentioning 'Macedonia'. Having few Serbs has saved it from Milosevic's hegemonistic schemes, but economic progress has stuttered under a socialist-dominated coalition government; while if the demands of western Macedonia's Albanian minority for enhanced status are not met, they may ultimately seek union with Albania.

Table 8.5. Croatia: Elections to Chamber of Deputies, August 1992

Party	% Votes	Seats
Croatian Democratic Alliance (HDZ)	42.6	85
Croatian Social Liberal Party (HSLS)	17.7	14
Party of Democratic Renewal (SDP) (former League of Communists)	5.8	11
Croatian Party of Rights (HSP)	6.4	5
Croatian National Party (HNS)	6.9	5
Serbian People's Party	1.1	3
Croatian Peasant Party		3
Independents	19.5	6
Regional parties		6
Total	100.0	138

Bulgaria

Until 1989 Bulgaria was ruled by a Party which steadfastly and uncritically supported the CPSU and never let its people forget Russia's role in Bulgaria's liberation from the Turks in 1876–78. Todor Zhivkov consolidated his rule at the eighth Party Congress in November 1962 and maintained it till 1989. Bulgaria got the highest Soviet aid *per capita* in Europe and of all Comecon's European members traded most with the USSR and least with the West. It test-marketed Soviet foreign policy options and some Soviet economic experiments, such as agro-industrial complexes.

A low initial level of economic development meant relatively high growth through to 1985. Then problems mounted and the first signs of dissidence emerged. But it was an inner-Party coup that ousted Zhivkov in November 1989. A month later he was expelled from the Party, and then arrested. In September 1992, though no more guilty than others like him, he was imprisoned for seven years for embezzlement of state funds and inciting ethnic hostility against Bulgaria's Turkish population.

Romania

Bulgaria's slavish conformity with Soviet wishes contrasted with Romania, whose deviant foreign policy attracted undeserved western support well into the 1980s, despite Nicolae Ceausescu's increasingly obnoxious domestic policies. Divergence from bloc policy began under Gheorge Gheorghiu-Dej in the late 1950s, and in April 1964 the Party issued its *Stance on the Problem of the International Communist and Working-Class Movement* (often called its Declaration of Independence from Moscow). Thereafter, Ceausescu made opposing the Soviets an art form in a bid for domestic popularity that reached its peak when he denounced WTO intervention in Czechoslovakia in August 1968.

Ceausescu's personality cult was unrivalled in post-Stalin Europe. By March 1974 when he became president of the Republic, he was already chairman of the Council of State, commander-in-chief of the Armed Forces, chairman of the Front of Socialist Unity and Democracy, and headed a vast array of Party and state committees and commissions. He was a great domestic and foreign traveller. Unwilling to delegate responsibility, he poked his finger into every domestic pie, but errors were invariably attributed to others. By the late 1970s his father-image was wearing thin, which made his publicity machine work even harder.

Nepotism was common in bloc countries, especially Albania and Bulgaria, but Ceausescu's went so far as to be called 'socialism in one family'. His wife Elena became his acknowledged number two and the power behind the throne. Some 50 relatives held significant posts. Four were Party Central Committee members in 1977.

Living standards were then dropping drastically and a manic drive from 1982 to repay Romania's accumulated economic debt to the West made malnutrition endemic, especially among the young, whose numbers were high due to severe anti-abortion laws. Many children ended up in orphanages, where large numbers became HIV-positive after injections with infected blood as a treatment for malnutrition.

Romanian society was to be transformed by a policy of 'systematisation'. Draconian rules were enforced in all spheres of life. Though it was claimed that rural living standards were to be raised by knocking down crumbling villages and replacing them by urban-style centres, the real goal was to destroy the last remnants of private agriculture by moving the peasants from their individual houses and plots of land to soulless blocks of jerry-built flats, with the vacated land taken over by the vast, inefficient state farms. This destruction of the rural community particularly affected Transylvania where the ethnic Hungarians were already struggling to preserve their distinctive cultural identity.

By 1989 a sixth winter of energy-saving meant reduced street lighting, a single 40-watt bulb in barely heated houses, and short-time working. The economy depended on guaranteed cheap energy, and the drop in domestic supplies from exhausted oil wells and the high cost of imports meant that factories and the over-large petro-chemical industry ran short. Drastic penalties for unfulfilled targets in militarised coal-mining inevitably meant low-grade output. At the same time thousands of buildings were being destroyed in Bucharest to accommodate a grandiose new city centre, in which an eight-lane Avenue of the Victory of Socialism led up to the Ceaucescus' ostentatious new House of the Republic.

Ceausescu's excesses were belatedly recognised by western governments. In June 1987, the United States removed the most favoured nation status unique to Romania among bloc countries. Yet the Ceausescus felt to the end that they could defy the tide of change sweeping the bloc. At the Fourteenth Party Congress in late November 1989, the policies of the 'Conducator' were (as always) rapturously approved. Despite demonstrations and violence in Transylvania and western Romania, Ceaucescu then set off on a three-day state visit to Iran. On his return he was deposed, and on Christmas Day executed along with Elena.

Poland

Events in Poland and Hungary presaged the end of communist party rule in the bloc. Poland had undergone many trials since Gomulka fell after massive strikes in the Baltic seaports in December 1970 following a 30 per cent rise in basic food prices. His successor Edward Gierek announced a two-year price freeze, and an import-led investment boom induced a false sense of prosperity. Real wages and Poland's foreign debt both increased dramatically. Gierek planned to repay the debt through higher quality output, which never materialised. Huge price rises of 60 per cent in basic foods announced in June 1976, with immediate effect, brought a rerun of the 1970 events. Workers' strikes and demonstrations were again put down harshly. Severe sentences for their leaders led intellectuals to form the Workers' Defence Committee (KOR), which united dissident workers and intellectuals for the first time in post-war Poland and led during the 1980 strikes to the creation of Solidarity, the bloc's first independent trade union. Solidarity, which was led by former Gdansk shipyard electrician Lech Walesa, attracted almost 10 million members, including many Party members, over the next year and a half before President Wojciech Jaruzelski declared martial law to avert a real threat of Soviet intervention. But the regime had lost all credibility and was sustained only by Poland's geopolitical situation. The problems remained unsolved when Gorbachev became CPSU General Secretary in March 1985.

In October 1987 the economic situation forced Jaruzelski to announce a programme of radical reconstruction. A referendum asked Poles to approve a short sharp shock to get it off the ground and to reduce Poland's US$35 billion foreign debt. (As in most bloc countries, the bulk of the creditors were western countries and banks.) In return he promised a parliamentary Upper House and expanded civic rights. Solidarity advised a 'no' vote and the Catholic Church was silent. Less than half of those eligible to vote approved the programme, but Jaruzelski went ahead with it. Rising inflation caused wage strikes in Spring and Autumn 1988, and he turned to Lech Walesa for help. This led to the 'Round Table' meetings between Party, Solidarity and Church leaders in early 1989 which agreed that parliamentary elections would be held in June 1989, with 65 per cent of the Lower House seats reserved for the Party and its allies. Solidarity swept the board in the new Upper House and won all seats it was allowed to contest in the Lower one.

Hungary

In Hungary change began within the Communist Party itself. Janos Kadar, ever mindful of the limits of Soviet toleration, had been the first bloc leader to try to reduce direct Party control while maintaining its leading role. From the late 1970s his regime flirted increasingly with small-scale privatisation. Garden plots worked by families in the evening and at weekends produced a third of the gross agricultural product. Groups of workers in state enterprises rented their machinery in the evenings and worked at higher rates negotiated with management. The more orthodox Party leaders became worried about society's ideological scepticism and indifference.

After 1985 economic problems mounted and Gorbachev's reforms in the USSR made Kadar seem increasingly conservative. Imre Pozsgay, his most radical Party critic, was demanding faster and more radical political and economic change. Hungary's debt to the West was rocketing and to curb consumerism in 1987 Hungary adopted the bloc's first western-style income tax and VAT. Opposition mounted and the Hungarian Democratic Forum was formed in September 1987. A May 1988 Party Conference shunted Kadar into an honorary Party Chairmanship. Eight of the thirteen Politburo members were replaced by much younger men, who faced the impossible task of trying to reconcile political pluralism and the Party's leading role.

Further opposition groups emerged – the Alliance of Young Democrats (FIDESZ) in March 1988 and the Alliance of Free Democrats (AFD) in November. The Independent Smallholders, the Free Democrats and the Social Democrats, which had been disbanded or absorbed in the late 1940s, were recreated. In March 1989, the Party and the opposition groups agreed that there should be free multi-party elections. In May Kadar lost his honorary Party chairmanship. In July, Imre Nagy's remains were taken from an unmarked grave and reinterred, and he was honoured by a great ceremony on Heroes' Square. An October Party Congress condemned the Soviet invasion in 1956 and removed 'Workers' from the Party's title, leaving it as a Hungarian Socialist Party committed to multi-party parliamentary democracy and a free-market economy.

Czechoslovakia

Despite Czechoslovakia's democratic heritage, de-Stalinisation – revived in the USSR in 1961 – began in Prague only after the 12th Party Congress of December 1962. It was also a response to severe economic problems in a country that had always seen itself as the region's most developed. By 1966 the economist Ota Sik was telling the Party leadership that genuine economic reform was impossible without political change; in response the New Economic Mechanism came into force in January 1967, but entrenched habits of bureaucratic interference greatly reduced its impact.

Demands also came from Slovaks for the rehabilitation of their leaders purged for 'bourgeois nationalism' after 1948 and for an end to Slovakia's subordination to Prague rule. In September 1963 Antonin Novotny – Czechoslovak Party (CPCz) First Secretary since September 1953 – was forced to dismiss some leading Stalinists, including the two leading Slovak supporters of Prague rule. The Czechoslovak prime minister, Vilem Siroky, was replaced by Jozef Lenart, a Slovak proponent of 'controlled liberalisation', while the much-hated Slovak Party first secretary, Karol Bacilek, was replaced by Alexander Dubcek. Demands for greater autonomy grew steadily over the next five years.

Dissent also mounted in Czech and Slovak cultural organisations, and ultimately the pressures coalesced. Novotny was replaced as CPCz first secretary by Dubcek in early January 1968. Within three months Novotny had to give up the presidency also, intra-Party democracy was being promoted from the top, censorship had been abandoned, and a mood of change was becoming infectious. In this 'Prague Spring' lesser parties and the trade unions began to establish a more separate identity from the CPCz, and a host of new, independent bodies emerged like KAN, the Club of Committed Non-Party members. Church grievances began to be redressed, and religious freedom to be re-established.

In April 1968 the Party adopted an Action Programme. Its preamble admitted grave errors since 1948 and promised 'a new, profoundly democratic, Czechoslovak model of socialist society'. It looked back to the pre-1948 national-communist period and saw Czechoslovakia as a bridge between East and West. Its notions of separation of powers and civil rights echoed the views of Imre Nagy in Hungary 12 years earlier, and the Soviets again responded by invasion, though now backed by WTO members other than Romania. Soviet tanks in the streets forestalled the Fourteenth Party Congress which had been expected to adopt new rules on intra-Party democracy and hasten the realisation of the Action Programme. The Party's remaining hardliners were expected to lose their posts, and the Soviets rightly saw this as foreshadowing the beginning of the end of Party rule.

Intervention met only passive resistance. Secret protocols to the Moscow agreements forced Dubcek to reverse the reform programme and 'normalise'. The Soviet government justified its action by declaring that bloc member countries had the right and duty to intervene if socialism was threatened in any other member state (the 'Brezhnev Doctrine'). After May 1969, Gustav Husak prolonged normalisation for 20 years. Most Czechoslovaks retreated into political and social apathy during the 1970s and most of the 1980s. But small groups of intellectuals, stimulated by the Helsinki Accords of 1975, publicly protested at the suppression of democratic freedoms in such documents as Charter 77. Though there was widespread sympathy for them, they aroused little active backing until Honecker's fall in East Germany, when students demonstrated against the regime in Prague. A political grouping of anti-communist forces called 'Civic Forum' was founded, and – led by Vaclav Havel – it swiftly and bloodlessly overthrew the communist regime in a so-called 'velvet revolution' in November–December 1989.

East Germany

From August 1961 the East German government built their 'Anti-Fascist Protection Wall' (Berlin Wall) round West Berlin to stem the flood of East Germans, who had previously crossed the border to West Germany in spite of all efforts to stop them. The wall was a symbol to the West of the failure of the communist regimes of the eastern bloc to fulfil the aspirations of their citizens, but it stabilised the regime. Some still tried to escape over it, and were machine-gunned in the attempt. American President Kennedy came to Berlin in 1963 and declared his support for the beleaguered West Berliners with the declaration '*Ich bin ein Berliner*' (which in local usage means 'I am a doughnut', but the Berliners knew what he meant).

East Germans were forced back on their own resources, as head of state Walter Ulbricht tried with some success to turn a rump territory into a *bona fide* state. Though statistics were somewhat padded, the German Democratic Republic (GDR) was accepted as a leading industrial country, and a wide-ranging social security system provided excellent benefits, especially for mothers and young families. This supported the fullest possible employment of women in a country from which many of the best young workers had emigrated before the wall was built.

Figure 8.2. Memorial to a wall-builder (cartoon on the death of Erich Honecker, who supervised the construction of the Berlin Wall, *Guardian*, 3 June 1994)

Ulbricht's opposition to the Four-Power Agreement on Berlin led to conflict with Brezhnev and his replacement in 1971. His successor Erich Honecker's policy of *Abgrenzung* (separation) claimed that the building of socialism had created a distinctive East Germany in which West Germans should be treated as foreigners. But little sense of separate East German nationality developed, and by the mid-1980s the GDR had become so economically dependent on the FRG that it could no longer afford to antagonise it. Honecker, however, did achieve international recognition for the GDR – partly through a massively funded, highly selective and ethically flawed sports programme designed to produce world champions.

Honecker tried to ignore Gorbachev's policy of openness and democratisation, and the German editions of some Soviet journals were ultimately banned. But demands for political change grew, stimulated by meetings of new informal organisations (many sheltering under the umbrella of the churches) from which New Forum emerged as the leading organiser of demonstrations. There was also a flood of emigrants to the West after Hungary opened its borders with Austria. A 'Chinese solution' (i.e. sending in the tanks as in Tiananmen Square, June 1989) is said to have been considered, but was rejected after Gorbachev told the leadership in October 1989 at the GDR's 40th birthday celebrations that the USSR would no longer bail them out of any difficulties. Days later Honecker was removed from office.

Towards 1989

Several sources of tension were growing within the bloc during the 1980s. One was the continuing influence of religion, despite all the years of state-supported atheism. In Poland the regime had always been aware that the institution to which the bulk of the population devoted genuine deference was the Roman Catholic Church. The communists maintained an uneasy stand-off with this ideological rival, but increasingly the Church's influence undermined people's respect for the regime. The Pope's 1979 visit to his homeland gave dissidence an enormous boost. He was seen by millions at vast rallies and on television. As one writer said, the lasting impression was of a nation united with its Church; the Party seemed forgotten and almost irrelevant. Many parish priests became active supporters of KOR and Solidarity, and during martial law their churches – the only places where more than three people could meet openly without breaking the law – often doubled as pro-Solidarity political forums. Yet Cardinal Glemp managed to convince the regime of the Church hierarchy's support sufficiently for it to allow the Pope's much-delayed second visit in June 1983.

The Church's position in Poland was paradoxical. Most people identified it with rebellion against authoritarian constraints. But the Church hierarchy saw its role more as that of a mediator in disputes between Party and people. The

Church had to be accepted by the regime as a partner, undertaking many social, educational and cultural functions normally handled by the state in socialist countries. If it stuck to purely religious functions, it was relatively unhampered, as church attendance and the large number of churches under construction in the mid-1980s showed. But priests who got involved in politics were greatly harassed by the authorities. Most of them worked in the cities. In October 1984, one of the most radical Warsaw parish priests, Father Jerzy Popieluszko, was murdered by state security agents. Popular revulsion was such that they had to be tried and sentenced to prison terms, but the Party's treatment of the episode was thoroughly cynical, and contributed further to public disillusionment.

In East Germany the Evangelical Church established an informal agreement with the regime in 1978 which, while far from resolving all issues between them, recognised the Church's social role and provided cover for its youth activities. The Church established discussion groups focusing on Christian goals, Green issues and an autonomous peace movement, and maintained close contacts with West German churches. The GDR's smaller Roman Catholic Church also became more politically active in the late 1970s.

Another source of tension was the growing impact of ethnic divisions (some of which were strongly connected with religious loyalties). If an ethnic minority was of a different faith from the majority of a country's population coercion was more likely, as with Bulgaria's attempt in the mid-1980s to force its Turkish citizens to adopt Bulgarian names and renounce Islam. Notice also that the crisis of the Ceausescu regime began with the threatened eviction of a Hungarian priest from his parish in Timisoara. Despite the communist parties' formal adherence to internationalism, nowhere in the bloc was an effort made to resolve the disputes between territories and peoples created by the post-First World War settlements. Minorities in countries with a predominant nationality could at best expect second-class status, while efforts might well be made forcibly to assimilate them. Despite the myth of 'proletarian internationalism' national stereotypes remained entrenched, and nationalism remained a primary motivating force. It is fair to say that no ethnic issue that existed overtly or latently within or between countries in this region at the end of the Second World War was solved in the period to 1989, and thereafter many resurfaced more openly in the freer interplay of political forces. Even the Romanian claim to Southern Dobrudja has recently re-emerged to complicate relations with Bulgaria.

The economic system was also breaking down, and economic problems were accumulating throughout the bloc. It was becoming apparent by the early 1980s that bloc members could do little to solve each other's economic problems. The Council for Mutual Economic Assistance (Comecon), which was supposed to coordinate economic activity in the bloc, had been established in 1949 as a response to the Marshall Plan but was largely redundant until Khrushchev, in the late 1950s, realised that the autarchy encouraged in the Stalin era was dysfunctional and attempted to introduce an 'international socialist division of labour' in a move towards integration. This had little appeal when one member (the Soviet Union) was so much larger and more powerful than all the others.

Moves towards integration were resisted, particularly by Romania, which made use of the 'unanimity principle' adopted at the body's founding meeting. All subsequent Soviet efforts to promote integration foundered and Comecon remained a body whose many activities covered relatively slender achievements. Neither of the two Comecon banks did much to foster intra-bloc trade. This was largely because the so-called 'transferable ruble' never lived up to its name, and member states relied on annual bilateral barter agreements. Generally low-quality production made member states loath to see a positive balance with one country offset by imports from another and they increasingly tended to demand hard currency for deliveries outside the annual protocols. This became particularly true of the fuel and raw materials imported from the USSR (on which the other member countries' industries were so dependent). Such primary products had world standards so they could more readily be priced than manufactured goods, which were often outdated and qualitatively vastly inferior to western and latterly East Asian ones. So the fact that the USSR was prepared to accept such products shielded Comecon members from outside competition, but also meant that there was little impetus towards efficiency and innovation until the 1980s.

By the end of that decade, above-norm fuel deliveries were hardly available at any price because of falling Soviet production, and latterly there were even cutbacks in agreed deliveries. This was awkward for countries which had always used a lot more energy per unit output than the West, where energy-saving since the mid-1970s had increased the differential. Energy-saving and anti-pollution measures are both very recent in central and eastern Europe.

By the late 1980s Soviet economic output was falling ever further behind the West both quantitatively and qualitatively. An American journalist likened the USSR to a banana republic which nevertheless could incinerate the world. Within the country, jokers turned Khrushchev's old slogan of catching up with the West into one of catching up with Africa. As Henry Kissinger, a former American secretary of state noted, the USSR faced two crises – a political one if it changed the system, and an economic one if it did not.

But the bloc crisis was precipitated by the loosening of the Soviet political system after Gorbachev's accession to power. The later Brezhnev years had been marked by growing economic stagnation and frustration. Even defence spending slowed from the late 1970s, when the USSR was bogged down in Afghanistan, repeating America's errors in Vietnam. The increasing momentum of economic decline made Gorbachev realise that the USSR could no longer afford to pursue the Cold War or impose its will on central and eastern Europe by military force. The extent and significance of on-going change in the domestic and foreign policy priorities of the Soviet leadership was masked at first by uncertainty and conflict in the higher reaches of the CPSU and was poorly appreciated or disregarded by most bloc leaders, though it began to make an impression on their peoples. After Hungary announced that it was acceding unconditionally to the UN Convention on Refugees in March 1989 and symbolically cut the barbed wire on its border with Austria, the rush to emigrate to the West began. In September the Hungarian government announced that East German 'tourists' were free to cross Hungary's border with Austria and head for the FRG, and it began to seem that momentous events in that year might not be restricted to Poland and Hungary.

Table 8.6. GDR: Elections to National Assembly, March 1990

Party	Percentage of votes	Seats
CDU	40.82	163
DSU	6.31	25
Democratic Awakening	0.99	4
Free Democrats	5.28	21
SPD	21.88	88
PDS	16.40	66
Alliance 90	2.91	12
Others	5.41	21
Total	100.00	400

Table 8.7. Central and eastern Europe: basic data, January 1993

	Population (m)	Labour force (m)	Unemploy- ment (%)	Per cap. GDP (US$)	Agriculture % of GDP	Industry % of GDP	GDP (% growth)
Bulgaria	8.5	4.5	18.9	1,052	11.3	46.9	−13.9
Czech Rep.	10.4	5.3	2.6	2,526	n.a.	n.a.	−6.7
Hungary	10.3	5.2	12.3	3,594	17.4	29.0	−4.0
Poland	38.3	19.2	12.9	1,883	30.0	30.6	−0.4
Romania	23.2	11.6	8.5	529	19.3	46.8	−10.5
Slovakia	5.2	3.0	10.4	1,837	n.a.	n.a.	−14.7
Slovenia	2.0	0.8	11.6	6,052	4.9	32.5	−6.5
Russia	148.8	71.6	1.5	435.9	n.a.	n.a.	−20.0

Source: Business Central Europe, June 1993, p. 64; EIU, World Bank, IMF, national statistics.

The immediate effect in the GDR was dramatic. Demonstrations became more and more threatening, and the government announced that the wall and all border-points would be opened. Berliners from both sides of the wall were soon tearing it down and selling bits of it as souvenirs to tourists. The East German government opened discussions with New Forum and promised free elections. In the March 1990 elections the influence of the West German political parties was decisive, and pressure for union with the West became overwhelming. Negotiations for economic and monetary union between the two Germanies took place immediately, and full union was achieved on 3 October 1990.

Developments since 1989

All post-communist states claim to be creating a market economy and a western-style democratic political system, but their levels of commitment vary, and both people and politicians have been sorely tested by the consequences of rapid market reform. Social services have had to be greatly pruned, many workers have been made redundant, and others fear redundancy in countries where full employment was the norm. Significant proportions of the population are living on or below the poverty line, while a smaller group, including many of the old *nomenklatura*, has become very rich.

In the German *Länder* formed from the GDR on unification in October 1990, these pressures on the population have created enormous tensions as pay remains below that elsewhere in Germany. Target dates for parity have been dropped, but prices are identical and creches, kindergartens and other services have been closed or threatened with closure. Unemployment is still rising, and to many the hopes of 1989 seem betrayed.

Western-style political institutions were quickly introduced in all countries, but their functioning is often uncertain as old habits linger. Political cultures change slowly, and the strains of the rush to market have shortened tempers and hindered progress towards a civil society based on tolerance of other views. Western democracy is impossible without decent living standards for the population at large, and the threat to the fledgling democracies is less from old-style communism (for the mainstream of the communist parties have predominantly turned to democratic socialism) than from the extreme right, which can more readily generate ethnic hatred in troubled times.

Poland

In Poland, which has made the most direct and successful dash for capitalism, Tadeusz Mazowiecki's initial Solidarity-dominated government was bound at some stage to upset the movement's rank-and-file as price rises under economic reconstruction pinched. Solidarity's populist chairman Lech Walesa realised this and neither ran for election nor accepted any government post. Opposed by his old allies in the Democratic Union, he became Poland's first-ever popularly elected president in December 1990. Within six months, he had revived memories of Marshal Pilsudski's inter-war dictatorship by threatening to dissolve a parliament which opposed his proposals for increased presidential powers. He largely got his way on this, but not on a party-list system for parliamentary elections; voting for individual candidates was retained.

The low (43 per cent) turnout in the October 1991 elections showed how the public was getting disillusioned with politics. The Democratic Union (DU) won with only 12 per cent of the votes, followed by the Union of the Democratic Left (SLD – largely ex-communist) with 11.9 per cent, which gave Walesa great leverage in his nomination of a new prime minister for the Sejm's approval. After several failures, Jan Olszewski of the right-of-centre Liberal Democratic Congress was chosen.

Olszewski had run against Walesa for the presidency, and they quickly clashed over the large numbers of ex-communists and secret police collaborators who remained in important military and security posts. Walesa engineered a parliamentary vote of no-confidence and nominated the youthful Waldemar Pawlak in Olszewski's place. His government fell after a month, whereupon the disparate ex-Solidarity parties cobbled together a coalition government under Hanna Suchocka, Poland's first woman Prime Minister, who held on till May 1993, when her refusal to break budgetary guidelines to meet health and education workers' salary demands lost her a no-confidence vote.

September elections returned the ex-communists of the SLD and their old allies in the Polish Peasant Party (PSL) to power as the population voted to slow down reform and emphasise social welfare. The DU now won only 10.6 per cent of the vote compared to the SLD's 20.4 per cent. None of the six parties backed by the Catholic Church passed the threshold for Sejm representation. A law restricting abortion had been passed in January 1993 as a result of Church pressures, and this aroused suspicion of the Church's political influence, especially among women.

Walesa set up a range of presidential councils of prominent personalities outside day-to-day politics in fields including culture, the media, ecology, rural problems, science, business, legal issues and Polish–Jewish relations and submitted a Charter of Rights and Freedoms to the Sejm. But the PSL leader Pawlak, restored to the premiership, enhanced his position after clashing with the SLD over the sacking of Deputy Finance Minister Stefan Kawalec and the resignation of Deputy Prime Minister and Finance Minister Marek Borowski following a public outcry over the government's undervaluation of the newly privatised Bank Slaski, whose shares (sold at half a million zloty) quickly rose to 6.9 million.

The coalition, which had been shaky from the start, has survived to Summer 1994, but with the SLD leader Aleksander Kwasniewski losing ground to Pawlak, further friction seems inevitable; and while the SLD has 171 Sejm

Table 8.8. Poland: Elections to National Assembly, September 1993

Parties	Sejm % Votes	Sejm Seats	Senate Seats
SLD (ex-communists) (Alliance of the Democratic Left)	20.4	171	37
PSL (Polish Peasant Party)	15.4	132	36
UD (Democratic Union)	10.6	74	4
UP (Union of Labour)	7.3	41	2
KPN (Confederation for an Independent Poland)	5.8	22	–
Non-party Bloc Supporting Reform	5.4	16	2
"Fatherland" Catholic Election Committee	6.4	–	1
Solidarity	4.9	–	9
Centre Alliance	4.4	–	1
KLD (Liberal Democratic Congress)	4.0	–	1
Real Politics Union	3.2	–	1
Self Defence	2.8	–	–
Party X	2.7	–	–
Coalition for the Republic	2.7	–	–
Others	3.9	–	6
Total	100.0	456	100

deputies compared to the PSL's 132, it is the weaker partner because no other Sejm party would enter a coalition with it. As a leading candidate for the 1995 presidential elections, Kwasniewski can expect no support from Walesa. The PSL meantime has been flirting with the Catholic Church and the right-wing Confederation for an Independent Poland.

Pawlak and Walesa are currently mutually supportive. Walesa's main aim is to win the 1995 presidential elections and increase presidential powers in a new constitution. Pawlak's demand for a deputy minister in two of the three presidential ministries – defence, interior and foreign affairs – has been met. An April 1994 poll on choice of president saw Kwasniewski in the lead with 17 per cent, followed by Pawlak with 10 per cent. Walesa – now much less popular – came seventh equal with three others on 5 per cent.

In June 1994, the Sejm and Senate both approved a bill greatly liberalising abortion once more. (Cardinal Glemp commented that 'this Sejm was born in a time of national sickness'.) President Walesa then vetoed it, and the Sejm may have difficulty finding the two-thirds majority needed to override his veto. (It may be worth noting that Proctor and Gamble have opened a large nappy factory in Warsaw, with Walesa's backing; it aims to produce two billion babies' nappies per year, mostly for the Polish market. This TNC is one of the biggest investors in Poland.) Soon afterwards, with a poll of less than 30 per cent in most districts, right-wing parties made a comeback in local elections. Kwasniewski welcomed this as 'an element of normality'.

Poland's economy continued to prosper in the first half of 1994. Industrial production in June was 9.2 per cent up on June 1993 while real wages were 4.7 per cent higher. The private sector's contribution to total turnover rose from 29 per cent to 34 per cent in the year to May 1994. January–June inflation was 12 per cent and unemployment seemed to have stabilised at around 16 per cent. Exports grew by 12 per cent in the first four months of 1994 and imports by only 0.5 per cent. By the end of May, the budget deficit amounted to only 21 per cent of the sum projected to December.

Czechoslovakia

After its 'velvet revolution', Czechoslovakia was led by an interim government with a tiny non-communist majority until June 1990, when Federal and Republican elections which reverted to the party-list system used between the wars and in May 1946 were contested by 22 political parties. Fourteen were eliminated by a 5 per cent threshold in the Czech Republic and the Federal elections (a 3 per cent threshold operated in Slovakia). Civic Forum and its Slovak equivalent 'Public Against Violence', won by wide margins. In its two-year term, the federal parliament was expected to decentralise and establish the basis for democratic pluralism. Important issues required a 60 per cent majority, with members from the Czech Lands and from Slovakia voting separately in each House. But due to the surge of Slovak nationalism, the two could rarely agree, and neither Civic Forum nor Public Against Violence would cooperate with the communists or the Slovak National Party. Relations were strained even with the Christian Democrats within the coalition government. Havel was re-elected president for what he said would be a final two years.

Demands for Slovak independence steadily mounted, and when Vladimir Meciar's Movement for a Democratic Slovakia won 37 per cent of the votes for the Slovak National Council in the June 1992 elections and formed a coalition government with the Slovak National Party, early separation became inevitable. The running thereafter was made by the Czech Prime Minister Vaclav Klaus who wanted to end the Slovak drain on Czech resources as quickly as possible. On 1 January 1993 the Czech Republic and Slovakia became independent sovereign states.

The split was relatively painless, but tensions arose thereafter. The currencies were separated in early February 1993 after initial agreement on a single currency. By the time of the split, virtually all shares in the first companies privatised under the government's voucher scheme had been sold, but in March the Czech government announced that shares due to Slovak investors would be held as security until the two governments had agreed on

Table 8.9. Czechoslovakia: Elections to Federal Assembly, Czech Lands, June 1992 Turnout: 85%

Party	House of the People		House of the Nations	
	% vote	Seats	% vote	Seats
Civic Democratic Party–Christian Democratic Party	33.9	46 + 2	33.4	34 + 3
Left Bloc*	14.3	17 + 2	14.5	13 + 2
Czechoslovak Social Democratic Party	7.7	8 + 2	6.8	2 + 4
Association for the Republic–Czechoslovak Republican Party	6.5	5 + 3	6.4	3 + 3
Christian Democratic Union–Czechoslovak People's Party	6.0	5 + 2	6.1	3 + 3
Liberal Social Union**	5.8	3 + 4	6.1	3 + 2
Civic Democratic Alliance	5.0	–	4.1	–
Civic Movement	4.4	–	4.7	–
Moravia-Silesian Association	4.2	–	4.9	–
Others	12.3	–	13.1	–
Total	100.0	99	100.0	75

* The Left Bloc comprised the Communist Party of Bohemia and Moravia, the Democratic Left Movement, the Left Alliance and the Movement for Social Justice.
** The Liberal Social Union comprised the Czechoslovak Socialist Party, the Agrarian Party and the Green Party.

Table 8.10. Czechoslovakia: Elections to Federal Assembly, Slovakia, June 1992 Turnout: 84%

Party	House of the People		House of the Nations	
	% vote	Seats	% vote	Seats
Movement for a Democratic Slovakia	33.5	23 + 1	33.9	31 + 2
Party of the Democratic Left*	14.4	8 + 2	14.0	12 + 1
Slovak National Party	9.4	5 + 1	9.4	7 + 2
Christian Democratic Movement	9.0	4 + 2	8.8	7 + 1
Hungarian Minority Coalition**	7.4	4 + 1	7.4	5 + 2
Social Democratic Party in Slovakia	4.9	–	6.1	4 + 1
Civic Democratic Union	4.0	–	4.0	–
Civic Democratic Party	4.0	–	3.7	–
Association for the Republic–Czechoslovak Republican Party	0.4	–	0.3	–
Others	13.2	–	12.4	–
Total	100.0	51	100.0	75

* The Party of the Democratic Left (SDL) was the new name of the Communist Party of Slovakia.
** The Hungarian Minority Coalition comprised the Hungarian Christian Democratic Movement, Coexistence (which included other ethnic minorities) and the Hungarian People's Party.

the division of property and on their shares of the assets and liabilities of the former State Bank. Although it was reversed after two months, this decision both soured mutual relations and slowed the privatisation process in the Czech Republic. Border controls were also tightened and travelling between the two countries became decidedly time-consuming.

The Czech Republic

The Czech Republic has excellent long-term prospects, both politically and economically, and has further attracted German and other outside investors and joint venture partners since the break. It rivals Poland as front-runner for full EU membership. When Havel, elected president in January 1993, visited Germany that April, Chancellor Kohl pledged to support the application. Germany promised to look at ways of compensating Czech victims of Nazism, and the Czech government promised to consider possible forms of compensation for Sudeten Germans expelled at the end of the war, though Havel was criticised for this at home.

The Czech Republic has functioned without an Upper House (Senate) since an attempt to fill it with former Federal Assembly deputies failed in early 1993. It was eventually agreed that elections to it should be held in Autumn 1994 along with local elections; there has been deadlock since then on the necessary electoral law. A Constitutional Court has been established in a move towards a greater separation of powers. Both Havel and Prime Minister Klaus's Thatcher-style government have enjoyed considerable public support, but that for parliament has dropped sharply. Klaus's Civic Democratic Party (ODS) still heads opinion polls by a considerable margin, while at the Communist Party's July 1993 Congress reform-minded members broke away to set up a Party of the Democratic Left. Support for the Social Democratic Party rose to 13 per cent, reflecting mainly an influx of other dissatisfied Communist Party members.

Some parties are promoting a federal system for Bohemia and Moravia, but the major coalition parties fear a repetition of the Czech–Slovak split. This will have to be resolved for local elections to take place as scheduled in Autumn 1994. There has also been controversy over whether all or only part of confiscated Church property should be returned, while the former communists were aggrieved by a July 1993 law which declared the 1948–89 regime illegitimate and criminal and lifted the statutory time limitations on prosecutions for ideologically motivated crimes committed in that period.

The second wave of voucher privatisation got under way in Autumn 1993 and was as popular as the first. The private sector produced more than half of the Czech Republic's GDP by the end of 1993. Exports were 16 per cent up on 1992 and there was a trade surplus of about US$350 million. Inflation dropped to around 1 per cent per month, but wage rises exceeded those in productivity. At 3.5 per cent, unemployment was among the lowest in Europe, but is likely to rise as businesses are further rationalised. By mid-1994, the Republic's hard currency reserves had reached US$5.3 billion, and in August the Czech National Bank decided to repay in advance an IMF US$471 million loan due in 1996–99. An insurance system replaced the old health service.

It is the fragmentation of the left rather than its own cohesiveness that has kept the fragile four-party coalition in power. Klaus's rather abrasive personality often upsets the ODS's coalition partners, whom he attacks for putting their own interests above those of society. The ODS's November Congress saw the first significant vote against Klaus's chairmanship of the party, but continued economic success may ensure his continuance in office.

Slovakia

Slovakia's economic and political prospects may be poorer. Czech traditional democratic values point towards a classic western-style democracy, whereas the long-repressed Slovaks, who embraced clerico-fascism in the 1930s, may lapse towards authoritarian rule. After the break, constraints on the Slovak media and governmental attitudes towards minority rights seemed to point in this direction.

There was a growing rift in the Movement for a Democratic Slovakia. By May 1993, defections left it only 66 of the 150 Lower House seats and it had to rely on the support of the ex-communist Party of the Democrat Left. Meciar struggled and many colleagues found it impossible to work with him. In February 1994, Foreign Minister Jozef Moravcik and Deputy Premier Roman Kovac left the government to set up the Alternative for Political Realism (APR). In March, Meciar lost a no-confidence vote and Moravcik became prime minister, heading a five-party coalition government. In April the Alliance of Democrats merged with the APR to form the Democratic Union of Slovakia (DU). Between them, the Movement for an Independent Slovakia and the Slovak National Party now had only 65 Lower House seats. Early elections were scheduled for 30 September–1 October, with the second round two weeks later, as all parties agreed that to wait until the due date of mid-1996 would be politically destabilising. This gave Moravcik little time in which to achieve economic improvement or appeal to the MDS's rural supporters.

Moravcik's policies were decidedly more moderate than Meciar's. He admitted that opinion polls before the June 1992 elections showed more than half the Slovak population opposed to Czechoslovakia's division, and said that while he himself had voted for the split, he expected both the Czech Republic and Slovakia to become EU members by the end of the century and forecast the closest possible contacts between them and cooperation based on 'European' values.

Around 30% of Slovakia's assets had been privatised by June 1992, but privatisation ground to a halt under Meciar with only 3% added. Restarting it meant tight and unpopular policies to reduce the budget deficit in order to gain IMF credit facilities. It was not surprising therefore that the privatisation campaign flopped.

The Slovak economy has deteriorated steadily since the split, and the Slovak crown has depreciated by about 15% against the Czech one. Czechs have preferred to buy German and Austrian imports and new markets for Slovak exports have been hard to find. Inflation is around 20% and unemployment 15%. Much of Slovakia's industry was militarily-linked and has lost its previously assured markets and is making massive losses.

Moravcik opened a dialogue with the ex-communists of the Hungarian Socialist Party after their victory in the May 1994 elections and better relations seemed assured if he stayed in power, but this also proved grist to the MDS's mill. The three ethnically Hungarian parties formed an electoral coalition to enhance their joint chances of beating the threshold which for a 3-party coalition was 7% of the vote. They got 10.1%, but the success of Meciar's MDS was a major blow to their aspirations.

Of the 150 parliamentary seats, MDS won 61 and the ultra-right, neo-fascist Slovak Nationalist Party 9, leaving a possible coalition between them six short of a majority. It took two months for Meciar to draw in the recently created old-style socialist Workers' Association of Slovakia which won 13 seats. Moravcik meantime led a lame duck government.

President Kovac set no deadline for Meciar forming a government and Meciar seemed happy just to make life difficult for Moravcik in parliament. President Kovac declared parliament's second session provocative and ordered an investigation into the constitutional legality of the steps taken, while Moravcik refused to sign the law cancelling the direct sale privatisation projects and delayed a draft budget which parliament would inevitably reject.

A meeting of about 10,000 people in Bratislava to commemorate the fifth anniversary of the 'velvet revolution' turned into a anti-Meciar rally, but the size of his electoral victory suggests that Slovaks, worried about the prospect of further widespread redundancies, are backing his stance of propping up old-fashioned, inefficient factories with continued subsidies. Older members of society looking back nostalgically to the perceived certainties and security of the pre-1990 system also back him. MDS got a quarter of the votes in Bratislava, and 44% in central Slovakia. The SNP got many of its total votes in Bratislava. Votes for the Hungarian coalition came largely from the region bordering Hungary.

Meciar's government took over on 13 December 1994 and immediately announced the postponement of the second wave of voucher privatisation. Juraj Schenk, the new Foreign Minister promised no major change in orientation, but the government has clearly lost international credibility. An expected EU loan was refused at the end of November despite improved economic performance under Moravcik. Relations with Hungary are again in jeopardy and media independence is threatened. How much of its term the government will survive is uncertain.

Hungary

In the March/April 1990 general elections, the Hungarian Democratic Forum (HDF) got 42.5 per cent of the vote and its president, Jozsef Antall, headed a three-party coalition. (The Hungarian Socialist Party came fourth with 8.5 per cent.) The HDF is a centre-right grouping, but nationalist and ultra-right elements in it have caused internal tensions and lost it public support. These tensions came to a head at the party's January 1993 Congress when Antall was challenged by the ultra-nationalistic, anti-semitic Istvan Csurka, and had to give the right a quarter of the seats on the party's Central Presidium. By June there was an open rift in the course of which Csurka and four other deputies formed the Hungarian Justice Party.

The HDF tried to put party loyalists in charge of the media and armed forces. Not for the first time, this put the rather authoritarian Antall at odds with President Arpad Goncz who, despite formally limited powers, used his public popularity to block such a reversion to 'political' appointments. The issue was put before the constitutional court, to which the opposition has also referred most controversial legislation.

Despite earlier fears, Peter Boross settled smoothly into the premiership on Antall's death in December 1993, and parliament's four-year term ended peacefully in April 1994. President Goncz urged such deputies as would be re-elected in May to pass much-needed legislation on the media, parliamentary representation for minorities and a human and minority rights ombudsman.

Hungary's relative lack of economic progress and the growing gulf between rich and poor helped the Socialist Party to gain steadily in opinion polls from late 1993. Hungary had been closer to a market economy than any other bloc country in 1989, but had the highest per capita debt to the West. Political deadlock has hindered economic development, and privatisation has gone relatively slowly, limiting outside investment. IMF credits were suspended in 1992, when unemployment more than doubled. Living standards of much of the population have declined and much-needed social legislation has been bogged down in parliament's endless bickering. Hungary's budget deficit is

Table 8.11. Hungary: Elections to National Assembly

March/April 1990			May 1994		
Party	% of Vote	Seats	Party	% of Vote	Seats
Hungarian Democratic Forum (HDF)	24.71	164	Hungarian Socialist Party	54.0	209
Alliance of Free Democrats (AFD)	21.38	92	Alliance of Free Democrats	18.0	70
Independent Smallholders' Party	11.76	44	Hungarian Democratic Forum	9.8	37
Hungarian Socialist Party	10.89	33	Independent Smallholders' Party	6.8	26
Federation of Young Democrats	8.94	21	Federation of Young Democrats	5.3	22
Christian Democrats	6.46	21	Christian Democratic People's Party	5.3	20
Agrarian Alliance	3.15	1			
Independents and Others	12.71	10	Independents and Others	0.6	2
Total (not incl. 8 seats for minorities)	100.00	386	Total	100.00	386

the worst in the region apart from Serbia's. The Socialist Party headed the first-round polls in May's general elections with 32 per cent of the votes, while its possible coalition allies, the Alliance of Free Democrats (AFD), came second with 19 per cent. The HDF came third with 12 per cent. The turnout of 69 per cent reflected the public's feeling that it was time for change. None of the extreme right- or left-wing parties broke the 5 per cent threshold. The Socialists did even better in the second round, winning 54 per cent of the votes and their leader Gyula Horn headed a new government coalition with the AFD.

Hungary submitted the ex-Comecon countries' first formal application for EU membership on 1st April 1994, followed a week later by Poland.

Tension has increased over policy towards Hungarians in Serbia, Romania and Slovakia, the latter exacerbated when that country (under Meciar) began diverting the Danube on completion of the Gabcikovo hydroelectric dam, but Moravcik seems more inclined to reach an accommodation with Hungary.

Bulgaria

Two months after Todor Zhivkov had been ousted, Bulgaria's communist party changed its name to the Bulgarian Socialist Party (BSP). An extraordinary Congress then made major changes in its leadership. The Party also offered to share power with the new opposition parties until elections to the 400 National Assembly seats in June 1990. Half the deputies were elected by a first-past-the-post system, with a second ballot between the two leading candidates if the winner failed to get over half the votes; and the other half were elected according to party lists. A 4 per cent threshold was set.

The BSP's victory owed much to the advantages provided by its established organisation. It won 211 seats, while the Union of Democratic Forces (UDF) got 144, the (Turkish) Movement for Rights and Freedoms (MRF) 23 and the Bulgarian Agrarian National Union 16. Most non-Turks who voted for other opposition parties in the first round switched to the UDF in the second. The UDF did well in major cities, but was outgunned in the countryside, where it failed to establish an adequate support network. It refused to enter a BSP-led coalition government, but its leader, Zhelyu Zhelev, was soon elected president by the new National Assembly deputies, and tried to mediate between the minority of opposition deputies and the passive BSP majority. Ignoring constitutional uncertainties, he quickly initiated legislation to depoliticise the army, police and part of the civil service. The National Assembly then created a Political Consultative Council to regulate its dealings with the president.

The BSP's reform programme was unlikely to satisfy the younger generation's demands for western-style democracy. Economic reform never really got off the ground and the government fell. Close-run elections in October 1991 gave the UDF a four-seat majority over the BSP. The MRF won 24 seats in a National Assembly now of 250 seats. The UDF made inroads into BSP support in smaller towns, but the BSP kept much of its rural backing; and its strong anti-Turkish line made more impact in eastern Bulgaria than the UDF's tolerance of the Turkish community's rights. The BSP won enough seats to block further constitutional reform and to resist any moves to strip deputies of their immunity to prosecution.

Table 8.12. Bulgaria: Elections to National Assembly, October 1991

Party	Percentage of votes	Seats
UDF	34.36	110
BSP	33.14	106
MRF	7.55	24
Agrarians	3.86	0
Others	21.09	0
Total	100.00	240

In the first quarter of 1992 a range of small shops, businesses and housing were denationalised, and an amended land law effectively abolished collective farms, though this proceeded slowly as the farms resisted claims by former owners. Plans to privatise large enterprises got bogged down in a UDF–MRF rift. The slow pace of reform led to a number of serious strikes organised by the major trade union amalgamations – the Confederation of Independent Unions and Podkrepa.

Re-elected president in January 1992, Zhelev urged the UDF in August to abandon its 'war against everyone' and seek compromise with the unions, the press and the opposition. By late October, relations between the UDF and MRF were at breaking point and the MRF voted with the BSP to bring down the government. Human rights legislation had not improved the worsening economic and social plight of the Turks and gypsies in Bulgaria's south where redundancies were heaviest. Many of these emigrated. In December the MRF agreed to support a 'non-party government of experts', whose February 1993 Action Plan was for further austerity after 100 per cent inflation the previous year. (It had been 334 per cent in 1991.) Gross output dropped by 15–20 per cent and unemployment reached 13 per cent. In June UDF demonstrators accused President Zhelev of favouring the BSP and ex-communists. His vice-president resigned. In the same month, ex-communists and other left-wingers set up the Civic Alliance for the Republic in preparation for future elections.

In February 1994 Prime Minister Lyuben Berov survived his fifth no-confidence motion and got his budget passed with MRF support after promising higher state purchasing prices to MRF-voting Turkish tobacco growers and giving vague assurances about future financing to the main trade unions, the military, teachers and other professional groups. Berov suffered a heart attack in early March 1994 after a heated meeting of the country's Council of Ministers, but was back in harness within a month. The EU agreed to provide a further US$46 million credits, but the lev dropped sharply against the dollar. Bulgaria became the first country to recognise Macedonia's independence, and strengthened relations with Turkey, while trying to allay Greek fears of irredentist aspirations.

The economy picked up later in the year, with the first increase in industrial output since 1988. Bulgaria's foreign debt was largely rescheduled and its trade balance moved from deficit into surplus. But Berov's hold on power was fragile and his government finally fell in early September. The extreme factionalism, defections and embittered relations among National Assembly deputies and parties over the previous three years meant that many deputies would be dropped from the party lists for the mid-December elections and lose their parliamentary immunity. But their fears of prosecution for their activities up to 1989 diminished when the BSP, promising to slow down economic reform and increase social security, won 43.5% of the votes and 125 of the 240 National Assembly seats. The UDF dropped to 69 seats after defectors had joined the agrarians in a People's Union, which won 18 seats. The MRF had also split and dropped to 15 seats. A Bulgarian Business Bloc won the remaining 13 seats, but is unlikely to stay together.

Romania

In Romania a National Salvation Front (NSF) replaced the Communist Party, and its chairman Ion Iliescu became interim president. Most members were erstwhile Ceausescu supporters, though Iliescu had been in conflict with him since the mid-1980s. Fears that the Party apparatus had simply changed its name grew when the Front quickly announced its intention of fighting the May elections rather than just supervising them. It abandoned systematisation and acknowledged the grave economic situation, but intended to leave major reform until after the elections. Mass protests by the numerous opposition parties, including the re-formed National Liberals and National Peasants, forced the Front to share interim power with representatives of 29 other parties in a Provisional Council for National Unity.

The opposition parties protested against the NSF's electoral advantages of access to CP assets and control of radio, TV, the secret police and the local authorities. Despite this, western observers validated the NSF's 66 per cent of the votes and Iliescu's 85 per cent of those for president.

Within a month, the regime ordered a police crackdown on an anti-government student and worker protest in central Bucharest. Iliescu finally invited 30,000 Jiu valley miners to crack some heads and end the demonstrations. The West then suspended all non-humanitarian aid and put Romania's request for Council of Europe membership on the back burner.

The NSF had promised gradual reform without economic upheaval, but most of the IMF's demands for rapid restructuring were quickly accepted. Continual price rises reduced real wages by about 40 per cent in a year and were met by frequent strikes. In September 1991 the Jiu valley miners were back in Bucharest, but this time demonstrating against the government and bringing it down. A six-months price freeze was announced on staple items. Former finance minister Theodor Stolojan dedicated his NSF-majority coalition government to stabilising the economy, improving Romania's international image and organising long-overdue local elections as well as fresh general and presidential elections the next spring, though the latter were later postponed.

In local elections the NSF vote dropped to 33 per cent, while the Democratic Convention (DC) formed in July 1991 obtained 24 per cent. Soon afterwards the NSF split. Pro-Iliescu elements set up the Democratic National Salvation Front (DNSF). The National Liberal Party (NLP) withdrew from DC (later the Democratic Convention of Romania – DCR) but then failed to reach the 3 per cent threshold in the September 1992 general elections, while some members established a counter NLP which rejoined DCR. Iliescu retained the presidency with 61 per cent of the second-round vote, while the DNSF won the general elections but, with DCR second and the NSF third, could achieve only a narrow parliamentary majority in coalition with the chauvinistic Greater Romania Party and the Socialist Labour Party, both of which seek a return to national communism, and the right-wing Party of Romanian National Unity.

Table 8.13. Romanian General Elections, September 1992: Percentage of Votes

Party	Chamber of Deputies	Senate
Democratic National Salvation Front	27.71	28.29
Democratic Convention of Romania	20.01	20.16
National Salvation Front	10.18	10.38
Party of Romanian National Unity	7.71	8.12
Hungarian Democratic Union of Romania	7.45	7.58
Romania Mare (Greater Romania Party)	3.89	3.85
Socialist Labour Party	3.03	3.18
Democratic Agrarian Party	–	3.30
Others	20.38	15.14
Total	100.00	100.00

The economy continued to cause grave concern. GDP dropped a further 16.5 per cent in 1992; 42 per cent of families were destitute and 16 per cent were living below subsistence level. There were major anti-government demonstrations in Bucharest in mid-February 1993 and a month later the government lost a no-confidence motion on its economic programme. Unemployment reached 9 per cent and real wages dropped to two-thirds of those three years earlier. The lei began 1993 at 460 to the US dollar and reached 1,074 by early December.

Privatisation and real reform remained stalled, with Prime Minister Nicolae Vacaroiu a leading conservative force in the DNSF (which was renamed the Party of Social Democracy (PSDR) at its July conference). President Iliescu tried to hold the middle ground between a more reform-minded group and the PSDR's dominant hardliners and their nationalist allies, among which Gheorghe Funar's Party of Romanian National Unity (PRNU), was pushing hard but unsuccessfully for Cabinet seats. In November, it formed a National Unity Bloc with the Senate's Democratic Agrarian Party. The main opposition alliance, the DCR, has remained fragmented, and a drive to rehabilitate Marshal Antonescu seems likely to enjoy further success. Yet Romania signed an association agreement with the EU in February and was admitted to the Council of Europe and had Most Favoured Nation status with the USA restored, both in October. In January 1994, it became the first ex-WTO member to sign a framework agreement with NATO on the Partnership for Peace programme, while the World Bank encouraged foreign investment by announcing a loan of US$175.6 million to update the country's oil and gas extraction and processing.

Relations with Hungary remained poor, partly because of the provocative treatment of Hungarians by Funar, the mayor of Cluj, Transylvania's leading city. Minorities prudently placed few hopes in Romania's Council of National Minorities which was set up to facilitate Council of Europe membership, and in March 1994, the Senate approved by 100 to 2 a PRNU amendment to a war veteran pensions bill denying state benefits to citizens who had fought against the Romanian army, which primarily affected the Transylvanian Hungarians conscripted into the Hungarian army in the Second World War. In June a promise by Gyula Horn to support the 'striving for autonomy' of Hungarians in the diaspora received short shrift from a Romanian presidential spokesman. There has been a general rise in racial tensions with a revival of anti-semitism and some nasty attacks on Transylvanian gypsies by both Romanians and Hungarians. Both Bulgaria and Ukraine fear Romanian irredentist claims to parts of their territory, while Moldova, although ethnically Romanian, currently rejects any idea of union with Romania and has drawn closer to Russia.

Conclusion

Central and eastern Europe as a whole still confronts awesome problems. However, one is struck by some positive signs. The post-communist systems may be fragile, but democracy has certainly been strengthened. Though the rules of the game have still to be fully established, competition has taken root both in politics and in economics. There may be some reversals in the years ahead, and prospects vary from country to country, but the overall picture still gives grounds for optimism. Cooperation with and within sub-regional, regional, European and international organisations has grown steadily, and while many issues still divide contiguous states, real efforts are frequently being made to resolve them. The observer not blinded by euphoria in 1989 may feel more real grounds for optimism in developments since. The problems of many of the constituent parts of the former Yugoslavia are, of course, of another order and may yet engulf other areas of the Balkans and beyond.

Table 8.14. Presidents of Central and Eastern European States

	Elected by	Term in years	Incumbent	Year Elected
Albania	Parliament	5	Salih Berisha	1992
Bulgaria	Popular vote	5	Zhelyu Zhelev	1990
Croatia	Popular vote	5	Franjo Tudjman	1992
Czech Republic	Parliament	5	Vaclav Havel	1993
Hungary	Parliament	5	Arpad Goncz	1990
Macedonia	Popular vote	5	Kiro Gligorov	1991
Poland	Popular vote	5	Lech Walesa	1990
Romania	Popular vote	4	Ion Iliescu	1990
Slovakia	Parliament	5	Michal Kovac	1993
Slovenia	Popular vote	5	Milan Kucan	1990
Yugoslavia	Parliament	4	Zoran Lilic	1993

Source: J. McGregor, 'The Presidency in East Central Europe', *RFE/RL Research Report*, Vol. 3, No. 2, January 1994, p. 30.

Further Reading

Brown, J. (1991) *Surge to Freedom: The End of Communist Rule in Eastern Europe* Adamantine, Twickenham.
Brown, J. (1994) *Hopes and Shadows: Eastern Europe after Communism,* Longman, Harlow.
Glenny, M. (1993) *The Rebirth of History: Eastern Europe in the Age of Democracy,* 2nd edn., Penguin, Harmondsworth.
Letgers, L. (ed.) (1992) *Eastern Europe: Transformation and Revolution, 1945–1991,* Heath, Boston, MA.
Schopflin, G. (1993) *Politics in Eastern Europe, 1945–1992,* Blackwell, Oxford.
Staar, R. (1989) *Communist Regimes in Eastern Europe,* 5th edn., Hoover Institution Press, Stanford, CA.
Stokes, G. (1993) *The Walls Came Tumbling Down: The Collapse of Communism in Eastern Europe,* Oxford University Press, Oxford.
Swain, G. and Swain, N. (1993) *Eastern Europe since 1945,* Macmillan, Basingstoke.
White, S. *et al.* (eds) (1993) *Developments in East European Politics,* Macmillan, Basingstoke.
The most useful journal is the weekly *Transition,* OMRI (Prague)

9 Managing development: markets and planning

Introduction

The variety displayed in the economic organisation of the European states is one of the most striking features of the continent's diversity. The dramatic transformations that have occurred in the early 1990s are both a cause and a consequence of many countries' decisions fundamentally to change how their economic systems work. This chapter will examine the original diversity and offer some explanation of the economic causes of the recent changes. In so doing, it will look at the principles underlying terms such as 'command economy', 'mixed economy', 'social market' and 'free economy' which can confuse rather than illuminate discussion. The chapter will focus first on two extreme models, the market economy and the planned economy, using these models to interpret the functioning of all the economic systems of Europe lying at various points between these extremes. First, however, it is necessary to examine what economic systems do.

The economic problem

All societies confront the same basic economic problem – that their citizens would like to have more goods and services than can be made with the available resources, so that choices have to be made about what is to be produced, including how this is to be done, and who is to receive the goods and services when they are available. Consider, for example, the inhabitants of Europe in the late Stone Age. They grew crops, such as grain, and they made various tools, including polished stone axes. In order to quarry the stone and then shape it to make the axes, they needed to devote labour and other resources to the task. The axes were used to help to clear the ground for the cultivation of new areas; and so more axes enabled more food to be grown in the long term. At any one time, however, the resources used to make axes had to be diverted away from other activities, such as growing grain and making it into bread. The problem confronting any Stone Age family in any year can be considered in a stylised way as the choice between making axes and making bread, as represented in Fig. 9.1.

In Fig. 9.1 the curve, known as a production possibility curve, represents the range of possibilities open to a family or community at any one time – for example, if it chooses to make no axes it can have up to 10 loaves (point A). It could also have only seven loaves (point B), but in that case it would not be using all its resources and would therefore be operating inefficiently. Another economically efficient combination is at point C, where there are four loaves and three axes. The production possibility curve can be used to identify how much of any one commodity the family has to give up to have more of the other. Look at Fig. 9.2, which repeats points A, B and C from the first diagram. Starting at A, if the family wants one axe it has to give up one loaf of bread (because at D there is one axe but only nine loaves). A second axe (point E) requires a greater sacrifice of bread, because devoting enough resources to make two axes leaves the family with only enough to make seven loaves, so in moving from D to E the extra axe requires resources that could have made two loaves. Except in very unusual circumstances, the efficient combinations will all lie along a curve, as in Figs. 9.1 and 9.2. When axe production is very low (point D), axes can be made using labour that is not very useful for baking bread and by quarrying the stone from land that is not good for growing wheat; but when more axes are made (point C), the labour and other resources diverted are more and more efficient at making bread, so more bread is lost for each extra axe as axe production rises.

It should be noted that 'efficient' is here being used in the quite restricted sense that at any time with predetermined resources as much is produced as

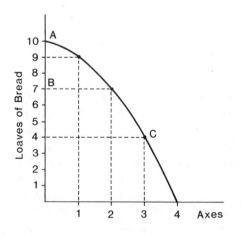

Figure 9.1. The production possibility curve

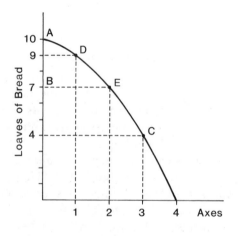

Figure 9.2. Trade-offs on the production possibility curve

possible, or any achievable output is made with as few resources as possible. It usually excludes problems such as the depletion of natural resources or pollution, because it limits itself to relatively immediate matters. It also assumes that resources are available in the right mix and of the right quality to be fully used, and that what is produced will be demanded. Neither part of this assumption is necessarily valid, so there may be unemployment (see Chapter 2).

Bearing these qualifications in mind, one can conceive a production possibility curve, drawn in multi-dimensional space to allow for a whole range of commodities, as representing the set of choices of goods open to the family. If it is operating efficiently, it can select any combination on the curve, but cannot go beyond the curve unless its options are increased. One way of enlarging the choices is for the family to trade with others – the implications of this will be considered in Chapter 10. At present, it is assumed that the family is self-sufficient. In that case, it can obtain goods in greater quantities if it increases the resources available to it – if more of its members can work, or it acquires more of other means of production, like more axes to clear more land. The choices between bread and axes can be regarded as illustrating the choice between consuming as many goods as possible now – bread – or forgoing some present consumption to increase resources – axes – to enable more bread to be consumed in the future. Pushing the curve out, by increasing the resources available, or by improving technology so as to enable more to be made with given resources, or both, is the process of growth.

Somehow, every society, whether a Stone Age family or a modern industrialised economy, has to determine what goods to choose to make and what to choose to forgo. In the case of the family, the decisions might have been made by the head of the household, but in modern societies the matter is more complex. One method is for the government to decide what should be made; it might, for example, determine what goods and services society should have (including communal services such as national defence), arrange that the relevant goods and services are made, and allocate them to its citizens on some social principle such as Marx's 'to each according to his needs'. This would be done for all goods in a pure planned economy. Alternatively, the government might believe that it is not its business to decide what should be produced and who should receive the goods, and such decisions should be left to individuals to determine for themselves – a market economy. In reality, no modern government adopts either of these extreme positions, but operates somewhere on a spectrum between them. Before discussing why this is so, it is helpful to consider briefly exactly what happens if the decisions are left to individuals.

The market and its limitations

Whether in prehistoric society or in a modern one, families play two economic roles. They are consumers of the goods and services that are available, and they make (or help to make) them. In the Stone Age society, our family was producing simply for its own needs, and, since it was self-sufficient, made everything for itself. One can imagine an economy which is similarly self-sufficient in total but in which households do not produce for themselves everything they wish to consume. In that case, the households will wish to exchange their surpluses of unwanted goods 'for goods of which they would like more. Those with surpluses wish to supply goods, and those who want more demand them. This exchange can happen in two ways.

The more straightforward method of exchange is barter – the swapping of goods at some agreed rate – for example, one axe for 10 loaves of bread. However, simple bilateral swaps may not be possible. For example, in the early 1950s most international trade had to be conducted by barter because of currency restrictions, but even so it often had to take a multilateral form. In one deal, chemicals were exported from Britain to East Germany in exchange for an assortment of china, glass and textiles which were sent to Argentina, which in turn sent pork to Britain; the pork was condemned by the British authorities as unfit for human consumption but was re-exported, some to the Netherlands (where it was canned and sent to East Germany in exchange for cement which was eventually sold to Canada) and the rest to Austria in exchange for prefabricated houses.

Because of the difficulties of barter, economies have evolved the use of a specialised good – money – to act as a medium of exchange. Whether with a barter system or a monetised one, the principles are similar – those who demand goods and those who wish to supply them meet to try to arrive at a deal. This process of meeting, whether it takes place physically in a market place or without buyer and seller ever coming into direct contact with each other, is called a market. Figs. 9.3 and 9.4 illustrate the principles.

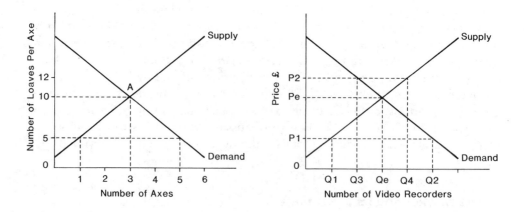

Figure 9.3. Supply and demand in a barter economy

Figure 9.4. Supply and demand in a modern economy

Figure 9.3 shows the operation of barter in the Stone Age community. The family that wants to supply axes and receive bread will be willing to supply more axes the more bread it gets for each axe, so the supply curve for axes slopes upwards from left to right. The family that wants to obtain axes and to barter its surplus bread for them will demand more axes the fewer the loaves it has to pay for each axe, so the demand curve for axes slopes down from left to right. If, as in the diagram, the two curves intersect, it is possible to find the equilibrium price for axes in terms of bread – 10 loaves, so at the equilibrium point A three axes will be exchanged for 10 loaves each, 30 loaves in total. At any other price, one or both of the families will not be satisfied – for example, if the price of each axe was five loaves, only one axe would be supplied but six axes would be demanded, so there would be excess demand of five axes. Similarly, if the price were above equilibrium, for example at 12 loaves per axe, there would be excess supply of axes.

Figure 9.4 illustrates exactly the same principle for a modern economy – the price in the UK of video recorders. The equilibrium price is Pe and quantity Qe; at prices below equilibrium, such as P1, there will be excess demand (Q2 – Q1); and at prices above equilibrium like P2 there will be excess supply (Q4 – Q3).

Thus if a government leaves it to market forces to determine what is made and who is to receive the goods, the outcome depends on the willingness of producers to make and supply goods and of households to demand them. However strongly they want goods, households will be able to buy them only if they can afford to do so. What they can afford depends on their income. In a market system, people's income depends on the labour and other services producers wish to buy from them. Producers buy factor services to enable them to make goods. They make goods only if they can sell them to households. So there is a circular system – households pay for goods from income they earn because producers want to use their services to make goods to sell to them. The market system is thus complete and will in practice always arrive at an equilibrium solution for all markets, determining simultaneously how much (if any) is produced of each good (Qe) and who receives it (everybody who is willing to pay at least Pe for it). (It is theoretically possible for markets not to arrive at an equilibrium solution, but the circumstances in which this happens are unlikely to occur in practice.) The market solution avoids waste, because there is no excess supply of any product, and it works automatically regardless of how complex the economy becomes.

The outcome may, however, not be best in practice. There are three major reasons for this. The first is implied by the limited definition of 'efficiency' – the market system does not consider third party interests, and so takes no account of environmental considerations such as pollution which have no direct impact on buyers or sellers.

Second, the description here assumes that the participants in the market all have roughly equal say in the outcome; but there may be only a few suppliers, who are therefore able to distort prices in their favour (by cutting output). The position where there is only one supplier (or very few suppliers) is called monopoly (or oligopoly). There are particular problems when the market is that for labour, and when (as is common in most towns) there are a lot of workers but only very few employers, because in this case the price which is distorted is wages, which the few employers try to push down to increase their profits. Attempts by workers to protect themselves against this power have often taken the form of workers grouping together to form trade unions, where the union tries to distort wages back into its favour. Two distortions pushing in different directions do not, however, necessarily arrive at anywhere near the outcome that would emerge if neither existed – a problem analysed by economists as 'the theory of the second-best'.

The third reason is that the market system contains no guarantes of social equity; households' income depends on what services producers want to buy from them, and not on their needs. Thus the distribution of income depends on two sets of considerations: the ability and willingness of households to offer labour of various kinds, and their capacity to provide other factor services. The main factor service other than labour in modern economies is finance (which enables companies to undertake investment); and the ability of households to buy shares or lend money to financial institutions depends on their savings and on their inherited wealth. Inheritance, both financial and genetic, is also part of what determines whether households can offer skilled and well-educated (and therefore usually well-paid) labour. Thus in a market system income is likely to vary from household to household, and these variations to some extent reflect chance rather than merit or need.

The resurgence of markets

In practice, every society which depends on the market system moderates the effects of markets to some extent, to limit the power of monopolists by legislation, and to provide some income to those who are unable to earn it (by a system of state social security). Similarly, every country wishes to provide some services collectively – typically law and order, national defence, the basic administration of government and perhaps education. For these reasons, all governments require some say in the allocation of resources.

At the other extreme, it is too cumbersome in practice for any government normally to make all the decisions about what is to be produced. Unless (as in wartime Britain or in the USSR in the 1930s) there are clear overriding priorities, there are simply too many decisions for any planning authority to make. In practice, therefore, in the centrally planned European economies, informal markets have usually been allowed to operate for goods and services relatively peripheral to the main activity of the economy – for example, farmers selling their surplus vegetables on a free market, or the making of craft products (in East Germany in 1988 a quarter of a million people were employed in private firms in what was designated as the craft sector).

It is, however, important to understand that fundamentally all economies must opt for either the market or the planned approach, because if the economy is to operate coherently one or other system must determine the basic allocation of resources. There are two issues which it is easy to confuse – ownership of the means of production and the mechanism for determining what is to be made. The means of production can be owned privately or communally (e.g. by the state). Except in a system of slavery, labour power is always privately owned and it is up to individuals to determine how much labour to offer for wages or other reward (though they may not always have a choice of occupation).

The touchstone of socialism is that a substantial part of the other means of production is owned not by individuals but by the state or collectives. Collective or state ownership means that market signals of rate of return on capital need not determine how resources are allocated, but there is no reason in principle why the administrators acting on behalf of the state should not allocate capital to its different uses in response to information coming from consumer markets. Resource allocation in a socialist system can, therefore, be driven as if by markets. Indeed, the market-inspired Conservative governments in the UK from 1979 have tried to simulate market disciplines in the public sector. They try to ensure efficient management by compulsory competitive tendering for the provision of some services to central and local government, and by provisions such as the Citizen's Charter for ensuring the management's sensitivity to public demands on services. Similarly, private ownership of the means of production is not inconsistent with planning – private companies can be told what to make (and how to make it) and allocation to consumers can be controlled by rationing, as, for example, in the UK in the Second World War.

The distinction between how capital is owned and how the economy is operated is crucial to understanding the options available to the centrally planned economies of Europe up to 1989; in practice, they have all combined measures of privatisation (selling state enterprises to private ownership) with the movement to a market mechanism, but in different ways in different cases. It was Yugoslavia which tried the longest to combine a market mechanism with communal ownership of the means of production; from 1952 it pursued a distinctive path, with increasing development of 'market socialism' and decentralised decision-making. Its markets, however, were really just using western European prices to guide planning decisions as to what was to be made and who would be able to buy it, and did not try to reflect what prices would prevail in freely operating Yugoslav markets.

Greater sensitivity to local circumstances was displayed in Hungary, where from the late 1960s the planners calculated 'shadow prices' to try to reflect what market prices in Hungary would be, and used these to determine the allocation of (predominantly state-owned) resources. However, 'shadow prices' are based on resource-use and are not very sensitive to changing consumer demand, as the sharp price changes after the liberalisation of markets in Hungary in 1990 demonstrated.

Within the market economies of western Europe, the most consistently 'planned' system has been that of France, which since 1947 has regularly published five-year plans, in a manner which is at first sight similar to the USSR and its satellites. However, these were indicative plans – plans which set out what the government's economists believed could be achieved if industry produced the relevant output. But the merely persuasive influence of the indicative plans on the French economy was probably never very great, and by the mid-1970s the planners were merely going through the motions.

Figure 9.5 is a stylised version of where European economies (of the mid-1970s and the mid-1990s) lie on the spectrum between pure market economies and pure planned ones. The figure clearly shows that there has been a general trend in Europe towards the free market end of the spectrum, with particularly dramatic changes in countries like Russia and Poland. Why this is so is partly a matter of politics but has also had economic causes and consequences.

Consider first the market economies. Their move to the right along the spectrum has been mainly in the form of the transfer, from the state to the private sector, of responsibility for the production of certain goods and services. This process of privatisation was led by Margaret Thatcher's UK government (1979–1990), which was motivated by a mixture of considerations. Three of the major economic motives are discussed below, but it is proper also to recognise that there was a political reason, the demonstration of the collapse of socialism by an explicit rolling back of the state from the economy and reassertion of the importance of personal freedom.

The most fundamental economic consideration is that the Thatcher government believed that the profit motive provides the best stimulus to efficiency in production – competition between different producers means that those who are weakest financially will fail, and financial strength comes from a record of success in producing the goods customers want at a price they are willing to pay. State-run enterprises are not exposed to competition in any very direct way, and hence they lack profit-driven motivation to efficiency. So unless they have some other spur, such as high requirements for return on

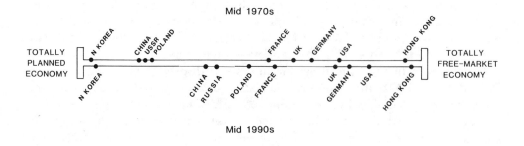

Figure 9.5. The spectrum from planned to market economies

capital, it is easy for the managers of state-run enterprises to slide into the use of excessive quantities of the factors of production, particularly labour. It is, however, difficult for any agent outside the industry, including the government, to be very confident of exactly what would be a proper requirement of return on capital, so there is danger of either waste of resources or unattainable targets. Privatisation makes it much easier to avoid these problems. Critics dispute this view on the grounds that private monopolies can (perhaps in different ways) be as damaging to the economy as public monopolies; the various 'watchdogs' for the privatised industries, such as Ofgas for British Gas, try to deal with these problems.

A second reason for privatisation's appeal to the Thatcher administration was the government's desire to cut taxes. They expected privatisation to help here in two ways. One of the factors influencing the level of taxation was the payment of subsidies to finance the operations of state enterprises. If privatisation were to remove the need for such subsidies, taxes could be cut. Furthermore, the national debt could be reduced by the profits from the sale of state enterprises, and this too might enable taxes to be cut.

The third major economic reason for the appeal of privatisation is that it can help to reduce interest rates and hence, in the long run, inflation. The more the government borrows, the higher the rate of interest it has to pay to persuade savers to lend it the money. Privatisation can reduce government borrowing in two ways. As mentioned above, it can cut the existing national debt. Furthermore, once an industry is privatised, its investment needs are met by the private sector and not by government borrowing.

Where the UK led, with such privatisations as British Petroleum, British Telecom and British Gas, other western European economies followed. The West German government sold its shares in Volkswagen. In France, a wave of nationalisation under a socialist government in the early 1980s was thrown abruptly into reverse in 1986 when the socialist government lost office and the new government under Jacques Chirac published a bill to privatise 65 firms, including those that had been nationalised five years earlier. In February 1988 under a new socialist government the privatisation programme was partially halted, but the election of a new conservative government in 1993 has restored it to a high position on the political agenda; for example, the Balladur government plans to sell its share of the Renault car firm.

Whilst Fig. 9.5 illustrates the move of the western European economies towards greater reliance on the market, its most striking feature is the more dramatic shift in central and eastern Europe, where what was basically a planned system has been superseded by what is basically a market system. This shift is much more fundamental in scale. For example, at the time of unification there were about 6,000 enterprises in the former GDR which were candidates for privatisation.

Planning and its limitations

To understand some of the problems of the USSR and most of the other
central and eastern European economies in 1990–91, it is useful to consider
what happens if the market equilibrium solution is not allowed to emerge.
Since the late 1920s, the governments of the USSR had generally set low and
stable prices for most products regularly demanded by consumers and
producers. So long as those prices did not diverge too far from
market-equilibrium prices, this was no great problem. But the system was
inflexible, particularly when external forces (such as the increases in inflation
caused by oil price rises in 1973–74 and 1979–80) produced pressure for price
rises.

Suppose that, to try to maintain or increase its popularity, the government
still wishes to keep prices down, and does this by imposing price ceilings in
individual markets. In Fig. 9.6 Pe is the equilibrium price, and Qe the
equilibrium quantity. The government wants price to be below Pe, say Pmax.
There is therefore excess demand, because producers are willing to supply
only Q1 but Q2 is demanded.

When excess demand occurs, there are queues of people who want the
good but are unable to obtain it, and shopkeepers can choose to whom to sell
the good (perhaps their favoured customers). In some circumstances, as in the
USSR in 1990, the central or local government tries to override shopkeepers'
preferences by introducing its own allocation system. One such system is
rationing, whereby people wishing to buy a good need both the money and a
government-issued coupon. The number of coupons would be set to equal
total supply, Q1, and the coupons distributed to households in what the
government regards as a fair way – for example, local authorities might use
rationing to limit purchases to local residents. Exactly that device was adopted
by St Petersburg to cope with shortages in late 1990 and 1991 by restricting

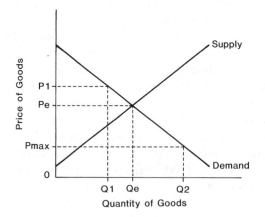

Figure 9.6. Price controls

Figure 9.7. St Petersburg ration coupons of 1990–91. From top, coupons for one person for wine and strong alcoholic drinks (March 1991), two sets for strong alcoholic drinks (August/September 1991), tea (February/March 1990) and soap (March–June 1990)

sales of consumer goods to local citizens. Figure 9.7 shows coupons for wine, strong alcoholic drinks, tea and soap. The coupons for strong alcoholic drinks, issued for the same period by different district offices were obtained from one family, showing how trade in coupons quickly developed.

Any government which tries to control a market, whether or not it operates a rationing policy, faces the prospect of its price ceiling being violated. Usually, it is relatively simple for a planning authority to control fairly completely what is produced, so output is unlikely to be much more than Q1, but it is much more difficult for the government to control the distribution

Figure 9.8. 'Can you remember? Are we working in a meat shop or a fish shop?' (Viktor Bogorad, *Smena*, St Petersburg, 1991)

network, and so to stop the good being sold at prices higher than Pmax on the black market. If all the supply available, Q1, were sold on the black market it would command a price P1, even further above Pmax than the market-clearing price Pe. If only some of the supply is diverted to the black market, the price there can be even higher than P1. How far the government chooses to tolerate black markets depends on the circumstances; in the USSR by 1990–91 a vast variety of meat and produce was being sold openly by individuals in city centres, and the government did nothing to prevent this because the availability of extra produce to cities helped to reduce social unrest.

Figure 9.9. 'God! You're such an optimist!' (Viktor Bogorad, *Smena*, St Petersburg, 1991)

The decision of a government to operate official price ceilings but to acquiesce in the existence of a black market can serve both to make most of the good available at low prices to those who are prepared to queue, *and* to make small quantities (sometimes of superior quality) available at a much higher price to those who are prepared to pay for it. It does not, however, address the basic problem that the overall quantity of the good is kept artificially low (Q1 rather than Qe). A further problem of shortages is that, when durable goods are available, buyers hoard them. This is true both for producers, hoarding supplies of raw materials, and for households. The average Soviet family in 1990, fearing even worse shortages or sharp price rises was storing about 6 kg of soap and washing powder and vast holdings of toilet rolls and sugar. The confusion in the retail market turned Soviet flats effectively into small warehouses. Hoarding serves, of course, only to make the shortages worse for those who are not holding stocks. The shortages of consumer goods were one cause of the dissatisfactions underlying the developments discussed in Chapter 8.

Introducing markets to planned economies

It is clear that limited black markets and free markets for some goods can be consistent with an overall planned economy and indeed facilitate its operation. What has happened since 1990 in all the countries of the former Soviet bloc is a much more radical abandonment of planning and its substitution by a broadly market system. This has caused major disruption, particularly to the countries formerly in the USSR which had been accustomed to central planning for up to 70 years.

The reason for this is that demand has adjusted much more quickly than domestic supply, because producers used to being told what to make (and, sometimes, how) find it difficult to learn how to adapt output to demand. The problem is illustrated in Fig. 9.6. If the official price was Pmax, and when price controls are abandoned supply is unchanged at Q1, the equilibrium price is not Pe but P1. Eventually, once supply adjusts, price will fall, but the initial price rise is very steep. Although some of the data is only approximate, Table 9.1 illustrates the prices of basic foodstuffs in Russia. The first date in the table, January 1990, shows the old controlled prices. About 90 per cent of retail prices and 80 per cent of wholesale prices were freed on 2 January 1991 and left to market forces. The January 1992 figures in the table show two influences – general inflation (which was running at about 20 per cent a month in 1991, so that prices generally rose about ninefold during the year) and further changes in relative prices as market equilibrium was established. So in real terms bread and beef became cheaper during 1991 and milk, tomatoes and especially cheese more expensive.

Table 9.1. Prices of staple products in St Petersburg 1990–92

Price	2/1/90	2/1/91	2/1/92
Bread, 1 kg	13 kopecks	65 kopecks	2.92 rubles
Cheese, 1 kg	3 rubles	9 rubles	144 rubles
Beef, 1 kg	2 rubles	7 rubles	60 rubles
Tomatoes, 1 kg	50 kopecks	9 rubles	120 rubles
Milk, 1 litre	36 kopecks	65 kopecks	7 rubles

Inflation has continued to be very rapid: in 1993 it was about 940 per cent, and the target set for 1994 was around 400 per cent. Actual monthly inflation in January 1994 was 22 per cent. By February it had dropped to 9.9 per cent and by June to 4.8 per cent. An Academy of Sciences report predicted that monthly inflation would not rise above 10 per cent by the end of the year, but a government economic research centre has forecast 12–14 per cent by then.

Some price rises, like those for bread and beef in 1992, would be relatively unimportant if incomes rose in step with prices, but the conservatism which makes the producers reluctant to change output also makes them unwilling to adjust wages in step with prices (roughly, the rise in wages in the two years to June 1993 was 86-fold and of general prices 96-fold, so wages had fallen over 10 per cent in real terms) and many households could not afford the high prices. On one estimate, in May 1993 the income of about a third of Russian households was below the government-calculated minimum needed for survival – the problem being particularly acute for families with young children and only one wage-earner.

Falling demand makes it less attractive for producers to expand output and prolongs the problem. Furthermore the government, knowing that prices should fall when output grows, will be reluctant to see incomes rise very far because of the inflationary consequences. This is compounded by a further problem. To meet the excess of demand over supply, more goods are imported – for example, in Russia in early 1993 much of the supply of vodka and spirits, and nearly all paper handkerchiefs, were imported, as were vast quantities of consumer durables. For reasons to be discussed in the next chapter the growth in imports, together with inflation, caused rapid devaluation of the ruble. Such poor economic performance has fuelled popular dissatisfaction with 'economic reform'. Writing about the USSR in 1990, Levada comments:

> In recent years and months in the Soviet 'post-traditional' society (the society of developed perestroika) the nature of shortage has changed. Instead of merely being in short supply, whole categories of consumer goods, raw materials etc. abruptly disappear from circulation. It is impossible to adjust to this type of shortage, and it gives rise to a different

type of social relations: tensions, protests, explosions. This is no longer the producer dictating to the consumer, but black market diktat (in Ellman and Kontorovich (eds) 1992: pp. 60–1)

The problem for consumers in Russia by early 1993 had become not shortages but what they regarded as high prices.

In some ways the incorporation of the former East Germany into a united Germany is an even more interesting case, one of trying to transform almost overnight a planned to a market economy. West Germany had itself been the market system's obvious European success story, with its 'economic miracle' of 8 per cent growth a year throughout the 1950s to become by 1990 Europe's largest, and the world's third largest, economy.

Meanwhile East Germany, though advanced by the standards of the other planned economies, was lagging further behind West Germany. Political discontent produced a trickle of East Germans in May 1989 crossing the newly opened Hungarian border into Austria and then West Germany, and later a flood, especially after the breaching of the Berlin Wall. For this situation the only economically and politically acceptable solution was unification of Germany. The initial phases of unification did nothing to slow the collapse of the East German economy, industrial output in which is estimated to have fallen by 80 per cent in the year from July 1990 to June 1991.

The next chapter will consider the monetary aspects of the union; our concern here is that when there was a common currency the East German industries were opened to the full force of competition from their counterparts in West Germany. Since output per worker in East Germany was typically only about half of that in West Germany, the problems for firms in the former East Germany would have been immense even if they had been familiar with a competitive system. Welfens summarises the problem neatly:

> Firms in East Germany that had been used to soft budget constraints, easy market conditions in the form of monopolistic positions plus structural excess demand (as a consequence of low state-administered prices) and cheap credits all of a sudden faced a new environment: an economy with non-rationing, functional competition and market interest rates on loans of three times the former 3 per cent. ... It is clear that German unification implied a coincidence of massive supply and demand shocks for East Germany where production has to adjust to relative world market prices and global competition. (Welfens 1992: p. 13)

But the support of the West German government meant that average output per head in the combined country fell only to 80–85 per cent of the previous West German level.

It is, however, clear that raising the productivity of the former East German *Länder* and guiding the process of privatisation will preoccupy Germany for the next few years. Consequently, western Europe will be able to look less than in recent years to Germany for economic leadership.

The fundamental problem for all the former centrally planned economies is that it is not sensible to try gradually to introduce markets. As Dornbusch says: 'The lesson of the post-war period is that those countries which pushed reform most aggressively soon showed the best results, even if the transition period was very hard. The market is already there. The only choice is whether to work with the market or to lose out in a fight against the market' (in Welfens (ed.) 1992: p. 135)

Gradualist approaches had been tried in Czechoslovakia (although with little sustained enthusiasm) and in Hungary on and off from 1968. Learning from their lack of success, Poland in 1990 adopted a radical programme to introduce the market system overnight and freed all prices. This process was supported externally, most notably by the IMF. Painful though the adjustments were, by the beginning of 1992 when Russia was planning to undergo a similar transformation, the Polish example was being used as a model of quick success.

After its first free elections in 1990, Hungary swiftly liberalised prices, trade and foreign exchange, allowed foreign direct investment in the economy and opened a stock exchange to deal in shareholdings, but privatisation has lagged. Romania in 1990 tried a gradualist approach, but in 1991, again initially with IMF support, moved to a market system. Such abrupt transitions, however, produce great economic strains in the short term, and thus impose a social and political cost. Further, they require political as well as economic will.

Figure 9.10. Bus driver to standing passengers in bus which has fallen apart, except for rail to hold on to: 'Next stop – developed capitalism'.

Economic structure and performance

One of the motives for economic reform in the former Soviet bloc has been popular dissatisfaction with the typical performance not just of individual markets for consumer goods but of the economy as a whole, and the belief that a market system would do better. To assess the realism of this view, this section will start with a brief review of the record.

Table 9.2. Macroeconomic performance in Europe, 1985–1990

	GDP per head US $000	GDP % growth 1985–90	Inflation 1985–90 %	Balance of payments % of GDP	Unemployment rate %
Austria	20.647	3.3	2.3	0.7	3.6
Belgium	19.807	3.5	2.2	1.2	9.3
Bulgaria	1.270*	3.7*	11.2	–5.2	n.a.
Cyprus (Greek)	7.647	7.3	3.3	–3.3	2.3
Czechoslovakia	2.839	0.9	2.5	2.0	2.6
Denmark	25.458	2.3	4.2	1.1	8.6
Finland	27.586	3.5	5.5	–4.9	3.5
France	21.107	3.2	3.3	–0.4	8.9
Germany (West)	18.878	3.4	1.4	3.0	6.4
Greece	6.566	1.8	24.5	–5.4	8.1
Hungary	3.103	1.0	19.7	–4.8	n.a.
Iceland	22.595	2.4	30.4	–1.8	0.7
Ireland	11.952	3.5	3.5	1.5	14.0
Italy	18.575	3.0	6.4	–1.2	12.0
Luxembourg	27.320	5.1	1.8	with Belgium	n.a.
Malta	6.559	6.1	1.5	–0.2	3.7
Netherlands	18.541	2.6	0.7	2.8	4.9
Norway	24.960	1.6	7.1	3.8	4.9
Poland	1.729*	–0.3*	1115.0	–2.1	4.5
Portugal	5.670	4.6	14.2	0.4	5.0
Romania	1.164	n.a.	n.a.	–12.0	9.0
Spain	12.476	4.9	7.4	–3.2	16.3
Sweden	26.356	2.1	7.0	–1.2	1.4
Switzerland	33.955	2.9	2.6	4.8	1.1
United Kingdom	16.926	3.0	6.7	–2.2	5.8
Yugoslavia	4.757	–1.3	445.0	2.1	15.9

Source: The Economist Pocket Europe, Century Business, London, 1992.

Notes: Gross Domestic Product (GDP), converted into US$ for ease of comparison, is used as the measure of total output unless otherwise indicated. In cases marked with an asterisk, the data is of Net Material Product (NMP) – this is the equivalent concept in Marxian social accounting, but ignores certain elements, particularly services, included in GDP. NMP is about 80–90 per cent of GDP, and may grow at a different rate from GDP. Growth rates are not available for Romania as it has changed from one system to the other.

GDP per head is a good indicator of output, but not necessarily of living standards, for which the cost of living in each country is relevant, and the country ranking of which is a little different from that for GDP per head.

The percentages quoted for the balance of payments are for the current account (i.e. excluding loans and borrowings). A positive figure means a surplus, a negative sign a deficit.

Differences in the way countries measure unemployment rates mean that the figures in the last column should be interpreted with some caution.

No data are available for Albania, Estonia, Latvia, Lithuania or Russia or for the countries formed from the former Czechoslovakia and Yugoslavia. Unless otherwise indicated, all data refer to 1990 or 1989.

Table 9.2 presents some basic data about European economic performance 1985 to 1990, when pressure for reform was mounting. Of the 26 countries in the table the bottom 6 in output per head in 1990 were (in descending order) Yugoslavia, Hungary, Czechoslovakia, Poland, Bulgaria and Romania.

Although the comparisons should be made with care because of definitional problems, Romanian output per head was under a 20th of that of Switzerland (the highest in Europe) and a little under a 10th of that of the UK (which was about the median value). In terms of growth, Bulgaria did well (growing faster, for example, than the FRG or the UK) but the other planned economies were doing badly, with falls in real output in Poland and Yugoslavia. Bulgaria's quite rapid growth owed much to its role as an economic satellite of the USSR, exporting agricultural produce and manufactures to the USSR (about two-thirds of its exports in 1989). As a result, however, it is confronted with even more acute restructuring problems in the 1990s than other former planned economies. Inflation was rampant in Poland and Yugoslavia, over 10 per cent in Hungary and Bulgaria, but quite low in Czechoslovakia. Romania had a current balance of payments deficit of 12 per cent of total output, but the other planned economies had less alarming deficits, or were even in surplus (in the case of Czechoslovakia and Yugoslavia). Although the planned economies were in general not performing very well, the data give only limited evidence of impending crisis. To understand the real problems, it is necessary to look behind the data.

One of the economies not included in Table 9.2 (because of the difficulties in obtaining agreed data) is the USSR. Some information for one year, 1988, is presented in Table 9.3. It highlights the strong diversity in economic structure and level of output per head within the USSR. Using official Soviet data for total net material product (which is analogous to the western measure of total output, but has certain exclusions, particularly of services) and making its own estimate for 1989, annual Soviet growth of income per head in 1981–85 and in 1986–89 can be estimated at 1.8 per cent and 2.2 per cent respectively. Total

Table 9.3. Republics of the USSR: economic data 1988

	Employment % of USSR total	Employment structure Agriculture %	Industry %	NMP % of USSR total	NMP per head % of USSR total
Armenia	1.1	13.8	32.2	1.0	87.3
Azerbaizhan	1.9	27.1	18.6	1.9	75.8
Belorussia	3.8	22.0	30.0	4.2	116.0
Estonia	0.6	13.7	31.0	0.7	121.7
Georgia	1.9	22.3	20.2	1.7	89.4
Kazakhstan	5.2	21.9	20.7	4.1	71.3
Kirgizia	1.1	28.3	20.3	0.8	56.2
Latvia	1.0	16.2	29.8	1.2	123.9
Lithuania	1.4	18.7	29.3	1.4	109.8
Moldavia	1.5	32.6	21.4	1.3	82.8
Russia	55.1	13.2	30.9	59.8	115.4
Tadzhikistan	1.1	32.0	15.8	0.8	44.5
Turkmenistan	0.9	35.4	11.2	0.8	67.5
Ukraine	18.7	20.6	30.8	16.8	92.4
Uzbekistan	4.6	32.0	16.8	3.5	50.3

Source. D. Cohen 'The Solvency of Eastern Europe', *European Economy* special edition number 2, 1991, Commission of the European Communities Directorate-General for Economic and Financial Affairs, Luxembourg.

Note: USSR total population was 286.7 million and employment 128.9 million.
The USSR average employment structure was 18.5 per cent in agriculture and 29.0 per cent in industry, and average Net Material Product (NMP) per head was 2197 rubles.

product grew by about 2 per cent per annum in 1983–88 but fell by 9 per cent in 1989–90; overall in the decade to 1990 it fell by about 3 per cent. More telling is the evidence of the use to which the extra output available in 1985–89 was put.

According to estimates by the Central Intelligence Agency (whose definition of consumption includes public services such as housing, health and education), the annual growth in consumption per head has steadily declined since 1951; from 4.2 per cent in the 1950s, 3.8 per cent in the 1960s, and 2.4 per cent in the 1970s to 1.6 per cent in the 1980s. If the estimated 9 per cent fall in output in 1989–90 is added, one can imagine the frustration of households' expectations of rapid growth in the quantity and quality of goods made available to them.

Three further factors compounded the problem. First, a government decision to accelerate output growth by increasing investment in capital equipment by about a third brought about a decline in the growth of consumption in the late 1980s. Investment could not be increased as rapidly as that, so construction periods lengthened and the balance of payments worsened, while there were no immediate fruits in the form of an increased supply of consumer goods. Second, the money supply (liquidity) was allowed to grow very fast, and at an increasing rate, throughout the 1980s. Inflation was rising, and was expected to continue to do so. Ellman identifies the consequences:

> Whereas an increase in the liquidity of a western economy leads mainly to increased prices for housing, land and stocks (i.e. shares), in the USSR in 1981–90 it led primarily to increased shortages of food products, longer queues at grocery stores, increased income for people in the trading apparatus who were able to divert scarce food on to the [black] market, and (ultimately) the introduction of rationing. ... Even at the end of the decade, when basic goods such as bread and vodka were scarce in state shops, an abundance of food was available in the free markets. (Ellman and Kontorovich 1992: pp. 109–10)

Third, all this took place against a background of rising expectations. Gorbachev's 1986–88 investment programme led to a popular belief that a rapid growth of consumer goods would follow. In his attempts to dismantle the state bureaucracy, he gave much more independence on economic decision-making to state enterprises, which promptly raised wages. Families had higher incomes, but there was steadily less for them to buy at the official prices, so they saved more; but the value of their savings was being eroded by inflation.

It seems, then, that central planning is just too rigid to adapt to the changing demands of a sophisticated economy. This arises from the lack of sufficient innovation and from their isolation from the international trading economy. So centrally planned economies suffer a gradual decline relative to free market economies.

The motivation for popular dissatisfaction in the 1980s with the economic performance of the USSR, and of the eastern and central European countries that had attempted reform, is thus plain. Table 9.4 offers a rather longer perspective by putting the growth performances for those European countries for which information is available into the context of the period 1955–85, divided at its mid-point 1970. It details growth of output and growth of population, identifying the broad significance of population change (including migration) for economic growth. As comparison with Tables 9.1 and 9.3 makes plain, most of the European economies experienced slower growth in the 15 years after 1970 than in the previous 15 years, as did the USA and Japan. This can partly be explained by special factors, such as the disturbance of the two major oil price rises in the mid-1970s and early 1980s and anti-inflationary policies pursued in the wake of these events. The major European economies appeared, however, to be less resilient than the USA. The period 1985–90 (Table 9.2) was relatively immune from major external disturbances, and so a better growth performance might have been expected.

Table 9.4. Long-term annual average growth trends in European countries, 1955–85

	Growth of output (GDP)		Growth of population	
	1955–70 %	1970–85 %	1955–70 %	1970–85 %
Austria	4.9	2.8	0.4	0.1
Belgium	4.1	2.3	0.6	0.1
Cyprus	5.0	4.2	0.1	0.1
Czechoslovakia	–	3.5	–	0.5
Denmark	4.6	2.4	0.7	0.2
Finland	4.7	3.3	0.6	0.4
France	5.5	2.7	1.0	0.6
West Germany	5.6	2.2	1.0	0.6
Greece	6.7	3.5	0.7	0.8
Hungary	–	3.8	–	0.2
Iceland	4.0	4.4	1.9	0.9
Ireland	3.2	3.9	0.1	1.2
Italy	5.8	2.9	0.7	0.4
Luxembourg	3.8	2.5	0.7	0.6
Malta	4.6	7.2	–0.3	0.8
Netherlands	4.8	2.2	1.3	0.7
Norway	4.2	2.2	0.8	0.4
Portugal	5.5	3.5	0.3	0.6
Spain	5.4	2.9	0.9	0.9
Sweden	4.1	1.9	0.7	0.3
Switzerland	4.6	1.4	1.5	0.3
United Kingdom	2.7	1.9	0.5	0.1
Yugoslavia	6.6	3.9	1.0	0.8
Japan	9.8	4.2	1.0	1.0
USA	3.3	2.7	1.4	1.0

Source: Calculated from *International Financial Statistics Yearbook*, 1982 and 1992, International Monetary Fund, Washington DC, 1982 and 1992

Notes: The data for Yugoslavia in the first two columns are for 1960–70. All data of gross domestic product (GDP) are calculated at constant (1975 or 1985) prices. No reliable data exist for output growth for Czechoslovakia and Hungary in the period 1955–70. Note that for some of the countries of central and eastern Europe the data are of material product or of social product, the growth of which is probably a little slower than that of GDP.

The rates of growth of income and population can be compared both to measure the change in real income per head (growth rate of GDP minus growth rate of population) and to give some indirect indication of how far the growth in income is attributable to the presence of a larger labour force (because of natural increase, or net immigration, or both).

The table must be used with caution to interpret the changing growth rates over time of individual countries or groups of countries, as no attempt has been made to correct the figures either for the stage of the trade cycle or for special shocks such as the two major oil price rises (which reduced growth for most countries in the table in 1970–85). The relative position of countries between the two periods does, however, give some indication of how far they became stronger or weaker in world terms over the whole period. Countries starting with low income levels can be expected to grow more quickly because of the extent to which they are 'catching up'.

As Table 9.4 shows, there was some marginal improvement in most European countries, but in most cases growth was still poor by the standards of the 1960s, despite increasing availability of labour, particularly as the proportion of women offering themselves for employment rose. Further, European growth looked mediocre in comparison with that of its major industrial competitors, Japan and the USA, which achieved growth of 4.2 per cent and 3.0 per cent respectively per annum throughout the 1980s.

For many of the central and eastern European economies, the political upheavals since 1989 were the culmination of a series of social and ethnic tensions that had affected their economic performance for much of the 1980s. Even in those with less acute tensions, such as Hungary, bloc trade inter-dependence produced difficulties, so weak growth or actual decline in 1985–90 is understandable. This poor performance involved a painful mix of low growth, rising unemployment, rising inflation, falling real wages and balance of payments problems. Many of these difficulties should, however, be relatively short-lived and transitional.

It is less easy to account for mediocre economic performance and high unemployment in western Europe, particularly when compared with Japan's past growth record. Just as the economic problems of the USSR had knock-on effects on its trading partners in central and eastern Europe, which in turn aggravated the difficulties of the USSR, the weakened growth of the West German economy led to a general slow-down in western Europe.

The effects of government policy are debatable, but the tendency to devise macroeconomic policy primarily to reduce inflation certainly meant eschewing measures which might have boosted output and employment growth in the short run. This anti-inflationary stance was led by West Germany and supported, with varying degrees of enthusiasm, by the other western European governments. As the next chapter shows, one of the features of the EU, as of any successful customs union, has been convergence of rates of inflation towards the lowest rate among the major member countries, and the convergence has in practice been towards the 0 per cent–3 per cent experienced by West Germany throughout the 1980s. How far the greater integration of the EU economies through the Single European Market and possible extensions of the EU by the addition of new members can reasonably be expected to stimulate growth in Europe is an issue of great importance.

Development in all economies means not just *more* goods and services but *different* goods and services. This is partly a matter of technical progress making more sophisticated goods available both to producers and consumers. For example, some production processes are being revolutionised by computer-aided design and manufacture. Computer technology is also having profound effects on household leisure gadgets. But economic growth is associated with two further major trends – increasing international specialisation and changing patterns of household consumption.

The basic rationale of international specialisation is explored in the next chapter, so the discussion here is limited to some of its consequences. Because it is relatively cheap for them to do so, transnational companies increasingly undertake their large-scale production processes in newly industrialising countries (NICs) such as Taiwan and Malaysia rather than in Europe. This has two major consequences for European economies. First, their workers lose job opportunities in relatively unskilled manufacturing activity, so to maintain employment levels the European countries have to adapt and retrain their labour force. Second, since they have to import increasing quantities of their manufactured goods, to avoid balance of payments problems they have to increase their exports of other goods and services – a further reason to change their pattern of production.

The influence of changes in consumption as incomes rise is even more profound. The Stone Age family will have had few goods, because the business of growing enough food to stay alive probably absorbed most of its labour. In modern European households, the pattern of consumption depends on income, but for most families a fairly small proportion of income is spent on food. In 1988, the median proportion of total personal expenditure per head which was spent on food and drink was about 25 per cent, with a range across all countries between 16 per cent (Netherlands) to 50 per cent (Yugoslavia). As incomes rise, households spend a lower proportion of their income on basic foodstuffs and more on consumer durables and services – for example,

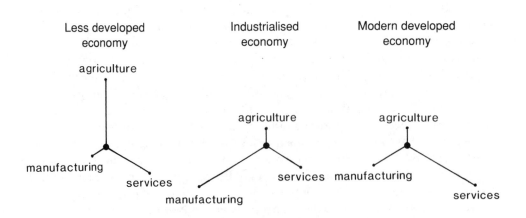

Figure 9.11. The structure of production and development

they eat less at home and more in restaurants, while if they eat at home increasingly their food is a commercially prepared frozen meal heated in the microwave.

The combined effect of these two influences is that as economies grow more prosperous their pattern of production changes, in a way stylised in Fig. 9.11. Initially, agriculture is the dominant product. When the economy undergoes its industrial revolution, manufactures and other industrial products become most important. The industrial revolution raises income and stimulates further growth. As income goes on rising, two results have been evident for the developed economies. First, as their workers are better paid they become uncompetitive in terms of wages with NICs. Second, as mentioned above, their increased prosperity means that demand changes towards services, many of which cannot be imported. As a result, the pattern of production changes again, so that services become the dominant sector.

Table 9.5 shows the current structure of production in European economies (see Table 9.3 for the USSR in 1988), and shows very clearly that in the western European economies services are dominant, accounting for 50–70 per cent of total output (and, if anything, a rather higher share of total jobs). The data for the central and eastern European economies can be compared with those for western Europe only with caution, but it is clear that the service sector is much less developed there. This is partly a natural consequence of their relatively low income levels, but the planning mechanisms for these countries tended artificially to curb the development of service activities, which can therefore be expected to expand rapidly in the 1990s.

There are, however, dangers in an excessive dependence on the service sector. Some economists fear that certain European economies – for example that of the UK – may be damaging their export prospects by allowing their manufacturing sector to decline too drastically. An economy specialising in producing services may have difficulty in exporting enough to pay for its imports. The combination in Spring 1994 of large balance of payments deficits with high unemployment in the UK is perhaps a sign of this. Usually, imports rise as income rises (because more goods, including imports, are being bought) and fall when income is relatively low; so low income and therefore high unemployment should be associated with balance of payments surpluses, not deficits. Moreover, it is questionable how quickly skilled labour displaced from manufacturing can retrain to find a comparable quality of work in services, so rapid restructuring can bring with it the social and economic cost of unemployment.

Tables 9.4 and 9.2 also highlight those economies in which agriculture is still particularly important. If employment shares are used as a rough criterion of importance, it emerges that agriculture accounted for over 10 per cent of all jobs in all countries of the eastern bloc and in Cyprus, Greece, Ireland, Portugal and Spain – so these are the economies for which actually or potentially the EU's controversial Common Agricultural Policy is most beneficial. They are also the economies which probably have most to gain

Table 9.5. Structure of production (employment) in European economies, 1989 or 1990

	Agriculture		Industry		Services	
Shares of GDP						
(Employment)						
Austria	3.7	(1.0)	38.3	(37.3)	58.0	(61.7)
Belgium	2.1	(2.7)	30.7	(28.2)	67.2	(69.1)
Cyprus	7.1	(14.6)	27.0	(29.6)	60.7	(55.7)
Denmark	4.3	(5.5)	28.1	(27.8)	67.6	(66.7)
Finland	7.2	(8.5)	35.0	(29.7)	57.8	(61.8)
France	3.7	(6.4)	31.1	(28.5)	65.2	(65.1)
Germany	1.6	(3.4)	39.0	(47.8)	59.4	(48.8)
Greece	17.0	(25.1)	27.2	(27.3)	55.8	(47.6)
Hungary	20.4	(20.5)	35.5	(38.0)	44.1	(41.5)
Iceland	3.9	(5.8)	44.0	(38.3)	52.1	(55.7)
Ireland	11.0	(14.7)	37.0	(28.8)	52.0	(56.5)
Italy	5.0	(9.3)	37.1	(32.2)	56.6	(58.6)
Luxembourg	1.9	(3.4)	32.3	(31.1)	58.0	(65.5)
Malta	3.9	(4.4)	40.5	(48.5)	55.7	(47.1)
Netherlands	4.7	(1.5)	33.3	(27.5)	61.9	(71.1)
Norway	2.6	(6.4)	31.6	(24.9)	65.8	(68.7)
Portugal	6.2	(19.0)	38.0	(35.0)	55.7	(46.0)
Spain	5.2	(11.8)	37.7	(33.4)	57.1	(54.8)
Sweden	4.5	(3.6)	42.1	(29.5)	53.4	(67.0)
Switzerland	3.5	(5.1)	34.5	(34.2)	62.0	(60.7)
United Kingdom	1.5	(1.2)	35.5	(29.0)	62.9	(69.8)
Yugoslavia	15.8	(4.7)	51.4	(48.6)	33.0	(46.6)
Shares of NMP						
(Employment)						
Albania	n.a.	(50.5)	n.a.	(23.8)	n.a.	(18.5)
Bulgaria	11.2	(18.6)	68.7	(46.0)	20.1	(35.4)
Czechoslovakia	10.3	(12.1)	68.7	(46.1)	21.0	(41.8)
East Germany	n.a.	(10.8)	n.a.	(47.1)	n.a.	(39.6)
Poland	13.0	(9.1)	60.0	(45.1)	27.0	(45.8)
Romania	15.2	(31.5)	66.4	(51.3)	18.4	(17.2)

Source: The Economist Pocket Europe 1992, Century Business, London.
Figures for East Germany from Welfens (1992)
Notes: Net Material Product (NMP) excludes certain services included in Gross Domestic
Product (GDP). NMP is some 80–90% of GDP, most of the differences being in services.
This must be borne in mind in any comparison of data between Bulgaria, Czechoslovakia,
Poland, Romania and all the other countries in this table.
    Data are not available for Estonia, Latvia, Lithuania and Russia, nor for the separate
components of the former Czechoslovakia and Yugoslavia.

from restructuring to modernise their farming methods and to redeploy labour to industrial or service activities.

Further reading

Ellman, M. and Kontorovich, V. (1992) (eds) *The Disintegration of the Soviet Economic System*, Routledge, London.

Ferguson, P. R. (1988) *Industrial Economics: Issues and Perspectives*, Macmillan, Basingstoke.

Lange, P. and Regini, M. (eds) (1989) *State, Market, and Social Regulation: New Perspectives on Italy*, Cambridge University Press, Cambridge.

Meade, J. E. (1970) *The Theory of Indicative Planning*, Manchester University Press, Manchester.

Nove, A. and Nuti, D. M. (eds) (1972) *Socialist Economics: Selected Readings*, Penguin, Harmondsworth.

Smith, A. H. (1992) 'Integration under Communism and economic relations after Communism in eastern Europe' in Dyker, D. (ed) *The European Economy*, Longman, London.

Szarka, J. (1992) *Business in France: an Introduction to the Economic and Social Context*, Pitman, London.

Welfens, P. J. (ed.) (1992) *Economic Aspects of German Unification*, Springer-Verlag, Berlin.

10 Team trials: the problems of trading and trading blocs

Introduction

One of the most striking features of modern Europe is its organisation into groups of countries to achieve economic and political goals. Some of the present groupings are of very long standing, for example, Benelux, which dates back to 1948. One of the most important trading blocs, the Council for Mutual Economic Assistance (Comecon) dating from 1949 and active from the mid 1950s, was dissolved in 1991. As documented in Chapters 3 and 4, the biggest bloc, the European Union (EU), lurched in the early 1990s through a series of fundamental debates about its future, but now seems likely eventually to embrace all the countries of Europe. At the same time some European countries are breaking apart to form separate countries, which must make decisions about their economic relationships with the rest of the world.

This chapter examines why countries group together for economic reasons, the tensions generated by the process, and the main implications of trading blocs for non-members. To make these matters clearer, the chapter starts with a brief discussion of the economic relationships between countries.

Why countries trade

Chapter 9 examined the production possibility curve representing the combinations of goods that a Stone Age family could produce, and found that its position depended on the technology available to the family and on the resources it could command. Even in Stone Age society the mix of resources available would differ from one family to another – for example, one family might be living on flat land good for growing corn, whereas another might be living fairly high up a mountain whose rock is ideal for making axes. In these circumstances, it would obviously make sense for the family on the flat land to bake more bread than it needs and exchange some of its surplus bread for axes, while the family on the higher ground makes more axes than it needs and exchanges its surplus axes for bread. This is the principle of the division of labour where each family makes the products for which its resources are best suited and surpluses are exchanged. When one considers not Stone Age families but modern countries, there will usually be quite big differences between countries in the kind of resources available, and these differences are the basic reason why trade is mutually advantageous.

This can be illustrated by the example of Tayside in Scotland and Bordeaux in France. The climate and the soil conditions in Tayside are such that the only way to grow grapes is to do so in a greenhouse, but raspberries grow very well in the fields. In Bordeaux, raspberries grow quite well, but grapes flourish in the vineyards and hence wine can readily be produced. The options for each region are illustrated in a stylised way in Fig. 10.1, where on diagram (a)

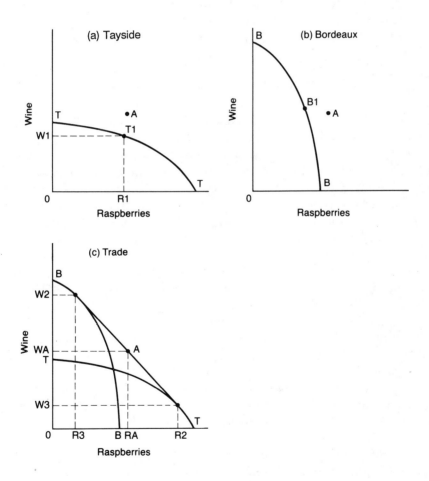

Figure 10.1. Production possibility curves for (a) Tayside, (b) Bordeaux and (c) both regions

TT represents the production possibility curve for Tayside and on diagram (b) BB represents that for Bordeaux.

If there were no trade between Tayside and Bordeaux, each region would at most be able to choose some combination of raspberries and wine on its curve, like for Tayside point T1 (with R1 raspberries and W1 wine) and for Bordeaux point B1. However, both regions can probably do better for themselves if they trade. In diagram (c) in Fig. 10.1, the curves TT and BB are repeated from diagrams (a) and (b). Suppose, to simplify the analysis, consumers in both regions would like the combination of wine and raspberries represented by point A, where each region would have RA raspberries and WA wine. This point is not available to either region without trade, because it lies outside the range of possible combinations on both TT and BB, but point A can be reached by trade.

A can be reached if Tayside grows R2 and Bordeaux R3 raspberries, Bordeaux makes W2 and Tayside W3 wine, and Tayside sells to Bordeaux RA-R2 raspberries in exchange for WA-W2 wine. As common sense would suggest, Tayside grows more raspberries – the product in which it has an advantage over Bordeaux – than it wants to consume and exports the surplus to Bordeaux. At the same time, Bordeaux makes more wine that it wants to consume, and exports the surplus to Tayside for raspberries.

Although Fig. 10.1 portrays a very simplified analysis, its results generalise into the real world of many products and many countries. Where countries differ from each other in the mixes in their basic factor-endowments, trade can always make available combinations of goods that are otherwise unattainable. If these new combinations are what the citizens of participating countries want, trade will be mutually beneficial by making more goods available to everybody. This can happen because trade lets each country specialise in making the products at which its resources give it a relative advantage: like the Stone Age households, countries adopt the principle of division of labour.

Once the division of labour has occurred, its advantages may be compounded by economies of scale, which occur if the average cost of production declines as output grows. Economies of scale do not exist for all products (indeed in some cases average costs may actually rise as output grows), but they are a common phenomenon and hence frequently add to the benefits available from trade.

In advanced modern economies trade can take sophisticated forms, including that of intra-industry trade in which the same product in variant forms is both imported and exported. Most western European countries both import and export cars, exporting those they produce themselves (perhaps under licence arrangements from another European country or Japan) and importing different models. Intra-industry trade seems paradoxical; if France is relatively good at producing Renault cars, why is it not also relatively good at producing Audi cars? It is, however, readily explicable by a mixture of accidents of history (which determine where goods were made in the first instance), economies of scale (which perpetuate the accident of initial location), and the extent to which the citizens of prosperous countries demand a wide range of goods (so that some Germans want Audis and some want Renaults).

Financing trade

The previous chapter illustrated the complexities of conducting trade on a barter basis. To overcome these problems, international trade usually entails financial transactions rather than direct swaps of goods. The financial arrangements for international trade are one step more complicated than those for the purchase of goods and services in any one country. Consider, for example, a group of Tayside farmers selling raspberries. They will want payment in pounds sterling. Households in Bordeaux buying the raspberries will want to pay in francs. So the farmers (or an agent acting for them) must convert the francs into sterling. Each time an item is sold from one country to a country with a different currency, there is a foreign exchange transaction as well as the transaction of selling the good or service. If the foreign exchange rate is determined by the operation of market forces, the price of any currency in terms of any other depends on the interaction of supply and demand like any other price.

Figure 10.2 illustrates the effect on the exchange rate between sterling and francs of the sale by the Tayside raspberry farmers to Bordeaux. The vertical axis in Fig. 10.2(a) shows the price of francs in terms of pounds sterling, and the horizontal axis the quantity of francs, with supply and demand intersecting at the exchange rate £0.1 (1 franc = £0.1 or 10p, 10 francs = £1). A rise in the exchange rate from, say, £0.1 to £0.2 represents an appreciation (i.e. a rise) in the value of the franc (1 franc = £0.2 or 20p, 5 francs = £1). The supply curve represents the transactions of people who currently want to sell francs and buy sterling, that is, UK exporters to France like the Tayside farmers. The more francs are worth, and therefore the less sterling is worth, the more attractive it is to convert francs into sterling now rather than wait, so the supply curve slopes up from left to right. It is, however, quite steep – most UK exporters will want to convert their francs into sterling more or less regardless of the exchange rate. The demand curve represents the transactions of people who currently want to sell sterling and buy francs, that is, French exporters to the UK, like the Bordeaux wine makers. It slopes down steeply from left to right because if sterling is worth relatively few francs, some people holding sterling are likely to postpone converting it into francs in the hope of being able to do so at a more favourable rate later.

Now, the raspberry farmers make their sale to France and want to convert francs into sterling. Fig. 10.2(b) illustrates the result. Their sale of raspberries results in an increase in the number of people supplying francs, so the supply curve shifts from S to S1. As a result, the price of francs falls, to, say, £0.09 (11 francs = £1) – the franc has depreciated (i.e. fallen in value) against sterling because of the import to France of British goods. The converse effect if France exports more to the UK is seen by looking at Fig. 10.2(c), which illustrates what will happen if the Bordeaux wine merchants sell more wine to Tayside. They will have received payment in sterling, and wish to convert it to francs, so they represent an addition to the people who are supplying sterling and demanding francs, and so the demand curve shifts from D to D1, with the price of francs accordingly rising to, say, £0.11 (9 francs = £1) – the franc has appreciated against sterling.

In reality many exchange transactions are taking place in any one day, and the value of transactions from francs into sterling is normally nearly equal in any day to the value of transactions from sterling into francs. The difference

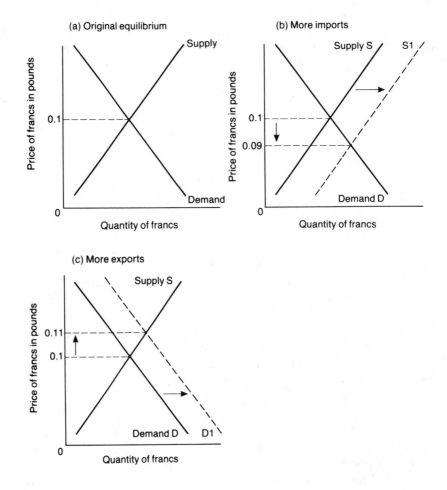

Figure 10.2 The exchange rate between francs and pounds (a) in equilibrium, (b) after an increase in imports to France, and (c) after an increase in exports from France

between the two flows is what causes the exchange rate to alter, so normally there is very little movement from day to day in the exchange rate. Where dramatic changes do take place, as for sterling on 'Black Wednesday' in September 1992, it is because the small changes resulting from trading flows are swamped by speculative transactions. To understand speculation in currency markets, it is important to consider what activities (besides trade) produce foreign exchange transactions.

Besides importing and exporting goods, firms and households can also import and export factor services. For example Irish labourers might work for a French company on constructing the Channel Tunnel. Such services form an export from Ireland to France – instead of providing goods to France, Ireland is providing labour. The Irish workers will be paid in francs, and will want to convert some of it to Irish punts, perhaps to send money home while they are working in France and to take their savings home at the end of the contract. Imports and exports of labour are, however, small in volume in comparison with the international flow of financial capital. When a British company issues shares, some of the shares may well be bought by people in other countries – such as Spain. The initial transaction – the purchase of the share – is an 'export' from Britain to Spain, and money has to be converted from pesetas to sterling to pay for the share. When dividends are paid on the share, the flow is the other way (an 'export' from Spain to Britain because the dividend is payment for a factor service provided by Spanish finance) with sterling being converted to pesetas.

Some of the financial flows are very volatile, because they represent surplus cash which is being lent out for short periods (often a matter of days) to whoever gives the highest return. The return on money is the rate of interest, so to attract financial flows a country should offer a rate of interest a little higher than that prevailing elsewhere. However, this may not be enough, because international currency lending also raises the question of what is happening to the exchange rate.

Suppose a Spanish household has some spare cash, the best interest rate available to it in Spain is 10 per cent per annum and it therefore decides to lend it to the British government for a year. It does so by buying some savings certificates, which offer interest of 15 per cent per annum – for each £100 the household lends, it will get £115 in a year's time. Provided the rate of exchange between the peseta and sterling is constant, the family will obtain a return of 15 per cent in terms of pesetas (pta). If, however, the exchange rate alters, it will do better or worse than this. Suppose that when it made the loan £100 was worth 20,000 pta. If, when the loan matures, sterling has depreciated against the peseta, so that £100 is worth only 15,000 pta, the £115 will give the family only 17,250 pta, a loss of 14 per cent on the investment. But if sterling has risen to a rate of 25,000 pta to £100, the £115 gives the family 28,750 pta, a return of 44 per cent.

To simplify the arithmetic of the illustration, 25 per cent appreciation/devaluation is assumed, which is quite a high figure even over a year, but it is not unrealistic for currency movements to swamp interest differentials. To see why, it must be remembered that the really volatile financial flows are lent for periods of days, not years, so the interest they attract is normally measured in fractions of a percent, and can easily be outweighed by quite small changes in the exchange rate. That is why, in currency crises when a country is trying to stave off a devaluation, it is not uncommon for interest to have to be offered for one-day loans at 100 per cent or more, because 100 per cent per annum is under a third of a percent per day, not much return if the currency is expected to depreciate tomorrow.

Exchange markets exist, then, to facilitate trade both of products and of factors. Because of the extra risks (of unfavourable exchange rate movements) implied by foreign trade, various arrangements have been developed to insure traders against the risk. If the raspberry farmers are worried that the pound might depreciate against the French franc before they are paid, they can obtain protection against that risk by operating in a futures market: they commit themselves today to buying sterling for francs which they promise to deliver in, say, three months' time. Then, when the farmers are paid in francs for the raspberries, they use the francs to pay for the sterling they have agreed to buy. Thus the farmers know now how much sterling they will get for the francs they have not yet received, whatever the exchange rate becomes. Of course, the farmers have to pay for avoiding the risk of devaluation, because the extra transaction will involve extra brokerage fees and the future price they are quoted may be unattractive, but if the currencies are volatile the protection may be thought to be worth the payment.

Futures markets were thus created to facilitate trade, but once they exist their nature changes; agents buy and sell foreign currency as a commodity in its own right and not because of trade flows. Such agents are speculators, who make their living by anticipating movements of the exchange rate. For example, a speculator who thinks that sterling will depreciate against the franc will buy francs for sterling now, and then sell the francs for what he or she expects will be more sterling in the future. Thanks to the existence of futures markets, speculators do not have to pay for the francs now, and thus can operate in terms of a set of contracts to buy and sell large amounts of currency which they do not in fact have, because all that will have to be paid for is any net loss on the contracts. Speculators can have a powerfully destabilising effect in the short run on currency markets, whenever they share opinions which (because they are shared) become self-fulfilling.

If most speculators expect sterling to depreciate against the franc, they sell it and buy francs. As they do this, the price of sterling in terms of francs falls – that is, the 'market sentiment' has produced exactly the outcome the speculators expected. Such speculative activities have been important, as will be seen later, in the recent history of monetary union in Europe. However, market sentiment is unlikely to hold strongly to some opinion without having some underlying basis in the economic or political realities, so most of the time speculation simply hastens the inevitable.

Volatility in exchange markets is not welcome to those trying to trade products or factor services, because of the uncertainty it causes for them. Nor is it welcome to governments, who are jumpy both about the country's trade and about its international capital markets. They also attach prestige to the strength of the currency. For these reasons, it is not uncommon for countries to intervene in the operation of currency markets.

This intervention can take many forms. It can be short-term action in particular circumstances to nudge the exchange rate in the desired direction (usually the government or the central bank using foreign exchange reserves to buy the country's own currency to push the exchange rate up). It can involve bilateral or multilateral international agreement to fix exchange rates at some particular level and to use appropriate instruments to ensure that the level does not change. It can be an attempt to control the market directly, by imposing exchange controls such as preventing citizens and visitors from taking more than a minimal amount of currency out of the country; in this way clamping down on free-market transactions (and even possibly reducing the conduct of foreign trade to barter terms again). Until the end of the 1980s nearly all the former Soviet bloc's internal trade, and a high proportion of its external trade, was based on swapping commodities; the Soviet ruble, Polish zloty, and so on were either not convertible at all to other currencies or were convertible only at official rates that bore very little relationship to reality.

Currency inconvertibility leads to all the complications of barter trade. If currency is convertible, but only at rates which do not reflect market forces, there is the potential problem of excess supply or excess demand discussed in Chapter 9; and for currencies, as well as for goods, black markets can emerge as a result. This can be illustrated by considering the official, black market and free market exchange rate between the Soviet ruble and the US dollar in the period 1990–93 as in Table 10.1.

Table 10.1. Ruble/Dollar exchange rates, 1990–93

Ruble/Dollar exchange rate	31/12/90	31/12/91	31/12/92	31/12/93
Official rate	0.55:1	1.8:1	415:1	1,250:1
Commercial rate	1.8:1	1.8:1*	–	–
Tourist rate	5.5:1	18:1	–	–
Free market rate	10–18:1	170:1	–	–
Black market rate	20–40:1	170:1	–	–

*5.4:1 for centralised imports from 10/2/92

The table shows that in 1990 there were five exchange rates, all different from each other. The official rate valued the ruble highest (at 0.55 rubles to one US $) and the black market rate valued it lowest (and the $ highest), at 20–40 rubles to the dollar. By the end of 1991 the official and commercial rates were the same, but there was still a huge gap between these rates and the free market/black market rate. Because the free market was operating so as to find equilibrium, although the black market still nominally existed it was in fact offering the same rate as the free market. By the end of 1992, the artificial setting of official, commercial and tourist rates had ended, so there was only one rate. The other conclusion to be drawn from the table is the rapid devaluation of the ruble – from (using the black market rate) about 30 rubles to the dollar at the end of 1990 to 1,250 rubles to the dollar at the end of 1993 and over 2,000 on 6 July 1994. The acting finance minister Sergei Dubinin then forecast a fall to 3,000–3,500 by the end of the year, stating that this was necessary in order to boost exports. The State Duma had two weeks earlier voted to raise the minimum monthly wage from 14,260 rubles to 20,500 (US$10), the first increase since December. (It had been 70 rubles in 1990.) The average wage in April was 175,000 rubles. The ruble touched 4,339 to the dollar on 20/2/95.

Free trade and restrictions on trade

The advantages of specialisation are considerable, but they cannot be realised unless trade occurs. There is thus a very powerful case for permitting trade to take place without hindrance. Yet the history of any European country gives numerous examples of devices adopted to prevent free trade. This section briefly considers why countries can perceive trade as threatening their national interest.

The literature on international trade gives long lists of rationales for intervening in trade flows, but they all fall under one or other of three policy headings – strategic and social, industrial, and macroeconomic. Strategic and social policy reasons lead quite commonly to the prevention of free trade in certain materials or ideas: for example, those which are regarded as important to national defence (e.g. embargoes during the Cold War on the export from western Europe to the USSR of products incorporating advanced computer technology), or those which are seen as socially undesirable (such as restraints on the import of pornographic films).

For reasons of industrial policy, countries frequently seek to protect their home producers from competition. This may be from what they regard as 'unfair' competition (e.g. dumping, where surplus stocks of a product are sold abroad at less than the cost of production). Also common, but less so in Europe than in some other parts of the world, is the protection of infant industries, where a country prevents or limits imports of products which it is starting to make for itself but not yet in sufficient quantity to develop economies of scale.

But in modern Europe most of the restraints on trade have been for reasons of macroeconomic policy. There are two different ways in which a country's trading balance affects its macroeconomic position. The more direct impact is the immediate effect on total output. When a country exports goods and services (including factor services), the total demand for its products exceeds that represented by the home market, so exports cause the country's output to rise. Conversely, when households or firms buy imported goods and services not only is there no stimulus to the country's output but some of the country's demand for goods and services has leaked abroad, so its output is less than if the imports had not occurred. Therefore, the difference between the total of exports and the total of imports – the balance of payments – is one of the determinants of total output in the country. If the balance of payments is in surplus, exports are greater than imports, and output is boosted. If the balance of payments is in deficit, the country is losing more sales to other countries than it is gaining in export orders, and so output is reduced. So if a government wishes to boost output, perhaps because the economy is in recession, one attractive route is to reduce imports and try to stimulate exports.

Trading may have a less direct effect on the macroeconomic position by way of the exchange rate. As discussed earlier, the balance of payments affects the exchange rate, causing it to depreciate if imports are greater than exports (balance of payments deficit) and to appreciate if there is a balance of payments surplus. Exchange rate movements help to solve the original problem. (Depreciation, for example, makes exports more competitive and imports dearer, and so helps to reduce the original balance of payments deficit.) But exchange rate fluctuations bring with them their own macroeconomic problems because the volatility of international financial flows tends to magnify the effects. Hence governments have an added reason to try to reduce imbalance, either way, between imports and exports.

Practical action in restraint of trade can take many forms. It can be an outright ban on the export or import of goods or services administered through the legal system. There are, for example, legal penalties imposed on people found guilty of importing certain addictive drugs to the UK, and in recent years British firms violating trade embargoes to Iraq or to Serbia have been liable to prosecution. At the other extreme, bureaucratic devices can reduce trade to a trickle, even with no official restrictions at all – as when France curbed the import of Japanese video-recorders (to protect its own infant industry) by processing the documentation and inspection of all such imports through a small customs post in Poitiers. Sometimes also – but only in exceptional circumstances – producers who feel threatened by imports may take the law into their own hands and physically prevent imports. For example, both British and French fishermen have blockaded fishing ports. The more common forms of restraint on trade are, however, operated through governments and are 'voluntary' agreements, quotas, tariffs and non-tariff barriers.

'Voluntary' export restraint agreements are bilateral arrangements between exporting and importing countries; in recent practice, they have usually been between Japan or South Korea as exporter and the USA or European countries as importer, and have taken the form of such agreements as limiting the number of Japanese cars imported in any year to a particular country to some prescribed level. There are major problems in agreeing and unambiguously defining such arrangements. For example, when Nissan cars are manufactured in Britain, does France regard these as British or Japanese? Quotas, similarly, identify a maximum number of items of any particular product that may be imported to a certain country in a particular year, but usually apply on the same basis to all potential exporting countries.

Tariffs are special taxes levied on imports. Their main intent is to make imports more expensive and hence to make home produced goods appear more competitive in the domestic market. Tariffs do, however, have an incidental effect of increasing the government's tax revenue, which makes them more politically attractive. The so-called 'non-tariff barriers to trade' are much more subtle, and take the form of requirements imposed (at least apparently) for reasons quite different from trade protection – for example, the 1992 German requirement that all packaging must be recyclable – but which discriminate in favour of home producers because there may be an extra expense to exporting countries of meeting the standards. As mentioned in Chapter 4, the demolition of many non-tariff barriers within the EU is the object of the Single European Act.

Although theoretically there are many measures countries can take to protect their home markets from foreign competition, their freedom of manoeuvre is usually fairly limited. In the short term, the most powerful force is probably the fear of retaliation. If a country feels it is being treated unfairly in one of its export markets it may itself threaten to discriminate against the 'offending' country. For example, in 1992 the USA announced that it would impose tariffs on EC agricultural exports such as French wine in retaliation against what it regarded as unfair levels of subsidy to EC farmers. A sequence of such retaliations in a trade war could in theory reduce each country to its own production possibilities and make points like A in Fig. 10.1 unattainable.

However, the recognition of the advantages of free trade has sometimes caused countries voluntarily to forgo means of restraining trade flows by entering into agreements to reduce barriers to trade. The Cecchini Report of 1988 estimated (perhaps optimistically) the substantial gains to the income of EC countries which it expected from the demolition of barriers to trade among them consequent upon the Single European Act. The geographically most wide-ranging international compact on the reduction of trade barriers is the General Agreement on Tariffs and Trade (GATT) which, since its establishment in 1947, has bound its signatories not to increase existing barriers to trade and periodically to negotiate agreement to reduction of barriers. The reductions take place after complex and protracted 'rounds' of discussion named after the initiator or the place in which discussion started. The 'Uruguay round', which started in 1986 and went on till 1994, proved particularly difficult because it addressed problems of agricultural subsidies; it involved head-on clashes between the USA and EC, both of which subsidise farmers but in different ways. In addition to membership of GATT, European countries have chosen to enter into much closer trading relationships with each other in various forms of groupings.

Forms of trading groupings

The possible forms of trading groupings can be regarded as lying along a spectrum in which (in order from the loosest to the tightest relationship) there are: free trade areas, customs unions, common markets, monetary unions, and economic unions. Although the boundaries between the different types are sometimes a little unclear, they can be distinguished sharply in principle. In a free trade area, member countries abandon internal barriers to trade. A customs union is a free trade area with common external barriers. A common market is a customs union with freedom of movement for factors of production. A monetary union is a common market with what is *de facto* a common currency. An economic union is a rather more nebulous concept, but is probably a monetary union with common fiscal and other macroeconomic policy. The further countries proceed along the spectrum, the more they are ceding to whatever organisation controls the grouping powers which are theoretically part of their national sovereignty. Whether in practice they would have been free to exercise those powers is, however, another matter.

Countries entering into such arrangements agree to act in some spirit of commonality of interest which will tend to have political as well as economic implications. Unless the structure is a free trade area, this commonality also applies to policy towards non-members. This can make problems for new members of a customs union, who have a set of pre-existing special arrangements which are inconsistent with those of the union. Such difficulties were, for example, evident for France, the UK and, to a lesser extent, Italy and the Netherlands, for all of whom membership of the EC cut across previous trading relationships with countries formerly in their empires. Whilst compromises may be found, as in the Lomé Conventions whereby the EU preserves special relationships with some of the less developed former colonies, the difficulty highlights the extent to which trading groups are second best to free trade and distort trade to the ultimate disadvantage of some producers and most consumers.

As compared with free trade, they systematically disadvantage producers in low-cost non-member countries. However, to assess their effects in reality, their outcome must be compared not with a hypothetical free trade position but with what is likely otherwise to have occurred – which is determined, among other things, by the different positions from which their members started. This question has been examined in several ways with respect to the EU, and all the studies have concluded that on balance not only EU members but all countries have gained from its creation (although they differ in their estimates of the magnitudes).

However, even within the EU the benefits are spread unevenly; the member countries on its periphery show little capacity to catch up even in growth rates with its core countries. Non-members, likewise, are affected in different ways and to different extents. This chapter will look shortly at some evidence about the trade flows in the EU, and note that the shares of the EU countries' trade with developing countries have fallen markedly since the EC was formed. The tables that will be considered are too aggregative to show fine detail, but it is clear that some of the developing countries not protected by the Lomé Convention, and some developed British Commonwealth countries, have lost export markets to EU countries. The overall effect on the trade flows affecting different countries of a customs union or free trade area cannot be adequately assessed. It is difficult to separate out from the complex of factors determining international transactions the influences of regional integration.

Europe contains an interesting range of trading groupings. The Nordic Council, founded in 1953, contains some element of cooperation on economic matters between its members but on a fairly *ad hoc* basis. A similar function has been performed since 1947 for what is now all the European countries, plus Canada and the USA, by the Economic Commission for Europe. By contrast the European Free Trade Area (EFTA), established in 1960, to some extent as a counter-weight to the EC, performs for manufactures and some agricultural products exactly the functions its title implies. Most of its members are in the process of being considered for membership of the EU, and EFTA and the EC have agreed to form a European Economic Area as an interim measure.

Comecon (now defunct) covered the eastern bloc and functioned partly as a customs union and partly, reflecting USSR dominance, as a kind of economic union. Its planning sought to enable each member to enjoy economic growth by specialising in the products in which (relative to the other members of Comecon but not necessarily in world terms) it had most advantage. This policy left some its former members specialising in products in which they were not efficient in world terms, as discussed in the last chapter with regard to Bulgaria.

The EU is a common market, with ambitions to become a monetary and possibly also an economic union. Unified Germany is a very interesting case of a full economic and monetary union created almost overnight from very limited prior cooperation.

Table 10.2. Percentage share of European areas in EFTA countries' total trade, 1964 and 1990

Imports

Country	EFTA		EC		European planned economies	
	1964	1990	1964	1990	1964	1990
Austria	14.6	7.1	58.8	68.6	10.6	6.8
Denmark	35.8	–	35.4	–	3.9	–
Finland	32.1	19.4	29.7	46.2	20.9	11.7
Iceland	–	16.3	–	49.9	–	6.7
Norway	41.1	21.5	28.9	46.6	3.4	2.6
Portugal	21.6	–	33.1	–	1.3	
Sweden	31.9	18.2	37.4	55.2	4.1	3.0
Switzerland	15.0	7.2	62.0	71.7	2.0	1.2
UK	13.4	–	16.6	–	3.4	–
EFTA members	20.6	13.0	30.1	61.0	4.6	4.3

Exports

Country	EFTA		EC		European planned economies	
	1964	1990	1964	1990	1964	1990
Austria	19.1	10.1	47.5	65.2	14.9	10.4
Denmark	47.0	–	28.0	–	4.1	–
Finland	34.2	19.9	30.6	45.6	17.1	13.7
Iceland	–	8.6	–	67.8	–	3.0
Norway	44.8	15.7	26.2	64.9	4.5	1.3
Portugal	25.7	–	20.6	–	1.3	–
Sweden	41.4	19.0	31.6	54.2	4.6	2.3
Switzerland	19.5	6.6	40.5	58.1	2.4	3.2
UK	14.4	–	20.6	–	2.4	–
EFTA members	24.6	13.4	27.2	58.0	4.4	5.3

Note: the EFTA totals are for those countries that were members in the year in question. The percentage shares for Denmark, Portugal and the UK are presented on a consistent basis in Table 10.3.

Source: EFTA Trade 1964 and EFTA Trade 1990 Economic Affairs Department, European Free Trade Association, Geneva

Table 10.3. Percentage shares of trade of central and eastern European planned economies

Imports from:	Rest of group	Other developed countries	Asian planned economies	Other developing countries
All countries				
1975	54.05	33.97	1.39	10.60
1988	63.60	22.37	3.22	10.81
USSR				
1975	44.30	38.35	1.52	15.83
1988	51.52	29.13	4.44	14.91
Other countries				
1975	61.34	30.69	1.29	6.68
1988	72.91	17.17	2.28	7.64

Exports to:	Rest of group	Other developed countries	Asian planned economies	Other developing countries
All countries				
1975	57.36	26.29	2.54	13.19
1988	56.63	21.85	4.38	16.66
USSR				
1975	49.38	28.77	3.30	18.51
1988	48.87	21.85	6.84	22.33
Other countries				
1975	63.40	24.42	1.96	9.17
1988	64.77	21.85	1.81	10.72

Source: World Economic Survey 1991, Department of International Economic and Social Affairs, United Nations, New York, 1991

Tables 10.2, 10.3 and 10.4 present some basic information about the pattern of trade of EFTA, the central and eastern European members of Comecon and EC/EU countries with other members of their blocs and with third parties. Table 10.2 considers EFTA as it was constituted in 1964 and 1990 and identifies the trade of each member with other EFTA members, with the EC and with central and eastern Europe. As former members such as Denmark, Portugal and the UK left EFTA and joined the EC one would expect to see the EC share of EFTA countries' trade rise over the period, and the table clearly shows the extent to which trade with EC countries has grown to dominate the EFTA countries' trade even more than expected, although trade with the former planned economies of Europe remained important for Austria and Finland up to 1991.

In terms of trading patterns, the evidence of Table 10.3 is that Comecon was more successful than EFTA; starting from high initial levels intra-group trade grew in importance between 1975 and 1988, as did trade with the Asian planned economies, albeit always at low absolute levels. The division in the table between the USSR and the other European Comecon countries shows that the USSR was markedly less dependent on trade within the group than were its other members.

Table 10.4 disaggregates EC countries' trade in 1958 and 1991 into trade within the bloc, trade with the EFTA countries, and trade with developing countries. The data here are corrected for changes in EC membership. The apparent anomalies about Irish trade arise from the heavy (but declining) dependence of the Irish economy on trade with the UK. Otherwise the table shows a clear pattern (except for Denmark, whose Nordic Council partners are in EFTA, not the EU) of growing shares of intra-EU trade, relative stability of the shares of trade with EFTA, and declining trade with the rest of the world. The focus of the EU countries has been on trade with each other and, to a lesser extent, with other European partners. The focus of EFTA members has been increasingly on trade with the EU. Comecon, except for the USSR, became increasingly reliant on internal trade, but how far this would have been true if trade flows had been less strongly dependent on planning decisions (coupled with acute shortages of hard currency) is impossible to assess.

The contrast between the EU on the one hand and Comecon and EFTA on the other is striking. The economic difficulties of the planned economies and the disintegration of the USSR discussed in Chapters 8 and 9 are perhaps all that is needed to explain the collapse of Comecon and its members' applications for admission to the EU. But why is EFTA steadily losing members to the EU? This seems particularly puzzling in the light of the travails of the EU over monetary union. The answer must lie in the extent to which the EU dominates European trade.

When the exporters of non-member countries become more and more reliant on EU markets, so membership of the EU becomes more and more attractive to them. If their countries were in the EU they would be free from any barriers the EU applies to imports from their country. They would enjoy the benefits that EC industrial or agricultural policy confers on their competitors in member countries, and, if the EU were to become a monetary union, they would not have to worry about exchange rate movements because there would be none. The disadvantages to them of EU membership might be

Table 10.4. Percentage shares of selected areas in trade of EC countries, 1958 and 1991

Imports from:	EC		EFTA		Developing countries	
	1958	1991	1958	1991	1958	1991
Belgium/Lux	55.5	70.5	7.7	5.8	13.5	7.0
Denmark	60.0	54.2	18.6	23.6	5.6	7.1
France	28.3	64.2	6.7	7.3	25.9	8.3
W Germany	36.3	54.5	15.2	14.9	17.2	8.5
Greece	53.7	60.3	11.5	7.6	7.9	7.5
Ireland	68.9	69.1	3.4	3.8	8.6	3.8
Italy	30.2	57.7	13.1	10.9	15.5	7.9
Netherlands	50.7	59.0	7.2	6.8	12.9	9.5
Portugal	53.4	71.9	8.6	6.3	21.3	8.3
Spain	31.8	59.8	8.4	6.0	14.3	11.3
UK	21.8	50.1	8.7	11.8	23.4	10.1
EC average	35.2	58.6	10.1	10.4	18.7	8.6

Exports to:	EC		EFTA		Developing countries	
	1958	1991	1958	1991	1958	1991
Belgium/Lux	55.4	75.2	8.7	6.4	18.0	10.0
Denmark	59.3	54.1	16.6	23.8	9.3	9.0
France	30.9	63.6	9.0	7.4	46.9	16.7
W Germany	37.9	53.8	22.7	17.9	20.9	11.0
Greece	50.9	63.5	10.3	9.7	7.2	13.5
Ireland	82.4	74.5	0.9	5.7	1.6	5.4
Italy	34.5	59.0	18.9	11.6	26.2	14.3
Netherlands	58.3	76.2	11.9	7.5	17.6	7.8
Portugal	38.9	75.1	5.1	9.9	42.3	7.4
Spain	46.8	66.4	12.4	5.2	18.4	18.6
UK	21.7	56.3	9.1	9.4	33.6	15.8
EC average	37.2	61.6	13.7	11.4	27.4	12.8

Note: Developing countries are defined to exclude OPEC countries. The Irish figures include some substitution of trade with the UK by trade with other EC countries between 1958 and 1991.

Source: European Economy, May 1992, Commission of the European Communities Directorate-General for Economic and Financial Affairs, Luxembourg

twofold. They might meet higher barriers to trade in some of their traditional markets; but as they trade more with the EC these markets are becoming less important to them. They might also be disadvantaged by changes in their country's macroeconomic policy required by membership of the monetary union.

Monetary unions

In a monetary union countries do not necessarily have to have a single currency, but if there are different currencies the exchange rates between them must be fixed. This can be achieved only if monetary policies are harmonised, so that the different countries follow agreed plans about the rate of expansion of their money supply, and operate and maintain agreed interest rate differentials.

The history of the EU's Exchange Rate Mechanism (ERM) from late 1992 to Summer 1993 amply illustrates the difficulties that occur if these conditions are not met. One of these problems was that the exchange rates were not quite fixed: each currency could move up and down within a prescribed range (usually 2.25 per cent) against the ECU (a weighted average of all EU member currencies). The fact that movement was permitted at all enabled the market to read signals into the extent to which currencies persisted at the top or bottom of the permitted range, because if there is a big underlying anomaly speculators may be able to predict what the monetary authorities will do. On this basis speculators will push the currency to the limit until they either see the action they expect or are forced to make losses by powerful countervailing action by the monetary authorities.

Consider, for example, early September 1992. The ERM was fully operating, with sterling at the bottom of the range for some time, partly because of market belief that the UK economy was weak and partly because UK interest rates were low relative to those in Germany. Germany had a stronger currency which was in no danger of devaluation, but it maintained high interest rates for domestic macroeconomic reasons related to German unification. In the UK interest rates had been cut, for macroeconomic reasons, to try to stimulate economic growth. Market sentiment was that sterling was over-valued, and so speculators sold it. By the rules of the ERM, when sterling reached the critical level, the governments of the UK and the other member countries had to act. They tried to support sterling, by buying it in exchange for other currencies, but the reserves available were small relative to the strength of speculative selling. The UK government raised interest rates in a single day from 10 per cent to 12 per cent and then to 15 per cent, to try to strengthen sterling by encouraging financial inflows. But by then it was too late for the move to be credible to the markets, so later that day sterling had to be devalued (in fact by leaving the ERM rather than changing its parity within it). Similar pressure in early August 1993 on the French franc led not to simple devaluation or floating of the franc but to drastic modification of the whole ERM.

The outcome in Summer 1993 was more fundamental for the ERM for three reasons. First, evidence had accumulated over the previous year of the effects of speculative selling of individual currencies. Second, the French government was more committed than the British to avoid devaluation (all the main political parties were committed to a *franc fort* policy). Third, Franco-German unity was central to the development of the EU. A successful monetary union requires a degree of policy harmonisation which the ERM evidently lacked overall in its successive crises from September 1992 to August 1993, and the decision in August 1993 to allow a movement up or down of 15 per cent in each currency remaining in the ERM was, if not an outright abandonment of the ERM, at least a severe setback to the exchange rate stability which was its objective.

Despite such difficulties, even countries which are not in a monetary union may wish to behave as if they were in one, in order to maintain stability of the exchange rate to help their exporters. Such a policy is much more difficult because, as already mentioned, monetary unions include provisions whereby all members act together to maintain the fixed exchange rates by concerted use of their pooled reserves in the foreign exchange markets. Thus whilst non-members trading even with an incomplete monetary union (like the EC in 1992) frequently find that it is in their best interests for their exchange rate to 'shadow' that of the union, they have to bear the burden of administering this on their own, and thus at greater cost than if they were members. So full membership might actually give more, not less, scope for independence of macroeconomic policy. That is why the issue of the extent of loss of sovereignty for a country in joining is rather complex.

The last form of economic grouping to be considered is the most striking of all – full monetary and economic union, of which the most dramatic recent European example is Germany. Chapter 9 considered some aspects of the impact of the union on individual markets, but the concern here is with the macroeconomic implications. Because East Germany was by far the smaller party in the union, the effects there are greater than in West Germany, so the following discussion will concentrate on the East German experience.

One of the first questions which arises when countries decide to enter a monetary union is at what exchange rate they should merge their money supplies. In the case of German monetary union on 1 July 1990, political considerations led to a decision to use what, on all economic criteria, was at best a compromise rate. Considering exchange rates in terms of what currencies can buy, in the long term they should reflect what is known as purchasing power parity: a representative collection of goods is identified, and the exchange rates should be such that the amount of one currency needed to buy it is equal to the amount of the other currency needed to buy it. Various German economic institutes tried in early 1990 to estimate what purchasing power parity would imply, and concluded that a rate of about one East

German Mark (Ostmark, OM) to one West German Mark (DM) was about right. This assumed existing relative prices for different goods, but taking likely price changes induced by unification into account led to much the same answer.

Another way of looking at it, however, was to consider supply considerations, by comparing the productivity of factors of production in export industries in the two Germanies, and to set a rate at which East German exporters could compete with those in West Germany. On this basis, the right rate was about OM4.4 to DM1. More generally, factor productivity suggested a rate of about OM2 = DM1. To add to the confusion, whilst the (pegged) official exchange rate was OM1 = DM1, the black market rate in early 1990 was OM7–11 = DM1 (the black market was, of course, heavily influenced by political uncertainties, and a more normal value was about OM6 = DM1).

The basic choice confronting the two German governments was, then, whether to try to protect East German exporters (by going for a rate of OM4–5 = DM1), to protect East German production generally (by a rate of about OM2 = DM1) or to protect the savings of East German consumers (by a rate of about OM1 = DM1). In fact they opted for two different rates. For current transactions (prices, wages etc.) the conversion rate used was OM1 = DM1. Most financial assets and liabilities were converted at the rate OM2 = DM1, but up to a certain limit household savings by East German families were converted at OM1 = DM1. The overall average for all financial assets and liabilities was about OM1.8 = DM1. As perhaps could be expected, the compromise created complications for producers and both gains and losses for consumers in the former East Germany.

The consequences for producers could be predicted from the earlier analysis: industrial production in the former East Germany fell in the last six months of 1990 by about 50 per cent. Part of this fall was presumably due to the switch from a planned to a market economy and the consequential drastic relative price changes. A reasonable estimate based on the experience of other countries such as Poland is that these microeconomic effects account for about half of the fall in industrial output. The other half of the fall is attributable to two factors. One is East German loss of trade (previously 65 per cent of its foreign trade) with its former Comecon partners because of their economic difficulties. The other is the combination of the initial over-valuation of East German production implied by the failure of the exchange rate to reflect productivity, with rapid rises in costs for former East German producers from wage inflation.

In deciding what rate to use to convert East German Marks into Deutschmarks for general current payments purposes such as calculating prices and wages, the two German governments tried to balance issues of labour productivity against the need to make sure that wages in the East were high enough to prevent any further outflow of labour from the East into West Germany. Wages were initially converted at OM1 = DM1, which, since East German money wages were about a third of the West German levels, would have been consistent with East German labour productivity being a third of that of West Germany.

What is important for wage inflation is not so much the initial exchange rate but the expectations of both workers and employers. The two German governments had promised to reduce the gap in living standards between West and East Germany, so it was reasonable for workers and employers in the former East Germany to expect subsidies from the new German government (i.e. in practice from West German taxpayers) to cover the period until their capital equipment and their labour training levels were brought up to previous West German levels. The strength and persistence of these expectations can be seen from the extent of industrial unrest in May 1993 in response to employers' failure to honour an understanding to raise wages in Eastern German engineering firms. (High and growing unemployment failed to deter the strikers.) Money wages in East Germany (as measured in DM) rose by about a third in 1990. In consequence, however, existing capital equipment became uneconomic very quickly (because using obsolescent equipment causes labour productivity to be low, and unless wages are correspondingly low, producers cannot cover their costs). Thus capital equipment required urgent replacement at once across nearly all of the former East German economy. The impossibility of doing this meant that the former East German *Länder* simply could not produce competitively, even with generous subsidies. The fall in total East German output in 1990 was about 30 per cent – less severe than the decline in industrial production because of transfers from the West, particularly to government services – and, with some lag, employment fell by a comparable amount.

Unemployment is a blow to consumers – if members of the household lose their jobs, household income falls. Those in work, however, benefited from the wage rises. Average income rose by some 5 per cent in 1990. Living standards also improved because west European and especially West German goods were much more readily available and could be substituted for inferior East German or Soviet bloc products – for example, people bought second-hand Volkswagen cars instead of new Trabants. But the real income of many households fell because of the loss of free or heavily subsidised services, especially assistance for newlywed couples to set up house and for families with young children to use creches and kindergartens.

The other major impact on East German households was on their wealth. In terms of purchasing power parity, the average rate of OM1.8 = DM1 reduced the wealth of East German households by about a third. (The effect varied from family to family, with the wealthier families losing more.) The effects of this wealth loss are more widespread than might be expected at first sight, because in East Germany, as in the other planned economies, the economic stresses of the late 1980s meant that most households had accumulated considerable savings because of the shortages of goods available to buy.

Furthermore, in a socialist economy, they could not spend their money to buy other financial assets (like company shares) or real assets (such as houses).

After unification they converted some of their savings from money into assets such as shares. In the process they pushed up the prices of the shares, thereby losing a bit more of the real value of their wealth. So Germany's economic and monetary union reduced household wealth in the East German *Länder*, and thereby the willingness of East German households to buy goods and services. In general the experience of East German households was very diverse, some clearly gaining and others losing from the union.

German economic and monetary union is obviously a very special case, because of its abruptness and because it combined a planned and a market economy. Some of the lessons apply, however, to any monetary union, such as the Treaty of Maastricht's proposals to convert the EC into a full monetary union. In particular, the choice of the exchange rates for initial conversions in the monetary union is important. The obvious technique seems to be to try to achieve a gradual reduction in the volatility of rates over time, to head towards stability at some exchange rate sanctioned by the market. This was the method adopted by the EC in its progress towards full Economic and Monetary Union (EMU), but gradualist approaches do not always work and in the case of the EMU they failed spectacularly in 1992/93.

Nevertheless, the insistence in the Treaty of Maastricht on the importance of convergence of key macroeconomic variables as a precondition of monetary union seems justifiable, because the absence of such convergence between the two Germanies has led to acute difficulties for East German producers. Perhaps, then, some convergence followed by a sudden union is the best method.

In the light of these problems, it is proper to conclude by asking why countries might want to join monetary unions rather than stopping at some earlier stage in the process of economic integration. The answer lies in the extent to which a successful economic integration leads to a desire for increasingly closer links. If, for example, as Table 10.4 shows, the countries of the EU become increasingly inter-dependent in trade, it is more and more in the interests of their producers and consumers to cut out avoidable costs in transactions between member countries. This means first dismantling the tariff and non-tariff barriers to trade – completed, for the EC/EU, by the Single European Act. Once this has been done, exchange costs are the obvious next barrier to remove, together with impediments such as different systems of taxing goods and different tax rates on goods – hence the centrality of these matters in the Treaty of Maastricht. Governments may worry about the loss of sovereignty over economic matters, but in practice they are gradually ceding sovereignty to the EU by the extent to which achieving exchange rate stability requires them to make their monetary and fiscal policy coherent with those of their EU partners (or, more strictly, those of the strongest currency countries in the EU, like Germany). If a customs union is working well, it takes major national political events like the need to ratify the Treaty of Maastricht, or major externally induced problems like the partial collapse of the ERM in late 1992, to engender serious questioning of this gradual apparent inevitability of monetary union.

It is appropriate to conclude the general messages of this chapter by quoting from Wijkman's comments on the formation of the European Economic Area:

> When the EEA is in place and the EC has completed the internal reforms that are presently under discussion, the Europeans will have at their disposal a pattern of institutions representing four circles or levels of integration. The outermost circle is represented by a free trade area in industrial goods ... The second circle is a free trade area encompassing industrial goods, services, capital and persons characterised by equal conditions of competition and with some common administrative institutions but without common decision-making institutions and with no common policies *vis-à-vis* third countries. This is represented by the EEA. The third circle is a common internal market for all goods, for services, capital and persons, with common internal and external policies and common decision-making institutions. This level of integration is represented by the EC of '1992'. Finally, the innermost circle is the economic, monetary and political union into which the EC may develop ... Countries starting out on the transition to market economies may find this variety of options particularly attractive. It would mean that ... they would have the opportunity to progress gradually through the various levels of integration. (Wijkman 1991: p. 5)

However, the route is not necessarily one-way. Europe in the 1990s provides us with many examples of the disintegration of economic unions – the USSR, Yugoslavia and Czechoslovakia have broken up economically as well as politically. In all of these cases, the changes are too recent for any economic analysis of their effects to be feasible, and in some of them – particularly in what used to be Yugoslavia – the process has been so violent that the economic damage will in any case take a long time to repair. Even where the break-up of former economic unions has been relatively peaceful, as in the former USSR, the new countries (other than Russia, which as the dominant member of the USSR inherited much of the old arrangements) have had to decide almost from scratch how to run their economies – for example, should they have a currency separate from the Russian ruble? If so, what should they call it and what should its initial exchange rate be? What economic relationship do they wish to have immediately and in the longer term with Russia, with each other, and with other countries? Contemporary Europe is indeed an exciting place in which to study the formation and break-up of trading blocs.

Further reading

Cecchini, P. (with Catinat, M. and Jacquemin, A., shortened text written by Robinson J.) (1988) *The European Challenge: 1992: The Benefits of a Single Market*, Wildwood House, Aldershot.

De Grauwe, P. (1992) *The Economics of Monetary Integration*, Oxford University Press, Oxford.

Dyson, K. (1994) *Elusive Union: the process of economic and monetary union in Europe*, Longman, London.

Giersch, H., Paqué, K. and Schmieding, H. (1992) *The Fading Miracle: Four Decades of Market Economy in Germany*. Cambridge University Press, Cambridge.

McDonald, F. and Dearden, S. (eds) (1994) *European Economic Integration 2nd edn.*, Longman, London.

Nielsen, J.U., Heinrich, H. and Hansen, J.D. (1991) *An Economic Analysis of the EC*, McGraw-Hill, London.

Sinn, G. and Sinn, H. (1992) *Jumpstart*, MIT Press, Cambridge, MA.

Swann, D. (ed.) (1992) *The Single European Market and Beyond: A Study of the Wider Implications of the Single European Act*, Routledge, London.

Wijkman, P.M. (1991) *The EEA Agreement – At Long Last!*, EFTA Trade 1990 Economic Affairs Department, EFTA, Geneva.

11 And nation shall speak unto nation: the communications network

Introduction

When people try to do something together, everything depends on how they communicate with each other. We can send messages into deep space in the hope that some extra-terrestrial beings might find them and interpret them; but the project of setting up a Joint Galactic Research Programme in High-Energy Physics or Forms of Social Organisation is blocked by the fact that it will take about 22,000 years or more for one message to travel from sender to receiver. Similar – though less drastic – difficulties for centuries reduced effective European contact with China to very limited exchanges of trading information. But even where the technical possibility exists of passing information quite quickly from A to B, in practice that technology may be so expensive or cumbrous to install that it does not in practice operate as a network. Royal messages might be carried on selected routes by relays of fast horses kept in readiness along the route, but for ordinary traders in the grain-market towns of eighteenth century Poland or the coastal wool ports of northern Spain, messages depended on the pace of barges on the River Vistula or schooners on the Bay of Biscay, or at best on the efforts of a single messenger managing one horse on a difficult journey over bad roads. The peasants in their villages hardly heard anything of the events of the world outside a radius of about 30 kilometres.

Gradually, communications improved in Europe, but for a while only along limited routes of communication, from city to city by state postal systems for example. What has happened to Europe in the twentieth century is a transformation of its communications into an ever speedier and wider spread fast network, in which very many messages pass very quickly in many different directions. The tendency of any such network is to produce a loose and fluid exchange of understanding spreading through the whole network. One effect of this – wherever it becomes established – is to change drastically the underlying structure of political and social life, of economic activity, and of culture.

But for Europe – as opposed to the USA and Canada – any such tendency meets a counter-tendency: the effects of Europe's division into separate units – separate countries, separate strategic and economic regions, and so on. These divisions are associated with another major barrier to communication – language differences. The tendency of technology is towards a uniform, swift and transparent network of communication, producing a correspondingly swift and uniform framework for the European economy and commerce and tending towards a unified structure of political power. But the cultural differences of Europeans – reinforced by political power – divide this network into partially separated smaller ones because of the problems of understanding one another across these divisions. Of these cultural barriers the most substantial – but not the only one – is language difference.

Language difference and the sense of identity

People tend to feel a strong emotional bond with those they understand, and with whom they share ideas, attitudes, social activities and jokes. All these depend on language, so it is not surprising that people often have a sense of their own identity as members of groups (e.g. nations) which are defined by speaking a common language. Also, for any job except unskilled labouring, carrying out your work tends to require a knowledge of the language of those with whom you have to cooperate, both those working in the same organisation and in other organisations. In this way, people's career-paths also tend to be determined by language; you can hope to get a job or be promoted, generally, only in organisations which use a language in which you can write and speak fluently. So all these factors – emotions, sense of identity, interest – tend to steer people into groups of those who share a language; and all these factors also interact with each other. Thus there is a strong tendency towards nation-states with a common language, a tendency first identified (and proclaimed as a political programme) by Johann Gottfried Herder in the eighteenth century.

Nevertheless, strong though these tendencies are, reality is much less tidy. Once a population has an established language, that language becomes very deep-rooted, and cannot easily be eradicated even by the determined efforts of the state to make people speak some other language (even a closely related one). For example, Spanish governments from the eighteenth century to the 1960s tried to eradicate the Basque language from its north-eastern provinces and the Catalan language from its eastern province of Catalonia. But they failed completely, and only aroused greater resentment and greater determination to preserve their own identity in the oppressed Basques and Catalans. Soviet governments from the 1930s to the 1980s downgraded and disadvantaged languages other than Russian in the USSR with a very similar result; when the Soviet regime began to disintegrate in the late 1980s (partly because of these national resentments) many non-Russian peoples demanded increasing degrees of independence and recognition for their own languages. Union republics established their own sovereign states and made their languages official within them; while in Russia itself, after the break-up of the Soviet Union in 1991, most regions of the Federation have been trying to make their own language the leading one on their territory. However, it should be remembered that languages may die or fade away to an insignificant status: Manx (in the Isle of Man, UK), Dalmatian (in Croatia), and Jutish (in northern Germany) are examples, while the position of Scottish Gaelic, Friulian (in northern Italy), and Sorb (in east Germany) – to mention only a few examples – looks somewhat insecure.

So the idea that every nation-state has its own language unique to that nation is a myth (one which some nation-states themselves sedulously promote). In fact virtually all states contain minority populations whose native language differs from the official one, or else have two or more different official languages spoken by substantial elements of the population, as in Switzerland (official languages: French, German, Italian, Romansh) or Belgium (French and Flemish). Moreover, many of the languages are spoken (in various forms or dialects) by substantial populations of two or more different states of Europe. That applies to English (UK, Ireland, Malta); French (France, Belgium, Switzerland, Luxembourg); German (Germany, Austria, Alsace in France, Luxembourg, part of eastern Belgium, the Netherlands, Silesia in Poland, Romania, and Südtirol in Italy); Albanian (Albania, the Kosovo province of Serbia and FYROM Macedonia); Hungarian (Hungary, Slovakia, Transylvania in Romania and Vojvodina in Serbia); Turkish (Turkey, Bulgaria, and Greece); Swedish (Sweden and Finland); Finnish (Finland, Sweden and Russia); and Russian (in the Baltic states and in every state of the CIS). Then there are states where a once dominant older language and a more recently established one are both official languages (like Ireland with Irish Gaelic and English). There are others where a variant of the older official language now enjoys official status for some purposes, for example Spain with Spanish and Catalan, and France with French and Occitan (Provençal).

It can be seen from these examples how far reality is removed from the myth that one language goes with one nation-state. Taking into account also that there are about 30 million people in Europe who are immigrants from countries not adjacent to the state in which they have settled – immigrants from other European countries and from all over the world, speaking more than 100 different languages – it is clear that what is normal (i.e. nearly always the case) for a 'nation-state' is, in fact, to be *multi-lingual*. In Britain, for example, about 100 minority languages are in regular use by residents.

Nevertheless most states do exert pressure in the direction of one official language. The reasons are obvious enough. Economic efficiency within a state is promoted by easy exchange of information; the legal system works better if everyone in the courts understands what is being said; the armed forces and the civil service work better if they use the official language and can recruit the personnel they want from the entire population; and in times of crisis the state is more likely to be able to call on a loyal population (ready, for example, to sacrifice its blood on the battlefield) if its people have a sense of loyalty to 'their country' which is greatly promoted by a shared language and culture. Modern states can promote the official language in many ways: through the education system; through the influence of the legal system, and of the civil service, on the language needed for commerce; through the prestige and influence of the armed forces; through the broadcasting system (both radio and television), especially if it is a public (government-controlled) broadcasting system, but also by influence and legal controls exerted on commercial broadcasting. The way in which these forms of pressure are in some circumstances becoming less powerful will be considered later. States may also take steps to *define* the official language, as with the activities of the French Academy, though many states are content to leave this to organisations like universities and publishing houses which are anyway usually closely involved with state policy, power and organisation.

It is important to see that the very definition of one 'language' is nearly always (in the developed world) the outcome of this official determination of what the official language of some state is. In the beginning of any such process there are just a lot of overlapping dialects, usually mutually intelligible in neighbouring villages and regions, but becoming more different from each other as distance between them increases. One of these dialects is reduced to writing, which is extended and developed by dictionaries, with terms for specialised uses, refinements of grammatical rules, and so on; and it then receives the enormous boost which comes from the backing of a state. (In the earlier history of Europe the backing was very often more from the Church, and associated especially with the language used for translations of the Bible.) But it remains the case that the official language is different (to varying degrees) from the various dialects of most people who 'speak that language'.

For these reasons the definition of a dialect as a 'language' rather than merely a dialect of some other language is a *political* matter, fraught with political consequences and fought over by adherents on each side. Slovak was distinguished as a separate language by native nationalists in the second half of the nineteenth century, but was not recognised by their Hungarian masters. In the same period the similar speech form of Czech (readily comprehensible to Slovaks) was defined as a separate language by Czech nationalists, trying to establish recognition for Czech identity within the Austrian Empire. In both cases the establishment of defining written forms of the language by new national literature was of central importance.

When the power of both Austrians and Hungarians was overthrown by the First World War, the victorious powers at Versailles (trying to apply the 'national principle' of one-language-one-state) were persuaded by the Czech leader Tomas Masaryk to treat the two speech forms as one language and so to constitute Czechoslovakia as a unitary state with Czechoslovak (undefined) as its official language. Since power was centred in Prague there might have been a tendency for a predominantly Czech unitary language to become established and accepted (as happened in England through the Middle Ages with the gradual fading to dialect status of Northern English forms). But in 1939 the Nazis pressured the Slovaks to set up a clerico-fascist independent Slovak state, promoting Slovak as a separate language, and after the war Slovak – now more thoroughly established – was treated as a speech form and written form parallel with Czech. (On television two newscasters – one Czech and one Slovak speaker – would sit together and take it in turns to read news items, both of them understood well enough by both Czech and Slovak viewers.) So a sense of both political and linguistic separateness developed together. When democracy arrived in 1989 the Slovaks soon separated themselves from the Czechs as the independent state of Slovakia and established international recognition of Slovak as a separate language, even though by the criterion of linguistic science (i.e. languages are the same if mutually comprehensible to a reasonably high degree) the two are one language.

In a rather similar way, the state of Yugoslavia was founded in 1919 on the idea that the Serbs and the Croats spoke essentially the same language ('Serbo-Croat'), which – because of the accidents of history – were written in two different scripts, the Roman for Croat, and the Cyrillic (like Russian) for Serbian. But from the late 1980s it became clear that the Serbs and the Croats did not regard themselves as one people, and consequently in the world outside some have come to regard Croatian and Serbian as two separate languages, partly just because of that difference in scripts. As for the Serbs and Croats, many Serbs would still like to think that they have a single Serbian language with Croatian forms, but most Croats have for a long time thought of Croatian as a different language.

The status of Catalan as a separate language from Spanish (though closely related) became established in a similar way through political pressure associated with semi-independent status for the province of Catalonia within Spain. On the other hand the dialect of Ruthenian has no official status within Ukraine; the Provençal (Occitan) dialect of French has a literature and some limited official recognition, but is regarded as a dialect; and the dialect of Scots English has no recognition at all within the UK.

The many dialects of German (grouped into the 'High German' of south Germany, Switzerland and Austria, and the 'Low German' of north Germany) are not treated as separate languages, and official German (a version of High German) prevails everywhere as the written form. But in Switzerland, for example, the spoken Swiss dialect is so different from the official written German that Swiss children have to be taught both – as separate linguistic skills – in schools; while in Luxembourg the local German dialect – Letzebürgisch – enjoys official recognition as one of the three languages of the state along with French and standard official German, which all Luxembourgers are taught.

In Norway (which had been part of Denmark until 1814 and then of

Sweden until 1905) an official language related to the linguistically similar Danish had been set up, in the eighteenth and nineteenth centuries, called the Riksmål ('the King's tongue') or the Bokmål ('the book tongue'). In the later nineteenth century some Norwegians trying to establish their separate national and linguistic identity came to think that the Riksmål was too Danish-influenced and too different from the speech of the people (especially in the country districts); so they defined and promoted the Landsmål ('the country tongue'), also known as Nynorsk ('New Norwegian'). Today both forms of Norwegian are officially recognised and taught.

Among the south Slav dialects the speech of the Macedonian region might be regarded as a dialect of the official language Serbian, or of the official language Bulgarian, or as a separate official language in the state of Macedonia (FYROM); and which decision is taken has major political implications in a region tense with the potential for ethnic conflict. (The Greeks, for example, are determined that Macedonia proper is part of Greece, and that its proper language is Greek. They are therefore opposed to recognition of the Slav dialect as a Macedonian language.)

The official languages of Europe are often quite recent creations (as with Norwegian), and associated with the establishing of political rights or separate statehood. Finnish was defined and recognised as part of the nationalist movement against the Russians in the nineteenth century and up to 1914, as were Estonian, Latvian and Lithuanian. Modern Greek, Romanian, Bulgarian, Hungarian, Serbian, Slovenian, Czech, Albanian, Maltese, and Icelandic were all defined and established as official, separate languages in the nineteenth and twentieth centuries, in association with separatist movements and (later) the backing of state power. By contrast, Romany (the language of gypsies), Sardinian (in Italy), Corsican (in France), Kashubian (in north-west Poland), Lapp (in Norway) and many others, receive little official recognition and are consequently not flourishing.

Disputes about linguistic recognition and official support for languages can arouse very serious political tensions. In 1968 the government of Belgium fell because of protests by the Flemings (Flemish-speaking Belgians) about state backing for a French-speaking university (the University of Louvain). Post-Franco Spanish governments have staved off political trouble from their separatist provinces (frequently seeking recognition and official status for their language/dialect) by granting substantial provincial power (including power over language policy) to certain provinces. In the Russian Federation where several hundred different languages are spoken, 89 administrative territories are accorded powers as 'subjects'. But there are considerable pressures in many of these territories for greater powers; one factor encouraging this has been their determination to promote their own language above Russian as the territory's official language.

Organisations like the European Union which seek to promote cooperation and inter-communication across several European countries also have an interest in ensuring that all workers in Europe – more generally all people living in Europe – are treated in a way which enables them to realise their full potential and to play their full part in the life of Europe. This interest is partly economic, to maximise the efficiency of work, and partly political, to reduce the chances of political conflict arising from discontent. The powerful trans-national corporations (TNCs) may share these concerns, favouring not only the recognition of minority languages but also a general mastery of the languages most used for international commerce, English, French and German. (Russian is spoken as a first language by about 150 million people in Europe, as compared with roughly 60 million each for English, French and German, but the role of Russian in commerce outside the CIS is so far small. Spanish is a major world language, but mainly because of its widespread use in South and Central America; in Europe its role is smaller than that of English, French or German.)

In addition, one motive for the founding of the EC/EU was to reduce the potential for destructive wars in Europe by promoting human rights. Thus the EU, the TNCs and other similar organisations should be expected to favour rights for minority languages and to promote the teaching of languages so as to produce a sizeable population speaking at least one or two of the major languages. In fact the Treaty of Rome did not mention languages or education. The EC only gradually recognised the importance of language issues, despite the enormous translation and interpretation costs of conducting its own business in all the official languages of the EC. (In 1990 60 per cent of the costs of the European Parliament were absorbed by translation of documents, and 2,000 people were employed by the EC in translation and interpretation.)

Language issues have been neglected until recently because national governments are particularly touchy about their own languages, and the politicians drafting the Treaty of Rome and subsequent EC directives and treaties were trying to avoid stirring up a hornets' nest. So the EC itself absorbed the ever-rising costs of recognising all the official languages of member states as official EC ones. They relied on commercial pressures to determine the dominating language in the European economy.

But in 1977, migration pressures provoked an EC directive pledging member states to 'take appropriate measures', as far as consistent with domestic requirements, to provide free and adequate tuition to the children of migrants to teach them the official language of the country, and also to provide teaching in their mother tongue. An EC directive is binding, but member states differ in the extent to which thus far they have implemented this directive. In 1990 the EC established the LINGUA programme of encouraging bilingualism (or multi-lingualism) in EC countries. Article 126 of the Maastricht Treaty stresses the Community aim of developing 'the European dimension in education, especially through the learning and the development of the languages of the member-states'. But the Treaty also expects (and endorses) continuation of linguistic diversity, specifically mentioning its value and its connection with national cultures. But of course, it leaves the content and organisation of education to member states. Still, it is significant that education and language are seen as sufficiently important to appear in this Treaty. We may expect growing pressures to develop these policies, so the EU is unlikely to retreat from this position. Indeed, with every new member, the cost and delay of translation and interpretation increases hugely; it seems likely that soon the EU will have to simplify its rules.

As the structure of European commerce, quasi-governmental activity and society becomes more international, so the influence of the major European languages will surely grow. The power of governments of nations with minor languages to influence the language of their citizens may be expected to diminish. Three-quarters of the world's letters and 80 per cent of electronic databases are in English, while simplified and technical forms of English have been developed for universal use in air and sea traffic control and for much of scientific and technical interchange. (These figures are, of course, heavily weighted by North America; for Europe alone the balance between English, French and German is much more equal, with German especially significant in eastern Europe.) Thus for those with jobs involving international commerce, the language crucial for personal advancement is likely to be one of the major languages, perhaps together with the language of one's own country. For this reason, the Dutch, the Danes, and the Finns have a very large proportion of speakers of two, three or more languages, and devote large proportions of their education time to language learning. Other small and medium-sized countries in Europe are likely to develop similar policies. The inhabitants of countries such as Norway, Poland, Portugal and Hungary are increasingly becoming used to material in one of the major languages. Television and magazines – as well as scholarly and scientific publications which the advanced student must study at university and even at school – have much wider coverage in the major languages. In such ways the power of the state to influence its citizens to adopt its own official language exclusively is diminishing. In countries using the major languages – UK, Ireland, France, Belgium, Germany, Switzerland, Austria – this trend to multi-lingualism is much less marked, but even so it is considerable, since no one language is really adequate for anyone whose work has an international dimension.

Modern communications technologies

Languages determine what people can understand, but what messages can reach them is determined by the communications available. In the mid-nineteenth century people communicated by letters, and by newspapers, pamphlets and books. By 1960 Europeans generally had added to these radio, television, telephones and telex, films and posters, and newspapers were adapted for mass circulation and carried hot news (i.e. the previous day's). Notice how far these developments worked by enabling *one* sender of messages to send the same messages to *very many people* – that is what 'broadcasting' means for radio and television, but the same effect worked for films and for mass circulation newspapers. The effect of such a dominating one–many system of communication is to centralise the sources of information and ideas (and thus cultural power) in a smallish elite, usually located in capital cities. Because of these technologies, information and ideas spread much more widely, and quite a lot faster. The culture of Europe changed accordingly.

Effects of development of communications technology to 1960

The principal effect of new communications technology pre-1960 was that commerce became much easier: orders could be sent more quickly, invoices sent out and payment received, problems with delivery of orders chased by telephone messages, and so on. Markets could be built up and secured by advertising campaigns. As a result, trade increased sharply and on a more international scale, the market reacted faster to conditions, and the major firms became larger and more powerful.

Another effect was that cultures became more evenly spread and more pervasive within their areas of effective influence. For many countries – though not for some smaller ones – the effective range of the mass communication of information and ideas was the nation-state. Radio and television transmitters were controlled by each nation-state, and each set up its own state broadcasting corporation to communicate its culture to its own people, such as BBC (UK), TF1 and Antenne 2 (France), ARD and ZDF (Germany), BRT (Belgium, Flemish language), RTBF (Belgium, French language), RTVE (Spain). This arose partly because setting up broadcasting facilities was hugely expensive, and partly because the technology then available permitted only a few non-interfering radio frequency channels and television transmitting channels, which had to be shared out between the European states. Differences of language between the populations of some European states and their neighbours stopped them from listening to the broadcasts of other states. In this way, state broadcasting corporations provided an opportunity to promote the sense of national identity and solidarity among their citizens. Newspapers in many states also assumed a national range, although the regional press remained influential.

Thus cultures became more national and more sharply separated from those of other nations, while within each state they became more uniform. These effects were always less marked in smaller states, especially if their populations shared a language with other states. Viewing figures to foreign-language broadcasts reached about 13 per cent in some smaller states by the mid-1980s. But for the larger states there was a great concentration of effective cultural communication within the country.

Because broadcasting systems were controlled by the state, they were thought of as agents of education and of the promotion of national

consciousness. Thus they tried to encourage and develop (a) 'high' culture –
programmes about the history of painting, serious drama, classical music and
so on; (b) especially the *national* achievements of high culture – Shakespeare
and Galsworthy for the British, Molière and Anouilh for the French, Dante
and Betti for the Italians, and so on; (c) a folk culture specific to that nation –
for example comedy programmes like 'The Goon Show' full of British humour
and in-jokes about British characters and history; (d) sport, especially
international contests seen from the point of view of whether one of 'ours' is
playing; (e) political information, focused on the politics of the state
concerned – so that in Germany a listener or viewer would become familiar
with the views of German politicians like Adenauer, in Hungary with those of
Hungarian politicians like Kadar; (f) political and social history of the nation
concerned; and sometimes (g) outright propaganda, either by cutting out any
information about embarrassing events, like the attacks by police on Algerians
in Paris in 1960, or by promoting distortions and lies, as in the Portuguese
broadcasting corporation's optimistic version of Portugal's efforts to put down
revolts in its African colonies, or in Czechoslovak radio's happy tales about the
contented and progressive Czech and Slovak people under communism. But
even where the state broadcasting corporation did not go in for crude
propaganda, such national educational broadcasting policies strongly
promoted a sense of national identity and loyalty (and to some extent support
for the government) by reinforcing the distinctive elements of the national
culture like the language, the style of humour and the pool of shared
knowledge of literature and of broadcast shows.

Developments in communications technology 1960–94

During these years there has been an extraordinary (and continuing)
revolution in communications technology. To understand these developments
it is necessary to look more closely at the technology itself.

Technological advances have come mainly in four areas; (a) the *physical
medium* of transmission of messages; (b) the *coding of the message*; (c) *switching* –
the systems for controlling the passage of different messages in different
directions; (d) the *interfaces* – instruments for transposing voice, video-image,
keystrokes and so on into radio-waves or electric impulses along a wire, and
vice versa.

The physical medium
Fibre-optic cable is a (sheaf of) glass-fibre thread, along which the signal is
transmitted as laser-controlled pulses of light. It transmits at 565 megabits per
second (565,000,000 electric blips per second), that is, 4,000 times as much
information per second as copper cable carries (1993, and still improving). In
1956 the transatlantic telephone cable (copper) carried 36 telephone
channels; the 1988 fibre-optic one carried the equivalent of 40,000.

Geostationary satellites (i.e. satellites which travel at the same speed as the earth beneath them, thus remaining always above the same point of the earth's surface) receive radio signals (including television signals) from a transmitter (an uplink) and retransmit them from their own transmitters (transponders) over a wide area of the earth's surface (the satellite's footprint). They can be received either by a special large receiver and retransmitted by cable, or directly by private consumers using a small satellite dish receiver; the latter method (DBS – Direct Broadcast by Satellite) requires a larger and more powerful satellite.

The coding of the message

The old method was analogue representation; the new method is *digital representation*, in which every represented feature of the message is coded (ultimately in a binary code of blip-or-no-blip-in-a-position). Digitisation makes possible better interfaces and more efficient transmission of the messages, which can be interleaved with each other along transmission lines within microsecond 'packets', so utilising the greatly increased speed of transmission for carrying many more messages along the same line (cable or radio). This makes possible the use of the same transmission line for different kinds of message; thus teletext, interactive videotex, network services and so on can be carried on the same line as the ordinary telephone. This is the idea of integrated services; so the information technology made possible by digitisation is called ISDN (integrated services digital network).

Switching

The old electro-mechanical systems of rotating cogs are now superseded by electronic switching by large computers switching digitised messages in 'packets' in accordance with codes on the front end of each message. These make possible a great increase in the volume of information passed through the system.

Interfaces

Among many developments, some of the most important are cellular mobile telephones, fax transmission of documents, fax transmission of graphics, videophones (cheaply available now for the deaf as outline representation), videoconference, consultation of computerised databases, direct transmission of data from one computer to another, teletext, and interactive videotex.

Character of the new communications technology

Telecommunications have become more plural; they do not have the same tendency to be dominated by a few people or by the state. Partly this is because telecommunications are not a one–many kind of communication, but a many–many network, with messages going in many different directions between many different senders and many different receivers. The more efficient and widespread the telecommunications network becomes, the less will the technology allow a few powerful controllers of communications to exercise an effective monopoly over the messages in the culture. This is partly because the technology now permits a much larger number of radio or television channels to be utilised without interfering with each other; so there can be many different message senders available for any individual to receive. It is also partly because some of the technology is relatively cheaper; desk-top publishing allows anyone who owns a small computer to design and print high quality pamphlets, flyers or magazines, and it is not too hard to make one's own video.

The number of communications has become so large that nobody could control it. The demand for television programmes has grown by a factor of 10 to 20. Local radio stations are spreading fast. Newspaper sales have increased, and the size of newspapers – and thus the information they carry – has also grown enormously. Similarly, telecommunications traffic has grown so greatly that state organisations cannot monitor it effectively, even if they should wish to do so (except in the case of specially targeted telephones used by people already identified as suspicious). The speed of communication in 1994 is no greater than it was in the best cases in 1960 (e.g. in ship-to-shore radio). But so much more of it gets through, to so many more destinations, at great distances, and so much more reliably, that there has been a transformation in everybody's way of life and of working and in the character of their relations with other people. In effect, we now have a fast and dense network.

Effects of the application of this technology in Europe

Telecommunications

A modern economy hinges on its communications. According to the World Bank, investment in telecommunications produces for the economy as a whole a better rate of return than any other type of investment. In 1986 the average number of telephone lines per person in the world was about 9; in the EC it was 36, in Japan 37, in the USA 50. So investment in telecommunications (mainly fibre-optic cable and big computer switching stations) is a major priority.

Within the EU telecommunications are unevenly distributed, as you would expect in the light of the division between core and periphery; hence the EU has a policy (STAR – Special Telecommunications Action for Regional Development) of targeting regional aid onto the establishment of a modern telecommunications infrastructure in the peripheral parts of the EU – Ireland, Portugal, most of Spain, Corsica and Sardinia, southern Italy, and Greece. The policy is having some success, but development in the core regions and countries of the EU is proceeding even faster, and the public telecommunications corporations are being privatised, so it is doubtful whether the peripheral regions are really catching up. Since the opening up of the European Economic Area and the growing links between the economies of eastern Europe and the EU, the problem of imbalance in telecommunications facilities has become even larger. Eastern Europe was more out of date in this field than in any other. At present (1994) Germany is making strenuous and successful efforts to establish modern telecommunications in the former East Germany, but the rest of central and eastern Europe is lagging, though major efforts are now getting under way to bring their telecommunications up to date.

The markets for the industries which will supply telecommunications equipment and services will be very large indeed. Their sales amount to about 400,000 million ECU at present, while computing (170,000 million ECU) and consumer electronics (100,000 million ECU) provide further very large related markets. These markets are growing faster than any other major sector. But in all these sectors Europe is at present only third to the USA and Japan.

Telecommunications used to be the kind of business that provided a basic service to as many customers as possible, for which they paid only the basic subscription and a call charge. The old pattern was suited to public provision, and that was the structure of the service throughout Europe, usually linked to the Postal Service. Hence each state set up corporations for posts, telegraphs and telephones (PTTs). Now, however, information technology makes available many 'value-added services', that is, optional facilities. The new need for large-scale risk investment and the opportunity for sales of value-added services now favour a private competitive structure, and the PTTs are being privatised throughout the EU. The companies involved will increasingly face American and Japanese competition, and of course will compete with each other. The boldest development so far into ISDN (see above) – the French system of interactive teletext and videotex, 'Minitel' – is publicly funded. It was established in 1985 with free terminals for users, linking them to privately provided services (e.g. banking, databases of information like share prices, train timetables, teleshopping, electronic mail and the like – altogether more than 4,000 services in 1989). But whether this state-organised system is the pattern for the future or the swan-song of the old ways remains to be seen. It is businesses, not private individuals, which make the most extensive use of the new communications technology; increasingly, modern business operates through intensive use of databases, tele-negotiated deals with faxed back-up, transfer of computer data, videoconference to save the travel time of executives, and so on. By the year 2000 some 60 per cent of European jobs will be in information-related activities. Partly for this reason, and partly because of the application of EU competition policy, the telecommunications sections of the western European PTTs were rapidly privatised in the years 1993–95.

The effects of better communications on the European economy have been accentuated by further developments in these tendencies to greater speed and more effective circulation. But the many-to-many pattern of recent trends has had an effect on the character of the economy. The network of communications is so large and various that it cannot be so tightly controlled by centrally organised structures like states or firms. This does not mean that these organisations have ceased to matter; rather, they now exercise their power more loosely, by a more devolved system of management and by interlocking relationships with each other. Thus the dominant pattern of economic organisation is one of various inter-connected firms. The links may be by partial shareholdings held in common, by finance companies or banks, or by agreements to operate under licence to share markets. Thus the firms form loose networks rather similar to the communications network itself (see Chapter 1).

Television

The main effect of recent technical developments in television is an increase in the number of possible available channels: both terrestrial channels (broadcast from a transmitter on the ground) and satellite channels. The number can be further increased if the signals reach the viewer's home via a cable (which can of course also carry telecommunications); this is the simplest way of transmitting satellite channels, and at present is spreading fast in western Europe.

The role of the state public broadcasting corporations

Broadcasting as domination of cultural space

Nation-states use their control of the space of their territory to promote within it a national culture which will strengthen the sense of national identity for the population; thus a state will promote the national language(s), national history, national styles of literature and film, and so on. In effect, nation-states have for about 200 years operated as culture dominators within their own territories. Broadcasting which crosses national boundaries (especially satellite broadcasting with a broad footprint) or which broadcasts programmes predominantly of some other culture, threatens this cultural domination. Many people think that the space determined by the range of a widely watched television channel *is* a cultural space, just as a nation used to be; and that it is important for their own (or their nation's) cultural identity that this space be dominated by the right culture. Larger countries (with some prospect of controlling their own 'audiovisual space') may make strenuous efforts to combat foreign culture within it. The French are particularly committed to this, promoting the idea of a *pays audiovisuelle français* (or thinking globally, in resistance to American and other English-language cultural domination, *pays audiovisuelle latin*). This policy tends to cost France heavily. But note that the French are promoting French culture against *any* other.

The EU tends rather to promote European culture against American or Australian culture. This partly derives from the EU's keenness to promote

European cultural integration and partly because of the drive to protect European markets for European programmes, broadcasting control, and equipment provision. This partly overlapping campaign also had strong French support in the 1980s, and nearly led to the breakdown of the GATT Talks in 1993, when the Americans tried to insist on open access for their programmes to European markets. Jack Lang (French minister of culture in the early 1980s) especially publicised the idea of a *guerre des images* (a war of the television images). He was thinking especially of French versus American television programmes, seeking at that time to preserve French public broadcasting control of television channels. In this he failed; it proved commercially impossible to maintain the range of state television channels he wanted. Control of audiovisual space by nation-states within the EU, then, is very difficult, and it seems can succeed only to a limited extent.

Increasingly, many programmes are made with dubbing or voice-over provided in various languages for versions aimed at different language groups. Thus there is a tendency for the major languages to dominate a cultural space, even without any state controls intended to produce this result.

These issues are complicated by the issue of high culture versus low (or popular) culture. In the past, the idea of high culture has always been defined as part of national cultures and associated with national elites. Thus the defence of high culture tends to be also the defence (now often a losing battle) of national cultures in their elite forms. Hence the partial rejection of high culture (as expressed in viewing figures) partly reflects the rejection by the people of their middle-class national elites, the classes which have dominated them in the past.

Low or popular culture is commonly associated with the USA. What is the reason for the almost universal appeal of American culture as reflected in Westerns, pop music, police thrillers and soaps? Some alternative (but not necessarily exclusive) answers to this are: (a) taste not guided by an aspiration towards excellence tends to sink towards the crude, kitschy, and superficial; (b) for Europeans American culture seems free from the traditional culture of established – and oppressive (i.e. snobbish) – national power; (c) American culture actually *is* European culture (because of the large-scale immigration from Europe into America), but more go-ahead, less tied to tradition; (d) American tastes *actually are* world tastes; (e) American culture has a crucial edge in the production market for programmes because of its large financial backing and large home market.

But all these considerations are cut across by the suspicion that television broadcasting does not in fact determine a 'cultural space' in any important sense. For viewers attend to television in a much less focused and absorptive way than to books they study (especially if these are reinforced within an educational system) or even to newsprint; they chat to family and friends, go in and out of the room, and tend to retain only a vague general impression of the material of the telecast. And they don't just swallow the attitudes of the programmes they see; very often they watch with a detached and ironic stance based on more deeply embedded aspects of their minds and their cultures. So it is not clear that cultural space should be fought over in the way it has been (at least in connection with television). Perhaps the crucial factors are, rather, the education systems and career-paths.

A public service broadcaster may buy in foreign programmes and so not really be the standard-bearer of national high culture. The largest proportion of American programmes on a British TV channel is on BBC 1. Czech state TV broadcasts on two channels: on one channel many programmes are controlled by IP Praha, which is half owned by Information Publicité (French independent), broadcasting, for example, 'Dallas', 'Derrick' (German crime series), 'Walt Disney Presents', children's programmes sponsored by Mattel toys, and so on; and on its other channel, broadcasting programmes in French, English and German (not Czech) from La Sept (French), CNN (American), Screensport (British), RTL Plus (German), MTV Europa (French). Such a public service broadcasting corporation is driven to become just another player in the commercial market by the difficulty and expense of finding sufficiently interesting programmes, and it is totally wrong to take it as a force for Czech culture or national feeling. Alternatively, a corporation which tries to preserve its tradition of trying to inform and educate people risks becoming so boring to the majority of the population that few watch it. They tend instead to watch broadcasts from neighbouring foreign countries (this happened to Norway).

Programme production

In the effort to preserve national culture in the television its people watches, a country may require by law that a specified proportion of the programmes shown are made in the country, or have been originally made in the country's native language. France requires, for any channel broadcasting in France that 50 per cent of audiovisual broadcast material must be originally made in French, 60 per cent must originate in an EC country, 120 hours of French-produced programmes must be broadcast between 18.00 hrs and 23.00 hrs each year; 15 per cent of turnover must be spent on original French production. But five out of seven French TV channels are operating at a loss, often a very big loss – one private channel became bankrupt and had to be sold in 1992. Producers say this is partly *because* of the quota regulations.

But now a large proportion of programmes is co-produced, by privately backed or public-corporation-backed groups; a consortium of mostly public broadcasters was set up in 1985, comprising Channel 4 (UK), RAI (Italian), ORF (Austrian), ZDF (German), Antenne 2 (French), SRG (Swiss), and RTVE (Spanish). In 1989 442 co-productions were in progress. Thus it seems to make more sense (within the EU) to require that a given proportion of programmes originates in *some* European country. The EU does require this, hoping not only to preserve something of Europe's 'audiovisual space' against the Americans and Australians, but also to foster the European production industry. In addition some EU aid (Eurimage) assists European co-productions. But of course this does not adequately protect individual national cultures and production industries. Moreover, any such rules are very hard to enforce; very many productions use contributions and editing from different studios in different countries. At present there is not much American–European co-production. But it might easily develop – there is quite a lot of American–European co-ownership of broadcasting companies, especially for satellite broadcasting in eastern Europe. Thus the trend is quite strongly towards a broadcasting regime of private channels financed by advertising, competing with each other.

In spite of the tendency to pluralism inherent in modern communications technology, at present the control of major communications (especially television broadcasting, telecommunications networks, and newspapers) is becoming concentrated in the hands of a small number of private companies, and a smaller number of powerful individuals ('media moguls') each of whom controls or exerts influence over a considerable number of these companies. Well-known figures include:

- Rupert Murdoch – Australian by birth, now an American citizen; controls especially (but not exclusively) English-language broadcasting and newspapers, in Europe and North America;
- Silvio Berlusconi – Italian; controls most of Italian television and a lot of its publishing and newspapers, a big slice of Spanish television, some French and German television, and has major interests in Poland, Hungary, and other countries; now (1994) elected as Italy's prime minister on the basis of a campaign which utilised his control of the media;
- Robert Hersant – French; controls much of Hachette;
- Karl-Heinz Bertelsmann – German; interests in RTL Plus (German language independent based in Luxembourg) and in CLT (another Luxembourg-based company);
- Leo Kirch – German; extensive interests in German television and newspapers.

However, these men and their organisations normally focus only on profit, and do not promote particular political viewpoints (except for Berlusconi's campaign). This commercialism may, of course, indirectly affect the political messages conveyed; for instance, advertisers must not be offended, and the audience attracted should feel relaxed and inclined to think in terms of spending money on a high standard of living.

European integration

These and other tendencies have led some people to promote the idea of a European identity – a 'European village' (Delors), or a 'European space' (Felipe González). The public justification for the idea of an overarching

European sense of identity is usually the need to overcome the old, bitter national conflicts of European nations. But a powerful consideration is the attempt to gather together European resistance – especially economic resistance, most notably in the communications industries – to the economic power of America and Japan. How far this attempt to organise a sense of identity for an entity which was previously just a (vaguely defined) geographer's conception will succeed is doubtful. But, more than the discovery of European traditions, the decisive considerations are likely to be the extent to which Europe as a power-bloc – especially an economic trading bloc – operates as a unity which needs to strengthen the loyalty of its population in a similar manner to the way the nation-states operated in the past.

Further reading

Crystal, D. (ed.) (1987) *Cambridge Encyclopaedia of Language*, Cambridge University Press, Cambridge.

Katzner, K. (1977) *Languages of the World*, Routledge, London.

Negrine, R. and Papathanassopoulos, S. (1990) *The Internationalisation of Television*, Pinter Press, London

Noam, E. (1992) *Telecommunications in Western Europe*. Oxford University Press, Oxford.

Noam, E. (1992) *Television in Western Europe*, Oxford University Press, Oxford.

Packer, J., Myttin, K. and Abo Akademi Institute for Human Rights (1993) *The Protection of Ethnic and Linguistic Minorities in Western Europe*, Abo Akademi University, Turku, Finland.

Tunstall, J. and Palmer, M. (1991) *The Media Moguls*, Routledge, London.

Ungerer, H. 1990 *Telecommunications in Europe*, revised edn. The European Commission, Luxembourg.

12 How Europeans see themselves: culture, belief and writing

Introduction

The Introduction to this book discussed how the idea of Europe is partly a cultural one, based on a set of ideas of what a true European country or society is like; and how this idea is associated with a group of countries which might be called the ideal heart of Europe. These countries are pictured in an idealised, but not wholly unrealistic way, as embodying these cultural ideals.

This chapter considers that cultural tradition with which people seek to identify. Not surprisingly, different people hold different views about the essential character of European-ness. So it is important to examine competing conceptions of what it means to be European, and to consider what is genuine in them and what is myth or propaganda. It is also necessary to examine how these cultural traditions have developed since 1945 in Europe – how Europeans have tried to understand their own situation and who they are. The cultural development described here will be mainly focused on three of the biggest and richest states of the 'heart' of Europe, though for the period from 1945 to about 1968 there was a different cultural area operating separately, that of the eastern bloc, and some of its thinkers will be considered as well.

The European cultural tradition

From 600 BC to 200 BC the ancient Greeks built up an extraordinarily fertile intellectual tradition: one of rational inquiry into the causes and explanations of everything, and of development of the individual spirit as free, self-understanding, and valuable in itself. The Romans took over this intellectual tradition as their own culture, and spread it throughout their empire, adding Roman Law and a political tradition of disciplined participation in the state. From the Near East came the Hebrew tradition, which in a fruitful junction with Greek thought produced Judaism and

Christianity, religions in which the individual spirit is seen as having its own individual responsibility and destiny within the Creation. So at the roots of European culture are the curiosity, open-mindedness and rationality of the Greeks, the civic responsibility and political individualism of the Greeks and Romans, and the sense of the significance of the free individual spirit to be found in the main tradition of Christianity.

In the sixteenth and seventeenth centuries Europeans discovered and conquered North and South America, and their trading posts and privileged trading towns were established in remote parts of the coasts of Asia and Africa, in India, Arabia, China, the islands of the East Indies and Japan. Old certainties cracked open; the authority of tradition was rejected in favour of new attempts to make sense of the world from out of the newly strengthened conception of the power of individual reason; and the Europeans tried to make sense of their own dominance and advanced civilisation as against the more stagnant cultures of the East, of Africa, of Islam, and of the native Americans. For many of them the crucial European cultural possession was Christianity. For others, who saw the churches as conservative opponents of the typically European reliance on individual reason, it was reason itself, as developed from the Greeks and preserved in classical culture. For others it was the Roman virtue of self-reliant and socially responsible republicanism.

In modern times the Europeans have understood themselves precisely as the centre of modernity. Modernity began in the eighteenth century in the movement also known as the Enlightenment, at the time when confidence in reason as the power which could enable European civilisation to master the world reached its peak. Thinkers of France, Britain, Germany, Sweden, and Switzerland built up the idea that all of nature, as well as human beings and their societies, could be understood as a rational system. The one who would do the understanding was the individual person, the free thinking mind which developed its own fulfilment in understanding, the subject for whom the whole world was object.

In the Enlightenment view, tradition is of little interest and certainly need not guide people, since they can start at the beginning and by rational effort reach a complete understanding of everything. Not only can the enlightened mind understand everything and communicate everything in clear and coherent language; it can also construct society so as to make it produce the best outcome, which is of course the happiness of each individual member of it. And if the existing social and political arrangements include features now seen as non-rational, like monarchies, aristocracies, traditional religions and classical forms in the arts, then that only shows that we need to get rid of these cobwebs from the dusty past, if necessary in a revolution. Meanwhile we shall continue to develop our scientific knowledge, in an advance in which everything will always get better, because all progress is ultimately an expression of ever-developing knowledge. All structures of the world around us, therefore, are merely provisional; change will move endlessly onward, and is not to be feared or resisted because history itself moves us onward and upward. Politically the confidence of the Enlightenment in human reason tended to line it up with liberal causes – with defence of human rights and with democratic forms of government and society.

This Enlightenment creed is far from dead. It was originally a specifically European creed (even though it was soon exported to America), expressing Europe's sense of its own pre-eminent destiny in history as the bearer of 'progress'. But since the French Revolution of 1789 ended in the Terror and then in the military imperialism of Napoleon, and since the Romantics came to see the meaning of the individual's life, not in an attainable happiness but in an agonising yearning towards an unattainable infinite dream, modernity has been shadowed by a sense of loss and failure. Maybe, people thought, the constant shifting of the structures of the world is not guaranteed to lead always onward and upward; maybe our efforts to build our lives for ourselves in the modern world only lead us into destruction and the release of dark forces of the human mind. The controversial findings of Freud concerning the mysterious workings of the unconscious (the role of instinct, repression, neurosis), further discredited the view that individuals were capable of exercising reasoned control to achieve a progressively more harmonious society. Europe's self-confidence then came to seem to some Europeans a dangerous over-confidence, a belief in rational mastery which betrays the modern consciousness and casts it back into the unsolvable puzzles of life. But this mood of doubt did not appear as a rejection of modernism, but rather as an assertion of the true nature of modernity. So modernism came to mean both the individual mind's drive to understanding (the Enlightenment), and its shadowing by a sense of incompleteness and doubt.

Even in this aspect of negativity and uncertainty, however, a crucial element of the confident Enlightenment was retained: the idea that the centre within which we must wrestle with the problems of doubt is the individual soul or spirit. Whether in its confident 'Enlightenment' mode, or in its mode of doubt, modernism saw the issues as lying *within* the human mind, free even when it was struggling with its own incapacities. It is not surprising, then, that the mood of incompleteness and doubt is politically ambivalent. Some expressions of it have led to a rejection of reason and thence to the conclusion that political authority needs to be asserted above the carping of critics in democratic argument; while other expressions of it have led to a reassertion of true democracy as against the mere appearance of it (discerned by this spirit of suspicion) where it cloaks a subtle form of dominance or imperialism. The irrationalist fascism of the 1920s and 1930s is an example of the former, reactionary kind of critique of the Enlightenment. The Critical Theory of Society originating in the same period (Adorno and Marcuse), and some aspects of the Feminist Movement are examples of the latter, left-wing kind.

Around the beginning of the twentieth century this loss of confidence in the power of reason was coupled with a tendency to question the adequacy of language to express any objective reality. Thinkers and poets – especially those involved in the symbolist, expressionist and surrealist movements – began to regard the use of language in a plain and obvious way as a trap, the kind of trap which had led a whole generation into thinking that such an insanity as the slaughter of millions of men in the First World War was based on rational and sensible decisions. To use language in the traditional straightforward ways was to go along with war-time patriotism's crude propaganda and traditional society's complacent authority structures. To use it was to give way to the illusory objectivity of language which only blocked any possible access to reality as it is actually to be reached: fragmentary, subjective, filtered through dreams and images. Such writers sought new ways to use language, and their writing has shifted the sensibility and understanding of Europeans in ways that have affected the rest of the twentieth century.

The tradition of Christianity generally stood apart from the brasher expressions of the Enlightenment, but has by no means always taken up the mood of doubt and incompleteness. Sometimes it has fostered rather a rejection of the Enlightenment in favour of the assertion of authority and the rejection of democracy (especially in southern Europe, as in the clerical Fascism of Franco in Spain or the Colonels' regime in Greece). But in northern Europe some Christian thinkers have stood out as critics of the materialist capitalist society. And perhaps we should attribute to the Christian background of European culture the fact that even wholly secular thinkers tend to regard the question of the meaning of life as a meaningful question which each individual man or woman must face, even where they think the question cannot be answered. For that failure seems to them a ground for agonised meditation, not for a shrug of the shoulders.

It is in the second half of the twentieth century especially that the sense that the pride of Europeans led them into the worst disasters has been most acute. After two terrible world wars, after the overthrow of democratic values and democratic politics in many of the most advanced states of Europe, in Germany, Italy, Spain; after the building of extermination camps equipped with official gas-chambers for the scientific liquidation of whole peoples; after the burning of tens of thousands of people in bombed cities; after purges, grotesque show-trials, and hysterical panics about spies and foreign contamination; in the midst of a 'Cold War' in which Europe seemed to be irretrievably divided between over-simplified ideologies accusing each other of crimes, and all the peoples of Europe – and maybe of the whole earth – were threatened with extermination if their nuclear weapons were unleashed; how could anyone in Europe feel that the modern European spirit could be relied on to lead humankind towards happiness? So it is not surprising that much of the culture of Europe since 1945 has been a culture of doubt, of criticism, of a search for radical rethinking.

Critics and activists

This stress within contemporary European culture has shown itself most clearly in the work of artists, writers and thinkers. In some cultures artists and thinkers have generally been the ideological props and cheerleaders of society and of its political power structures. But in modern Europe the most significant artists and thinkers have usually been critical or oppositional in temper; they have registered in their own emotions the strains of the culture, and tried to find a way for society to be less oppressive, less fragmented into lonely individuals struggling against each other, less inclined to promote aggression and the drive for mastery. These concerns have often been embodied in the political left, in which they find expression in a political programme of some kind based on support for the poorer and (individually) less powerful in society, the workers and peasants, often linked to the hope of a politically driven transformation in society, a 'revolution'. Horror at the results of Fascism and Nazism during the Second World War gave a strong impetus to the left in the period from 1945 to 1968. European civilisation was in crisis; its power structures and culture seemed to have proved deeply and irremediably flawed. For many artists and thinkers the need for some kind of hope in the face of this sense of crisis was overwhelming.

The left

For the left this aspiration had to be centred on the hope of a revolution to enable Europeans to start building a good society from a different base than the old corrupt power structures. The most influential left-wing ideas about the possibility of forming a good society were those of Marxist-inspired cultural critics of capitalist society who had little connection with the Soviet model, the eastern bloc or the Leninist movement. For instance, an Institute of Marxist research had been founded in Frankfurt in 1923, producing notable work before 1934, when all its members had to flee. Most spent the war years in the free-wheeling atmosphere of California. It was there that Theodor Adorno and Max Horkheimer wrote their penetrating critique of the Enlightenment as an essentially imperialist, domination-justifying system of thought, *The Dialectic of Enlightenment* (1947).

It was particularly the Frankfurt School (as it came to be called after Adorno and Horkheimer had returned to Germany after 1949 and refounded the Institute) that established that kind of critique of the Enlightenment confidence in reason, which has been so influential ever since. Indeed much of European thought since then can be seen as successive attempts to identify a way of thought not trapped in the totalitarian dominance strategies which, according to Adorno and Horkheimer, hide behind the apparent liberal openness of Enlightenment thought. In their view, the whole structure of a modern, late-capitalist society is a kind of anonymous system, which oppresses, restricts and distorts the lives of everyone living in it, but which is not consciously operated by anyone or any class as a system of control and exploitation of others. Thus the oppression and alienation is as much cultural as economic, and it operates as destructively for managers and professionals living at quite a high standard of living as it does for unskilled labourers earning very little. The task of a writer, then, is to be a critic of culture, awakening the consciousness of people living in the midst of this system to its destructive, all-pervasive grip, provoking them to what the Italian writer Italo Calvino called a 'Challenge to the Labyrinth'. For example, the linguistically experimental texts of the German poet Hans Magnus Enzensberger, who was familiar with Adorno's ideas, sought to expose the insidiously mendacious nature of so-called normal language, particularly that of bureaucracy and advertising.

But whether such a challenge could result in a social or political revolution seemed dubious to the writers of the Frankfurt School; they were too deeply aware of the way the system absorbs all challenges against it, turning them into what critics called 'radical chic' (i.e. expressions of radical style and opinion which are really no more than gestures to make a smart impression on others). However, the ideas of this 'Critical Theory of Society' (as it was called) spread widely. The most influential Frankfurt School writer in the 1960s was Herbert Marcuse, who had stayed in California; his influential *One-Dimensional Man* of 1961 presented the critique of late-capitalist society as one which made its members atrophy into just one dimension when their real human potential should have enabled them to develop many dimensions of life.

It was from about this time (and partly because of Marcuse's vivid book) that the mood of these critics of 'The System' or 'The Establishment' changed from mere analysis to the thought that revolt might overthrow it. And a few years later factors such as acute student discontent in practical matters, for instance hopelessly over-crowded lecture theatres and soulless campuses, came together with this steadily developing intellectual attitude of anti-Establishment revolt to generate the mass rallies, demonstrations, and riots of 1968 in Paris, Berlin, London and other university cities of western Europe as well as the USA whose overtly imperialist Vietnam policy further kindled the anti-authoritarian fire. The hope among students for socialist revolution continued into the early 1970s in many western European countries, fuelled by the protest songs of dedicated left-wingers such as the Spanish singer, Paco Ibañez, who set to music politically committed poems by Gabriel Celaya and others.

But throughout the post-war years, right up to 1991, the left was bedevilled by the question of the Soviet Union: was Soviet communism the model for the left and the cause to which it should be loyal, or was it some kind of perversion of the socialist ideas of a good society? Already in the late 1940s the British socialist writer George Orwell pinpointed in ferocious satires the dangers of socialist revolutions. Gradually it became more and more difficult to believe in the Soviet Union as a progressive force. News of the purges and mass imprisonments of the 1930s became harder to deny or minimise; eastern

Europe under the domination of the Soviet Union looked less and less like a model of happy socialism and a beacon of hope. New purges and show trials and a revolt suppressed by tanks in East Berlin were followed by Khrushchev's account at the twentieth CPSU Congress in February 1956 of some at least of Stalin's crimes. This contributed to the causes of the Hungarian uprising later that year and further Soviet army intervention. Those who still believed in Soviet socialism were further disillusioned in 1968 by the suppression by WTO (mainly Soviet) tanks of the Prague Spring, which was feeling its way towards a humane form of socialism.

The political left increasingly turned to the attempt to bring about a socialist revolution in western Europe in a direction wholly different from that of the Soviet Union. This movement, however, always suffered from a tendency to be merely a movement of the intellectuals and students; the political weight of the workers as a mass force never settled into a clear focus on bringing about a socialist revolution, but directed itself more to short-term aims. When the student revolt of 1968 failed to take with it any substantial support from the workers, this kind of socialism ceased to be a basis for practical hope; and even the reformist socialist programmes of the big parties of western European countries (in any case less satisfying to those who are looking for a major change on which to pin their hopes), ran into all kinds of difficulties in the 1970s and 1980s.

To those within central and eastern Europe the situation seemed very different. Before 1968 some thinkers, especially in East Germany, Czechoslovakia and Hungary, tried to think constructively within the framework of Marxist socialism, to help their own societies to a better, freer society, 'socialism with a human face' as the programme of the Prague Spring was called. But one after another, after more or less of a struggle with the regime, they felt forced to abandon this hope, either by leaving eastern Europe altogether, or by writing in a more and more critical or individualist way and courting yet harsher sanctions. Bertolt Brecht the playwright and Ernst Bloch the philosopher, author of *The Principle of Hope*, returned from war-time exile in the USA to live in and identify with communist East Germany. Brecht was assigned a prestigious position in Berlin theatre, Bloch one in the University of Leipzig. But when they criticised the government for its suppression of the East Berlin uprising of 1953, Brecht's work was severely restricted and Bloch was forbidden to publish or teach and was put under house-arrest. In 1961 he finally gave up hope for the East German regime, and escaped to the West, where his work became one of the inspirations of the 1968 student revolt. Wolf Biermann the folk-singer and political poet followed a parallel course a few years later; his voice was also silenced while he lived in the East, so he returned to the West. Rudolf Bahro in 1977 published in the FRG (not in the GDR where he lived) a book describing a humane socialism, *The Alternative*; he was given an eight-year gaol sentence. Christa Wolf the novelist remained in East Germany, but her writing became more and more individualist, more distant from any clear kind of political hope.

Karel Kosik, the Czech philosopher, published analyses of Marxism in the early 1960s which helped to inspire the programme of the Prague Spring; after the suppression of that programme he stopped all publication. Agnes Heller and Ferenc Feher of Hungary, followers of the Marxist philosopher Georg Lukacs, continued to pursue their left-wing political thinking, but in a way more and more remote from the reality of communist power in their home country, and increasingly they worked in the West.

Worthwhile writers in the Soviet Union tended more frequently to be dissidents or outright opponents of the regime, writing in defence of the freedom of the individual and against the oppression and terror of the Gulags (the prison-camps). Consequently they were more likely to be subjected to serious harassment or imprisonment by the government. Such were Andrei Sakharov the nuclear physicist and Alexander Solzhenitsyn the novelist. But the outcome for such dissidents was often that they left the Soviet Union (voluntarily or involuntarily), their homeland where people understood their feelings and their language, and lived in exile. Andrei Tarkovsky the film-director, Rudolf Nureyev the dancer, Mstislav Rostropovich the cellist and conductor, were other Soviet artists who followed this road to exile. Sometimes (as for Milan Kundera the Czech novelist) exile in the West seemed to be a solution for these artists. But for some – like Solzhenitsyn and Tarkovsky – their creative power diminished away from their home country. In the 1980s, however, some thinkers made their protest and stayed in the East, often in prison or in preventive detention, as symbols of defiance for their people. Sakharov did this, as did Vaclav Havel, the Czech playwright, who called on people to resist the lies they were expected to subscribe to in his *The Power of the Powerless* of 1985. Havel subsequently became president of Czechoslovakia and then of the Czech Republic, and Sakharov a key figure in the more genuine Soviet parliament of 1989.

But for thinkers and artists of the West the fading of hopes of a revolutionary transformation of society left them more uncertain about where they stood. A common reaction was to stand aside from large-scale, positive political programmes, but to engage critically with the system of European society and its established power structures, and with its terrible history. Much of this work took the form of a focus on individuals trying to live their lives and give them meaning in the deadening framework of ideologies and power structures in which the weight of Europe's history imposed its force against any divergence from the norm. Gunther Grass the German novelist, in *The Tin Drum* of 1959, encased his 'individual', with bitter humour, in the character of a dwarf who even when he grows up has the mental age of a young child (thus retaining his 'innocence' and avoiding adult entanglement in the corruptions of society), but whose tin drum disrupts the music of the military-political brass band and whose magically piercing scream breaks the shop-windows of capitalist cities.

Although Germany's neighbour, Switzerland, had maintained an official position of neutrality throughout the Second World War, the Swiss writer Max

Frisch appeared fully involved in the contemporary socio-cultural crisis, exposing in his satirical plays the insidious phenomenon of self-delusion and complacent complicity with evil totalitarian regimes. His compatriot Friedrich Dürrenmatt in his play *The Physicists* (1962) used paradox and parody to identify courageous personal endeavour to fulfil one's obligations to humankind as the only possible line of conduct, however futile, in a materialistic world embarked on a crazy course to self-annihilation. Primo Levi, the Italian chemist and later novelist, survivor of the Auschwitz extermination camp, wrote of the decency of following the rational and useful structure of chemistry within a world in which decency was constantly lost.

One field of this struggle was precisely the issue of how recent European history should be understood, and in particular the horror of Hitler's Germany and the Nazi Holocaust. That such atrocities were possible at all overwhelmed many thinkers. Ever since 1945 successive writers have revealed the crimes of the Nazis, the extent of collaboration with them, and other awful crimes of the period.

Cases of hitherto-concealed collaboration especially aroused the greatest shock: Rolf Hochhuth's 1963 play *The Representative*, which portrayed the war-time Pope as agreeing to the extermination of the Italian Jews; Victor Farías's revelation of the extent of the involvement of the admired philosopher Martin Heidegger with the Nazi cause; the discovery of the extent of the French collaboration with the occupying Germans during the war, and with their extermination programmes, and so on. Trials of some of those responsible took place, sometimes 50 years after the crimes, as in the trial of the French collaborator Klaus Barbie in 1992. In Austria the Chancellor Kurt Waldheim was brought into disgrace when his war-time military record in the German Army was revealed. In Germany the attempt to gain any kind of sympathetic understanding of the actions of Germans who had gone along with the government during the Nazi period caused outraged controversies, as in the row over Chancellor Kohl's tribute to the dead soldiers of the war at the Bitburg Cemetery, while the philosopher Jürgen Habermas led the protest against sympathetic (or, fellow-travelling) history of the period in the 'historians' controversy' of 1986–89. The wounds left in European consciousness by that terrible time still hurt 50 years after the end of the war.

Existentialism

This sense of the life of the individual as the place of freedom apart from society, but also of suffering and of struggle to achieve meaning, could also be the focus of concern for writers in itself. This was the character of the extraordinary success of existentialism in the years after the Second World War, from 1945 to about 1955 or 1960. Existentialism arose especially in France, where it was the label given to the ideas of Jean-Paul Sartre who tried to give a direction to European culture by which it could avoid the feebleness of liberalism (as he saw its pre-war character) and the brutality of fascism.

Sartre argued that the self has no fixed being and no preordained destiny, but has always to be created by each individual person, following no rules, no prescription about how to live or how to understand oneself; each individual has his or her own freedom to live up to even while being perpetually threatened by the absurd. The self has its most fundamental meaning just in preserving its own integrity, in not going along with the norms of society or the requirements of others, even when these requirements are perhaps morally right. In existentialist plays and novels the characters who do this are often defeated, and their cause often fails, sometimes even in a way which shows it was perhaps the wrong cause; but if, in failing, they stick to their own sense of what their path in life is, while not trying to impose it on other people, then they have kept true to their own humanity. So there came to be a great fashion for the *film noir*, in which the heroes are killed and utterly defeated after everything they hoped for has turned out to be betrayed, or to have been a mistake; often these films were literally *noir* (black) or at least dark, as they often used night-scenes in the streets and alleys of cities, with figures appearing out of the shadows.

Perhaps it could be said that the fashion for existentialism reflected a deep sense in Europe that all grand talk, all messianic ideologies and great programmes for society, all claims to have seen the meaning of history, are illusions and frauds, which are used as covers for aggressive power structures like those of the Nazis. This is a rejection of the Enlightenment confidence about reason, a way of going over to the other side of modernism, the side of criticism and doubt. And what survives this scepticism about great causes and all-embracing interpretations of history and moral uplift, is just the sense of individual freedom and commitment preserved in the very heart of each individual person.

Existentialism seems at first like just the extreme negative side of modernism, the side of doubt and negativity, with all the positive, Enlightenment side eliminated. But it is not really like that. If it had been, then nothing at all would have been left, no hope, no meaning, no point in living in one way rather than another way. But the existentialists were really deeply, passionately committed to something. What they were committed to was just this belief in the value of human freedom, of the integrity and responsibility of the individual man or woman, lying behind all the religious creeds and political programmes and moral values, at the pure centre of the human consciousness. If everything else fails, if you go wrong in the pattern of all your actions and all your attempts to make sense of the world, still there will be, if you hold on to it bravely, this one thing, the freedom at the heart of your consciousness. It was a philosophy which struck an answering chord in post-war Europe, in which many people remembered how difficult it had been for those living in occupied Europe under the Nazis to keep faith with a belief in the victory of the Allies, and in some cases to die fighting for the Resistance without any certainty that the sacrifice would be of any use. Sartre wrote several plays and novels about just that situation, as did Albert Camus. For

Camus the notion of solidarity with others became increasingly significant, while Sartre remained suspicious of the potential that solidarity has for Fascist notions of blood and soil.

But that was in the years immediately after the war, when that sense of heroism and of the possibility of a socialist society was still fresh in people's minds. The hopes of social renewal faded, as people felt more the falseness of the ideologies of communism and of the anti-communist, capitalist West, both of them wielding the threat of horrible destruction which might be unleashed on the peoples of Europe, and responsible meanwhile for injustice and suffering. The ordinary entanglement of people's lives in selfish aims and corruption took hold, and the heroic style of existentialism came to seem less real. As a philosophy, it has died. Its over-blown faith in the being of transcendental consciousness, the self behind all particular contents of the mind, in control of its instrument – language – no longer convinces anyone. But its long afterglow is still with us in the form of pop culture.

Pop culture

Pop culture, the youth culture of our time, came originally from the USA. But it spread fast all over Europe. By the 1960s it was as thoroughly based in Europe as in North America. The Iron Curtain could not stop it; the young people of Moscow and Leningrad, Warsaw and Prague, took to the concerts, the songs, the records, the pop star cult, the discos, the jeans, in a way that the staid Party officials and the members of the *nomenklatura* could do nothing about. Pop culture has done more to dissolve the pompous prestige of official ideologies in Europe than any intellectual argument or great book. But how did it happen? Why did this culture of individual self-expression sweep Europe in the second half of the twentieth century when it had not done so before? People had always sung songs and listened to music when they could. But pop culture is different; it has a special individualist, anarchic style which the folk songs of the eighteenth century or the music-hall songs of the 1920s lacked. How did it come to have such an appeal to the generations of the 1960s, 1970s, 1980s and 1990s?

Pop culture has a style of approach to life which is like existentialism without the heroism and strong sense of commitment to action. Typically pop culture is anarchic, avoiding all involvement with causes, creeds, or moral rules imposed on others. Like existentialism, it takes each individual back to his or her own naked self, without rules or pretences or frameworks to guide life. But what is left at this centre of individual life, for pop culture, is not the drive towards commitment and responsibility, social or political action, which marked out Sartre's thought. Sartre's own political position was strongly left-wing, and he wrote a long and deep analysis of freedom and alienation in society (*The Critique of Dialectical Reason*) which pointed to the need for a Marxist revolution. One would not expect pop culture, since it is expressed mainly as song-lyrics, to include analyses of anything. And its style and tenor is far less earnest than Existentialism, more focused on the emotions and less on the possibility of action, on individuals and their immediate relations rather than the social or political.

This retreat from any sense of possible action to ameliorate the social conditions in which we all live is expressed also in a pervasive cynicism and materialism. The cynicism especially concerns political programmes or social causes involving politics. People feel that there are no great social or religious causes to identify with or believe in, that any political movements which exist are liable to be only fronts behind which self-seeking politicians can feather their own nests, and those who proclaim great causes are probably only in it for what they can get. More and more young people who, in a previous generation, might have been expected to be idealists passionately committed to a cause which might offer hope of some kind of New Jerusalem, were impressed by the thought that the consequences of attempts to establish a New Jerusalem were usually appalling. Instead, they increasingly focused their efforts just on getting a good job with a large salary. This combination of cynicism and materialism began to be noticeable in the 1960s, but after the failure of the 1968 students' revolt it was much more marked. Only time will tell whether it will continue to be so noticeable a feature of the Europe of the future. But it is worth noting that the collapse of the Italian political system in 1992–93 was essentially a product of this cynicism and materialism. Politicians, seeing that people expected little else from them, only nominally subscribed to political beliefs and used their power to feather the nests of themselves and their friends; but when the public became fully aware of this fraudulent power structure they overturned it in a general rage with all politicians.

Of course this cynicism and withdrawal from social commitment were never universal. Increasingly, from the time of the 1968 debâcle, people took up causes which might be called radical life-programmes: ideas for the reordering of attitudes and social action which were not total ideologies, not programmes for changing the whole social and economic structure, but which impinged on only one aspect or dimension of social life. It was in the 1970s that feminism took off in Europe. It built on the ideas of Simone de Beauvoir whose *The Second Sex* of 1949 inspired a whole generation of thinkers who argued for a deep-rooted change in consciousness and in ways of living to combat what they saw as a consistent suppression of women. A series of issues focused the more theoretical discussions on practical action: rights to abortion, rights to equal employment opportunities, rights to equal political representation. Such claims brought controversy to many countries in Europe and in turn further stimulated feminist thinkers and writers. It was in the 1970s also that active concern for the environment and for its degradation by the impact of modern human life and technology became widespread. These issues – altogether outside the structures of traditional politics – seemed to offer the possibility of really making a difference to life.

Literature and the language problem

Since the end of the nineteenth century rejection of the Enlightenment's overweening confidence in reason had been accompanied by a challenge to conventional assumptions about language – a challenge which was articulated above all in avant-garde poetry and theatre. This preoccupation with and exploration of the nature and status of language became more marked in the years after the Second World War, manifesting itself in novels as well as in poetry and plays. After the shattering experience of hypocrisy, propaganda, and violence, after the trauma of exile which often brought about separation from one's native language and confrontation with a strange new one, the notion of a logically consistent, pre-existing reality, in relation to which coherent individuals could have coherent thoughts which they could communicate in coherent language to other individuals capable of relating them to their own coherent world-view, seemed totally bankrupt. In many texts of the late 1940s, and of the 1950s and 1960s conventional linguistic and conceptual categories were dislocated to the point of virtual breakdown, articulating grotesque and disturbing hallucinatory visions of human isolation and degradation in a hopelessly fragmented, alien environment.

Such traits are present, for example, in the works of writers as diverse as Fernando Arrabal, a Spanish playwright who wrote in French during self-imposed exile from Franco's dictatorship, Eugène Ionesco, a dramatist of mixed Romanian and French origin, and Paul Celan, a German-speaking Romanian Jew, who settled in Paris after living through the deportation of his parents to a death-camp. Major questions and dilemmas haunt the works of poets like Celan – the possibility that there may be no way of escaping sufficiently from the corrupting effect of established language systems to articulate anything original or, alternatively, the possibility that the attempt to operate on the fringe of these systems may render texts so opaque and private that they are inaccessible to others. However, there are also hints of hope that the complex layers and networks of meaning generated by the experimental language will somehow open up new perspectives to humanity.

In the novels and plays of Samuel Beckett, an Irishman who spent much of his life in France and who wrote in both English and French mainly in the 1940s and 1950s, experimentation with language became a major feature and indeed a central theme. So also did exploration of its communicative power, and its relationship not only with thought and reality, but also with personal identity. In Beckett's trilogy of novels, parody of logically ordered language presented a vision of absurdity which pointed not only towards the meaninglessness of the world, but also called into question the integrity of the individual who confronts it. Beckett's characters are caught between the basic need to encapsulate their unique identity and the impossibility of doing so. Identity can be expressed only within the framework of language, since to pass beyond language is to pass into silence and non-being, and yet language is hackneyed and impure. Thus the contours of 'characters' who are no more than fragile linguistic constructs become blurred, and identities become at least partially interchangeable. Now, not only is our world devoid of meaning and our actions ridiculously futile, our language is suspect and yet we are trapped within it, so that our very identity as individuals is a dubious fiction. This is far from the existentialist belief in the freedom to shape the self or to construct an original and coherent book. Apparently nothing is left but a tissue of language compulsively filling the void and questioning itself – and perhaps laughter at the crazy incongruity of it all.

Modernism and post-modernism

The following sections consider not so much the general movements of feeling and opinion which were widespread in Europe in these years, but how the leading writers and artists and the deepest thinkers were responding to the spiritual crisis of the age.

Structuralism

The end of existentialism came with the realisation that its secure fortress to which consciousness retreated, the freedom of the transcendental self at the heart of consciousness, is really a kind of dream, a piece of philosophical wishful thinking. For if there were such a centre of the self, it would have to be possible to discern it as it expressed itself in some pure expression of free consciousness, with all the illusory and uncertain structures of tradition and old philosophies and rational constructions wiped away to reveal pure consciousness itself alone. And this just cannot be done.

The impossibility of such a pure expression comes out in the impossibility of 'innocent' writing; that is, of writing which could be completely free of traditions and inherited value-systems and pre-specified ways of understanding. All writing is already involved with some such structures; and since our traditions are always involved with failure and the crimes and disasters of history, all writing is 'complicit' with these failures and crimes, however it may try to approach all issues with the best of good intentions, in a spirit of pure starting-from-scratch. That was what Roland Barthes meant when he denied the possibility of innocent writing. Equally, the idea that any writing can be the expression of just the fresh response to the world of this one consciousness, the author's, is also an illusion. An author does not have a fresh consciousness which could start from nothing but its own freedom; any more than any human being on earth has such a fresh consciousness. What an author writes should be understood, rather, as an expression of a development of already given structures of thought and value in response to the changing reality of the world. So a reader should not interpret a text by using it as a key to the state of mind and understanding of the author who expressed his or her

262 THE EUROPEAN MOSAIC: CONTEMPORARY POLITICS, ECONOMICS AND CULTURE

consciousness in it. Rather, a text should be read as an expression of cultural structures.

This line of thought began as a theory of literary criticism, first argued by Barthes in *Writing Degree Zero* in 1953. But it was never merely a theory about literature (if such theories are ever 'mere'). The reason why a text cannot be interpreted as the expression of a pure individual consciousness is that *nothing* can be so interpreted: no music, no painting, no face-to-face speech, no looking into the eyes of another person, no love-making – nothing. And since there is no way in which expression of any kind can be innocent, the very idea of a pure transcendental self can only be an illusion – a figment of metaphysical dreaming. It is not just the text which has to be interpreted as a net of structures of cultural tradition; the consciousness which lies behind it is itself nothing but such a net of shifting structures. The tissue and substance of the conscious mind (and of the unconscious mind too) is made up of structures of thought and value and patterns of desire; and behind them there is no transcendental self freely accepting or rejecting these structures as if they were goods on offer in a supermarket. There is no transcendental self at all.

This view, that texts and thought and the life of individuals should be understood in terms of the structures of the cultures in which they are embedded, is what is meant by 'structuralism'. It is essentially connected with the rejection of the idea of a transcendental self.

The structuralist overthrow of existentialism, then, went much further than just to propose a different method of interpreting texts in literature courses in universities. Its implication was that the author, as he or she had previously been conceived, does not exist at all. The author as the constructing, inventing consciousness behind the text, who expresses his or her own individual and original response to the world owing nothing to anyone, does not exist. Barthes expressed this view, melodramatically perhaps, as 'the death of the author'. 'Death' here carried the implication that the *idea* of the author, which for centuries has governed Europe's idea of the source from which ultimately all culture comes, has been destroyed by Europe's development to the point where it has given birth to structuralism. The shock, nostalgia and almost grief which this event produces is like the effect on a family of the death of a loved one on whom the family had relied. A few years later, in the 1960s, Michel Foucault expressed the full implications of the death of the author by speaking of the end of humanism and the end of the human race. The idea of individuals as the transcendental source of all culture, free in themselves, is now revealed as an illusion. And the effects on our understanding of ourselves, of our hopes, fears and values, are sure to be profound.

The general character of this change was a retreat from the subjective basis to which European culture had ultimately referred all issues. The positive side of modernism, the Enlightenment, the confident assertion of mastery by the advance of knowledge, is detached from the base on which it had previously rested – the faith in the capacity of the pure self to proceed by reason alone towards rational truth. But equally, the negative pole of modernism, the scepticism and doubt, had been understood as resting on the power of the free mind to detach itself from rational schemas and discern for itself that they could not be proved and that their grounds were unsound. The emotion and sense of personal meaning to which the doubting mind then retreated took its value from the idea that it was a genuine, totally individual response. With the advent of structuralism, none of this could still be maintained.

But if not, if the consequences of the 'death of the human race' were so radically destructive of the basic assumptions of European culture, where did that leave us? What is the outcome of a structuralist understanding?

At first sight it might seem that structuralism would lead to a depressing kind of determinism: to the belief that every thought and any feeling that anyone could have has already been determined by the causal forces of society and history. Human beings would really be marionettes, pirouetting around the stage of life imagining that they were important and really doing something, while all the time the forces of the structures of society and history were pulling the strings which moved them. And that may indeed have been the implication of the ideas of the anthropologist Claude Lévi-Strauss, who showed how the cultural life of any society is built on structures of meaning and metaphor; for instance, the pattern of food taboos of the Australian aborigines relates to the structures of their family relationships, of their myths and their picture of the world, to their idea of history, and to the inter-relations of the different tribes. Indeed, in a way all these structures are just one structure, translated into a different dimension each time. This seems to describe the aborigines' way of understanding the world and themselves, and their ways of acting, as not really the result of any conscious planned decisions by the aborigines themselves but rather as the outcome of these structures underlying their lives, which they themselves did not grasp in a theoretical way at all. But if all societies are like that – including our own – then indeed it seems that it is the structures of culture which really determine everything.

Lévi-Strauss's ideas had great influence on the first generation of structuralist thinkers. But the structuralists who followed him and who made such a strong impact in the 1960s – Barthes, Foucault, Althusser, Todorov – were not at all inclined to see cultural life in this determinist way. Still less were the novelists who wrote under the structuralist influence – Alain Robbe-Grillet, Nathalie Sarraute, Italo Calvino – inclined to think in a purely determinist way. Rather, they set up texts which are devoid of traditionally recognisable characters and sequential plots and where obsessive language patterns invite the reader to interact with them, so that they sense the close and intricate influence of the cultural structures. Precisely in this way the reader may be able to discern how the new, fragile and barely attained expression of freedom within and among these structures might be found.

In political terms one could say that these writers wanted to face without any wishful thinking the complexity of the structures of power in society and their capacity to 'recuperate' (i.e. turn to their own purposes) all attempts to overcome or mitigate them by a progressive social or political movement. Calvino called this pervasive power 'the Labyrinth'. But still he wanted, as arguably they all wanted, to reveal the possibility of a 'Challenge to the Labyrinth', not by escaping from it completely – that was impossible – but by a continued and constantly renewed effort of fighting for what could be seen to make some freedom possible, some renewal of humanity.

Post-structuralism

In 1967 three remarkable books were published by the French thinker Jacques Derrida. In them Derrida made clear that like the structuralists he rejected the idea of a transcendental self and a pure consciousness, and that he accepted the view of thought as a deep entanglement of traditions of cultural understandings. But the main focus of his thought was on the indeterminacy of the way these traditions exerted their continuing influence within texts; and indeed on the precarious, shifting nature of these traditions – the structures – themselves. He wanted, he later said, to make these structures *tremble*, or rather, to show that they already trembled and shook and were not fixed, and that there is a perpetual tendency to go wrong in interpreting tradition by thinking of it as if its meaning had finally been determined. The way to show this is to examine the texts themselves in which these structures appear, which carry the cultural traditions in which we live, and *deconstruct* them; that is, interpret them so as to show their shifting, fragile character, in which their own internal tensions break down all attempts to find fixed meanings for them.

The idea of deconstruction proved enormously influential. Derrida himself was not very attached to the label 'deconstructionist', which journalists applied to his work, because he viewed all such labels as misleading in suggesting that there is a clear doctrine and defined method for people to adopt, whereas (he thought) all thinking must be acutely aware of its own tendency to pretend to a fixity which it cannot have. People also labelled his thought 'post-structuralist', thinking that it was a new movement in philosophy and came after structuralism, and that its attack on fixity of interpretation must be an attack on structuralism with its belief in structures.

This is clearly too crude a view: the structuralists never wanted to see the structures they studied as determinate. But what is true is that Derrida brought into much clearer view a way in which thinkers could do what structuralists had always wanted to do: to reveal within texts the complexity of interplay of cultural structures and the element of possible freedom in the way new texts and new thinking can use their own traditions. So in that sense it is true that there is a movement which can be called 'post-structuralism'. At any rate, since 1967 philosophy, literary criticism and avant-garde writing could never be the same again. There is a new focus on difference as such; on the possibility of writing and thinking in a way which looks outside its own framework to the different.

Who, besides Derrida himself, could be said to be part of this movement? One should notice the appearance of an important group of feminist thinkers, who brought together Derrida's thought of difference with the idea that women as such think in a way which is more open to difference than the thought of most men. In the 1970s and 1980s a new generation of women thinkers and writers – Julia Kristeva, Luce Irigaray, Hélène Cixous – took up this idea and developed the theory that women's thought-styles can carry further the post-structuralist focus on difference and plurality.

Post-modernism

This section attempts to draw these threads together. The governing conception of Europe, as a cultural focus for the late twentieth century, is that of modernism. It has been shown how the overthrow of existentialism really undercuts both the positive side of modernism, and its sceptical and doubting negative side. The crucial question for late twentieth century European culture then becomes, how is modernism to be rethought; or, if we abandon modernism, what do we need to put in its place? This question remains open. But one answer has come into view. This is the thought that modernism has been succeeded by a culture of post-modernism. According to this view (put forward by the American Martin Berman and the French thinker Jean-François Lyotard), modernism, in bringing everything back to the basis of thought in a single self-determining consciousness, imposes a simple, one-centred system on all understanding, at least as the direction in which thought should go.

The overthrow of the idea of the transcendental self should be understood as the overthrow of this ideal of one-centred, single-picture understanding. Instead we have to get used to thinking of a world in which there are always many perspectives, many viewpoints, which are never resolved into one right one. Difference, multiplicity, relation to others whom we do not fully understand, is what a post-modern society is like for everyone in it, and not just for those who have not acquired the established, final, approved view of the elite who know. On this view, post-structuralism is really the philosophy of a post-modern condition of life.

Whether this view is right or fruitful, it is as yet too early to say. What is clear is that these movements will have a very marked effect on how the Europeans can conceive of their own imperfect unity-in-difference, in their renewed attempts to understand what it is to be European. To some extent there is already in a number of domains a shift in focus from the exploration of difference to the notion of the extension of consensus, but consensus which can never be other than provisional, multi-faceted, and problematic.

Further reading

(a) You should read a few of the notable *post-war European novels and plays* published since 1945, choosing some different countries. Possible authors you might read include George Orwell, Heinrich Böll, Gunther Grass, Christa Wolf, Friedrich Dürrenmatt, Simone de Beauvoir, Samuel Beckett, Albert Camus, Alain Robbe-Grillet, Italo Calvino, Milan Kundera, and Alexander Solzhenitsyn.

(b) You could usefully study the following books on movements of thought and culture:

Baumann, Z. (1992) *Intimations of Postmodernity*, Routledge, London.
Hoffmann, S. and Kitromilides, P. (1981) *Culture and Society in Contemporary Europe*, George Allen and Unwin, London.
Hughes, H.S. (1988) *Sophisticated Rebels: the Political Culture of European Dissent 1968–87*, Harvard University Press, Cambridge, Massachusetts.
Kearney, R. (1986) *Modern Movements in European Philosophy*, Manchester University Press, Manchester.
Maier, C.S. (1988) *The Unmasterable Past: History, Holocaust and German National Identity*, Harvard University Press, Cambridge, Massachusetts.
Ramet, S.P. (ed.) (1994) *Rocking the State: Rock Music and Politics in Eastern Europe and Russia*, Westview Press, Boulder, Colorado.

13 Living with diversity? Nation-states and national identities

A notable fact about human beings in modern political systems is their tendency to define themselves as part of an *identified group*, such as a nation, which goes far beyond the immediate communities, rooted in family, locality, or workplace, to which they tangibly belong. Both *nationalism* and a universalised *sense of national identity* are essentially modern phenomena. Of course, it is neither the case that a sense of national identity automatically makes one a nationalist; nor that even a 'shared' national identity will necessarily evoke the same response in different individuals. Two people may both 'feel' German or British; but whereas one may take pride in a perception of past or present national 'greatness', the other may feel shame and even pain in a perception of past or present injustices perpetrated in the country's name. National identity, after all, is a complex phenomenon – the product of complex interactions between social, economic, political, and cultural histories. Moreover, one's sense of national identity is rarely one's *only* politically significant identity, even when it is of prime importance to the individual: national identity co-exists with identities rooted in region, class, religion, gender, sexuality, and so on.

Identification with a nation need not be an identification with only one such group. For example, one might be proud to be Welsh as well as British: when Colin Jackson won the 110 metres hurdles at the World Athletics Championship in 1993 he draped himself in both the Welsh flag and the Union Jack to do his victory-run round the stadium. One might identify oneself as a supporter of the football club Juventus, a citizen of Turin, a Roman Catholic, and an Italian, all together; as well as a European perhaps. So these group identifications about which people feel so strongly can and do overlap, in *multiple identities*. Sometimes they reinforce each other: a citizen of the Irish Republic may feel Irish partly as a Roman Catholic, so that Catholicism and Irishness reinforce each other. Sometimes they challenge each other: an Irish Protestant, Jew, or atheist, living in what has been until recently a devoutly Catholic society, may struggle with an idea of Irish identity which conflates that identity with membership of one religious denomination.

Above all, group identifications change, as societies change. Nowhere does a sense of national identity remain static. As with all identities, national identity is constantly reinterpreted and reconstructed, even if some nationalist political movements, appealing to myths of racial or cultural 'purity', seek to obscure this fact.

Many of the more powerful group identifications are associated with institutions such as the church or the state. These institutions build up their strength by doing all they can to promote in their supporters a sense of identification and loyalty. The state in modern times takes measures on an extensive scale to build up a sense of nationhood in its citizens, to make people think of themselves as loyal Greeks or loyal Swedes and so on, and moreover to disseminate the belief that it is the state which embodies the sense of nationhood shared by at least a majority of those living within its boundaries. The success, or otherwise, of the state in disseminating this belief will critically affect the extent to which ruling elites enjoy political legitimacy (that is, a widespread acceptance, active or passive, of their right to exercise state power in the name of the collective group).

This relates to another characteristic of the modern era: the fact that most modern states tend to be nation-states, the territorial limits of which are justified by reference to the perceived common national characteristics of a majority of those inhabiting the state's territory. In so far as features of physical geography – such as oceans, seas, or mountain ranges – may contribute to cultural differentiation between peoples, the myth of 'natural state frontiers' may be deployed by those engaged in the process of nation-state building. Of course, the reality is that – geography notwithstanding – few, if any, states in modern Europe are ethnically or nationally homogeneous. There are few universally or even commonly perceived 'natural' frontiers. Furthermore, European history has been marked – and looks set to be marked for some time to come – by disputes between the rival aspirations of peoples and ambitions of their rulers, on the one hand, and by the increasingly necessary search for a means of defusing potentially violent conflicts and accommodating clashing identities within a 'common European home', on the other.

National feeling can arise in people even if they are not already united in a state. Often (but not always) demands may be made for some degree of national self-government, or even outright independence from an existing state. A group of people who have defined themselves as distinctive will have the institutional structure of a state to uphold and to maintain their own special features – language and culture, for instance, or a commonly shared religion, or sufficient respect for people who share their (perceived) racial characteristics. Frequently, the belief that economic prosperity and advancement will be facilitated by a degree of self-government or independence adds powerful stimulus to the emergence of a movement seeking to articulate a sense of national identity in terms of 'self-determination', that is, a nationalist movement.

Though many states have come into existence as a result of such nationalist movements, they are almost never ethnically uniform; there are nearly always different ethnic groups within the state, and often some of these groups identify themselves as being of different 'nations'. So a modern nation-state is a kind of paradox. It is supposed to be a state which is the institutional organisation of one nation on a definite territory whose borders it protects, but frequently it is also a state which holds together as citizens people of different ethnic groups, some of which may well think of themselves as separate nations. Thus Spain holds together the Castilians of the centre, the Basques of the north-east, the Catalans of the east, the Galicians of the west, and the Andalusians of the south; Switzerland holds together the people of the different cantons, speaking four different languages and of two different major religious groupings; the United Kingdom holds together England, Wales, Scotland and Northern Ireland; Russia holds together many different semi-autonomous nations and ethnic groups; Belgium holds together French speakers (Walloons) and Flemish speakers (Flemings), and so on. It is therefore normal for a state to have to operate with some potential for political danger arising from these separate national groupings within it.

How dangerous such tensions can be was shown in a terrible fashion when Yugoslavia broke up from 1991. People identified themselves as Slovenes, Croats, Serbs, Albanians, Montenegrins, Muslims, Hungarians, Macedonians, and Romanies (Gypsies), and among several of these peoples demands were voiced for separate states. Since peoples were inter-mingled in adjoining villages and in the same villages and towns throughout the southern Balkans, it was never completely obvious where the boundaries should be. Peoples fought each other to try to secure territory which could be regarded as Slovenia, or Croatia, or Serbia, and so on. In such tragic situations, even individuals who have no desire to participate in wars, and whose sense of belonging to a common humanity transcends the narrow confines of nationalism, are often forced to identify with one group or another. Only in that way can they obtain protection, by being regarded as potential citizens of one or another incipient or possible nation-state.

The basis of these identifications is quite various. It can be language, though most states have substantial minorities speaking different languages from the majority. It can be just a matter of decision when two people are regarded as speaking a different language rather than just variant forms or dialects of one language. Or the criterion can be religious; for example, when by the Treaty of Lausanne of 1923 it was agreed to end the Greek–Turkish war by resettling a million 'Greeks' in the territories designated as part of Greece and a million 'Turks' in the territories designated as part of Turkey, the criterion which determined whether a person was Greek or Turkish was whether they were Christian or Muslim. As a result, many Turkish-speaking Christians found themselves labelled Greek and removed to Greece. In the eastern parts of Poland the criterion determining whether someone was Polish or Ukrainian was partly linguistic and partly whether the person was Roman

Catholic or Orthodox (at least by family tradition). And in Bosnia the group whose ancestors had once favoured a Christian heresy and had largely adopted Islam subsequently, became identified as the 'nation' of Muslim Bosnians who later suffered such losses in the Bosnian war of the 1990s.

It has also often been supposed that another criterion for classifying peoples as belonging to one national group or another might be 'racial'. The use of this idea is always dangerous. Europe in the twentieth century has been scarred indelibly by the murder of millions of men, women, and children on the grounds of alleged 'racial impurity'. And in fact this notion of determinate characteristics of a race is an illusion or a myth. People do of course differ in their physical appearance, and this is to a large extent determined by their genetic inheritance. But every human being inherits a very mixed set of genes, and people's appearance (colour of skin, etc.), intelligence, and moral character vary very greatly, so that there are no coherent groups in which people can all be said to be of the same 'race' in the sense of physical, intellectual, or moral characteristics. Racism is therefore a myth, though a powerful one. It differentiates human beings from one another by constructing an entirely spurious hierarchy of 'superior' and 'inferior' peoples on the basis of what are supposed to be inherited genetic features, both physical and (in association with these physical features) behavioural qualities of 'character'. This view – allied to nationalism – has been symptomatic of the far right of the European political spectrum, especially its Nazi and Fascist variants.

Over and above these criteria of nationhood everything depends on what people *feel* themselves to be. It is important to pay attention to the *idea of a nation* which people care about and in which they believe, and to bear in mind that such ideas are obviously subject to historical change. Benedict Anderson (1983) calls a nation an 'imagined community'; imagined, that is, by people who go along with the idea of the nation. Its basis is a sort of vision of collective identity, history, and so on, but on this basis the community can become very real indeed. To establish such an idea which can grip people's imagination it is necessary to have a history, a tradition; or at least to believe in such a history or tradition (though many national traditions are in fact invented, exaggerated, or distorted ones, like the Spanish history of El Cid the medieval warrior who fought the Moors, or the Hungarian tradition of the horsemen of the Milky Way who will return to aid the Hungarians in their hour of need; and there are much more recent – and widely accepted – examples too).

So attempts to build up the idea of a particular nation often involve the invention or bolstering up of a tradition, as well as the accentuation of the special distinguishing features of a nation, like its language or its folk songs. The Finnish independence movement of the nineteenth century involved the collection of fragmentary ancient stories and myths and putting them together as a coherent set of stories, the *Kalevala*, to play the role of the national tradition of the Finns; while the folk-musical traditions of Finns were raised by the great composer Sibelius to the status of the national music.

Nationalist movements

It is clear that movements which make loyalty to a nation central to their purpose will have a very different character depending on whether they direct their appeal to the dominant national group in an existing nation-state, or to a minority which seeks separation to form its own state. The former might be called a *status quo movement*; its purpose will tend to be the assertion of the unity of the existing nation-state and therefore to play down other loyalties and other divisions within the state (notably class divisions and the status of ethnic minorities). The latter is a *disruptive movement*, which seeks to limit or break the power of the existing state in order to detach part of its territory. Status quo nationalist movements do not necessarily want to leave everything as it is. They may be opposed to forces in the state which emphasise divisions within it, like movements for social change or parties which represent the workers against the middle class. The Franco regime in Spain (1939–75), the Salazar regime in Portugal (1926–74), and the regime of the Greek colonels (1967–74) are examples of authoritarian regimes which invoked defence of the status quo and preservation of the existing nation-state in attempted justification of their repression.

The most dangerous status quo nationalist movements (at least for the rest of Europe) are those which add to their promotion of national unity in their state (a) hostility to particular minority groups within the state, and (b) aggressive hostility towards other nations in other states. European history can show many examples of nationalism of this kind, and there is ground for serious concern that manifestations of reaction and resentment against immigrants, now widespread in Europe, might develop into such more extreme forms of anti-democratic, aggressive, and minority-persecuting nationalism. The risks of such movements in contemporary Europe will be considered shortly. But it is important to remember that not all status quo nationalist movements, either on the right or the left, reach these extreme forms.

Disruptive nationalism – since it is based on the discontent of its supporters with their place within their own state – is sometimes apt to be more populist, invoking the loyalty of ordinary people whilst attacking the existing social, political, economic, or cultural hierarchy. Like status quo nationalism, such movements have milder and more extreme forms. In their mild form they shade off into cultural movements promoting minority culture in the form of language and literature, folk music, and so on. They assume a disruptive form (in the sense of demanding political change) when they seek some kinds of special rights for the minority (such as teaching in the minority language in schools) which can easily develop into demands for a degree of local self-government. Sometimes, perhaps in response to state repression or due to frustration with their inability to command sufficient support through democratic channels, such movements can produce an extreme wing which is prepared to use violence to secure total independence. The IRA (Irish

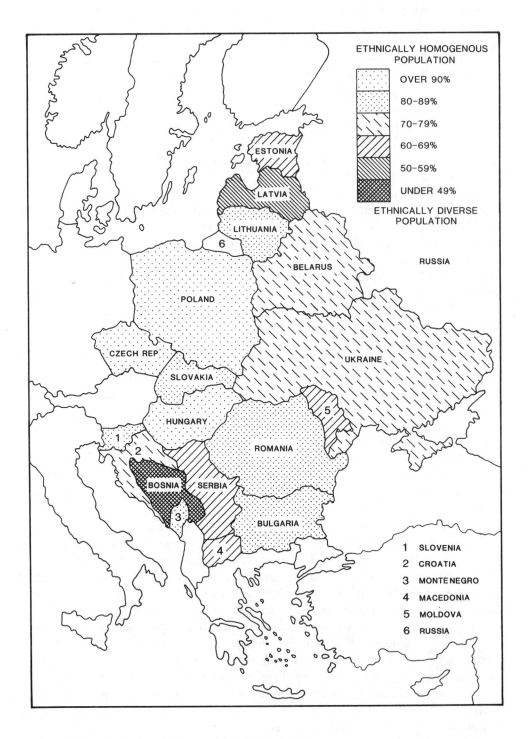

Figure 13.1. Ethnic diversity in central and eastern Europe

Republican Army) in Northern Ireland and ETA in the Basque lands of Spain are examples of such groups. In the 1990s the Corsican nationalist movement, though it has an extreme wing seeking separation from France through armed force, mostly operates as a movement seeking only a degree of local autonomy and recognition of the Corsican language.

On the other hand the nationalist movements in Latvia, Lithuania, and Estonia applied peaceful mass pressure to obtain total independence from the state exercising sovereignty over them (the Soviet Union) in 1991. Such movements (in so far as they use peaceful methods) may be tolerated by the existing state structure, and their demands to some degree conceded, as they have been by Spain and Belgium, which have tried in this way to defuse the potential danger from the separatist movements of the Basques, the Catalans, and the Flemings.

Alternatively, the state may resist the demands of ethnic groups and find itself confronted with demands for total secession backed by the threat of force. Such a situation may develop into one of endemic terrorism and state repression, as in Turkey in its relations with its Kurdish minority, or in Britain during the 1916–21 period in its relations with Irish nationalists.

Disruptive or revolutionary nationalist movements are often led and inspired by middle-class people who feel that their social, political, or economic ambitions are being thwarted within the existing state, and that they are being excluded, because of their nationality, from the important positions in society to which they feel entitled. To understand why this is so it is important to realise that the modern nation-state is (among other things) a way of organising the job opportunities and career-paths of people in a complex modern economy, in which many jobs require expertise so that candidates for them have to be found through some open competitive system (see Chapter 11). The state's institutional framework for this system of competition always favours the official culture and the official language, and in this way talented people with energy and organisational capacity may feel themselves to be held back by this power structure, and so come to support movements which give some kind of recognition to their own different culture; they may even reach the point of supporting revolutionary nationalism.

The question arises, then, how such movements will relate to social issues and class conflict. This is a question which has perplexed and confounded the European left throughout its history. Many socialists have argued that nationalist movements are regressive, opposed to socialist internationalism and to workers' interests, because their concern for the national issue leads them to submerge class divisions in society. But others have argued that they may represent the interests of workers because of their perceived anti-imperialist and democratic character, and that the class structure of modern states often operates by suppressing both minority cultures and the workers who share them.

State strategies for dealing with national or ethnic minorities

The paradox of the nation-state, described above, implies that virtually every state will have a more or less serious problem with minorities. How can they try to deal with it in contemporary Europe? Various strategies can be distinguished.

Melting-pot assimilation

This strategy involves submerging by every possible means any separate national feeling within the state, so as to strengthen as much as possible the new nation which is to be formed on the basis of the sense of identification with a new state. The classic example of this strategy in the nineteenth and twentieth centuries is the USA, which had such a large and various influx of immigrants that this seemed the only tactic which could build any sense of 'American-ness'. In Europe there is no real example of this since new states have always been based on one existing ethnic group. Lenin and the early Bolsheviks certainly envisaged in the immediate post-1917 period that the new Soviet Union would solve the problem of national and ethnic tensions through a process of 'melting-pot assimilation', the end product being a new Soviet national identity. But under Stalin especially, such ideals were all but reduced to empty rhetoric as Russian nationalism and Russian domination of other national groups took centre-stage again under the guise of Soviet patriotism.

One-nation dominance

The end goal of this strategy is apparently very similar; but the sense of national identity which the state seeks to promote is that of an existing nation or ethnic group, already present as the most powerful (and usually the majority) element in the state. In fact the two strategies operate very differently, since the dominance strategy places citizens on an unequal footing depending on whether they are, to start with, already members of the dominant ethnic group or are members of a minority group which it is the state's policy to extinguish as a separate group. It is thus more likely to arouse resentment.

Such a strategy has been applied by, for example, Poland, which after the end of the Second World War transferred great numbers of its citizens of Ukrainian background and language to a part of Poland (the north-west) remote from their former homes and from other Ukrainians, and dispersed them in isolated pockets while giving them purely Polish education. The idea was that in a generation or two they would feel themselves to be simply Polish, and so become loyal members of the Polish nation. It seems possible that the states emerging from the break-up of Yugoslavia may apply similar strategies under the slogan of 'ethnic cleansing'. It is also possible that such strategies might be applied in the Baltic states to discourage their large Russian minorities from exerting an unwelcome influence in states which were founded precisely to get away from the power of Russia (though present signs are that they will opt for more moderate strategies, partly in response to pressure from the Council of Europe).

But for most European states the nation has been established for a long time as based on its dominant ethnic group, with usually one official language and an education system and broadcasting system which favours that group and its traditions. For such long-established states a one-nation dominance strategy is unnecessary. For any state such a strategy is a high-risk option because it involves an active suppression of the special characteristics of the minority groups it seeks to merge into the dominant nation; for example, a suppression of their language, their religion, even sometimes their national dress (as in the suppression of Highland dress in Scotland in the late eighteenth century). If, in their resentment at this, they resist by founding nationalist movements, it involves active suppression of these movements, which as has been seen can lead to a vicious spiral of violence. At the time of writing (1994) it seems that there is a serious risk of such a development in the Kosovo province of Serbia; possibly also in the Transylvania province of Romania (which has a large minority Hungarian population), and in the Turkish parts of Bulgaria.

An extreme form of one-nation dominance strategy is the attempt to eliminate a minority (or all minorities) altogether from the territory of a state, by forced mass emigration or by genocide. The most recent large-scale European examples of mass expulsions at the time of writing are the expulsions of Germans from east of the Oder–Neisse Line (the new Polish border) and from Czechoslovakia in 1945–46, and the refugee exodus from the former Yugoslavia which had exceeded 600,000 by the end of 1993, with a further four million persons left displaced or homeless within the former state. It seems very likely that any settlement in Bosnia will involve further large transfers of population so as to produce ethnically uniform mini-states.

Genocide as a policy of one-nation dominance has cast its infamous shadow over European history in the Nazi Holocaust of the Second World War, in which six million Jews, about a million Poles, and 400,000 Romanies (not to mention trade unionists and socialists, homosexuals, and others who failed to fit the Nazi image of being a true German) were exterminated. But though the Holocaust is unique in its scale (so far), the strategy has been applied by other racially motivated nationalists, as by the Turks in 1915–16 against the Armenians and by the Serbs in the early 1990s ('ethnic cleansing') against the Muslim Bosnians. There is a continuing risk that any extreme nationalism could use the tactic; from the extremist's point of view, it has the great attraction of seeming to be a 'Final Solution' of the problem of minorities (though it is never really a final solution).

One-nation hegemony with tolerance

This strategy is different from the dominance strategy because it does not seek the active suppression of minority cultures. Instead it hopes that they will fade away, being gradually displaced by the officially-backed culture of the dominant nation. For instance, the language of the law courts, of government, and of the education system is the language of the dominant ethnic group; the best job opportunities in practice go to those with the right language (or dialect) and culture; the history and traditions taught in schools and favoured in the official broadcasting system are those of the dominant group. Such a policy relies on the minority group's language, traditions, and so on, fading away as the style of an older generation, without arousing too active a resentment.

This is the sort of policy followed by France and the United Kingdom. In these cases it may be said to have worked, so far, quite well. But one should remember that Britain's attempt to apply such a policy in Ireland in the period 1800 to 1916 failed; resentments were aroused, and discontent took a nationalist form, so that active nationalism arose and was forcibly suppressed. Italy has had a long-standing problem of a similar kind in the Austrian national feeling of many people in the Italian Tyrol (Südtirol). Attempts to assimilate these people led to bomb outrages in protest at Italianisation, but the situation was defused by the retreat of the Italian government from an assimilation policy to the strategy of regional pluralism.

Regional pluralism

Not all minorities occupy definite regions within a state. Indeed, many of central Europe's Romanies follow a wandering life all over the countryside, and most Jews in pre-war Europe were scattered over central and eastern Europe, living usually in towns. The problem of immigrant groups is also not one for which there could be a regional solution. But where a minority *does* occupy a particular region, one possible strategy for the state is to grant the region a substantial degree of self-government. Under such a system the regional government will support the culture and language of the ethnic group dominant within the region, but within the framework of the state which holds sovereignty over it. This solution has been applied quite widely in post-war Europe, and especially since 1980. Switzerland has long had a federal structure giving local power to its separate cantons, and it is in this way that a state containing four language groups and two main religions has been able to hold together. Similarly, in 1948–49 the representatives of the *Länder* who set up the constitution of the FRG reserved a great deal of power to the separate *Länder*.

Belgium has responded to growing tensions between its two language groups by devolving power in the state to three regions, a Walloon region, a Flemish region, and a Brussels central region. Spain, after the death of Franco,

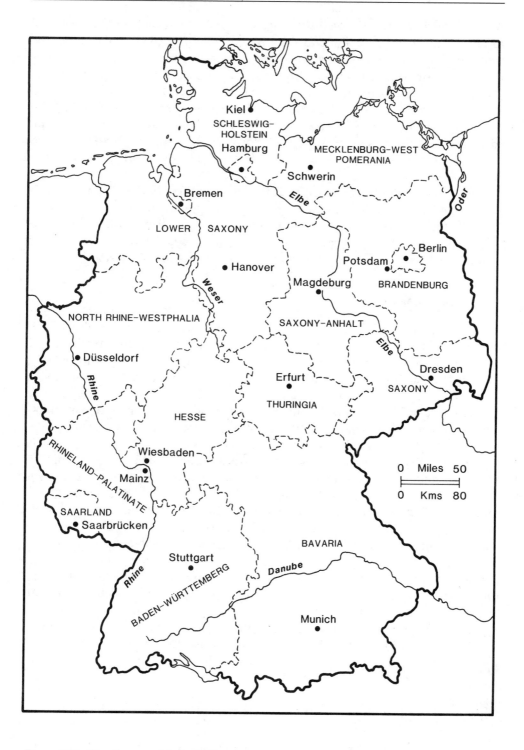

Figure 13.2. The German *Länder* 1990

decided on a strongly devolved structure, in which the strong sense of regional loyalties, especially in Catalonia, in the Basque region, and in Galicia could be satisfied. But such policies are also risky. They can easily develop in either direction. They can encourage the sense of separateness of regional ethnic groups as distinct nationalities, and so lead to the break-up of the state or to substantial clashes between separatists and the state (arguably, something like this happened in Slovakia's separation from Czechoslovakia). Alternatively, the sovereignty of the state can exert itself to make sure that the concessions to minority identity are just tokens and that the real power still rests with the dominant group.

The Soviet Union landed itself with the worst of both worlds. In the 1920s it encouraged the sense of separateness of its component nations, so that they came to feel more of a sense of separate nationhood as a result; while from the 1930s the separate nations were in fact suppressed, thus arousing resentments which ultimately contributed to the break-up of the state.

Cultural pluralism

This strategy tries to accommodate the policy of the state to the reality of the pluralist, multi-ethnic character of all states, and especially (perhaps) of modern European states. The aim is to acknowledge this reality and use the state as a legal framework holding together many different kinds of people with different cultures which should all – so far as possible – be recognised and encouraged. This leads to the idea that national identity is not ethnic – does not depend on particular cultural characteristics or possessions like language – but is simply that of a citizen of the state.

The idea fits well with the ideology of liberalism, which conceives of the state as a neutral legal framework within which people can pursue their own lifestyles. But in practice application of the strategy meets with severe difficulties. For one thing, the role of the state in a modern economy, as explained above, favours a single official language and a reasonably uniform education system to ensure reliable qualifications acceptable throughout the state. For another, the sense of identity on which modern states build the loyalty of their citizens tends to need more content than just the idea of a state with a particular name and flag. People associate the state with the dominant culture within it, and this tends to be thought of as the identity of the nation. So the old Soviet Union, though its constitution recognised many component nationalities within it, tended to be thought of as 'Russia' and its citizens as Russians even when they were Ukrainians, Lithuanians, or Uzbeks; and this corresponded to the reality that the Russian language and Russian culture were the ones which were promoted and encouraged by the state and by the CPSU, and the reality that ethnic Russians tended to occupy the best jobs and the most powerful positions.

Even apart from the direct influence of the state, minority languages have difficulty in maintaining more than a peripheral status in a modern economy, since all parents want their children to learn and use the language which will enable them to succeed in the job market, and time spent on minority languages is time not spent on chemistry, or geography, or some other 'useful' subject.

Sometimes a policy of cultural pluralism is legally entrenched as a system of minority rights; sometimes, indeed, such a system of legal minority rights is demanded by international pressure or treaty obligations. The League of Nations in the 1920s tried to protect Europe's minorities by requiring member states to grant specific rights to minorities. The policy failed, but it may be that it did so mainly because of the more general failure of the League of Nations. The most disastrous problems were those of German minorities in Czechoslovakia and Poland, and Nazi Germany was not interested in protection of Germans by the League, of which in any case it had ceased to be a member in 1934. Perhaps the prospects for protection of minority rights are better since 1945, but the policy is still fraught with dangers and difficulties.

Since 1975 the human rights clauses of the Helsinki Final Act have contained some provision for protection for minority groups, but these have not so far been very effective. The reason for this is not only lack of will; to implement any *general* form of protection for minorities is very difficult, since entrenched positions for special groups cannot be made available to every group, and it seems nearly impossible to formulate criteria for how big or how different or how vulnerable a group needs to be to deserve protection. Nevertheless, the prospect of possible future admission to, or association with, the European Union (with all its economic advantages) is sufficiently attractive for many states of eastern Europe that the Council of Europe and NATO are able to exert a considerable influence in favour of tolerance and liberal democratic standards.

The main problems of ethnic feeling in contemporary Europe

Regional self-government and inter-regional disputes

These problems are substantially different in the old communist bloc and in western Europe.

Central and eastern Europe
The removal of the old structures of authority with the fall of the communist governments has led to a situation in which people are uncertain what political authority may ultimately be established. In some cases people feel that the existing states may not be the ruling political structures in a few years' time, and in any case the political forces which will ultimately gain control over them are as yet uncertain. This uncertainty makes people afraid that their own national group may lose out, and this in turn makes them try to secure as

much independence as possible for any regional government which might be expected to protect them. In addition, the economy is unstable, and unemployment is high. It is a situation of fear; and fear produces prejudice and ultimately aggression against vulnerable minorities who may be made the scapegoats for society's problems by being portrayed as undermining the cohesion of the national group, or seeking to attack it or gain advantages over it.

Eastern Europe is ethnically very mixed; every state contains substantial minorities and the concept of ethnically 'natural' boundaries between one state and another is potentially a very dangerous myth. To add to the instability, the area has a confused and destructive history of national and ethnic conflicts, so that many families retain sad and bitter memories of past injustices which can easily give rise to present-day hatreds. Against this the main force preventing the descent of the whole area into conflict is the people's own awareness of how futile, destructive, and terrible such conflicts are. Moreover, common economic interests are beginning to pull countries of eastern Europe together into an array of regional organisations in the 1990s. There are a surprising number of possible conflicts in the area which have not (so far) got out of hand; the peaceful separation of the Czech Republic and Slovakia in 1992, the avoidance of *serious* conflicts arising from the presence of sizeable ethnic minorities in Romania and Slovakia, and so on.

Against these so far peaceful transitions to a more divided pattern of states must be set the terrible example of the war between Serbia and Croatia and the awful Bosnian war which began in 1992. It is possible that eventually a counter-movement of unification may set in, because of the substantial economic ties connecting the different regions and states making them mutually dependent on each other. But it seems likely that the pattern for any such overarching structure will not be a reunification of separate states into one larger state, but looser arrangements of economic connection.

Western Europe

In western Europe the people of richer regions may feel that poorer regions of the same state are parasitical and are holding them back; whilst the people of poorer regions may feel trapped in a relationship of under-development, exploitation and worsening dependency. For the richer regions, there are two possible tactics in this situation: to get control of the central government and make it reduce its subventions to the poorer regions by free market policies, or to split off the richer region from the state. The Northern Leagues in Italy is a movement which veers between these two approaches, combining a neo-liberal assault on central government's public spending with occasional calls for the rich North to secede from the rest of Italy so as to stop having to subsidise the South.

One possible development is that Europe may ultimately operate with the EU as its overarching structure (corresponding to the effective economic unit, the European market as a whole) while within it the units representing territorial interests could be of the size of (present-day) regions like Lombardy or Alsace or Jutland, while existing large states cease to exist or to be significant. Such a structure might be utilised either in the interests of the richer regions, entrenching their position, or as a structure to enable redistribution of wealth and resources from the richer to the poorer regions. But in practice it is mostly those who favour redistribution who tend to favour it. Such a 'Europe of the regions', embodying the 'principle of subsidiarity', would require very drastic changes in the present structure of the EU itself as well as to the entrenched political structures which depend on the existing states.

Of course, most of the larger European states, and some of the smaller ones, have already progressed some way on the road of regionalisation, following the model of Federal Germany. Spain has devolved a great deal of power to its regions, while France and Italy have devolved quite a lot of power; and Switzerland, Belgium and the Netherlands have long-established entrenched rights for their regions. (The UK under Conservative governments continues to centralise power in London, and stands out as the only large-scale centralised state in the EU.) However, if such a devolved structure is to serve as a basis for a redistributive polity, the control over its operation exercised by EU institutions themselves – especially the Social and Regional Funds – would have to be much stronger than at present. Of course these considerations provide part of the reason for the strong opposition of the political right to enlargement of the powers of the EU.

Racism and contemporary anti-semitism

Since the latter half of the 1980s there has been a perceptible growth in manifestations of racism and of anti-semitism in many European countries. Regrettably, this is nothing new; they have a long history in European culture, and 'the dark side of Europe' is as much part of Europe's political legacy as the Enlightenment ethos. How far Europe will outgrow them, and how far it is likely to become caught in a vicious spiral of racism and ethnic conflict, is one of the most important issues facing us today.

It is not so difficult, though, to discern some causes of the current wave of racism and anti-semitism. Continuing economic recession seems to have condemned many millions to long-term unemployment and has compounded social problems. The policies pursued by governments show little sign of being able greatly to improve the situation, and many people give up hope in democratic politics, identify closely with a narrow group of their own people, and take out their frustrations in hatred of outsiders.

Racism may appeal to those who feel their material security, or their sense of identity, or both, threatened by processes of change which are too complex to grasp or to control easily.

Racist ideology focuses on *difference* as constituting a threat. Those who are defined as different – the Outsider, the Stranger – are constructed as scapegoats for the resentments and frustrations of ordinary people. In fact, even the physical presence of minority groups is not always necessary for such 'scapegoat' hatreds to become established. It has been noted, for example, that strong anti-semitism has persisted in Poland, despite the fact that the Nazi Holocaust, followed by decades of discrimination at the hands of the Polish Stalinist regime, effectively reduced that country's Jewish community to a tiny handful (currently less than 5,000). Throughout the continent the Jewish community has once again been exposed to insult (manifested in the daubing of Nazi slogans on Jewish graves and synagogues and in attacks on Jews). However, the main targets of racist attacks in recent years have been immigrants, and these attacks have been associated with prejudices about those with different skin colour.

Immigration and immigrants

Since 1945 Europe has seen very substantial immigration into all the richer countries of western Europe. The immigrants came especially from southern Europe (Italians, Portuguese, Yugoslavs, Spaniards) and from North Africa particularly to France, from the West Indies, India and Pakistan to Britain, from Indonesia to Holland, and from Turkey to Germany. It proved impossible either to send them back again or to keep their families out (though Germany tried to operate both these policies for quite a while), so the outcome in each of these states was a substantial population of people of a different ethnic group from the dominant nation of the state.

In recent years the patterns of immigration have altered. It is estimated that between 1980 and 1992 some 18 million people entered western Europe as migrants. But many of these came as refugees from war and persecution, or in flight from economic collapse, from eastern Europe. It has been estimated that the war in Yugoslavia had left some four million displaced people by the end of 1993, with the international community struggling to prevent a mass exodus westwards.

The recent upsurge in racism is manifest in rising support for far-right political parties and in a sharp increase in physical (often murderous) attacks upon refugees and immigrants, in many western European countries (a 74 per cent increase from 1991 to 1992 in Germany, for instance). Far-right parties which openly advocated policies against immigrant peoples made substantial gains in elections in France, Germany, Italy, and Britain in the early 1990s, leading to the presence of neo-fascists in a European government in 1993 for the first time since 1945, in the government of Italy formed by Berlusconi. And the policies of many European parties on the 'respectable' right moved sharply in a racist direction in anti-immigrant policies adopted by, for example, the French Interior Minister Charles Pasqua in 1993.

In January 1994, the European Commission tried to promote a constructive European policy on immigration by issuing a Green Paper. As a result, the member states of the EU agreed to allow easier movement of immigrants between member states without the need for visas, to guarantee security of residence for immigrants and their families, and to outlaw racial discrimination at work. This is to accompany moves to reduce migratory pressure on the EU by improving economic and social conditions in the immigrant-exporting countries, and tough moves against illegal immigrants. Whether these agreements will eventually become law in the member states remains to be seen.

The meaning of Europe: an overarching identity?

It has been emphasised in Chapter 11 and at the beginning of this chapter that people's sense of identity is typically a multi-identity, with overlapping loyalties to different groups. Throughout the modern period the nation-state has been the largest, most inclusive, of the *political* groupings with which people have identified. But in Europe since the time of the Ancient Greeks people have also had some sense of being 'European' as a significant kind of identity (see the Introduction). The European leaders who set out to build up a European Community (as opposed to merely a pattern of arrangements for limited economic cooperation) sought to build on this sense of 'European-ness' by making the European Community a political unit, with which people could identify politically. Partly they did so to bind together the quarrelsome European nations and so reduce the risk of a recurrence of the European wars which had been so disastrous in 1914–18 and 1939–45. But the project also arose from a deeper sense that the age of the nation-state of moderate size was over; that the political and economic troubles of Europe of the 1930s had resulted from the attempt to organise life in separate units when in fact their activities intersected so much that they could not construct coherent policies as separate units, and instead fell blindly into destructive policies of injuring each others' interests. The technical, economic, and military conditions of the twentieth century made organised cooperation essential.

In this way the idea of Europe as an overarching political unit, encouraging a plurality of identities in its peoples, came to seem the best solution to Europe's problems. So from the start the European Community was conceived as an overarching entity, a unit of cooperation; not as a replacement for the European nations. It was envisaged that people would feel more vividly the plural character of their identities; that they would feel themselves to be both French and European (as well as, say, Breton, and a citizen of Dinard, etc.). Such a programme can work only if people feel happy to accept the overarching unit, 'Europe', and if they feel involved in it as participants.

From the perspective of the mid-1990s, it is clear that on the contrary there has been a tendency for the EU to be built from above, and that the decision-making processes of the EU are seen as technocratic and elitist, and often heedless of the needs and feelings of the different nations. Indeed, as the constitutional structure of the EU changes from unanimity to majority decisions the prospect of substantial clashes of policy between the government of a member state and the EU as a whole increases; and the larger the EU becomes, and the more extensive the range of competence of its policies, the more such clashes are likely to happen. Thus the sense of an overarching European identity is damaged or overthrown by a fairly widespread feeling that it is associated with structures which fail to respect national identities. The scene is thus set for an accumulation of grievances which nationalistic forces, and those nostalgic for the past, may seek to exploit.

So what policy might now be adopted for Europe? On the one hand, those who assume a *federalist* position argue that incremental progress in the direction of economic integration had reached the point where a relaunch of the EU along democratic federalist lines was necessary in order to safeguard and protect European democracy. They envisage a federal European Union, in which a European government elected by and accountable to the European Parliament would share power with regional and national governments and parliaments. Such a Union would have the power and the democratically based drive to operate a positive policy to ameliorate the ills of European society, to combat regional and sectoral imbalances and tackle the problems of mass unemployment and migration. On the other hand, others hold an *anti-federalist* position, arguing that we should construct an EU-wide free market based on free movement of labour, capital, goods and services. Following the Gaullist slogan of '*l'Europe des patries*', they seek to retain control over political and social matters at the level of the nation-state.

It is clear that the Maastricht Treaty on European Union leaves the EU's institutional framework inter-governmental rather than supranational in character. The European Parliament, for example, is still a long way from becoming transformed into a legislature; people refer to the 'democratic deficit': the fact that control of European institutions is a long way from the democratic control of the people, because the European Parliament has so little power.

David Marquand (1994) has argued that the European project now finds itself confronted by four paradoxes. The first is a paradox of *identity*. Born in the shadow of the Cold War, the identity of the EU was implicitly accepted, originally, as essentially western European, developed, and mainly Roman Catholic. Expansion towards the Protestant North and the non-western and underdeveloped East obviously forces reconsideration of a European identity. Clearly, what it is to be European as a citizen of the EU has now become more complex and problematic, culturally, socially and historically.

Second, there is a paradox of *territory*: the more the EU expands and grows, both economically and geographically, the greater the potential imbalance between its prosperous 'core' and its dependent 'periphery', with all the potential for political tension that brings. To overcome this paradox would require mechanisms of redistribution. As has been explained, redistribution requires some significant transfer of power from national governments to EU institutions.

Third, there is the paradox of *supranationalism*. So long as the political control of the EU remains substantially devolved to its member states, it can operate effective policies only if the more powerful of its member states (i.e. especially France and Germany) exert firm and dynamic pressure to get such policies accepted. But the result of the development of the EU is that these states 'have become stronger because they have created a chain of inter-dependencies which has made it impossible, or at the very least extremely expensive, for them to act unilaterally in certain key areas' (Marquand 1994, p. 24). Although they remain the focus for citizens' political loyalties, these inter-dependencies limit the capacity of nation-states to put in place policies which could effectively resolve the other paradoxes.

Finally, Marquand refers to the paradox of *functionalism*. The very success of the European project to date has brought us to the point where it is no longer clear that the hidden hand of economic integration can of itself deliver an answer to the question, 'What is Europe?'. But it is not clear how the political basis for a more extensive function for European institutions could be constructed.

Clearly, we cannot really speak of European culture, democracy, or civil society, unless we accept that there is more to 'Europe' than just a market place, and more to being a 'European' than just being a consumer – albeit a consumer of a greatly increased range of goods and services. As Jacques Delors, the former President of the European Commission, warned: 'You can't fall in love with a Single Market!'.

Yet the construction of the EU has, until recently, been guided largely by technocratic logic. Political elites in the EU have begun to show recognition of the fact that if substance is to be given to talk of a 'people's Europe', then new ways will have to be found of listening to the ordinary peoples of Europe – particularly the tens of millions of unemployed, low paid and marginalised who feel most threatened and betrayed by socioeconomic change; listening to them, and engaging them seriously with the project of the construction of Europe. This is likely to be the greatest political challenge in the years ahead. As European history shows, the price of failure could be high.

Further reading

Anderson, B. (1983) *Imagined Communities: Reflections on the Origin and Spread of Nationalism*, Verso, London.

Cohen, R. (1994) *Frontiers of Identity: the British and the Others*, Longman, London.

Cohn-Bendit, D. (1993) 'Europe and its borders: the Case for a Common Immigration Policy', in Ogata, S., *et al.*, *Towards a European Immigration Policy*, Philip Morris Institute, Brussels.

Harris, G. (1990) *The Dark Side of Europe: the Extreme Right Today*, Edinburgh University Press, Edinburgh.

Harvie, C. (1994) *The Rise of Regional Europe*, Routledge, London.

Hobsbawm, E. (1990) *Nations and Nationalism Since 1780: Programme, Myth, Reality*, Cambridge University Press, Cambridge.

Marquand, D. (1994) 'Prospects for a Federal Europe. Reinventing federalism: Europe and the left', *New Left Review*, No 203, Jan.-Feb., pp. 17–26.

Milward, A.S. (1992) *The European Rescue of the Nation State*, Routledge, London.

Ogata, S. *et al.* (1993) *Towards a European Immigration Policy*, Philip Morris Institute for Public Policy Research, Brussels.

Epilogue: A European identity?

It would be pleasant to be able to end with a clear message on where Europe is going, whether to a bright future or to disaster, whether to growing unity or to disintegration. When CPSU General Secretary Gorbachev invoked the idea of the 'Common European Home' in 1987, he was thinking in terms of a European family of nations based on its heart in the West, but including in its embrace eastern Europe and the Soviet Union. Meanwhile in western Europe some politicians and writers were committed to developing the idea of 'Europe' as based on the EC, and drawing ever more closely together within that framework. But the events of 1989–94 have proved traumatic, and the difficulties of putting such conceptions into practice have become more and more apparent. It is no longer possible to believe that Europe's persistent ethnic bitterness can be reliably contained by modern political structures, and the possibilities of united action – even in organising the economy – can now be seen to be more limited and more fraught with obstacles than had been generally understood in the mid-1980s.

As mentioned in the Introduction, the idea of Europe is not based on some naturally existing 'continent', but on a conception built on top of the national and ethnic identities of the peoples of the western peninsula of Eurasia. That is not to say that the conception is just a figment of over-heated imaginations. On the contrary, it has meant a great deal to Russians, Poles, Hungarians, Turks, and so on that they should be accepted as 'Europeans', just as the idea of being European as a member of a family of nations was invoked by Gorbachev. And similarly (but not in the same way) the west Europeans have felt a certain sense of being European, as against being American, or Japanese, or African. But how much weight does such an idea have now, in 1994? Does it really hold any peoples or states together where otherwise they would be separated? Or does it only operate as a label for certain limited common purposes (especially economic ones)? Is it still the case, as Raymond Aron claimed in 1954, that 'the European idea is empty; it has neither the transcendence of Messianic ideologies nor the immanence of concrete patriotism. It was created by intellectuals, and that fact at once accounts for its genuine appeal to the mind and its feeble echo in the heart' (Haas, 1958, p. 29)?

For any such supranational concept or identity to have any real weight, it has to work in two (related) ways: it needs to hold different national peoples together – at least to some extent, and for some purposes; and it needs to determine a sense of how there is a boundary between its members and those outside it: the distinction between insiders and outsiders.

The idea of Europe has always involved a contrast between insiders and outsiders, but such an idea carries two great dangers. First, it may lead to a spirit of exclusion against the outsiders, a lack of sympathy, an exclusion from benefits, perhaps sometimes even a hostility; in some cases even a kind of racism. The Ancient Greeks' understanding of themselves was based on their view of the inferior others who were called 'barbarians'; the very word carries a disdain combined with a fear which may lead quite easily – through the centuries – to colonialist contempt for the 'natives' and to stereotypes about the 'wily Oriental', the 'cruel Turk' and the 'brutal Black'. Second, the *application* of this insider–outsider division is not constant, and each time it is applied it raises new jealousies and new hostilities.

If there are to be insiders and outsiders, who are the insiders, and who are the outsiders? Are the members of the EU the insiders, the proper Europeans who carry the ideal of Europe within them, while the countries outside the EU are in some way not fully in Europe? Or should one think that since the end of the Cold War the Russians, Bulgarians, Norwegians and Portuguese are equally Europeans and only Americans and Japanese, and so on (among the rich) and the Muslims of North Africa and the Middle East (among poorer near-neighbours) are outsiders to this entity? Are the insiders Christians – or their secular descendants, vaguely defined as 'liberal'? If so, the exclusion of Muslims from that notion of European identity carries with it enormous potential for conflict, given that Turkey wishes to be regarded as part of Europe (and is so by most definitions already), and given the large and growing number of Muslims who have settled in Europe by immigration in the post-war years. Each time that the insider–outsider division is reapplied it seems to some people like a semi-fascist principle that treats some human beings with contempt. In the 1960s and 1970s the EC was characterised as 'the rich man's club' and more recently the EU has often been seen by outsiders as 'Fortress Europe'.

We must not suppose that the structures of European inter-connection or union can work without some exclusion of those outside them. In so far as the European identity is expressed in trading blocs, alliances, common defence policy arrangements, and so on, it necessarily carries with it barriers of exclusion against those who are not in it. The very idea of a trading bloc involves preferential tariffs and arrangements for commercial cooperation which work to the relative advantage of those within it and to the disadvantage of those outside it.

It is clear that economic and trading pressures are pushing Europeans towards closer organised links. But these networks of European connections are never purely economic. Which states are accepted into them is determined not only by commercial considerations, but also by their political-cultural character. Greece, Spain and Portugal could not be accepted as members of the EC or of most European organisations until their societies had become democratic, had recognised human rights and had accepted a democratic constitution. In the 1990s Bulgaria, Albania and Romania face similar obstacles; as applicants for the EU they are in a much worse position than Hungary or the Czech Republic precisely because they do not as yet sufficiently guarantee human and civil rights for their citizens, at least as seen by the EU. In this way the idea of European identity is seen as containing an ethical component: to be European is to be a member of a democratic society.

It seems, then, that understanding European identity in an exclusionary way is the result of understanding it in the wrong way. Being European is necessarily an identity which includes national identities within it, an overarching identity. Perhaps 'European-ness' can be understood in a more open and accepting manner. Gorbachev explained in his 1987 book *Perestroika: New Thinking for our Country and the World* that such an open identity was what he had in mind. In the modern world states find themselves willy-nilly involved in close inter-relationships with other states, so that the 'international community' (as it has increasingly come to be called) is a world of increasing inter-dependence. Perhaps people in the modern world need to think in terms of some kind of overarching identity which will not be entirely exclusive, but permeable to other groups. If that is right, then a critical issue for the future is just how the concept of being European comes to be understood – as strongly exclusive, or as an open-ended sense of identity.

Would such an overarching sense of identity need its own traditions, its own myths, just as national traditions seem to do? Do there need to be stories resonating in the European imagination the way the story of Joan of Arc resonates for the French or William Tell for the Swiss, or the works of national writers like Shakespeare for the English or Pushkin for the Russians? Perhaps that kind of national myth-making is not appropriate for an overarching and open kind of identity, since it tends to build up a heroic imagination of the community, which Europe cannot and should not be.

It is true that the founding fathers of the EC invoked the idea of the Europe of Charlemagne: an ideal western, Catholic Empire tolerating diversity, with multiple centres. But Jean Monnet remarked that 'Europe has never existed. It is not the addition of sovereign nations met together in councils that makes an entity of them. We must genuinely create Europe.' (Vaughan, 1976, p. 55) Such an identity can be created only by a change in the way Europeans come to see the world. In the late 1940s it was easier for a conception of Europe to settle in people's minds because the Cold War defined it for them – as the beleaguered West threatened by the Soviet East. But in the 1990s the Cold War is over and the question of the identity of

Europe is again on the agenda – without the visionary solutions which provided such an impetus in the immediate post-war years.

One should remember not only the benign image of Charlemagne but also more recent attempts to establish a kind of European unity which met with impassioned opposition: those of Napoleon and Hitler. Each of these leaders explicitly invoked the idea of Europe, but because they sought to establish it by conquest and to operate it as a kind of unified empire, their projects foundered in the stubborn defence of particular national identities by Spaniards, Portuguese, Prussians, Russians and British (in the case of Napoleon), and by (especially) Russians, British and Serbs in the case of Hitler. (Of course the opposition to Hitler was also in large part a defence against racist oppression and ideological perversion.) There is obviously a risk that the pursuit of an imperial kind of European identity in the late twentieth and the twenty-first centuries might meet with the same stubborn opposition. It is therefore quite inadequate to discuss 'European identity' and projects of 'European union' without defining also the *kind* of identity which is in question.

The attempt to develop a European identity has often been a protective measure against the threat of European quarrelsomeness. The US Secretary of State in the 1950s, John Foster Dulles, called Europe 'the world's worst fire hazard'. Thinking in terms of Europe as a whole has often been a way of trying to set up a fire-proof building that would satisfy the Fire Department's safety standards. The impetus for any such protective building project clearly wanes if the threat of major European quarrels diminishes; and perhaps that had happened by 1990. But there remains the cumulative experience of *being* a European, expressed by Churchill in his hopes for 'a Europe where men and women of every country will think as much of being European as of belonging to their native land and wherever they go in this wide domain will feel truly "Here I am at home" ' (Sampson, 1968, p. 4).

Further reading

Haas, E.B. (1958) *The Uniting of Europe*, Stanford University Press, Stanford.
Vaughan, R. (1976) *Post-War Integration in Europe*, Edward Arnold, London.
Sampson, A. (1968) *The New Europeans*, Hodder & Stoughton, London.

Appendix: European Regional Organisations

1	2	3	4	5	6	7	8	9	10	11	12	13	14	
x	x											x		Albania
x	x											x	x	Armenia
x		x	x			x				x				Austria
x	x											x	x	Azerbaijan
x	x												x	Belarus
x	x	x	x	x	x		x							Belgium
x										x				Bosnia & Hercegovina
x	x		x									x		Bulgaria
x	x	x												Canada
x										x				Croatia
x			x											Cyprus
x	x		x							x	x			Czech Republic
x	x	x	x	x	x			x	x					Denmark
x	x		x						x					Estonia
x			x	x		x		x	x					Finland
x	x	x	x	x	x		x							France
x	x											x		Georgia
x	x	x	x	x			x		x					Germany
x	x	x	x	x			x					x		Greece
x	x		x							x	x			Hungary
x	x	x	x	x		x		x						Iceland
x	x	x	x	x	x					x				Ireland
x	x		x	x	x		x			x				Italy
x	x												x	Kazakhstan
x	x												x	Kyrgyzstan
x	x								x					Latvia
x			x	x		x								Liechtenstein
x	x		x						x					Lithuania
x	x	x	x	x	x		x							Luxembourg
										x				Macedonia
x			x											Malta
x	x											x	x	Moldova
x														Monaco
x	x	x	x	x	x		x							The Netherlands
x	x	x	x	x		x		x	x					Norway
x	x		x						x	x	x			Poland
x	x	x	x	x	x		x							Portugal
x	x		x									x		Romania
x	x								x			x	x	Russia
x			x											San Marino
x	x		x							x	x			Slovakia
x			x							x				Slovenia
x	x	x	x	x	x		x							Spain
x			x	x		x		x	x					Sweden
x			x			x								Switzerland
x	x												x	Tajikistan
x	x		x									x		Turkey
x	x			x									x	Turkmenistan
x	x											x	x	Ukraine
x	x	x	x	x	x		x							United Kingdom
x	x	x												USA
x	x												x	Uzbekistan
x														Vatican

1	Conference on Security and Cooperation in Europe	8	Western European Union
2	North Atlantic Cooperation Council	9	Nordic Council
3	North Atlantic Treaty Organization	10	Council of Baltic States
4	Council of Europe	11	Central European Initiative
5	European Economic Area	12	Visegrad Group
6	European Union	13	Black Sea Economic Cooperation Council
7	European Free Trade Area	14	Commonwealth of Independent States

Source: Clarke, D. L. *Europe's changing constellations* RFE/RL Research Report, vol 2, no 37, 17/9/93, p. 14

Chronological Table

1917   Lenin and the Bolsheviks seized power in Petrograd (November).

1918   Civil war began in Russia and continued until the Bolshevik victory in March 1921 (May).
Armistice ended the First World War (November).

1919   Completion of Treaty of Versailles under which Germany surrendered Alsace and Lorraine to France and made other concessions over territory, reparations and armaments (June).

1920   Treaties of St Germain (with Austria) and Trianon (with Hungary) completed break-up of the Austro-Hungarian Empire (June and September).

1921   Treaty of Riga confirmed new Russo-Polish borders (March).
'Vidovdan Constitution' adopted in Yugoslavia, ensuring Serb dominance in inter-war period (June).

1922   Mussolini and the Fascists came to power in Italy (October).

1923   Coup d'état in Bulgaria toppled Alexander Stamboliski and ended democratic government (June).

1924   Death of Lenin (January). Stalin finally prevailed in ensuing five-year power struggle, and from 1929 embarked upon a drastic transformation of Russian economy at a huge cost in lives.

1926   Pilsudski seized power in Poland, ending Polish democracy. Beginning of Sanacja regime in Poland (May).
In Portugal, right-wing dictatorship came to power. From 1928, its leader and strongman was Antonio de Oliveira Salazar.

1929   Start of the Great Depression.
King Alexander of Yugoslavia began dictatorship, trying to suppress local nationalism and create a 'Yugoslav nationalism' (January).

1930   King Carol II of Romania began more personal regime ending with his dictatorship by 1938 (June).

1932   Gyula Gömbös became Prime Minister in Hungary and pushed Hungary to the right over next four years (October).

1933   Hitler became Chancellor of Germany (January).

1935   Germany repudiated military clauses of Versailles Treaty (March).
King Boris coup d'état in Bulgaria began period of 'benevolent dictatorship' until 1943 (April).
Elections in Czechoslovakia resulted in Sudeten German Party becoming largest party in Czech Parliament (May).
Italy invaded Abyssinia (October).

1936   Germany remilitarised the Rhineland (March).
Spanish Civil War began and continued until April 1939 (July).

1938   'Anschluss': Austria incorporated into Germany (March).
The question of the future of the Germans in the Sudetenland (in Czechoslovakia) came to a head, reaching its climax at the Munich conference at which Hitler's demands were largely satisfied by Britain and France (August–September).

1939   German troops occupied Prague, followed by German annexation of Czech areas with Slovakia becoming a German satellite state (March).
At end of March Britain and France guaranteed Polish independence, already under threat from Germany.
Spanish Civil War ended with defeat of the democratically elected Spanish government; Franco's dictatorship began (April).
In Yugoslavia central government made a special agreement ('Sporazum') with Croatia granting the Croats wide autonomy (August).
Germany and USSR signed Nazi–Soviet pact settling division of Poland and their future spheres of influence in eastern Europe.
Germany attacked Poland on lst. Britain and France declared war on Germany on 3rd (September).

1940   In series of whirlwind campaigns, Germany defeated Denmark, Norway, the Low Countries and France. Britain struggled to survive in the following 12 months, though with some moral and economic support from USA (April–June).

Fall of King Carol of Romania; period of brutal rule by 'Iron Guard' (1940–1) and regime of Marshal Antonescu (1941–44) (September).

1940-41 Hungary, Romania and Bulgaria drawn into alliance with Germany, Italy and Japan (Tripartite Pact)

1941 Germany invaded Yugoslavia and Greece. Independent Croatian State set up under Ustasha regime which began genocide of Serbs (April). Germany invaded USSR (June).
Reinhard Heydrich began 'regime of terror' in the Czech lands. Heydrich assassinated May 1942 (September).
German declaration of war on USA (December).

1943 German surrender at Stalingrad followed by defeat during summer in Battle of Kursk. Soviet forces advanced steadily westward thereafter (January).
Outbreak of civil war between factions of Greek anti-Nazi resistance movement (September).
Teheran conference between Stalin, Roosevelt and Churchill which did much to shape future of Europe (November–December).

1944 American and British forces landed in northern France and began their drive to victory from the west (June).
Bretton Woods Conference – 44 countries led by USA and UK devised plans for the post-war international financial system, including the establishment of the International Monetary Fund (IMF) and International Bank for Reconstruction and Development (World Bank) (July).
Warsaw uprising put down brutally by Nazis (August–September).
Germany's ally, Finland, concluded an armistice with the USSR (September).
Germans began to withdraw from Greece. Stalin agreed to assign country to British sphere of influence (October).
Fall of Admiral Horthy in Hungary; brutal rule of Fascist 'Arrow Cross movement' until April 1945.
British forces began to take action against the communists in Greece (December).

1945 Moscow recognised Lublin Committee as the provisional government of Poland (January).
Yalta conference on future of Europe attended by Stalin, Roosevelt and Churchill (February).
Leaders of old regime executed in Bulgaria (February).
Italy finally liberated from Fascism. Benito Mussolini executed by partisans (April).

Suicide of Adolf Hitler in Berlin (30 April).

Allied forces met in heart of Germany and war in Europe ended (8 May).

Labour Party, led by Clement Attlee, won British general election (July).

Allied leaders met at Potsdam, and United States tested and then used atomic bombs against Japan (July–August).

Potsdam: agreement on conditions for signing peace treaties with Hungary, Bulgaria and Romania (August).

Alcide de Gasperi became Christian Democrat prime minister of Italy (December).

1946   Forced merger of Social Democrats (SPD) with Communists (KPD) in Soviet Occupation Zone in Germany to form Socialist Unity Party (SED) (April).

Peace treaties negotiated with all former enemy states except Germany and Austria (April–December).

Italians rejected monarchy and voted in a referendum for establishment of a republic (June).

Constitution of French Fourth Republic promulgated (October).

Greek civil war began when communist resistance fighters, organised as the Democratic Army of Greece, refused to accept a right-wing royalist government under British tutelage.

1947   British and American occupation zones in Germany fused to form Bizonia (January).

Peace treaties signed with Italy, Romania, Bulgaria, Finland and Hungary (former allies of Germany) (February).

UK and France signed a 50-year friendship treaty (March).

Benelux states agreed to establish a customs union, commencing in January 1948.

Truman Doctrine formulated in general terms to assist 'free peoples in the struggle against communism'. It was prompted by British warning that it could not continue to back Greek government, and by fear of communist gains in Greece and Turkey.

Communists expelled from French and Italian governments with American encouragement (May).

First steps taken in the creation of the Marshall Plan, which, after departure of Soviet delegation, was directed to economic recovery of western Europe (June–July).

Cominform set up by USSR in response to Truman Doctrine and Marshall Plan (September).

Establishment of General Agreement on Tariffs and Trade (GATT) (October).

1948   Political crisis in Czechoslovakia left communists as dominant political force (February).
Brussels treaty signed by Britain, France and Benelux states providing for military cooperation (March).
Relations worsened rapidly between USSR and Yugoslavia.
USA granted massive economic and military assistance to right-wing forces in Greece.
Organisation for European Economic Cooperation (OEEC) set up in Paris (April).
Congress of Europe called for political and economic union of European nations (May).
American Senate approved Vandenberg Resolution which opened way to American defence cooperation with western European states (June).
East–West differences over German questions led to interruption of western supply lines to West Berlin (the Berlin blockade). West responded with airlift.
Cominform expelled Yugoslav Communist Party and approved Soviet model of industrialisation and agricultural collectivisation for the 'people's democracies' (July).
UK Labour government implemented major health and social security reforms, establishing National Health Service.

1949   Comecon set up by USSR and its partners (January).
North Atlantic Treaty (NATO) signed (April).
Southern Ireland became completely independent of British Commonwealth when Irish parliament promulgated Republic of Ireland Act.
Federal Republic of Germany (FRG – West Germany) adopted its post-war constitution (May).
Berlin blockade ended.
'Show trials' began in eastern Europe.
Statute of Council of Europe signed in Strasbourg by ten states.
First Soviet nuclear test (August).
Konrad Adenauer became first Chancellor of FRG (September).
Greek civil war ended with defeat of communist forces (October).
German Democratic Republic (East Germany – GDR) established.
Cominform denounced Yugoslav regime. Soviet bloc countries broke off diplomatic relations with Yugoslavia (November).

1950   Referendum in Belgium favoured return of King Leopold (March).
France proposed European Coal and Steel Community (Schuman Plan) (May).
Outbreak of Korean War (June).
'Workers self-management' introduced in Yugoslavia.

Start of western talks on West German rearmament (September).

France proposed Pleven Plan resulting in attempt to establish the European Defence Community (EDC) (October).

Growing East–West tension led to major increases in defence spending by NATO and a larger and firmer commitment by USA to defence of Europe (December).

1951   France, FRG, Italy, Belgium, The Netherlands and Luxembourg signed treaty establishing European Coal and Steel Community (ECSC) which operated from July 1952 (April).

Conservatives returned to power under Winston Churchill in UK (October).

1952   New constitution promulgated in Greece. But real power increasingly rested with the army which saw itself as custodian of status quo (January).

Greece and Turkey entered NATO (February).

USSR proposed German peace treaty based on withdrawal of foreign troops and neutralisation of Germany (March).

France, West Germany, Italy and Benelux states signed treaty to create EDC (May).

Yugoslav Communist Party renamed League of Communists of Yugoslavia (LCY) (November).

Right-wing forces won elections in Greece.

1953   First American thermo-nuclear test (first deliverable bomb tested in March 1954) (February).

First session of Nordic Council comprising Denmark, Iceland, Norway and Sweden (Finland joined in October 1955).

Death of Stalin (March).

Soviet intervention put down demonstrations in East Berlin and other cities in East Germany (June).

Korean armistice signed.

Soviet–Yugoslav diplomatic relations resumed.

Recently-appointed Prime Minister Imre Nagy introduced 'new course' in Hungary. Five Year Plan revised with priority switching from heavy industry to lighter industry and food production (July).

First Soviet thermo-nuclear test (August).

Death of Alcide de Gasperi, 'historic' leader of Italian Christian Democrats.

1954   French National Assembly refused to ratify EDC treaty (August).

London and Paris conferences opened way to creation of Western European Union, rearmament of West Germany, its membership of NATO and achievement of full sovereign status (September–October).

1955   Leadership struggle in USSR: Malenkov replaced by Bulganin (February) with Khrushchev (CPSU General Secretary) increasingly influential, taking over premiership in 1958.
Nagy replaced as prime minister in Hungary (March).
Churchill succeeded as UK prime minister by Anthony Eden (Conservative) (April).
Austrian Peace Treaty provided for withdrawal of occupation forces and establishment of a neutral Austria. The Warsaw Pact between USSR and its eastern European allies concluded in same month (May).
Khrushchev's rapprochement with Tito.
FRG became a sovereign state.
USSR cancelled friendship treaties with France and UK.
Messina Conference of Foreign Ministers of the six ECSC states discussed further European integration (June).
A Four-Power Summit in Geneva failed to reach any substantive agreements, but reflected a temporary easing of Cold War in Europe – the 'Thaw' or 'spirit of Geneva' (July).
Introduction of so-called 'Hallstein Doctrine' in FRG (December).

1956   Khrushchev denounced Stalin at 20th Party Congress (February).
Cominform dissolved (April).
Strains developed in Poland. Poznan riots. Gomulka restored to leadership in October (June).
Rakosi removed from Hungarian Party general secretaryship after visit of high-level Soviet delegation (July).
Nagy restored as prime minister in Hungary. Uprising ended with heavy bloodshed after Soviet military intervention occasioned by USSR's refusal to accept end of one-party rule and Hungary's departure from WTO (October–November).
Anglo-French action at Suez led to temporary crisis in Anglo-American relations, and deeper rift between Paris and Washington (November).

1957   Harold Macmillan (Conservative) succeeded Eden as UK prime minister (January).
Treaties of Rome signed, establishing the European Economic Community and the European Atomic Energy Community (March).
Moscow meeting of ruling communist parties other than Yugoslavia in vain attempt to restore movement's unity (November).

1958   Treaties of Rome came into force (January).
USSR agreed to withdraw troops from Romania (May).
Long-running crisis in French Fourth Republic came to a head with army coup in Algeria; Charles de Gaulle returned to power in France, promising end to colonial war in Algeria and return of political stability at home (May–June).

French referendum approved Constitution of Fifth Republic which inaugurated a strongly centralised presidential system of government (September).

A Soviet note on future status of Berlin led to period of intermittent and at times serious tension between East and West over Berlin (and Germany) until end of 1961 (November).

De Gaulle elected president of France (December).

1960   European Free Trade Association (EFTA) Convention signed in Stockholm by Austria, Denmark, Norway, Portugal, Sweden, Switzerland and United Kingdom (January).

Four-Power summit in Paris a dismal failure (May).

Growing evidence of a rift between communist China and USSR (June).

Cyprus became independent republic within British Commonwealth (August).

OEEC reorganised into Organisation for Economic Cooperation and Development (OECD) (December).

1961   USSR cancelled aid to Albania (April).

Denmark, Ireland and UK applied for EC membership (July–August).

Berlin Wall erected to stop growing numbers of East Germans going to the West (August).

22nd Congress of CPSU – Khrushchev renewed de-Stalinisation (October).

Move to 'goulash communism' in Hungary (December).

1962   French colonial war in Algeria ended. Algeria became an independent republic in July (March).

Norway applied for EC membership (April).

A Soviet attempt to deploy nuclear missiles in Cuba followed by most serious crisis in the Cold War (October–November).

De-Stalinisation began in Czechoslovakia (December).

1963   De Gaulle vetoed UK bid to enter EC. Franco-West German Treaty of Friendship and Cooperation signed (January).

Sino-Soviet rift made public (June).

Yaoundé Convention between the EEC and 18 African states and Madagascar (July).

FRG opened a trade mission to Poland (September).

GDR adopted New Economic System.

Alec Douglas-Home became Conservative prime minister of UK (October).

Ludwig Erhard succeeded his fellow Christian Democrat Konrad Adenauer as Chancellor of FRG.

In Greece, Centre Union, led by George Papandreou and his son, Andreas, won office (November).

New crisis in Cyprus: clashes between Greeks and Turks (December).

1964 Constantine II succeeded to throne of Greece (March).

Central Committee in Romania issued declaration asserting independence of all communist parties (April).

FRG opened trade mission in Hungary (July).

Hungarian Socialist Workers' Party Central Committee accepted principles of New Economic Mechanism.

Death of Palmiro Togliatti, leader of Italian Communist Party. Succeeded by Luigi Longo (August).

UK elections returned Labour government under Harold Wilson (October).

Khrushchev relieved of all his posts in USSR. Brezhnev shared power with Kosygin, but steadily became the more influential figure.

1965 Signing of Treaty (Merger Treaty) establishing a Single Council and a Single Commission of European Communities. Treaty took effect in July 1967 (April).

France began a boycott of EC institutions to register its opposition to various proposed supranational developments (July).

Constitutional crisis in Greece ended in defeat for elected government of George Papandreou when King Constantine forced its resignation to appease army.

1966 Luxembourg Compromise ended French boycott of EC institutions (January).

De Gaulle announced French withdrawal from military participation in NATO (March).

Rankovic dismissed in Yugoslavia (July).

Grand Coalition formed in FRG with Social Democrat, Willy Brandt as foreign minister (December).

Kurt Georg Kiesinger became third post-war Christian Democrat chancellor of FRG.

1967 FRG established diplomatic relations with Romania (January).

Military coup in Greece, designed to forestall democratic elections, led to establishment of 'Dictatorship of the Colonels'. In December, King Constantine left for exile in Rome having failed to remove colonels (April).

EC Brussels Merger Treaty came into force (July).

De Gaulle vetoed UK entry to EC again (November).

1968   Dubcek elected first secretary of Czech Communist Party. A wide variety of reforms followed, but 'Prague Spring' ended by Warsaw Pact invasion in August, the USSR once again fearing that matters were drifting out of control. In November so-called 'Brezhnev Doctrine' laid down that a socialist state was bound to intervene if socialism was threatened in another socialist state (January–November)
Paris rocked by strikes and demonstrations as students and workers revolted against the perceived authoritarian and paternalistic nature of de Gaulle's regime. Benefiting from fears of revolution, French right-wing won a parliamentary majority in general elections in June. Similar student protests elsewhere in Europe (May).
Completion of EEC Customs Union (July).
Marcello Caetano succeeded ailing Salazar as dictator of Portugal (September).

1969   De Gaulle resigned French presidency following defeat in referendum on constitutional reforms (April).
Georges Pompidou became president of France (June).
British troops arrived in Northern Ireland, ostensibly to keep peace between the province's Protestants and Catholics. A split in para-military Irish Republican Army (IRA) produced hard-line 'Provisional' IRA in August–December, which began serious campaign of violence against British presence in Northern Ireland (August).
Massive labour unrest in Italy led to trade union reforms and to forms of collective bargaining which increased strength of labour movement. An extreme right-wing backlash saw neo-fascist terrorist groups carry out some bombings.
Brandt became FRG chancellor heading an SDP-FDP coalition. In October he made overtures to USSR and Poland, and showed his desire to open a dialogue with GDR (September).
The Hague summit of EC leaders (December).

1970–   Nationalist disturbances in Croatia led to purges of LCs in Yugoslavia
1971

1970   First USSR–FRG agreement on supply of Soviet natural gas to FRG by pipeline (February).
Willy Brandt's 'Ostpolitik' led to first conference of FRG and GDR leaders (March).
Conservatives returned to power in UK led by Edward Heath (June).
EC membership negotiations reopened with Denmark, Ireland, Norway and UK.
USSR–FRG treaty of non-aggression (August).
Poland–FRG treaty of non-aggression and inviolability of borders (November).

Death of General Charles de Gaulle.

Riots occurred in Gdansk in Poland. Edward Gierek replaced Wladyslaw Gomulka as first secretary (December).

1971 Erich Honecker replaced Walter Ulbricht as general secretary of East German Communist Party (SED) (May).

Quadripartite Agreement on Berlin (September).

UK parliament approved EC membership (October).

1972 Enrico Berlinguer became leader of Italian Communist Party. Over the next four years, he articulated the ideology of Eurocommunism and sharply criticised the USSR (January).

President Nixon visited Moscow and signed first Strategic Arms Limitation Treaty (SALT 1) and Declaration on Basic Principles of Soviet–American relations (May).

FRG and GDR signed 'Basic Treaty' on mutual relations (December).

1973 Denmark, Ireland and UK joined EC (January).

In Greece, military dictatorship formally abolished monarchy (June).

Conference on Security and Cooperation in Europe (CSCE) opened in Helsinki, including representatives of all European States (except Albania), USSR, USA and Canada (July).

Student uprising against Greek dictatorship brutally suppressed (November).

FRG concluded a treaty with Czechoslovakia and established diplomatic relations with Hungary and Bulgaria (December).

1974 British Labour Party regained office; Wilson prime minister again (March).

Portuguese radical army officers overthrew right-wing dictatorship of Salazar–Caetano, initiating a period of revolutionary upheaval and ultimately consolidation of multi-party democracy. First free elections for 50 years held in 1976 (April).

UK Government demanded renegotiation of terms of accession to EC.

French President Georges Pompidou died; succeeded by Valéry Giscard d'Estaing (April–May).

Helmut Schmidt (Social Democrat) succeeded Willy Brandt as Chancellor of FRG (May).

Greek military intervened in Cyprus; driven back by the Turks. Cyprus divided into Greek and Turkish zones. Greek military regime collapsed (July).

In Greece, democratic elections (the first in which communists allowed openly to participate since the 1940s) returned centre-right New Democracy party led by Constantine Karamanlis to power (November).

Greeks voted by huge majority to abolish monarchy and declare a republic (December).

EC Heads of State and Government decided to meet regularly as European Council.

1975   First Lomé Convention between EC and 46 African, Caribbean and Pacific states (ACP states) (February).

Elections to a new constituent assembly in Portugal established socialists as biggest party (April).

UK referendum: two-to-one majority in favour of remaining in EC (June).

Greece promulgated a new constitution and applied for EC membership.

Final Act signed by eastern and western states at Helsinki Conference on Security and Cooperation in Europe (August).

General Franco died and transition to democracy began in Spain under King Juan Carlos. Free elections held in June 1977 (November).

1976   James Callaghan succeeded Harold Wilson as Labour prime minister of UK (April).

Portuguese general elections won by socialists.

Workers' strikes and demonstrations followed price increases in Poland (June).

Italian elections. Berlinguer-led communists polled 34 per cent of vote. So-called government of 'national solidarity', 1976–79, sought communist support in parliament in return for consultation. Communists, however, denied cabinet seats.

Socialist leader, Mario Soares, became prime minister of Portugal (July).

The Committee for the Defence of Workers (KOR) set up in Poland (September).

1977   Charter 77 formed in Czechoslovakia (January).

Legalisation of political parties began in Spain (February).

Portugal applied for EC membership (March).

A NATO summit agreed to increase defence spending by 3 per cent a year in real terms as confidence in detente weakened (May).

Spain's first free elections for more than forty years (June).

Spain applied for EC membership (July).

1978   China cut off aid to Albania (July).

Polish Archbishop Karol Woytila elected as Pope John Paul II (October).

1979   European Monetary System (EMS) came into operation (March).
        Margaret Thatcher led British Conservatives to election victory and
        became first female prime minister of UK (May).
        SALT 2 was signed but not subsequently ratified by USA (June).
        First direct elections to European Parliament.
        Second Lomé Convention between EEC and 58 ACP states
        (October).
        NATO took twin-track decision to negotiate with USSR on inter-
        mediate-range nuclear systems and, if Soviet SS-20s not removed by
        1983, to deploy Pershing and Cruise missiles in Europe (December).
        Soviet invasion of Afghanistan.

1980   Karamanlis became president of Greece (May).
        Death of President Tito of Yugoslavia.
        Price increases in Poland led to establishment of the Solidarity free
        trade union under leadership of Lech Walesa (August).
        Turkish government toppled by military coup (September).

1981   Start of Ronald Reagan's presidency in USA (January).
        Greece became 10th member of EC.
        Attempted military coup in Spain failed (February).
        Nationalist disturbances in Kosovo (March–April).
        François Mitterrand became first socialist president of French Fifth
        Republic, defeating Giscard d'Estaing. In June, Mitterrand's Socialist
        Party also won general elections. A left-wing government formed which
        included four cabinet ministers from French Communist Party (May).
        Giovanni Spadolini, a Republican, became Italy's first non-Christian
        Democrat prime minister since 1945. Christian Democrats continued
        to dominate the Government (July).
        Elections in Greece returned socialist party, PASOK, to power.
        Andreas Papandreou became prime minister (October).
        Further USSR–FRG gas pipeline agreement (November).
        Martial law declared in Poland by Jaruzelski. Solidarity leadership
        arrested. American sanctions against Poland and USSR followed. In
        1982 this led to serious controversy between USA and its European
        allies over handling of issue (December).

1982   Greenland referendum voted in favour of withdrawal from EC
        (February).
        Argentina invaded Falkland islands. Hostilities continued until UK
        victory in July (April).
        Spain joined NATO (May).
        FRG Chancellor Schmidt lost vote of confidence and was succeeded
        by Helmut Kohl, who led a CDU/CSU–FDP coalition government
        (September).

Brezhnev died. He was briefly succeeded by Yuri Andropov (1982–84) and Konstantin Chernenko (1984–85) (November).

1983   Reagan announced intention to proceed with Strategic Defence Initiative (SDI). The anti-nuclear movement became increasingly active in western Europe (March).
Conservatives under Thatcher returned to power in UK elections (June).
Martial law lifted in Poland (July).
Anti-communist Bettino Craxi, leader of Italian Socialist Party, headed CD-dominated government (August).
NATO began to deploy Pershing and Cruise missiles. USSR broke off East–West arms talks (November).

1984   Free trade area established between EC and EFTA (January).
Mitterrand shifted France to more pro-federalist position, implicitly recognising failure of 1982–83 'socialist experiment' largely due to pressure of world economic trends; in July, French communists left government in protest (June).
Death of Italian communist leader and father of Eurocommunism, Enrico Berlinguer; succeeded by Alessandro Natta.
FRG granted DM950 million loan to GDR in return for further relaxation of travel restrictions. By August there was a growing Soviet–GDR rift over détente and relations with FRG (July).
Third Lomé Convention between EEC and 65 ACP states (December).

1985   USA and USSR took the first steps towards renewal of arms talks (January).
Death of Enver Hoxha, leader of Albanian Communists since Party formed in 1941.
Mikhail Gorbachev became General Secretary of Central Committee of Communist Party of Soviet Union. USA–USSR arms talks renewed in Geneva (March).
Karamanlis resigned as Greek president (May).
Greek Socialists, led by Papandreou, returned to power in elections (June).
Electoral changes in Hungary led to election of some independents.
Geneva Summit between Reagan and Gorbachev marked beginning of end of 'Second Cold War' (usually dated as starting with Soviet intervention in Afghanistan in December 1979) (November).
Anglo-Irish Agreement gave Irish Government a consultative role in Northern Ireland.
European Council agreed principles of Single European Act (SEA) (December).

1986   Spain and Portugal joined EC (January).
        SEA signed in Luxembourg, fixing end of 1992 as completion date of
        Internal Market.
        Assassination of Swedish prime minister Olaf Palme (February).
        Mario Soares replaced General Eanes as president of Portugal.
        Right-wing parties won parliamentary majority in France, forcing a
        period of 'cohabitation' between Jacques Chirac as prime minister
        and Mitterrand as socialist president. This continued until May 1988
        (March).
        Major accident at nuclear power plant in Chernobyl, Ukraine (April).
        Gorbachev proposed 30 per cent cut in strategic nuclear arms (June).
        Stockholm Security Conference: agreements on observers and on
        notice of military movements (September).
        Reagan and Gorbachev met in Reykjavik. Western Europeans alarmed
        by USA's unilateral (though unsuccessful) proposals on strategic
        nuclear arms cuts (October).
        Riots in Alma-Ata after Kunaev replaced as CP first secretary in
        Kazakhstan by ethnic Russian Kolbin (December).

1987   FRG coalition government (CDU/CSU–FDP) returned to power in
        elections (January).
        USSR proposed Intermediate-range Nuclear Forces (INF) agreement
        (March).
        Gorbachev, in a Prague speech on 'a common European home',
        emphasised the shared history and culture of Europeans (April).
        Italian prime ministership passed from Bettino Craxi to the Christian
        Democrat Amintore Fanfani.
        Conservatives won third term of office in UK (June).
        Single European Act came into effect (July).
        Demonstrations in Baltic capitals on 48th anniversary of Molotov-
        Ribbentrop pact (August).
        Slobodan Milosevic became general secretary of the League of
        Communists of Serbia (October).
        Proposed economic reforms in Poland failed to win support of 50 per
        cent of the people. Strikes followed in Spring and Summer of 1988
        (November).
        INF treaty provided for elimination of all INF weapon systems in
        Europe within three years (December).

1988   Janos Kadar, Hungarian leader replaced; radical reforms promised
        (May).
        Mitterrand won second presidential mandate in France. Socialist
        Party also won general elections. Michel Rocard became prime
        minister.
        Rallies in former Baltic states calling for autonomy (August).

Lech Walesa invited to help end strikes in Poland.

1989   Independent opposition political parties legalised in Hungary (January).
Talks began between Polish communists and Solidarity; agreement reached in April on trade union, economic and political reforms.
Solidarity won all but one of the seats it was allowed to contest in June elections (February).
The Delors Report proposed three-stage progression to economic and monetary union (EMU) (April).
Hungary opened its borders to allow East German 'tourists' to cross to the West (May).
European Council of the EC agreed to begin Stage 1 of programme for EMU on 1 July 1990 (June).
Greek elections resulted in stalemate. A short-lived and unprecedented communist–conservative coalition took office to 'clean up' alleged corruption of outgoing socialist administration.
Human chain across Lithuania, Latvia and Estonia marked 50th anniversary of Molotov–Ribbentrop pact (August).
Solidarity-led government formed in Poland.
Hungarian government agreed to hold multi-party elections. Hungarian Socialist Workers' Party became simply Socialist Party. Party's leading role dropped from Constitution (October).
Soviet statement effectively ended the 'Brezhnev Doctrine'.
Massive demonstrations in East German cities (November).
GDR government promised free elections and free exit on 8 November. Within hours, Berlin Wall breached.
Zhivkov replaced in Bulgaria.
All-party government formed in Greece.
Coalition government formed in Czechoslovakia (December).
European Council of the EC agreed to convene an Intergovernmental Conference on Economic and Monetary Union and subsequently (June 1990) to establish an Intergovernmental Conference on Political Union.
Union of Democratic Forces formed in Bulgaria.
Romanian communist leader, Nicolae Ceausescu and his wife Elena executed.
Communist Party of Lithuania left CPSU.

1990   GDR government proposed unification of Germany (January).
Balcerowicz plan for economic shock therapy adopted in Poland.
First free general election in GDR. Christian Democrats won almost 50 per cent of vote, paving way for unification (March).
Lithuania declared its independence from USSR.

Free elections in Hungary produced right of centre coalition government led by Josef Antall's Hungarian Democratic Forum.

Centre-right New Democracy won one-seat majority in Greek elections. In May, Karamanlis returned as president (April).

Free elections in Slovenia won by DEMOS coalition.

Franco-German proposal for intergovernmental conference on political union.

Free elections in Croatia won by Democratic Union (April–May).

Free elections in Romania won by Iliescu's National Salvation Front (May).

Treaty between FRG and GDR on monetary, economic and social union.

Boris Yeltsin elected President of Russian Republic.

Free elections in Czechoslovakia won by Civic Forum and its Slovak counterpart Public Against Violence (June).

Free elections in Bulgaria won by Socialist (ex-Communist) Party.

Iliescu brought in Jiu Valley miners to end opposition demonstrations in Bucharest

Germany adopted single currency (July).

NATO Summit in London began to consider implications of post-Cold War era.

Group of seven states (G7) discussed integration of eastern Europe into world economy.

First stage of EC plan for economic and monetary union came into effect.

28th CPSU Congress. Yeltsin and others left Party.

State treaty on German unification signed by FRG and GDR (August).

New media law came into effect in Russia.

Treaty on Final Settlement on Germany signed by two German states and France, Soviet Union, United Kingdom and United States ('2+4' Treaty) (September).

Formal declaration of suspension of Four-Power rights in Germany (October).

Germany became a single state once again. Helmut Kohl (FRG chancellor) elected chancellor of reconstituted state in December and led a CDU/CSU–FDP coalition.

Margaret Thatcher forced from office in UK due to internal Conservative Party coup. John Major became party leader and prime minister (November).

Lech Walesa elected President of Poland (December).

Bulgarian government resigned following widespread strikes.

Elections in Serbia and Montenegro won by ex-Communists. Elections produced a weak coalition government in Bosnia-Hercegovina and a nationalist one in Macedonia.

Central Committee plenum removed hardliners from Albanian Party of Labour as anti-government demonstrations mounted.

Opening sessions of the two Intergovernmental Conferences on Economic and Monetary Union and Political Union.

1991   Harder line by Gorbachev reflected in OMON (para-military security force) attacks in Vilnius and Riga. Yeltsin recognised sovereignty of Baltic states (January).
Italian Communist Party (PCI), under leadership of Achille Occhetto, voted to dissolve itself and to give birth to the Democratic Party of the Left (PDS). A minority seceded to form rival Party of Communist Refoundation (PRC) (February).
Growing crisis in Yugoslavia.
Albanian Party of Labour (APL) won Albania's first free elections (April).
In France, President Mitterrand appointed a new socialist prime minister – Edith Cresson (May).
Albanian government replaced by coalition following widespread strikes. APL became Socialist Party of Albania (June).
Declarations of independence by Slovenia and Croatia.
Yugoslav army invaded Slovenia, but was forced to retreat. Serbia accepted Slovenian independence.
Comecon dissolved.
Bundestag voted Berlin capital of united Germany.
Warsaw Treaty Organisation dissolved (July).
Serbo-Croat war began in Croatia.
Attempted putsch failed in USSR. Gorbachev lost all credibility on return to Moscow. CPs banned and much of their property taken over by republican governments following Yeltsin's lead in Russia. Latvia, Lithuania and Estonia declared independence and Yeltsin urged world to recognise them (August).
Romanian government forced to resign. Coalition government formed (September).
Social Democrats defeated in Swedish elections; right-wing government came to power.
Indecisive Polish elections resulted in formation of weak coalition government under Olszewski in December (October).
Union of Democratic Forces narrowly defeated Socialists in Bulgarian elections.
Start of EC sanctions against Serbia (November).
Caretaker government formed in Albania (December).
EC association agreements with Czechoslovakia, Hungary and Poland provided for free trade within 10 years and possibility of eventual EC membership.
EC heads of state and government meeting in Maastricht agreed on a treaty framework for European Union incorporating agreements on political union and economic and monetary union, and introducing a new security/defence dimension to EC cooperation.

USSR replaced by Commonwealth of Independent States (CIS).

1992   EC recognised independence of Slovenia and Croatia (January).
Zhelyu Zhelev re-elected President of Bulgaria.
Broadly effective ceasefire in Croatia.
Treaty on European Union signed in Maastricht (February).
Democratic Party decisively won Albanian elections. Its chairman
Salih Berisha was elected executive President in April (March).
Proclamation of independence by Bosnia-Hercegovina.
Italian general elections confirmed crisis within corruption-tainted
Christian Democrats (who polled less than 30 per cent for first time
ever) and their Socialist allies. But the former Communists also
polled poorly, gathering a total of around 22 per cent. New parties
did well, especially right-wing secessionist Northern Leagues who
gathered 9 per cent of the total poll (April).
Start of serious conflict inside Bosnia-Hercegovina.
Conservatives returned to power in the UK, but with a much reduced
majority (May).
EC and EFTA signed treaty establishing the European Economic Area
(EEA).
Yeltsin won Russian presidential election. Leningraders voted to
restore name of St Petersburg (June).
Olszewski government fell in Poland. In July, Hanna Suchocka
formed a seven-party coalition government, which survived till May
1993.
General elections in Czechoslovakia. Strong performance of Meciar's
Movement for a Democratic Slovakia made early dissolution of
Federation inevitable.
Danish voters rejected Maastricht Treaty.
Tudjman's Croatian Democratic Union consolidated its grip on
power after lower house and presidential elections. This was
reconfirmed in February 1993 upper house and local elections
(August).
Iliescu re-elected President of Romania, but general election results
forced his Democratic NSF into a governmental coalition with three
hard-line nationalist parties (September).
French Referendum narrowly approved Maastricht Treaty.
Hungary referred dispute with Czechoslovakia over Gabcikovo dam to
International Court of Justice (October).
Brazauskas' Democratic Labour Party (former Communist Party of
Lithuania) won general election (October/November).
Hungary, Poland and Czechoslovakia (Visegrad group) signed free
trade agreement (December).
'Non-party government of experts' led by Lyuben Berov installed in
Bulgaria.

Dissolution of Czechoslovakia into Czech Republic and Slovakia at midnight on 31st December.

1993   EC formally became a single market (January).
EC opened negotiations with Austria, Finland and Sweden (and Norway – April 1993) on their applications for membership (February).
Attempt to impeach Yeltsin failed (March).
French general elections returned a parliamentary landslide for right-wing parties. Edouard Balladur became the new Gaullist prime minister, heralding new period of cohabitation with Mitterrand.
Following split within the New Democracy party in Greece, former foreign minister Antonis Samaras formed a new right-wing party, Political Spring.
Russian referendum; 59 per cent backed Yeltsin (April).
Danish referendum voted in favour of Maastricht Treaty (May).
Spanish general elections returned a minority Socialist Government, dependent on Catalan nationalist support (June).
DNSF changed name to Party of Social Democracy of Romania (July).
EC Finance Ministers agreed to alterations in EMS following turmoil in financial markets (August).
Polish elections. Ex-communists of Democratic Left Alliance returned to power in coalition government with old allies in Polish Peasant Party. Solidarity and church-backed parties did poorly. Pawlak became Prime Minister (September).
Attendance of members of government at reburial of Admiral Horthy in Hungary.
Yeltsin dissolved Russian Republic Supreme Soviet, intending to rule by presidential and governmental decree until elections to new State Duma on 12 December. Vice-President Rutskoi announced he had taken over presidency and was supported by Supreme Soviet, which also attempted to replace Defence Minister Grachëv by hard-liner Achalov. Deputies, led by Rutskoi and Speaker Khasbulatov occupied White House.
Army units stormed White House. Rutskoi, Khasbulatov and other leaders arrested (October).
Romania admitted as full member of Council of Europe.
Socialists, led by Andreas Papandreou, returned to power in Greece, inflicting a heavy electoral defeat on New Democracy. The latter elected a new leader, Miltiades Evert.
Maastricht Treaty on European Union formally came into effect (November).
Left-wing parties in Italian local elections scored big gains at expense of collapsing Christian Democrats. However, huge increase in neo-fascist vote registered in many cities, including Rome; in south of

the country neo-fascists seemed to replace CD in many areas as main right-wing party.

Elections to Russia's State Duma and Federation Council. Disarray among pro-Yeltsin parties and public apathy and disillusionment boosted Zhirinovsky's inappropriately named Liberal Democratic Party and also Communist Party of Russia. New Constitution approved in referendum (December).

Elections increased majority of Milosevic's Serbian Socialist Party.

Death of Prime Minister Antall increased problems of Hungary's Democratic Forum, which had suffered greatly from right-wing nationalist-populist defections in course of year.

117 countries agreed on treaty for liberalisation of world trade following seven years of GATT negotiations (Uruguay Round) (December).

1994   Second stage of economic and monetary union (EMU) came into effect with establishment in Frankfurt of European Monetary Institute (EMI) as a precursor to European central bank (January).

European Economic Area (EEA) came into existence creating a free trade zone comprising all EU member countries and 6 of the 7 EFTA countries – Switzerland having voted against participation in December 1992.

First meeting of new Russian Duma.

Pro-Russia Yuri Meshkov elected first President of Ukraine's Crimea.

Russia's State Duma granted amnesty to leaders of parliamentary resistance to President Yeltsin in October 1993 (February).

Croatia agreed ceasefire with self-declared Republic of Serbian Krajina (March).

Austria, Finland, Norway and Sweden agreed terms for joining European Union in January 1995.

Italian general elections confirmed collapse of old discredited Christian Democrat and Socialist parties; but hopes of the left-wing Progressive Alliance (led by former Communists) also dashed. The main beneficiaries of the crisis of the old party system were the neo-fascists, who won more than 100 seats in parliament, the right-wing Northern Leagues, and a new right-wing, pro-free market movement, *Forza Italia*, led by media mogul and billionaire, Silvio Berlusconi.

Slovak Prime Minister Meciar lost no-confidence vote and was replaced by Jozef Moravcik, leading a five-party coalition government.

Yeltsin's treaty on civil accord signed by representatives of 245 political and social organisations in Moscow.

Hungary and Poland became first former communist states to apply for membership of EU (April).

Spain's minority socialist government became mired in corruption scandals which brought down several cabinet ministers, involved senior public servants, and threatened the future of the prime minister Felipe Gonzalez (April–May).

Silvio Berlusconi became Italian prime minister. His government included five neo-fascist cabinet ministers, raising concern in many European capitals (May).

Hungarian Socialist Party (ex-Communists) won overall parliamentary majority in elections.

Gyula Horn of Hungarian Socialist Party (next Prime Minister) concluded talks with Alliance of Free Democrats on coalition government which would have large enough majority to change the Constitution if it wished (June).

Austrian referendum voted in favour of EU membership.

Russia joined NATO's Partnership for Peace and signed a 'partnership and cooperation' agreement with the EU, which, like one just signed by Ukraine, stopped short of setting full EU membership as the final goal. Some trade barriers lifted, but talks on Russia's inclusion in a free trade zone set only for 1998, and only on condition that market reforms continue. After being accepted as a full political partner at G-7 summit, Russia also seemed about to apply for admission to the Paris Club (of government creditors).

The Supreme NATO Commander in Europe and the Russian Defence Minister agreed to set up working groups to draft a programme of joint activities. NATO missions to be established in Russia and Russian military missions at NATO's European headquarters.

Jacques Santer appointed to succeed Jacques Delors as President of European Commission (July).

Tony Blair elected leader of British Labour Party.

Withdrawal of all American military forces from West Berlin after five decades of presence in the city.

Director of Russian foreign ministry's Department for European Cooperation stated that Russia proposed turning the CSCE into a central coordinating body overseeing the activities of the CIS, the North Atlantic Cooperation Council, the European Union, the Council of Europe, NATO and the Western European Union.

Italian anti-corruption judges resigned in protest at bail for prisoners on remand accused of corruption. Berlusconi's brother accused of corruption.

Italian ex-Prime Minister Craxi imprisoned for seven years for corruption.

Index

Page numbers in bold denote section/chapter devoted to subject. f denotes figure. t denotes table